THE ROUGH GUIDE TO

Barcelona

This eleventh edition updated by

Steve Tallantyre and Greg Ward

ROUGH GUIDES

roughguides.com

Contents

Introduction to
Barcelona

Barcelona – the past and potentially future capital of the independent nation of Catalunya, and the Mediterranean's most exciting destination – sets the standard for urban style, hip design and sheer nonstop energy. Time and again Barcelona has reinvented itself, from medieval maritime power to Olympic city, from neglected Franco-era backwater to dominant national force, with its dazzlingly inventive architecture as the most vivid expression of its tireless self-confidence. This is a place whose most famous monument, Antoni Gaudí's Sagrada Família, is an unfinished church of rapturous ambition; whose most celebrated street, the Ramblas, is a round-the-clock maelstrom of human activity; and whose vibrant restaurants, bars, shops and galleries are in the vanguard of European style and fashion. Whether you're visiting for the first time, expecting a traditional city break, or returning for the fiftieth, thinking you know it inside out, Barcelona never fails to surprise.

The impetus for Barcelona's almost overpowering self-promotion stems above all from its unique political and cultural identity. Its inhabitants leave you in no doubt that, whatever the map might show, you're not in Spain but in the autonomous province of **Catalunya** (Catalonia in English), which traces its history back as far as the ninth century. This makes Barcelona the capital of what many regard as a nation, and cranks the natural pride that locals feel for their city up an extra notch or two. Galleries and museums, for example, hold "national" collections of Catalan art and history, while the 1992 Olympics – which kick-started the dynamic rebuilding process – were indisputably Barcelona's Games, and not Spain's. The city fosters an independent spirit, setting itself apart from the wider country and single-mindedly pursuing its own social, economic and cultural agenda.

ABOVE VIEW OF PLAÇA D'ESPANYA FROM THE MUSEU NACIONAL D'ART DE CATALUNYA

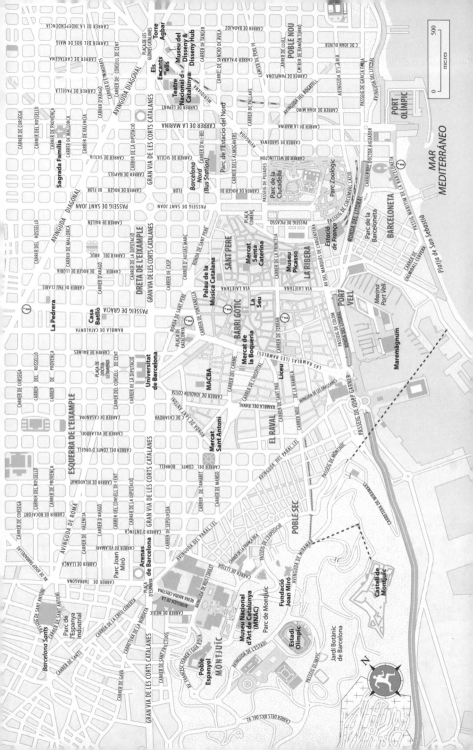

Nowhere is this more perfectly seen than in the otherworldly **modernista** (Art Nouveau) buildings that stud Barcelona's streets, dating from a previous era of renewal in the nineteenth century. **Antoni Gaudí** is the most famous of those who have left their mark in this way: his **Sagrada Família** church is rightly revered, but just as fascinating are the (literally) fantastic houses, apartment buildings and parks that he and his contemporaries designed.

Barcelona also boasts an extensive medieval **old town** – full of landmark monuments from an earlier age of expansion – and a stupendous **artistic** legacy, ranging from exquisite Romanesque treasures to major galleries celebrating Catalan artists Joan Miró and Antoni Tàpies, not to mention Pablo Picasso, who spent some of his formative years here. The city is equally proud of its cutting-edge **restaurants**, its late-night bars and clubs, and most of all its football team, the mercurial, incomparable **FC Barcelona**. Add a spruced-up waterfront, 5km of sandy beaches, and swathes of verdant parks and gardens, and even on a lengthy visit you could never see it all.

True, for all its go-ahead feel, Barcelona has its problems, not least a petty crime rate that occasionally makes the international news. But there's no need to be unduly paranoid, and you'll miss so much if you stick solely to the main tourist sights. Tapas bars hidden down alleys unchanged in centuries, designer boutiques in gentrified old-town quarters, street opera singers belting out arias, bargain lunches in workers' taverns, neighbourhood funicular rides, unmarked gourmet restaurants, craft workshops, restored medieval palaces, suburban walks and specialist galleries – all are just as much Barcelona as the Ramblas or the Sagrada Família.

BARCELONA ON A PLATE

In a town where lunch can go on until 5pm, and tapas is what you eat *before* dinner, not your dinner itself, dining out is a big deal. Word gets around quick if there's a hot new restaurant or bar, and Barcelona gourmets are pretty discerning customers – not for them the Ramblas tourist traps or fast-food chains. Embrace the local tastes and current trends and a whole new world opens up, from no-frills fishermen's favourites in **Can Maño** (see p.186) to inventive, cutting-edge bar snacks at **Tickets** (see p.188). Above all, if it's fresh, seasonal and straight from the market – that's Barcelona on a plate.

What to see

Despite being one of the largest cities on the Mediterranean (population 1.6 million, with a further 3.7 million in its metropolitan area), Barcelona is a pretty easy place to find your way around. In effect, it's a series of self-contained quarters or neighbourhoods, known as *barris*, stretching out from the harbour, flanked by parks, hills and woodland. The city centre and its major attractions – Gothic cathedral, Picasso museum, markets, Gaudí buildings and art galleries – can be explored on foot, while a fast, cheap, integrated public transport system takes you directly to the peripheral attractions and suburbs.

This guide starts, as nearly everyone does, with the **Ramblas** (*Les Rambles* in Catalan), a kilometre-long, tree-lined avenue – officially five consecutive avenues, hence the plural – of promenading pedestrians, pavement cafés and kiosks that splits the old town in two. East of the Ramblas, the **Barri Gòtic** (Gothic Quarter) is immediately recognizable as the medieval nucleus of the city, a labyrinth of twisting streets and historic buildings that include La Seu (the cathedral) and the palaces and museums around Plaça del Rei. A little further east lie the similarly venerable districts of **Sant Pere**, set around the terrific Santa Caterina market, and the fashionable boutique-and-bar quarter of **La Ribera** to the south, home to the Picasso museum. Over to the west of the Ramblas, the edgier, artier neighbourhood of **El Raval** contains the city's flagship museum of contemporary art (MACBA) as well as several of the city's coolest bars and restaurants.

At its southern end, the Ramblas reaches the waterfront. Walking east from the spruced-up harbour area here, known as **Port Vell** (Old Port), will take you past the aquarium and marina, through the old fishing and restaurant quarter of **Barceloneta**, past the **Parc de la Ciutadella** and out along the promenade to the cafés and restaurants of the **Port Olímpic**. This whole area is where Barcelona most resembles a resort, with city beaches lining the waterfront from Barceloneta all the way to the conference and leisure zone of Parc del Fòrum at **Diagonal Mar**.

OPPOSITE PARK GÜELL **ABOVE** *VASO DE ORO* (P.184)

The fortress-topped hill of **Montjuïc**, rising at the southwest corner of the city, was historically home to the city's Jewish population; now no longer a residential neighbourhood, it holds a host of remarkable cultural attractions, including Catalunya's vast and utterly unmissable national art gallery (MNAC), the Joan Miró museum, botanic garden and main Olympic stadium.

At the top of the Ramblas, Plaça de Catalunya marks the start of the gridded nineteenth-century extension of the city, known as the **Eixample** and divided into distinct "right" (**Dreta**) and "left" (**Esquerra**) neighbourhoods. Epitomizing the thrusting expansionism of Barcelona's early industrial age, the Eixample is home to some of Europe's most extraordinary architecture, including Gaudí's astonishing **Casa Batlló** and **La Pedrera**, as well as the ever-growing **Sagrada Família**.

Beyond the Eixample lie the northern suburbs, notably **Gràcia**, with its small squares and lively bars, and the nearby **Park Güell**, while you'll also come out this way to reach the famous **Camp Nou** FC Barcelona stadium. It's worth making for the hills, too, where you can join the crowds at Barcelona's famous **Tibidabo** amusement park – or escape them with a walk through the woods in the peaceful **Parc de Collserola**.

The good public transport links also make it easy to head further out of the city. The mountaintop monastery of **Montserrat** makes the most obvious day-trip, not least for the extraordinary ride up to the monastic eyrie by cable-car or mountain railway. **Sitges** is the local beach town *par excellence*, while with more time you can follow various trails around Catalunya's **wine country**, head south to the Roman town of **Tarragona** or Gaudí's birthplace of **Reus**, or north to medieval **Girona** or the Salvador Dalí museum in **Figueres**.

When to go

Barcelona is an established city-break destination with a year-round tourist, business and convention trade. Seasonal attractions range from summer music festivals to Christmas markets, but there's always something going on. In terms of the weather, the best times to visit are late **spring** and early **autumn**, when it's comfortably warm (around 21–25°C) and walking the streets isn't a chore. Evenings might see a chill in the air, but Barcelona in these seasons is often nigh on perfect. However, in **summer** the city can be unbearably hot and humid, with temperatures averaging 28°C but often climbing a lot higher. Avoid August, especially, when the climate is at its most unwelcoming and local inhabitants head out of the city in droves, leaving many shops, bars and restaurants closed. It's worth considering a **winter** break, as long as you don't mind the prospect of occasional rain. Even in December, when temperatures hover around 13°C, it's generally still warm enough to sit out at a café.

Beyond Barcelona, the weather varies enormously. On the coast it's best – naturally enough – in summer, but resorts like **Sitges** are packed from June to September. **Tarragona**, too, can be extremely hot and busy in summer, though **Girona** is much more equable at that time, and escaping from the coast for a few cool days is easy.

OPPOSITE FROM TOP PLAÇA DE LA SEU; CATALAN FLAGS ON THE RAMBLAS

things not to miss

It's not possible to see everything that Barcelona has to offer in one visit – and we don't suggest you try. What follows, in no particular order, is a selective taste of the city's highlights, from glorious modern architecture and world-class art to tapas bars and amusement parks. All entries have a page reference to take you straight into the Guide, where you can find out more.

1

1 LA PEDRERA
Page 106

Is it an apartment building or a work of art? Both, when the building in question – the undulating Pedrera, or "Stone Quarry" – is designed by Antoni Gaudí.

2 CITY BEACHES
Page 82

Barcelona has a golden seafront, with 5km of sandy beaches stretching from Barceloneta to Diagonal Mar.

3 A TAPAS TOUR
Page 179

Hopping from bar to bar, sampling the specialities, is the best way to experience some of Barcelona's finest food.

4 CAMP NOU
Page 132

The magnificent Camp Nou stadium is home to FC Barcelona, one of the world's premier sides, and has a cabinet full of trophies to prove it.

Itineraries

Architectural wonderland, gastronomic trailblazer, sun-kissed playground – Barcelona is all of these things and more. Let these one- to two-day itineraries lead you to its most emblematic sights, as well as those that sparkle below the surface.

FROM A GREAT HEIGHT

You can literally see it all in a couple of days with this jaunt that takes you from the summit of a mountain to the top of the city's culinary scene.

Transbordador Aeri Dangle high above the harbour on a daredevil cable-car ride between the beachside neighbourhood of Barceloneta and the Jardins de Miramar on Montjuïc (173m). **See p.78**

Tibidabo The journey up to the mountain-top amusement park is part of the fun, but the grand prize is the panorama of city, sea and sky that greets you at the summit of the 550m peak. **See p.137**

Mirablau Chic bar and restaurant in Tibidabo, where you can enjoy tapas and cocktails as night-time Barcelona glitters and glints in the background. **See p.204**

Arenas de Barcelona The rooftop terrace atop this bullfighting-ring-turned-shopping-centre affords grand views of Plaça d'Espanya and the domed Palau Nacional. **See p.113**

Park Güell It's hard to say which is prettier: architect Antoni Gaudí's extraordinary urban park or the spectacular city vistas you'll see from its famed terrace. **See p.126**

Dinner at Dos Cielos The Torres brothers take fine dining to new heights at this sleek, Michelin-starred restaurant on the 24th floor of the *Meliá Sky* hotel. **See p.187**

OFFBEAT BARCELONA

If you need a break from art museums and churches, try this one-day circuit of some of Barcelona's quirkier attractions.

El Gato del Raval After roaming Barcelona for more than fifteen years, artist Fernando Botero's giant bronze feline finally found a home on Rambla del Raval, where it has been vacantly staring down shoppers and tourists ever since. **See p.61**

Vintage shops If you're looking for something a little more unusual than an "I Love Barcelona" T-shirt, head to El Raval's Carrer de La Riera Baixa, where the secondhand shops brim with thrifty bargains and vintage fashion. **See p.230**

miba Motivation, laughs and inspiration are included in the entrance fee to this fun-filled museum dedicated to celebrating the power of invention. **See p.54**

Museu del Calçat Tucked away in Plaça Sant Felip Neri is a tiny museum that claims to be home to the world's largest shoe, as well as a range of other noteworthy footwear. **See p.52**

L'Antic Teatre Anything goes at L'Antic Teatre, a hub for experimental performance art where you'll also find one of the city's best bars and garden *terrassas*. **See p.209**

SAVING THE PENNIES

You can easily spend two to three days taking advantage of these inexpensive, if not free, attractions that are scattered around the city.

The beaches Unfurl a towel, slather on the sunblock and settle in for a relaxing day of golden sand and aquamarine waters at any of the city's eight beaches. **See p.82**

Mercat de la Boqueria It doesn't cost a thing to browse the colourful displays of fruits, vegetables, seafood and sweets inside Barcelona's most famous market. And who knows? Your stroll might yield a free sample or two. **See p.39**

La Seu Arrive in the morning or late afternoon, and you can wander around the ornate interior and lush cloister of Barcelona's grand Gothic cathedral for free. **See p.45**

Els Encants Vells If it's bargains you seek, then bargains you shall find at the city's main flea market, where spirited haggling is the name of the game. **See p.122**

Caixa Forum A superb collection of contemporary art fills the halls of Caixa Forum, an arts and cultural complex that's free to the public. **See p.89**

Font Màgica A gorgeous display of music, water and colour that's been attracting oohs and aahs since its debut during the 1929 International Exhibition. **See p.89**

STRICTLY CATALAN

The following places offer a deeper understanding of what defines Catalunya and its people.

Museu d'Història de Catalunya Journey from prehistoric times to the present day via engaging, interactive exhibits, housed inside a gorgeously renovated warehouse that overlooks Port Vell. **See p.80**

The sardana Performances of this dance – a graceful symbol of Catalan unity and identity – take place every Sunday afternoon at Plaça de la Seu. **See p.206**

Lunch at Can Culleretes Said to be the oldest restaurant in Barcelona (if not Spain), this wood-panelled gem serves quintessential Catalan food in a timeless setting. **See p.178**

Plaça del Pi's farmers' market Purveyors of locally made wine, cheese, pastries and more set up shop in the picturesque Plaça del Pi during this bimonthly farmers' market. **See p.51**

Palau de la Música Catalana From the music played within its walls to the allegorical decorations found both inside and out, this concert hall designed by *modernista* architect Lluís Domènech i Montaner is Catalan through and through. **See p.66**

Gràcia To experience small-town Catalunya without leaving the city, head to the charming squares and narrow streets of Gràcia, where the air is filled with the Catalan language. **See p.124**

TRAMVIA BLAU

Basics

Getting there

It's easy to reach Barcelona by air; budget airlines from regional UK and European airports compete with the Spanish national carrier Iberia to get you directly to the city, quickly and cheaply. There's also a fair amount of choice from North America, though you may well have to fly via Madrid or another European city to get the best fare.

To get the very cheapest fares on the budget airlines, you generally need to book weeks, if not months, in advance. Flights with Iberia and other major airlines tend to be more expensive and seasonal, with the highest fares from June to September, at Christmas, New Year and Easter, and at weekends all year.

If you're buying **online** be sure to check terms and conditions; most budget airline tickets are non-changeable and non-refundable. You can also still book via a general flight or **travel agent** – these have similar deals on flights and services, and some are particularly geared towards youth, student and independent travel. In addition, specialist **tour operators** can book you onto various city breaks or themed tours in Barcelona and Catalunya.

Travelling to Barcelona from elsewhere in Europe by **train** or **bus** inevitably takes longer than flying, and usually works out more expensive. However, if Barcelona and Spain are part of a longer European trip it can be an interesting proposition, and is an increasingly popular, green alternative to flying. **Driving** to Barcelona from the UK is something of an undertaking, and what with motorway tolls in France and Spain, fuel costs, cross-Channel ferry and Eurotunnel fares, it's certainly not a cheap option.

Flights from the UK and Ireland

Around a dozen **airports** in the UK and Ireland offer flights to Barcelona all year, including all the London airports, plus Birmingham, Bristol, Dublin, East Midlands, Edinburgh, Glasgow, Leeds-Bradford, Liverpool, Manchester and Southend, with a **flight time** of something between two and two and a half hours.

Airlines offering the route range from budget operators such as Ryanair (⑩ryanair.com), easyJet (⑩easyjet.com), Monarch (⑩monarch.co.uk), Jet2 (⑩jet2.com) and Vueling (⑩vueling.com), up to national carriers like Iberia (⑩iberia.com), British Airways (⑩ba.com) and Aer Lingus (⑩aerlingus .com). You can get a sense of current fares, and a full list of the relevant airlines, by using a comparison site such as ⑩skyscanner.net. For most of the year,

you can confidently expect to find one-way fares in any specific week starting at less than £50, and often significantly lower than that; even on the national airlines, however, taking check-in baggage is liable to cost extra.

With so many Barcelona options, it's only likely to be worth flying to any of Catalunya's other airports if you want to see more of the region than just Barcelona itself. Ryanair do however fly to **Girona**, 90km north of Barcelona, and **Reus**, 110km south of Barcelona, near Tarragona, from several British, Irish and European airports, including smaller UK airports like Bournemouth and Bristol. Both Girona and Reus are more than an hour's journey from Barcelona, via bus or train.

Flights from the USA and Canada

While most **direct scheduled services** to Spain from North America are to Madrid, there are a handful of nonstop flights to Barcelona, including American Airlines (⑩aa.com) from New York and Miami; US Airways (⑩usairways.com) from Charlotte and Philadelphia; and both Delta (⑩delta.com) and United (⑩united.com) from New York. European-based airlines like Iberia and British Airways can also get you to Barcelona, though you'll be routed via their respective European hubs. Flying time from New York is around seven hours to Madrid, eight to Barcelona direct, though with an onward connection it can take up to eleven hours to reach Barcelona.

Return **fares** are as much as US$1200 in summer, though outside peak periods you should be able to fly for under US$700.

Flights from Australia, New Zealand and South Africa

There are no direct **flights** to Spain from Australia, New Zealand or South Africa. However, a number of airlines do fly to Barcelona with a stopover elsewhere in Europe or Asia – flights via Asia are generally cheaper – and you can also fly to Madrid, and pick up a connecting flight or train from there. If your visit to Barcelona is part of a wider trip, it may help to discuss your route and preferences with a flight and travel agent like Flight Centre (⑩flight centre.com.au or ⑩flightcentre.co.nz) or STA Travel (⑩statravel.com.au or ⑩statravel.co.nz).

City breaks and tours

Three-night **city breaks** to Barcelona, flying from London, Manchester or Dublin, start from as little as

£200 (€270) per person. For this price, accommodation is likely to be in a two-star hotel, potentially on a room-only basis. For three nights' bed-and-breakfast in a three- or four-star hotel you can usually expect to pay more like £300–400 (€400–540). The bigger US operators, such as American Express and Delta Vacations, can also easily organize short city breaks to Spain on a flight-and-hotel basis.

A few British and Spanish operators offer rather more **specialist holidays** in and around Barcelona, concentrating on things like art and architecture, cooking classes, wine tours or rural Catalunya. Prices vary wildly, according to the standard of accommodation and services provided, from say £100 (€120) for a fully catered day out to several thousand pounds/euros for an all-inclusive luxury holiday. North American **tour companies** also tend to include a couple of days in Barcelona as part of a whirlwind escorted itinerary around Spain, starting from around US$1500–2000 for a standard two-week tour.

UK

Martin Randall Travel ☎ 020 8742 3355, ⓦ martinrandall.com. Experts lead small groups on annual, all-inclusive quality tours to Spain – tours and themes change each year, though a typical gastronomic tour of Catalunya might cost from £2750 for six nights' wining and dining.

SPAIN

Madrid & Beyond ☎ 917 580 063, ⓦ madridandbeyond.com. Classy, customized holidays and special experiences, from private gallery tours to expert-led walks through Gaudí's Barcelona.

A Taste of Spain ☎ 934 170 716, ⓦ atasteofspain.com. Interesting food-based tours from a company with offices in Barcelona and Madrid, including a three-day gourmet tour (land only, from €720), and a day's chauffeured excursion to Girona (from €300 per person).

USA

Olé Spain ☎ 1 888 869 7156, ⓦ olespain.com. Eight-day cultural walking tours in Catalunya (US$3295), beginning and ending in Barcelona, with time to explore the city.

Petrabax ☎ 1 800 634 1188, ⓦ petrabax.com. City breaks, escorted Catalunya tours or self-drive Spanish holidays, plus independent travel services such as accommodation bookings and car rental.

Saranjan Tours ☎ 1 800 858 9594, ⓦ saranjan.com. Upscale, fully guided, customized tours concentrating on Barcelona and its nearby wine country.

By rail

Although travelling **by train** to Barcelona can't compete in price with the cheapest budget-airline fares, it can be a real adventure. Your first stop for information should be the amazingly useful

ⓦ **seat61.com**, which provides route, ticket, timetable and contact information for all European train services.

Ultra-fast TGV Duplex now connect Paris with Barcelona in little more than six hours, making it possible to get all the way from London to Barcelona within a single, comfortable day's journey. All year round, you can leave London after 9am, change trains in Paris, and arrive in Barcelona just after 8.30pm. Fares for each individual leg of the trip vary widely, and are of course at their highest during peak times and seasons, so it's hard to predict total costs, but you're unlikely to find a full round-trip fare for much under £200. Either book the entire journey at ⓦloco2.com, or look around for cheaper individual segments by booking the London–Paris **Eurostar** service (ⓦeurostar .com) separately from the Paris–Barcelona legs (try ⓦvoyages-sncf.com, ⓦcapitainetrain.com or ⓦrenfe.com). Sadly, overnight sleeper trains no longer connect Paris and Barcelona, though of course it's possible to spend a night in Paris en route.

If you plan to travel extensively in Europe by train, a **rail pass** might prove a good investment. However, if you're just headed for Barcelona, Inter-Rail (ⓦinterrail.eu) and Eurail (ⓦeurail.com) aren't a good deal, and even if you intend to travel around Catalunya by train, rail travel in that part of Spain is fairly limited (and quite cheap), so you probably won't get your money's worth.

By bus

Eurolines (ⓦeurolines.co.uk) operates a year-round bus service three times a week to Barcelona from London, which takes up to 28 hours. It typically costs around £153 return, though by booking well in advance you may be able to bring that down below £100. Eurolines also sells Barcelona tickets and transport to London at all UK National Express bus terminals.

Driving to Barcelona

It takes a good two days, with stops, to drive the 1600km from London to Barcelona. Motoring organizations such as AA (ⓦtheaa.com) or the RAC (ⓦrac.co.uk) can advise on insurance, documentation and avoiding toll roads. If you're bringing your own car, carry your licence, vehicle registration and insurance documents with you; you should also have two warning triangles, a breathalyzer kit, and a fluorescent vest in case of breakdown.

Although many people use the various ferry links to get from England to France – principally Dover–Calais, though services to Brittany or Normandy can be more convenient – the quickest way across the Channel is the **Eurotunnel** service (Ⓦeurotunnel .com), which operates drive-on-drive-off shuttle trains between Folkestone and Calais/Coquelles.

Alternatively, Brittany Ferries (Ⓦbrittany-ferries .co.uk) operates car and passenger ferry services from Portsmouth (2–3 weekly; 24hr) and Plymouth to **Santander** (one weekly; 20hr), which is around 6–7 hours' drive from Barcelona, and from Portsmouth only to **Bilbao** (2 weekly; 24 or 32hr), which is more like 5–6 hours' drive. Expect to pay at least £200 each way for a car, two passengers and a cabin, and potentially much more in summer.

Once in Barcelona itself, you're unlikely to need a car (see p.24).

Arrival and departure

Whether you travel to Barcelona by plane, train or bus, it's usually possible to get to a city-centre hotel within an hour of arrival.

By air

Barcelona airport (☎ 902 404 704, Ⓦwww.aena.es) is around 15km southwest of the city centre at El Prat de Llobregat. The terminals hold tourist information offices that handle hotel bookings, as well as ATMs, exchange facilities and car-rental offices.

Metered **taxis** wait at the terminals, and charge around €30 for trips to the city centre, including the airport surcharge (plus other surcharges for travel after 8pm and at weekends, and for any luggage that goes in the boot).

Barcelona's metro system does not extend to the airport, but a cheap and efficient **airport train service** (daily 5.42am–11.38pm; journey time 19min; €4.10; ☎902 320 320) runs every thirty minutes to Barcelona Sants station (the main train station) and Passeig de Gràcia (best stop for Eixample, Plaça de Catalunya and the Ramblas). It departs from Terminal T2 – a free shuttle-bus to the station from T1 takes around ten minutes. Trains back to the airport run from Barcelona Sants on a similar half-hourly schedule (daily 5.13am–11.14pm). Zone 1 city travel passes (*targetes*) and the Barcelona Card are valid on the airport train service.

Alternatively, the **Aerobús** service (daily 5.35am–1.05am; €5.90 one-way, €10.20 return; departures every 5–10min; Ⓦaerobusbcn.com) from T1 and T2 stops in the city at Plaça d'Espanya, Gran Via–Urgell, Plaça Universitat and Plaça de Catalunya. It takes around 35–40 minutes to reach Plaça de Catalunya, though allow longer in the rush hour. Aerobús departures to the airport from Plaça de Catalunya leave from in front of El Corte Inglés department store (daily 5.30am–12.30am); note that terminals T1 and T2 are served by separate services.

Anyone flying into **Girona airport**, 90km north of Barcelona, can take the Sagalés Airport Line bus direct to Barcelona Nord bus station (€16 one-way, €25 return; journey time 1hr 15min; ☎ 902 130 014, Ⓦsagalesairportline.com). From **Reus airport**, 110km south of Barcelona, there's a connecting Hispano Igualadina bus to Barcelona Sants (€15.35 one-way, €26.50 return; 1hr 30min; ☎902 292 900, Ⓦigualadina.com).

By train

The main station for domestic and international arrivals – **Barcelona Sants**, 3km west of the city centre – holds a tourist office with an accommodation booking service, plus ATMs, an exchange office, car-rental outlets, a police station and left-luggage facilities. The metro station that's accessed from inside Barcelona Sants is called ⓂSants Estació. Line 3 from here runs direct to Liceu (for the Ramblas), Catalunya (for Plaça de Catalunya) and Passeig de Gràcia, while line 5 runs to Diagonal.

Some Spanish intercity services and international trains also stop at **Estació de França**, 1km east of the Ramblas and close to ⓂBarceloneta. Other possible arrival points by train are **Plaça de Catalunya**, at the top of the Ramblas (for trains from coastal towns north of the city), and **Passeig de Gràcia** (Catalunya provincial destinations).

Barcelona and Madrid are connected by the high-speed **AVE line** (Alta Velocidad Española), which takes between 2hr 30min and 3hr 10min and runs via Tarragona and Zaragoza. Arrivals and departures are at Barcelona Sants, though a second high-speed station is due to open at **La Sagrera**, east of the centre beyond Glòries, at some future point.

TRAIN INFORMATION

RENFE ☎ 902 320 320, Ⓦ renfe.com. For all national rail enquiries, sales and reservations. At Barcelona Sants station (Pl. dels Països Catalans, Sants; Ⓜ Sants Estació) there are train information desks and advance ticket booking counters, some with English speakers.

By bus

The main bus terminal, used by international, long-distance and provincial buses, is **Barcelona Nord** on c/d'Ali-Bei (☎902 260 606, ⓦbarcelonanord.cat; ⓜArc de Triomf), four blocks north of Parc de la Ciutadella. There's a bus information desk on the ground floor (daily 7am–9pm), plus a tourist office (daily 9am–7pm), accommodation agency, ATMs, shops and luggage lockers. Various companies operate services across Catalunya, Spain and Europe – reserve tickets in advance for long-distance routes, either online, or at the station a day before.

Some intercity and international Eurolines services also stop at the bus terminal behind Barcelona Sants station on c/de Viriat (ⓜSants Estació). Either way, you're only a short metro ride from the city centre.

By car

Driving into Barcelona is reasonably straight-forward, with traffic only slow in the morning and evening rush hours. Parking, however, is a different matter altogether – rarely easy and not cheap. If your trip is just to the city and its surroundings, our advice is not to bother with a car at all (see p.24).

Coming into Barcelona along any one of the motorways (*autopistes*), head for the Ronda Litoral (B-10), the southern half of the city's ring road. Following signs for "Port Vell" (coming from the south) or "Ciutat Vella" (coming from the north) will take you towards the main exit for the old town, though there is also an exit for Gran Via de les Corts Catalanes (C-31) if uptown Barcelona is your destination.

City transport

Barcelona's excellent integrated transport system comprises the metro, buses, trams and local trains, plus assorted funiculars and cable cars. The local transport authority, Transports Metropolitans de Barcelona (TMB; ⓦtmb.cat), has a useful website (English language available) with full timetable and ticket information.

TMB operates customer service centres at Barcelona Sants station, and at Universitat, Diagonal and Sagrada Família metro stations, where you can pick up a free public transport map. The map and ticket information is also posted at major bus stops and all metro and tram stations.

Tickets and travel passes

A transit plan divides the province into six zones, but as the entire metropolitan area of Barcelona (including the airport) falls within **Zone 1**, that's the only one you'll need to worry about on a day-to-day basis.

On all the city's public transport, including night buses and funiculars, you can buy a single ticket every time you ride (€2.15), but if you're staying for a few days it's much cheaper to buy a *targeta* – a **discount ticket** strip which you pass through the metro or train barrier, or slot in the machine on the bus, tram or funicular. The *targetes* are available at metro, train and tram stations, but not on the buses.

The best general deal is the **T-10** ("tay day-oo" in Catalan) *targeta* (€9.95), valid for ten separate journeys, with changes between methods of transport allowed within 75 minutes. The ticket can also be used by more than one person at a time – just make sure you punch it the same number of times as there are people travelling. It's also available at newsstands and tobacconists.

Other useful (single-person) *targetes* for Zone 1 include the **T-Dia** ("tay dee-ah"; one day's unlimited travel; €7.60); the **Hola BCN!** (two to five days' travel; €14–32); the **T-50/30** (fifty trips within a thirty-day period; €42.50); or the **T-Mes** (one month; €52.75) – for the latter, the station ticket office will need to see some form of ID (driving licence or passport). The Barcelona Card (see box, p.26) also includes city transport for between two and five days.

Heading for Sitges, Montserrat or further **out of town**, you'll need to buy a specific ticket or relevant-zoned *targeta* as the Zone 1 *targetes* don't run that far. Anyone caught without a valid ticket anywhere on the system is liable to an immediate fine of €100 (or €50 if you pay in cash on the spot).

The metro

The quickest way to get around Barcelona is by **metro**, which runs on eight lines. Metro entrances are marked with a red diamond sign with an "M". Its **hours of operation** are Monday to Thursday, plus Sunday and public holidays, 5am to midnight; Friday and evenings of public holidays, 5am to 2am; Saturday 24-hour service. There's a metro map at the back of this book, or you can pick up a little foldout one at metro stations (ask for *una guia del metro*).

Trains are fast and efficient, but note that changing from one line to another can involve a very long walk within what's nominally the same station. The system is perfectly safe, though buskers and beggars are common, moving from one carriage to the next.

Buses

Most buses operate daily, roughly from 4 or 5am until 10.30pm, though some lines stop earlier and some run until after midnight. Night bus (*Nit bus*) services fill in the gaps on all the main routes, with services every twenty to sixty minutes from around 10pm to 4am. Many bus routes (including all night buses) stop in or near Plaça de Catalunya, but the full route is marked at each bus stop, along with a timetable.

Trams

The tram system (W tram.cat) runs on six lines, with departures every eight to twenty minutes throughout the day from 5am up to as late as 3am on some segments. **Lines T1**, **T2** and **T3** depart from Plaça Francesc Macià and run along the uptown part of Avinguda Diagonal to suburban destinations in the northwest – useful tourist stops are at L'illa shopping centre and the María Cristina and Palau Reial metro stations. **Line T4** operates from Ciutadella-Vila Olímpica (where there's also a metro station) and runs up past the zoo and TNC (the National Theatre) to Glòries before running down Avinguda Diagonal to Diagonal Mar and the Parc del Fòrum. You're unlikely to use suburban lines T5 and T6.

Trains

Barcelona has a cheap and efficient commuter train line, the **Ferrocarrils de la Generalitat de Catalunya** (FGC; ☎ 932 051 515, W fgc.cat), with its main stations at Plaça de Catalunya and Plaça d'Espanya. These go to places like Sarrià, Vallvidrera,

Tibidabo, Sant Cugat, Terrassa and Montserrat, and details are given in the text where appropriate. The Zone 1 *targeta* is valid as far as the city limits, which in practice is everywhere you're likely to want to go except for Montserrat, Colònia Güell, Sant Cugat and Terrassa.

The national rail service, operated by **RENFE** (☎ 902 320 320, W renfe.com), runs all the other services out of Barcelona. Local lines – north to the Costa Mareseme and south to Sitges – are designated as **Rodiales/Cercanías**. The hub is Barcelona Sants station, with services also passing through Plaça de Catalunya (heading north) and Passeig de Gràcia (south). Arrive in plenty of time to buy a ticket, as queues are often horrendous, though for all destinations you can use the automatic vending machines instead.

Taxis

Black-and-yellow taxis (with a green roof-light on when available for hire) are relatively inexpensive – most short journeys across town run to around €9. There's a minimum charge of €2.10 and after that it's €1.07 per kilometre (€1.24–1.44 after 8pm, and on Sat, Sun & hols), with surcharges for baggage (€1 per piece) and pick-ups from Barcelona Sants station (€2.10) and the airport (€3.10). The taxis have meters so charges are transparent – if not, asking for a receipt (*rebut* in Catalan, *recibo* in Spanish) should ensure that the price is fair. Current rates are posted on W www.taxibarcelona.cat. Many taxis take credit-card payment.

Taxi ranks can be found outside major train and metro stations, in main squares, near large hotels and along the main avenues. You can call a taxi in advance, for an additional charge of €3.40–4.50 on top of the fare, but few of the cab company operators speak English.

TAXI COMPANIES

Barna Taxis ☎ 933 222 222, W barnataxi.com
Radio Taxi ☎ 933 033 033, W radiotaxi033.com
Servi-Taxi ☎ 933 300 300, W servitaxi.com

UP AND AWAY – FUNICULARS AND CABLE CARS

Several **funicular rail lines** still operate in the city, up the hills to Montjuïc park, Tibidabo funfair and the suburban village of Vallvidrera. Summer and year-round weekend visits to Tibidabo also combine a funicular trip with a fun ride on the clanking antique tram, the **Tramvia Blau** (see p.138).

There are also two dramatic **cable-car** (*telefèric*) rides: from Barceloneta right across the harbour to Montjuïc (see p.78), and then from the top station of the Montjuïc funicular all the way up to the castle. Both are great experiences, worth doing just for the views alone.

Driving

You don't need a car to get around Barcelona, but you may want to rent one if you plan to see any more of Catalunya. That said, in summer the coastal roads in particular are nightmarish, so if you just want to zip to the beach or wine region for the day, it's far better to stick to the trains. Driving in the city itself is not for the faint-hearted either. Parking is notoriously difficult, and vehicle crime is rampant – never leave anything visible in the car.

Most foreign **driving licences** are honoured in Spain – including all EU, US and Canadian ones. Remember that you drive on the right in Spain, and away from main roads you yield to vehicles approaching from the right. Speed limits are posted – maximum on urban roads is 60kph, other roads 90kph, motorways 120kph. Wearing seatbelts is compulsory.

Parking

City-centre display boards indicate which indoor **car parks** have free spaces. Central locations include Plaça de Catalunya, Plaça Urquinaona, Arc de Triomf, Passeig de Gràcia, Plaça dels Angels/MACBA and Avinguda Paral.lel. Parking in any of these is convenient, but it's also pretty expensive (1hr from around €3; 24hr from €30).

City-owned **long-term car parks**, run by BSM (Barcelona Serveis Municipals; **W** bsmsa.cat), are available for residents and visitors, and work out cheaper. The best option is the large Plaça Fòrum car park at Diagonal Mar (Pl. d'Ernest Lluch i Martin; **M** El Maresme-Fòrum or tram T4). Parking for between one and five days costs €39.90, plus €7.50 for each additional day. Closer to the centre, the 24-hour BSM car park at Barcelona Nord bus station (c/d'Ali-Bei 54; **M** Arc de Triomf) costs €18.40 per day.

FOLLOW THAT TRIXI

A fun way to get around the old town, port area and beaches is by **trixi** (**W** trixi.com), a kind of love-bug-style bicycle-rickshaw. They tout for business between noon and 8pm outside La Seu (cathedral) in the Barri Gòtic, though you can also flag them down if one cruises by or make an advance reservation. Fares are fixed (€18 for 30min, €30 for 1hr, longer tours available) and the *trixistas* are an amiable, multilingual bunch for the most part. As they say, "It's transportainment!".

Street parking is permitted in most areas, but it can be tough to find spaces, especially in the old town and Gràcia, where it's nearly all either restricted access or residents' parking only. The ubiquitous residents' **Área Verda meter-zones** (**W** areaverda .bsmsa.cat) throughout the city allow pay-and-display parking for visitors, for €3 per hour, with either a one- or two-hour maximum stay. Elsewhere, don't be tempted to double-park, leave your car in loading zones or otherwise park illegally – the **towing fee** is €150, plus a daily €20 charge, and no mercy is shown to tourists or foreign-plated vehicles.

Vehicle rental

Car rental is cheapest arranged in advance through one of the large multinational agencies. In Barcelona, the major chains have outlets at the airport and at, or near, Barcelona Sants station. Inclusive rates start from around €40 per day for an economy car (less by the week, and often with good rates for a three-day weekend rental, around €150). Drivers need to be at least 21 (23 with some companies) and to have been driving for at least a year. It's essential to take out fully comprehensive insurance and pay for Collision Damage Waiver, otherwise you'll be liable for every scratch.

Some local outlets, like Vanguard (**T** 934 393 880, **W** vanguardrent.com), rent out **mopeds and motorcycles**, though given the traffic conditions and the good public transport system, it's not really recommended as a means of getting around the city.

Cycling

The city council has embraced cycling, and is investing heavily in cycle lanes and schemes such as the much-touted **Bicing** pick-up and drop-off system (**W** bicing.com). You'll see the red bikes and bike stations all over the city, but Bicing is aimed at encouraging locals to use the bikes for short trips, rather than at tourists. Users can register online or at the **Oficina del Bicing**, Pl. Pi i Sunyer 8–10, Barri Gòtic, between c/de la Canuda and c/de Duran i Bas (Mon–Fri 8.30am–5.30pm).

In any case, **bike-rental outfits** all over town are more geared to tourist requirements, charging from around €6 for two hours, and €15 for a full 24 hours. Many cycle-tour companies (see opposite) can also fix you up with a rental bike.

BIKE RENTAL

Bicicleta Barcelona c/de l'Esparteria 3, La Ribera **M** Barceloneta **T** 932 682 105, **W** bicicletabarcelona.com

Biciclot Pg. Marítim 33, Port Olímpic ⓜ Ciutadella-Vila Olímpica ☎ 932 219 778, ⓦ biciclot.net
Budget Bikes c/d'Estruc 38, Plaça Catalunya ⓜ Catalunya ☎ 933 041 885, ⓦ budgetbikes.eu
Rent Electric c/del Pas de l'Ensenyança 1, Barri Gòtic ⓜ Jaume I ☎ 670 474 474, ⓦ rent-electric.com

City tours

The number of available tours is bewildering, and you can see the sights on anything from a Segway to a hot-air balloon. Bike tours in particular are hugely popular – at times it seems as if every tourist in the city is playing follow-my-leader down the same old-town alley – while other operators offer tapas-bar crawls, party nights and out-of-town excursions. Highest profile are the open-top sightseeing bus tours, whose board-at-will services can drop you outside every attraction in the city. Barcelona also has some particularly good walking tours, showing you parts of the old town you might not find otherwise, while sightseeing boats offer a different view of the city.

BIKE TOURS

Bike Tours Barcelona ☎ 932 682 105, ⓦ biketoursbarcelona.com. Find the red-T-shirted guides in Pl. de Sant Jaume in the Barri Gòtic, outside the tourist office (top of c/de la Ciutat) – tours last 3hr (daily 11am, plus April to mid-Sept Fri–Mon 4.30pm; €22), no reservations required.
Fat Tire Bike Tours ☎ 933 429 275, ⓦ fattirebiketours.com. English-speaking guides lead the way during these relaxed four-hour pedals past some of the city's most iconic sights (daily: mid-April to mid-Oct 11am & 4pm; mid-Oct to mid-April 11am; €24). No reservations required; tour meets at Pl. Sant Jaume on the side nearest to Las Ramblas. They also offer tours of Montjuïc on electrically assisted e-bikes, for which reservations are required (Tues, Thurs, Sat & Sun; €34).

BUS TOURS

Barcelona City Tour ⓦ www.barcelonatours.es. The red buses make a circular sweep through the city on two routes, east and west, from Pl. de Catalunya (daily 9am–8pm, departures every 10–20min). Tickets available on board and online: one-day €27, two-day €38 (under-12s €16/20 respectively, under-4s free), with a ten percent reduction for online bookings.
Bus Turístic ⓦ barcelonabusturistic.cat. The main official sightseeing service (departures every 5–25min) with over forty stops on three combined routes, linking all the main tourist sights. Northern (red) and southern (blue) routes depart from Pl. de Catalunya (daily 9am–7pm; April–Sept 9am–8pm), and a full circuit on either route takes two hours.

The green Fòrum route (daily April–Sept 9.30am–8pm) runs from Port Olímpic to Diagonal Mar and back via the beaches, and takes forty minutes. Tickets are valid for all routes, and cost €27 for one day, €38 for two days (children aged 4–12 €16/20 respectively, under-4s free). The ticket also gives discounts at various sights, attractions, shops and restaurants. Buy on board the bus, at Sants station or any tourist office or TMB customer centre, or online for a ten percent reduction.

WALKING TOURS

Barcelona Walking Tours ☎ 932 853 832, ⓦ barcelonaturisme .com. The Pl. de Catalunya tourist office coordinates a popular series of walks and tours, including a two-hour historical walking tour of the Barri Gòtic (daily 9.30am; €16). There are also Picasso tours that include an hour walking and an hour in the Picasso museum (April–Oct Tues–Sat 3pm; Nov–March Tues, Thurs & Sat 3pm; €22, includes museum entry); a two-hour *modernisme* tour (Wed & Fri: April–Oct 6pm; Nov–March 3.30pm; €16); gourmet tour (Mon & Fri 10.30am; €22, includes tastings); a three-hour tapas tour, with copious food and drink tastings (Mon–Sat 5pm; €59); and many other specialist itineraries. Times given are for the current English-language tours; advance booking essential (discounts for online bookings, and reductions for children/seniors).
My Favourite Things ☎ 637 265 405, ⓦ myft.net. Highly individual tours that reveal the city in a new light – whether it's where and what the locals eat, contemporary architecture or Barcelona in the movies. Tours (in English) cost €26 per person and last around four hours, and there's always time for anecdotes, diversions, workshop visits and café visits. Tour numbers are limited to ten, and advance bookings are essential – call or email for latest information or tailor-made requests.
Runner Bean Walking Tour ☎ 636 108 776, ⓦ runnerbeantours .com. Spanish-Irish couple Gorka and Ann-Marie, along with their team of passionate, well-versed guides, offer a couple of free walking tours (2hr 30min; donations accepted), one devoted to Gaudí and the other to the Old City, and also a longer programme of specialist tours and private excursions, including activity-packed tours for kids (€45 for one child and one or two adults).
Spanish Civil War Tour ⓔ nick.iberianature@gmail.com, ⓦ iberianature.com. Engrossing English-language tours on Barcelona and the Spanish Civil War, bringing to life the city that George Orwell knew so well. Tours are under the auspices of a local history society and led by Civil War enthusiast Nick Lloyd. Three-hour walks around the old town or a visit to the mass grave at Montjuïc cost €20 per person.

WATER TOURS

Catamaran Orsom ☎ 934 410 537, ⓦ barcelona-orsom.com. Catamaran trips around the port (May–Sept daily noon or 3.30pm; €15.50), plus jazz cruises (May–Sept daily 3.30pm; €16.50; July & Aug also Fri–Sun 8pm; €19.50). Both depart from the Moll de Drassanes, opposite the Columbus statue at the bottom of the Ramblas (ⓜ Drassanes); you can buy tickets there, but call ahead to be certain of departures.
Las Golondrinas ☎ 934 423 106, ⓦ www.lasgolondrinas.com. Daily sightseeing boats depart from Pl. Portal de la Pau, behind the Columbus monument (July–Sept every 30min; Feb–May, Oct & Nov at least 5 daily; none Dec & Jan; ⓜ Drassanes) – trips are either around

the port (40min; €7, under-10s €2.75, under-4s free), or port and coast including the Port Olímpic and Diagonal Mar (90min; €14.80, under-10s €5.35, under-4s free). Bad weather can force cancellations.

Information

The city tourist board, Turisme de Barcelona, is the best first stop for information about Barcelona, with a really useful English-language website that sells discounted tickets for most city museums and attractions (ⓦbarcelona turisme.com), and offices at the airport, Barcelona Sants station, Plaça de Catalunya and Plaça de Sant Jaume.

There are also **staffed kiosks** in main tourist areas, such as on the Ramblas, outside the Sagrada Família and at Plaça d'Espanya, which dispense information and sell discount passes and entrance tickets for popular attractions.

For information about the wider province of Catalunya, you need the Generalitat's information centre (Centre d'Informació de Catalunya) at **Palau Robert**, while events, concerts, exhibitions, festivals and other cultural diversions are covered in full at the Institut de Cultura in the **Palau de la Virreina** on the Ramblas.

The city hall (Ajuntament; ⓦbcn.cat) and regional government (Generalitat; ⓦgencat.cat) **websites** are absolute mines of information about every aspect of cultural, social and working life in Barcelona, from museum opening hours and festival dates to local politics and council office locations; they both have English-language versions. Also useful is ⓦ**barcelona-online.com**, with punchy reviews in English of all things Barcelona, plus links to scores of other websites.

For arts and events listings, the websites of the local newspapers and magazines (see opposite) are also very useful.

INFORMATION OFFICES

Turisme de Barcelona ☎ 932 853 834, ⓦ barcelonaturisme.com. Main office, Pl. de Catalunya 17, Ⓜ Catalunya (daily 9am–8pm); also at Pl. de Sant Jaume, entrance at c/de la Ciutat 2, Barri Gòtic, Ⓜ Jaume I (Mon–Fri 8.30am–8pm, Sat 9am–7pm, Sun & hols 9am–2pm); Airport Terminals 1 & 2 (daily 9am–8pm); Barcelona Sants, Pl. dels Països Catalans, Ⓜ Sants Estació (daily 9am–8pm); Pl. Espanya, Av. María Cristina, Ⓜ Espanya (July–Sept daily 8.30am–7.30pm; Oct–June daily 9am–3pm); Sagrada Família, Pl. Sagrada Família, Ⓜ Sagrada Família (July–Sept daily 8.30am–7.30pm; Oct–June daily 9am–3pm); Mirador do Colom, Pl. Portal de la Pau, Ⓜ Drassanes (daily 9am–8pm). The main Pl. de Catalunya office is down the steps in the southeast corner of the square, opposite El Corte Inglés. It's always busy and can be frustrating if you just

---

DISCOUNT CARDS AND PACKAGES

If you're planning to do a lot of sightseeing, you can save money by buying one of the widely available discount cards. Only you can know for sure which suits your needs, but the Barcelona Card is likely to be the best deal, as it includes public transport.

- **Barcelona Card** (3 days €45, 4 days €55 or 5 days €60; ⓦbarcelonaturisme.com). Covers public transport, plus admission to most of the major museums (except the Picasso museum), and big discounts at other museums, venues, shops, theatres and restaurants. A two-day version, called Barcelona Card Express, costs €20, and includes transport but no free museum admissions, only discounts. All are available at points of arrival, tourist offices and kiosks and other outlets, and there's a ten-percent discount if you buy online.

- **Articket** (€30, valid three months; ⓦarticketbcn.org). Free admission into the permanent and temporary exhibitions at six major art centres and galleries (MNAC, MACBA, CCCB, Museu Picasso, Fundació Antoni Tàpies and Fundació Joan Miró). Buy at participating galleries, at Barcelona tourist offices and kiosks or online. For most visitors, the Barcelona Card is a better option.

- **Arqueoticket** (€13.50, valid calendar year). In the same vein as Articket, offers free entry into four historical museums (Museu d'Arqueologia de Catalunya, Egipci, Historia de Barcelona and Marítim). Available at participating museums and tourist offices. It's only worth buying if you plan to visit them all, and don't have a Barcelona Card.

- **Ruta del Modernisme** (€12, valid one year; ⓦrutadelmodernisme.com). An excellent English-language guidebook, map and discount-voucher package that covers 116 *modernista* buildings in Barcelona and other Catalan towns, offering discounts of up to fifty percent on admission fees, tours and purchases. If you plan to visit several such sites, this will probably prove worth having as well as a Barcelona Card.

want a quick answer to a question. There's also a money exchange service, separate accommodation desk, tour and ticket sales and a gift shop. **Institut de Cultura** Palau de la Virreina, Ramblas 99 ☎ 933 161 000, ⓦ barcelonacultura.bcn.cat, Ⓜ Liceu (daily 10am–8.30pm). Cultural information office, with advance information on everything that's happening in the city, from events and concerts to exhibitions and festivals; you can also buy tickets here. The website has daily updated cultural news and web TV previews, or pick up the free *Cultural Agenda* (in English), a useful monthly what's-on listings guide.

Centre del Modernisme ☎ 933 177 652, ⓦ rutadelmodernisme .com. Offices at Institut Municipal del Paisatge Urbà i la Qualitat de Vida, Ajuntament de Barcelona, Av. Drassanes 6–8, planta 21, Ⓜ Drassanes (Mon–Fri 9am–2pm), and Pavellons Güell, Av. de Pedralbes 7, Pedralbes, Ⓜ Palau Reial (Sat & Sun 10am–2pm). The staffed information desks provide details of visits to the city's *modernista* buildings and monuments, and sell the Ruta del Modernisme package.

Centre d'Informació de Catalunya Palau Robert, Pg. de Gràcia 107, Eixample ☎ 932 388 091 or ☎ 932 388 012, ⓦ gencat.cat /palaurobert, Ⓜ Diagonal (Mon–Sat 10am–8pm, Sun & hols 10am–2.30pm). Information about travel in Catalunya, plus maps, guides, details of how to get around and lists of places to stay. Also exhibitions and events relating to all matters Catalan.

Barcelona Informació (Oficina d'Atenció Ciutadana) Pl. de Sant Miquel 3, Barri Gòtic ☎ 010, ⓦ bcn.cat, Ⓜ Jaume I (Mon–Sat 8.30am–8pm, except Aug Sat 9am–2pm). Citizens' information office, around the back of the Ajuntament in the new building. It's not really for tourists, but is invariably helpful about all aspects of living in Barcelona (though you can't count on English being spoken).

The media

You can buy foreign newspapers and magazines at the stalls down the Ramblas, and around Plaça de Catalunya, on Passeig de Gràcia, on Rambla de Catalunya and at Barcelona Sants station. If you can't find what you're looking for, try FNAC at El Triangle on Plaça de Catalunya (Ⓜ Catalunya), which has an excellent ground-floor magazine section.

Newspapers and magazines

The best **local newspaper** is the Barcelona edition of the liberal *El País* (ⓦ elpais.es), which has a daily Catalunya supplement and is good on entertainment and the arts. The conservative Barcelona paper *La Vanguardia* (ⓦ lavanguardia.es) has turned rather downmarket in recent years, but still has a good arts and culture listings section on Friday, while *El Periódico* (ⓦ elperiodico.com) is more tabloid in style, and also comes in a Catalan edition. *Avui* (ⓦ avui.cat) is the chief nationalist paper,

printed in Catalan. For wall-to-wall coverage of sport (for which, in Barcelona, read FC Barcelona), buy the specialist dailies *Mundo Deportivo* (ⓦ elmundo deportivo.es) or *Sport* (ⓦ sport.es).

The two most useful weekly **city listings publications** are *Guia del Ocio* (ⓦ enbarcelona.com), a small paperback-book-sized magazine (in Spanish), and the magazine-format *Time Out Barcelona* (English website at ⓦ timeout.cat), available all over the city.

English-language publications

Barcelona Metropolitan (ⓦ barcelona-metropolitan .com) is a free monthly magazine for English-speakers living in Barcelona, while another free monthly **Barcelona Connect** (ⓦ barcelonaconnect.com), contains an idiosyncratic mixture of news, views, reviews and classified ads. You'll find these and other free magazines in hotels, hostels, bars and other outlets; the online versions are pretty comprehensive too. For the style scene, look in newsagents for **b-guided** (ⓦ b-guided.com), a painfully cool quarterly magazine, while the excellent ⓦ **barcelona.lecool .com** is a hip cultural agenda and city guide, available online or as a weekly e-magazine.

Television

In Catalunya you can pick up two **national TV channels**, TVE1 and TVE2 (La 2), a couple of **Catalan-language channels**, TV3 and Canal 33, and the private Antena 3, Cuatro (ie, Four), Tele 5 and La Sexta (The Sixth) channels. Barcelona itself also offers the city-run **Barcelona Televisió** (ⓦ btv .cat), which is useful for information about local events, and news programmes on the otherwise subscriber-only Digital Plus channel. TVs in most *pensions* and small hotels tend to offer these stations, with cable and satellite channels available in higher-rated hotels.

Travel essentials

Admission charges

Admission charges for city attractions vary between €3 and €21, with most museums and galleries costing around €7–8. Many offer free admission on the first or last Sunday of every month, and most museums are free on the saints' days of February 12, April 23 and September 24, plus May 18 (international museum day). There's usually a reduction

ADDRESSES

Addresses are written as: c/Picasso 2 4° – which means Picasso street (*carrer*) number two, fourth floor. You may also see *esquerra*, meaning "left-hand" (apartment or office); *dreta* is right; *centro* centre. C/Picasso s/n means the building has no number (*sense numero*). In the gridded streets of the Eixample, building numbers run from south to north (ie lower numbers at the Plaça de Catalunya end) and from west to east (lower numbers at Plaça d'Espanya).

The main address abbreviations used in this book are: Av. (for Avinguda, avenue); Bxda. (for Baixada, alley); c/ (for Carrer, street); Pg. (for Passeig, more a boulevard than a street); Pl. (for Plaça, square); and Ptge. (for Passatge, passage).

or free entrance if you show a student, youth or senior citizen card. Several discount cards give heavily reduced admission to Barcelona's museums and galleries (see box, p.26) – worth considering if you're planning to see everything the city has to offer.

Costs

Barcelona is not a particularly cheap place to visit, and it tends to be more expensive than other major cities in Spain. However, it still rates as pretty good value when compared with the cost of visiting cities in Britain, France or Germany, especially when it comes to dining out or getting around on public transport. Hotel prices are the main drain on the budget. Realistically, you'll be paying from €80 a night for a room in a simple *pensió*, and from €140 for a three-star or budget boutique hotel. Still, once you're there, a one-day public transport pass gives you the freedom of the city for €7.60, and most museums and galleries cost €7–8 (though a few showpiece attractions charge much higher entry fees). A set three-course lunch goes for €10–15, and dinner from around €25, though of course the Michelin-starred destination restaurants are much pricier – even so, at around €100 a head, they're still a far better deal than the equivalent places in London or Paris.

Crime and personal safety

Catalunya has its own autonomous police force, the **Mossos d'Esquadra** (Ⓦ gencat.net/mossos), dressed in navy-blue uniforms with red trim. They have gradually taken over most of the local duties traditionally carried out by Spain's other police services, namely the **Policía Nacional** (Ⓦ policia.es) – the national police, in uniforms resembling blue combat gear – and the **Guàrdia Urbana** (Ⓦ bcn.cat/guardia urbana), municipal police in blue shirts and high-visibility jackets. There's also the **Guàrdia Civil**, a national paramilitary force in green uniforms, seen guarding some public buildings, and at airports and border crossings.

BUDGET BARCELONA

Boutique hotels, designer stores, gourmet restaurants and hip bars – life in Barcelona can get pretty pricey at times. But here's how to keep costs to a minimum while still having a great time.

- **Cafés and restaurants** Eat your main meal of the day at lunchtime, when the *menú del dia* offers fantastic value. Also note that there's usually a surcharge for terrace service.
- **Public transport** Buy a public transport travel pass, which will save you around fifty percent on every ride, or a Barcelona Card.
- **Discount cards** There are several useful city discount cards or packages, while you should bring along any student, youth or senior citizen card you're entitled to carry, as they often attract discounts on museum, gallery and attraction charges.
- **Special offers** Take advantage of the discount nights at the cinema (Mon & sometimes Wed), and at the theatre (Tues), and visit Tiquet Rambles in the Palau de la Virreina for half-price last-minute theatre and show tickets.
- **Museums and galleries** At many museums and galleries, admission is usually free one day a month, and most museums are free on saints' days (see p.27).
- **See the sights for free** Go to the Ramblas, Boqueria market, La Seu, Santa María del Mar, Ajuntament and Generalitat, Parc de la Ciutadella, Parc de Collserola, Port Vell, Port Olímpic, city beaches, Els Encants flea market, Diagonal Mar/Fòrum and Caixa Forum– all free.

EMERGENCY SERVICES

In an emergency, dial:
Ambulance, police and fire services ☎ **112**
Ambulance ☎ **061**
Fire service ☎ **080**
Police numbers:
Guàrdia Urbana ☎ **092**
Mossos d'Esquadra ☎ **088**
Policía Nacional ☎ **091**

In theory you're supposed to carry some kind of **identification** at all times, and the police can stop you in the street and demand to see it. In practice they're rarely bothered if you're clearly a tourist – and a photocopy of your passport or a photo-driving licence should suffice.

If you're robbed, you need to go to the police to report it, not least because your insurance company will require a police report. Don't expect a great deal of concern if your loss is relatively small – but do expect the process of completing forms and formalities to take ages.

The easiest place to report a crime is at the **Guàrdia Urbana station** at Ramblas 43, opposite Pl. Reial, ⓜ Liceu, ☎ 932 562 430 (24hr; English spoken), though there's a Guàrdia Urbana office in each city district (see their website).

However, to get a police report for your insurance you need to go to the **Mossos d'Esquadra station** at c/Nou de la Rambla 76–80, El Raval, ⓜ Paral.lel (☎ 933 062 300). You can fill in a report online (under "Denúncies", then "Denúncies per internet" on the website, English option available), but you'll still have to go to the office within 72hr to sign the document.

Electricity

The electricity supply is 220v and plugs come with two round pins – bring an adaptor (and transformer) to use UK and US laptops, cellphone chargers, etc.

Embassies and consulates

Most countries have an embassy in Madrid and maintain a consulate in Barcelona. You'll need to contact them if you lose your passport or need other assistance. Most consulates are open to the public for enquiries Monday to Friday, usually 9am to 1pm and 3 to 5pm, though the morning shift is the most reliable.

FOREIGN CONSULATES IN BARCELONA

Australia Av. Diagonal 433bis, Esquerra de l'Eixample ☎ 933 623 792, ⓦ spain.embassy.gov.au; ⓜ Hospital Clínic.

Canada Pl. de Catalunya 9, Dreta de l'Eixample ☎ 932 703 614, ⓦ canadainternational.gc.ca; ⓜ Catalunya.

New Zealand Trav. de Gràcia 64, Gràcia ☎ 932 090 399, ⓦ nzembassy.com; FGC Gràcia.

Republic of Ireland Gran Via Carles III 94, Les Corts ☎ 934 915 021, ⓦ embassyofireland.es; ⓜ María Cristina/Les Corts.

UK Av. Diagonal 477, Esquerra de l'Eixample ☎ 902 109 356, ⓦ ukinspain.fco.gov.uk; ⓜ Hospital Clínic.

US Pg. de la Reina Elisenda 23, Sàrria ☎ 932 802 227, ⓦ barcelona .usconsulate.gov; FGC Reina Elisenda.

Entry requirements

EU citizens need only a **valid national identity card or passport** to enter Spain. Other Europeans, and citizens of the United States, Canada, Australia and New Zealand, require a passport but no visa and can stay as a tourist for up to ninety days. Other nationalities (including South Africans) will need to get a **visa** from a Spanish embassy or consulate before departure. Visa requirements do change and it's always advisable to check the current situation before leaving home.

Most EU citizens who want to stay in Spain for longer than three months, rather than just visit as a

STAYING SAFE

Barcelona has a reputation as a city plagued by petty crime, but you don't need to be unduly paranoid. Take all reasonable precautions, and your trip should be a safe one. Sling **bags** across your body, not off one shoulder; don't carry wallets in back pockets; and don't hang bags on the back of a café chair. Make photocopies of your **passport**, leaving the original and any tickets in the hotel safe.

Be on your guard when on **public transport**, or on the crowded Ramblas and the medieval streets to either side – at night, avoid unlit streets and dark alleys. While you can take many **beggars** at face value, you should beware of people directly accosting you or who in any other manner try to distract you – like the "helpful" person pointing out bird shit (shaving cream or something similar) on your jacket while someone relieves you of your money.

tourist, need to register at the **Oficina de Extranjería** (Foreigners' Office; Pg. San Juan 189–193,
Ⓜ Joanic; Mon–Fri 9am–2pm), where they'll be
issued with a residence certificate. You don't need
the certificate if you're an EU citizen living and
working legally in Barcelona, or if you're legally
self-employed or a student. US citizens can apply
at a police station for one ninety-day extension,
but this must be done at least three weeks before
the initial entry period expires. Other nationalities
wishing to extend their stay will need to get a
special visa from a Spanish embassy or consulate
before departure.

Anyone planning to stay and live in Barcelona will
also need a **Número de Identidad de Extranjero**
(NIE), an ID number that's essential if you're to open
a bank account, sign a utilities, job or accommodation contract, and for many other financial
transactions.

As well as the Oficina de Extranjería, there's also a
telephone helpline on Ⓣ012 (Mon–Fri 9am–5pm)
that deals with all aspects of **residency and
immigration**, and you'll find more information at
Ⓦ gencat.cat.

Health

The **European Health Insurance Card** gives EU
citizens access to Spanish state public health
services under reciprocal agreements. While this
will provide free or reduced-cost medical care in
the event of minor injuries and emergencies, it
won't cover every eventuality – and it only applies
to EU citizens in possession of the card – so travel
insurance (see below) is essential.

For minor health complaints look for the green
cross of a **pharmacy** (*farmàcia*), where highly
trained staff can give advice (often in English), and
are able to dispense many drugs (including some
antibiotics) available only on prescription in other
countries. Usual hours are weekdays 9am to 1pm

and 4 to 8pm. At least one in each neighbourhood
is open daily 24 hours (and marked as such), or
phone Ⓣ010 for information on those open out of
hours – Farmàcia Clapes, Ramblas 98, Ⓜ Liceu
(Ⓣ 933 012 843, Ⓦ farmaciaclapes.com), is a convenient 24-hour pharmacy. A list of out-of-hours
pharmacies can also be found in the window of
each pharmacy store.

Any local **healthcare centre** (Centre d'Atenció
Primària, CAP) can provide non-emergency assis-
tance. In the old town, there's one at Passatge Pau 1,
Barri Gòtic, Ⓜ Drassanes (Ⓣ 933 425 549), and
another at c/del Rec Comtal 24, Sant Pere, Ⓜ Arc de
Triomf (Ⓣ 933 101 421); both are open Monday to
Friday 8am to 8pm, Saturday 9am to 5pm. Alterna-
tively, call Ⓣ010 or consult Ⓦ bcn.cat for a full list.

For emergency hospital treatment, call Ⓣ061
or go to one of the following **central hospitals**,
which have 24hr accident and emergency
(*urgències*) services.

HOSPITALS

Centre Perecamps Av. Drassanes 13–15, El Raval Ⓣ 934 410 600;
Ⓜ Drassanes.

Hospital Clínic i Provincial c/de Villaroel 170, Eixample Ⓣ 932
275 400; Ⓜ Hospital Clínic.

Hospital del Mar Pg. Marítim 25–29, Vila Olímpica Ⓣ 932 483
000; Ⓜ Ciutadella-Vila Olímpica.

Hospital de la Santa Creu i Sant Pau c/de Sant Antoni María
Claret 167, Eixample Ⓣ 932 919 000; Ⓜ Hospital de Sant Pau.

Insurance

Take out a comprehensive **insurance policy** before
travelling to Barcelona, to cover against loss, theft,
illness or injury. A typical policy will provide cover
for loss of baggage, tickets and – up to a certain
limit – cash or travellers' cheques, as well as cancel-
lation or curtailment of your journey. With medical
coverage you should ascertain whether benefits
will be paid as treatment proceeds or only after you

ROUGH GUIDES TRAVEL INSURANCE

Rough Guides has teamed up with WorldNomads.com to offer great travel insurance deals.
Policies are available to residents of over 150 countries, with cover for a wide range of
adventure sports, 24hr emergency assistance, high levels of medical and evacuation cover and
a stream of travel safety information. Roughguides.com users can take advantage of their
policies online 24/7, from anywhere in the world – even if you're already travelling. And since
plans often change when you're on the road, you can extend your policy and even claim
online. Roughguides.com users who buy travel insurance with WorldNomads.com can also
leave a positive footprint and donate to a community development project. For more
information, go to Ⓦ roughguides.com/travel-insurance.

return home, and whether there is a 24-hour medical emergency number. When securing baggage cover, make sure that the per-article limit will cover your most valuable possession. Most policies exclude so-called dangerous sports unless an extra premium is paid: in Spain this can mean most watersports are excluded, though probably not things like bike tours or hiking.

If you need to make a claim, you should keep receipts for medicines and medical treatment, and in the event you have anything stolen you must obtain an official statement from the police (see p.28).

Internet and wi-fi

Wi-fi (pronounced "wee-fee" in Barcelona) is widespread in cafés, bars and hotels, while Barcelona city council operates Spain's largest free public wi-fi network, with hotspots all over the city (🖢bcn.cat/barcelonawifi). While there are fewer internet shops around than there used to be, a stroll down the Ramblas, or through the Barri Gòtic, La Ribera, El Raval and Gràcia will still reveal plenty of possibilities.

Language schools

The Generalitat (the government of Catalonia) offers low-cost **Catalan classes** for non-Spanish speakers through the Consorci per a la Normalit- zació Lingüística (call ☎010 for information, 🖢cpnl .cat). Otherwise, the cheapest **Spanish** or Catalan classes in Barcelona are at the Escola Oficial d'Idiomes, Avinguda Drassanes 14, El Raval, 🖢Drassanes (☎933 249 330, 🖢eoibd.cat) – expect queues when you sign on. Language courses for beginners are also offered at Barcelona University, Gran Via de les Corts Catalanes 585, Eixample, 🖢Universitat (☎934 021 100, 🖢www.ub.es).

Laundry

Most youth hostels, and some *pensions*, offer inexpensive laundry services; hotels charge consider- ably more. Self-service laundries include LavaXpres, at eighteen city locations, including c/de Ferlandina 34, El Raval, 🖢Universitat, and c/Nou de Sant Francesc 5, Barri Gòtic, 🖢Drassanes (daily 8am–10pm; ☎933 183 018, 🖢lavaxpres.com), and Splash, at c/de la Diputació 199, Esquerra de l'Eixample, 🖢Universitat, and c/de Sicília 348, 🖢Sagrada Família (daily 8am–10pm; 🖢splashlaundry.es).

Left luggage

There are left-luggage offices (*consigna*) at Barcelona Sants train station (daily 5.30am–11pm; €3.60–5.20/ day) and Barcelona Nord bus station (daily 6am–11.30pm; €3.50–5.40). **Locker Barcelona**, near Plaça Catalunya at c/d'Estruc 36, Barri Gòtic, 🖢Cata- lunya/Urquinaona (daily: July–Oct 8.30am–10.30pm; Nov–June 9am–9pm; €3.50–10; ☎933 028 796, 🖢lockerbarcelona.com), lets you access your belong- ings throughout the day free of charge, and offers other services such as luggage weighing, boarding pass printing and internet access.

Libraries

The **British Council**, c/d'Amigó 83, Sant Gervasi, FGC Muntaner (☎932 419 700, 🖢britishcouncil.es), has Barcelona's only English-language lending library, and puts on a full arts and events programme.

The Catalan national library, the **Biblioteca de Catalunya**, is at c/de l'Hospital 56, El Raval, 🖢Liceu (Mon–Fri 9am–8pm, Sat 9am–2pm; ☎932 702 300, 🖢www.bnc.cat). A letter of academic reference is required, but there's a public library in the same building, the **Biblioteca Sant Pau-Santa Creu** (Tues, Thurs & Sat 10am–2pm, plus Mon–Fri 2.30–8.30pm). Barcelona's other public libraries are listed on 🖢bcn.cat – all have internet and wi-fi, and some have English-language books, international press, etc.

Lost property

Anything recovered by the police, or left on public transport, is sent to the **Oficina de Troballes** (municipal lost property office), at Pl. Carles Pi i Sunyer 8, Barri Gòtic, 🖢Jaume I/Catalunya (Mon–Fri 9am–2pm; ☎010). Most items are kept for three months. You could also try the TMB (public transport) customer service centre at Universitat metro station.

Mail

The main **post office** in Barcelona is near the harbour in the old town, while each city neighbour- hood also has a post office, though these have far less comprehensive opening hours and services. If all you need are **stamps**, however, it's usually quicker to visit a tobacconist (look for the brown- and-yellow *tabac* sign), found on virtually every street. These can also weigh letters and small

CATALAN NAMES

Traditionally, a person gets two surnames, one from dad and one from mum. They are not always used, but it explains why many of the names given in this book may be longer than those you are used to seeing. Thus, Antoni Gaudí i Cornet took Gaudí from his father and Cornet from his mother (the "i" simply means "and").

parcels, advise about postal rates and send express mail (*urgente*). Use the yellow on-street postboxes and put your mail in the flap marked *províncies i estranger* or *altres destins*. Letters or cards take around three to four days to European countries, five days to a week to North America.

POSTAL SERVICES

Main post office (Correus) Pl. d'Antoni López, at the eastern end of Pg. de Colom, Barri Gòtic ☎ 934 868 302, ⓦ correos.es; ⓜ Barceloneta/Jaume I (Mon–Fri 8.30am–9.30pm, Sat 8.30am–2pm). There's a poste restante/general delivery service here (*llista de correus*), plus express post, mobile phone top-ups, phonecard sales and bill payments.

Maps

The city tourist offices and kiosks charge €1 for their maps – you can pick up a good free one instead from the information desk on the ground floor of El Corte Inglés department store, right outside the main tourist office. With that, and the maps in this book, you'll easily find your way around.

You'll find a good selection of regional and national Spanish maps in most bookshops and at street newspaper kiosks or petrol stations. Map and travel shops in your home country should also be able to supply road maps of Catalunya or northern Spain (by Michelin, Firestone or Rand McNally). Alternatively, order from a map specialist like ⓦ stanfords .co.uk or ⓦ randmcnally.com.

Money

Spain's **currency** is the euro (€), with notes issued in denominations of 5, 10, 20, 50, 100, 200 and 500 euros, and coins in denominations of 1, 2, 5, 10, 20 and 50 cents, and 1 and 2 euros.

By far the easiest way to get money is to use your bank debit card to withdraw cash from an **ATM**, found all over the city, including the airport and major train stations. You can usually withdraw up to €300 a day and instructions are offered in English once you insert your card. Take a note of your bank's emergency contact number in case the machine swallows the card. Some European debit cards can also be used directly in shops to pay for purchases; you'll need to check first with your bank.

All major **credit cards** are accepted in hotels, restaurants and shops, and for tours, tickets and transport, though don't count on being able to use them in every small hotel or backstreet café. You can also use your credit card in an ATM to withdraw cash.

Spanish **banks** (*bancos*) and savings banks (*caixas*) have branches throughout Barcelona, especially along the Ramblas and around Plaça de Catalunya. Normal banking hours are Monday to Friday from 8.30am to 2pm, although from October until May most institutions also open Thursday 4pm to 6.30pm (savings banks) or Saturday 9am to 1pm (banks).

For out-of-hours banking you can use bureaux de change or a **foreign-exchange office** (*canvi, cambio*), found down the Ramblas (often open until midnight); at Barcelona Sants (daily 8am–8pm); or the El Corte Inglés department store, Pl. de Catalunya (Mon–Sat 9.30am–9.30pm). Exchange offices don't always charge commission, though their rates aren't usually as good as the banks.

Opening hours and public holidays

Basic **working hours** are Monday to Saturday 9.30 or 10am to 1.30pm and 4.30 to 8 or 9pm, though many offices and shops don't open on Saturday afternoons. Local cafés, bars and markets open from around 7am, while shopping centres, major stores and large supermarkets tend to remain open all day from 10am to 9pm, with some even open on Sunday. In the lazy days of summer everything becomes a bit more relaxed, with offices working until around 3pm and many shops and restaurants closing for part or the whole of August.

Most of the showpiece **museums and galleries** in Barcelona open all day, from 10am to 8pm, though some smaller collections and attractions close over lunchtime between 1 and 4pm. On Sundays most open in the morning only, and most are closed all day on Mondays. On public holidays, most museums and galleries have Sunday opening hours, while pretty much everything is closed on Christmas Day, New Year's Day and January 6.

Apart from the cathedral (La Seu) and the Sagrada Família – the two churches you're most likely to visit, which have tourist-friendly opening hours – other **churches** tend only to open for worship in the early morning (around 7–9am) and the evening (around 6–9pm).

Not all **public and bank holidays** in Spain are observed in Catalunya, and vice versa. On the days listed below, and during the many local festivals, you'll find most shops closed, though bars and restaurants tend to stay open.

BARCELONA'S PUBLIC HOLIDAYS

January 1 Cap d'Any, New Year's Day
January 6 Epifanía, Epiphany
Variable Good Friday & Easter Monday
May 1 Dia del Treball, May Day/Labour Day
June 24 Dia de Sant Joan, St John's Day
August 15 L'Assumpció, Assumption of the Virgin
September 11 Diada Nacional, Catalan National Day
September 24 Festa de la Mercè, Our Lady of Mercy (Barcelona's patron saint)
October 12 Dia de la Hispanidad, Spanish National Day
November 1 Tots Sants, All Saints' Day
December 6 Dia de la Constitució, Constitution Day
December 8 La Imaculada, Immaculate Conception
December 25 Nadal, Christmas Day
December 26 Sant Esteve, St Stephen's Day

Smoking

Smoking is forbidden in all Barcelona's public buildings and transport facilities, plus bars, restaurants, clubs and cafés. Compared to other countries with smoking restrictions in force, you'll find there's still some puffing going on, though the ban is generally observed.

Taxes

Local sales tax, **IVA**, is ten percent in hotels and restaurants, and 21 percent in shops. It's usually included in the price though not always, so some hotel or restaurant bills can come as a bit of a surprise. Quoted prices should, however, always make it clear whether or not tax is included. Note

---

CALLING HOME FROM ABROAD

Note that the initial zero is omitted from the area code when dialing the UK, Ireland, Australia and New Zealand from abroad.
Australia international access code + 61
New Zealand international access code + 64
UK international access code + 44
US and Canada international access code + 1
Ireland international access code + 353
South Africa international access code + 27

---

that there is also an additional tax on stays in tourist establishments in Barcelona of €0.65–2.25 (determined by the type of property) per person per night for up to seven days (under-16s exempt).

Telephones

Spanish **telephone numbers** have nine digits, and in Barcelona the first two digits of all landline phone numbers are 93 (the regional prefix), which you dial even when calling from within the city. Spanish mobile numbers begin with a 6 or 7, freephone numbers begin 900, while other 90-plus- and 80-plus-digit numbers are nationwide standard-rate or special-rate services. To **call Barcelona from abroad**, dial your international access number + 34 (Spain country code) + nine-digit number.

Most European **mobile phones** will work in Barcelona, though it's worth checking with your provider whether you need to get international access switched on and whether any extra charges are involved. Even though prices are coming down, it's still expensive to use your own mobile extensively while abroad, and you will pay for receiving incoming calls, for example.

Public telephones in Barcelona have instructions in English, and accept coins, credit cards and phonecards. Phonecards (*targetes/tarjetas*) with discounted rates for calls are available in tobacconists, newsagents and post offices, issued in various

---

AVERAGE MONTHLY TEMPERATURES

	Jan	Feb	Mar	Apr	May	Jun	Jul	Aug	Sep	Oct	Nov	Dec
Max/min (°C)	13/6	14/7	16/9	18/11	21/16	25/18	28/21	28/21	25/19	21/15	16/11	13/8
Max/min (°F)	56/42	58/44	61/48	65/52	70/61	77/64	82/70	82/70	77/66	70/59	61/52	56/46

denominations either by Telefónica (the dominant operator) or one of its rivals. Credit cards are not recommended for local and national calls, since most have a minimum charge which is far more than a normal call is likely to cost. It's also best to avoid making calls from the phone in your hotel room, as even local calls will be slapped with a heavy surcharge.

You can make **international calls** from any public payphone, but it's cheaper to use a calling card, or an internet application such as Skype.

Ticket agencies

You can buy tickets for concerts, exhibitions, sporting events and tourist attractions with a credit card via the **Servi-Caixa** automatic dispensing machines in branches of La Caixa savings bank, or online, in English, through **Ticketmaster** (Ⓦticketmaster.es; collect at Servi-Caixa terminals) or **Tel-Entrada** (Ⓦtelentrada.com; collect at Catalunya Caixa machines). There's also a concert ticket desk in the **FNAC store**, El Triangle, Plaça de Catalunya, while for advance tickets for all city council (Ajuntament)-sponsored concerts and events visit the **Palau de la Virreina**, Ramblas 99. The official tourist office website Ⓦ**barcelona turisme.com** also offers online ticket purchase for most city museums and attractions (click on "BCNShop"), with a five- to ten-percent discount.

Time

Barcelona is one hour ahead of the UK, six hours ahead of Eastern Standard Time, nine hours ahead of Pacific Standard Time, eight hours behind Australia, ten hours behind New Zealand and in the same time zone as South Africa. The clocks in Spain go forward in the last week in March and back again in the last week in October.

Tipping

In most **restaurants and bars** service is considered to be included in the price. Locals leave only a few cents or round up the change for a coffee or a drink, and a euro or two for most meals, though fancier restaurants will expect ten to fifteen percent. **Taxi drivers** usually get around five percent, more if they have helped you with bags or been similarly useful, while **hotel porters** should be tipped a euro or two for their assistance.

Toilets

Public toilets are few and far between, and only averagely clean. Bars and restaurants are more likely to have proper (and cleaner) toilets, though you can't guarantee it, even in the poshest of places. Ask for *toaleta* or *serveis* (*lavabo* or *servicios* in Spanish). Dones or Damas (Ladies) and Homes/Hombres or Caballeros (Gentlemen) are the usual signs.

Travellers with disabilities

The local tourist office devotes a separate website to the needs of travellers with disabilities (Ⓦbarcelona -access.com), featuring a full guide to accessible sights and facilities, and a thorough section on all forms of public transport. Barcelona's **airport** and **Aerobús** are fully accessible to travellers in wheelchairs, though the bus gets very busy and can be difficult if you have lots of luggage. **Barcelona Sants** has lifts to the platforms, though not all trains are accessible. There are access ramps at Estació de França and lifts to the platforms at Plaça de Catalunya's FGC and RENFE stations. Using the **metro** can be problematic, though improvements are ongoing – at present, lines 2, 9, 10 and 11 are fully accessible, with elevators at major stations (including Plaça de Catalunya, Universitat, Paral.lel, Passeig de Gràcia and Sagrada Família) from the street to the platforms. However, all **city buses** and trams are wheelchair-accessible, as is the sightseeing Bus Turístic. If you need a **wheelchair-accessible taxi** contact Radio Taxi (☎933 033 033, Ⓦradiotaxi033.com) or Taxi Amic (☎ 934 208 088, English rarely spoken).

Out on the streets, the number of acoustic traffic-light signals is slowly growing, while dropped kerbs are being put in place across the city. However, most old-town attractions, including the Museu Picasso, have steps, cobbles or other impediments to access. Fully accessible **sights and attractions** include MNAC, Fundació Antoni Tàpies, Fundacío Joan Miró, La Pedrera, Caixa Forum, CosmoCaixa, Museu d'Història de Catalunya and the Palau de la Música Catalana.

USEFUL CONTACTS

Institut Municipal de Persones amb Discapacitat Av. Diagonal 233 1°, Eixample ☎ 934 132 840, Ⓦ bcn.cat/accessible; Ⓜ Glòries. Information, some in English, on most aspects of life and travel in the city for disabled residents and visitors.

Water

Water from the tap is safe to drink, but it doesn't taste very nice. You'll always be given bottled mineral water in a bar or restaurant.

Women's Barcelona

Ca la Dona, c/de Ripoll 25, Barri Gòtic, Ⓜ Jaume I (☎ 934 127 161, Ⓦ caladona.org), is a women's centre hosting meetings for women's groups, and with a library and bar. The Ajuntament's official women's resource centre, the **Centre Municipal d'Informació i Recursos per a les Dones** (CIRD), c/de les Camèlies 36–38, Gràcia, Ⓜ Alfons X (☎ 932 850 357, Ⓦ bcn.cat/dones), publishes a monthly calendar of events online. The **Barcelona Women's Network** (Ⓦ bcnwomensnetwork.com) is a social, business and networking club for English-speaking women living and working in the city.

The Ramblas

It's a telling comment on the character of Barcelona that a single street – the Ramblas (*Rambles* in Catalan) – can count as a highlight. No day in the city seems complete without a stroll down at least part of what Spanish poet Federico García Lorca hailed as "the only street in the world which I wish would never end". Lined with cafés, restaurants, souvenir shops, flower stalls and newspaper kiosks, and thronged by tourists, locals and performance artists, it's at the heart of Barcelona's life and self-image. There are important buildings and sights along the way, not least the Liceu opera house and the acclaimed Boqueria food market, but undoubtedly it's the vibrant street life that is the greatest attraction along Spain's most famous thoroughfare.

The Ramblas derives its name from the Arabic *ramla* (sand), which refers to the bed of a seasonal stream that was paved over in medieval times. Benches and decorative trees were added, overlooked by stately balconied buildings, during the nineteenth century, and today – in a city choked with traffic – this wide tree-lined swath is still given over to pedestrians, with cars forced up the narrow strips of road on either side. There are **metro stops** at Catalunya (top of the Ramblas), Liceu (middle) and Drassanes (bottom), or you can walk the entire length in about twenty minutes.

The Ramblas splits the old town areas of Barcelona in half, with the Barri Gòtic on the east flank of the avenue and El Raval to the west. It also actually comprises **five separate sections** strung head to tail – from north to south, Rambla Canaletes, Estudis, Sant Josep, Caputxins and Santa Mònica – though it's rare to hear them referred to as such. However, you will notice changes as you walk down the Ramblas, primarily that the streets on either side become a little less polished – even seedy – the closer you get to the harbour. The businesses, meanwhile, reflect the mixed clientele, from patisseries to pizza takeaways, and stores selling handcrafted jewellery to shops full of sombreros, bullfight posters ("your name here") and football shirts. On the central avenue under the plane trees you'll find stallholders peddling ice cream, flowers, plants, postcards and books. You can have your palm read and your portrait painted, or while away time with the buskers and human statues (though if you play cards or dice for money with a man on a street, you've only yourself to blame if you get ripped off). Drag yourself home with the dawn, and you'll rub shoulders with the street cleaners, watchful policemen and bleary-eyed stallholders. It's a never-ending show, of which visitors and locals alike seldom tire.

Plaça de Catalunya

Ⓜ Catalunya

The huge **Plaça de Catalunya** square at the top of the Ramblas stands right at the heart of the city, with the old town and port below it, and the nineteenth-century Eixample district above and beyond. Laid out in its present form in the 1920s, it centres on a formal arrangement of statues, circular fountains and trees, and serves as the focal point for local events and demonstrations – notably the mass gathering here on New Year's Eve. The most prominent monument is the towering angular slab and bust that was dedicated in 1991 to **Francesc Macià**, leader of the Republican Left, parliamentary deputy for Barcelona and first president of the Generalitat, who died in office in 1933. It was commissioned from the pioneer of Catalan avant-garde sculpture, Josep María Subirachs, perhaps best known for his continuing work on the Sagrada Família church.

For visitors, an initial orientation point is the white-faced **El Corte Inglés** department store on the eastern side of the square, an amazing behemoth whose looks are half-Art Deco and half-Fascist, and whose ninth-floor cafeteria offers stupendous views. The main tourist office is just across from here on the square itself, while on the southwest side, over the road from the top of the Ramblas, **El Triangle** shopping centre makes another landmark. Incorporated in its ground floor is the **Café Zurich**, a traditional Barcelona meeting place, whose ranks of outdoor tables – patrolled by supercilious waiters – are a day-long draw for beggars, buskers and pan-pipe bands.

Rambla Canaletes and Estudis

The top two stretches of the Ramblas are **Rambla Canaletes**, with its iron fountain (a drink from which supposedly means you'll never leave Barcelona), and **Rambla Estudis**, named after the university (L'Estudi General) that was sited here until the start of the eighteenth century. This part is also known locally as Rambla dels Ocells, as it was until a few years ago home to a **bird market** (*ocell* being the Catalan for "bird").

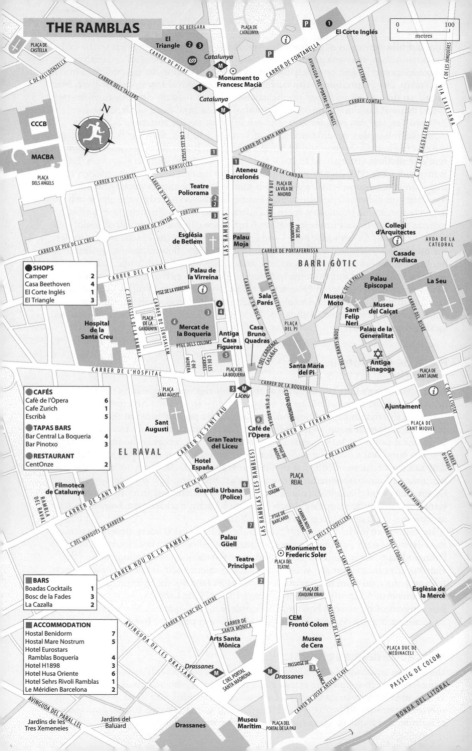

Teatre Poliorama

Ramblas 115 • ☎ 933 177 599, ⓦ teatrepoliorama.com • Ⓜ Catalunya

It seems hard to believe now, but the Ramblas was a war zone during the Spanish Civil War as the city erupted into factionalism in 1937. George Orwell (see box, p.40) was caught in the crossfire between the *Café Moka* – the restaurant that now occupies part of the ground floor is a modern replacement – and the Poliorama cinema opposite, now the **Teatre Poliorama**. This was built in 1863 as the Royal Academy of Science and Arts, and restored as a theatre in 1985.

Església de Betlem

Ramblas 107 • Daily 8am–1.30pm & 6–9pm • Ⓜ Liceu

The **Església de Betlem** was built in 1681 in Baroque style for the Jesuits, but was completely gutted during the Civil War as anarchists sacked the city's churches at will – an activity of which Orwell quietly approved. Consequently, the interior is plain in the extreme, though the main facade on Carrer del Carme sports a fine sculpted portal.

Palau Moja

Ramblas 188 • ☎ 933 162 740, ⓦ mhcat.cat/monuments/palau_moja • Ⓜ Liceu

Across the Ramblas from the Betlem church, the arcaded **Palau Moja** dates from the late eighteenth century and still retains an exterior staircase and elegant great hall. It's currently occupied by the city's cultural department, and not open to visitors. Take a look, though, at the illustrated tiles above the **fountain** at the start of Carrer de la Portaferrissa, which show the medieval gate (the Porta Ferriça) and market that once stood here.

Palau de la Virreina

Ramblas 99 • **Tiquet Rambles** Daily 10am–8.30pm • **Centre de la Imatge** Tues–Sun noon–8pm • Usually free • ☎ 933 161 000, ⓦ lavirreina.bcn.cat • Ⓜ Liceu

The graceful eighteenth-century **Palau de la Virreina** is set back slightly from the Ramblas. Commissioned by a Peruvian viceroy, Manuel Amat, and named after the wife who survived him, its five Ramblas-facing bays are adorned with pilasters and Rococo windows. Today the palace is used by the city council's culture department, and has a useful ground-floor **information centre** called "Tiquet Rambles" where you can find out about upcoming events and buy tickets. Under the overall name of the **Centre de la Imatge**, various galleries and studios towards the rear present interesting temporary **exhibitions**, with an emphasis on contemporary culture, social studies and photography.

The city's two official **Carnival giants** (*gegants vells*), representing the celebrated thirteenth-century Catalan king Jaume I and his wife Violant, are usually displayed behind glass at the back of the palace courtyard. The origin of Catalunya's outsized (5m-high) wood-and-plaster Carnival figures is unclear, though they probably once formed part of the entertainment at medieval travelling fairs. The first record of specific city giants is in 1601 – later used to entertain the city's orphans, they are now an integral part of Barcelona's festival parades (see box, p.218).

On a more mundane note, the complex also holds free public toilets.

Mercat de la Boqueria

Ramblas 91 • Mon–Sat 8am–8.30pm • ☎ 933 182 584, ⓦ boqueria.info • Ⓜ Liceu

Barcelona's glorious main food market, officially the Mercat Sant Josep but invariably known as **La Boqueria**, stands immediately west of the Ramblas, at the point where a sudden profusion of flower stalls marked the switch to **Rambla Sant Josep** (also known as Rambla de les Flors).

1

GEORGE ORWELL IN BARCELONA

Barcelona is a town with a long history of street-fighting.   *Homage to Catalonia*, 1938

When he first arrived in Barcelona in December 1936, English journalist **George Orwell** was much taken with the egalitarian spirit he encountered. Loudspeakers on the Ramblas bellowed revolutionary songs, café waiters refused tips, brothels were collectivized and buildings were draped in anarchist flags. After serving as a militiaman on the Aragonese front, Orwell returned on leave to Barcelona in April 1937 to find that everything had changed. Not only had the city lost its revolutionary zeal, but the various leftist parties fighting for the Republican cause had descended into a "miserable internecine scrap". From the **Hotel Continental** (Ramblas 138), where Orwell and his wife Eileen stayed, he observed the deteriorating situation with mounting despair, and when street-fighting broke out in May, Orwell was directly caught up in it. As a member of the Workers' Party of Marxist Unification (POUM), Orwell became a target when pro-Communist Assault Guards seized the city telephone exchange near Plaça de Catalunya and set about breaking up the workers' militias. Orwell left the hotel for the **POUM headquarters** (Ramblas 128) just down the street, sited in the building that's now the *Rivoli Ramblas* hotel – a plaque here by the "Banco Popular" sign honours murdered POUM leader Andrés Nin ("victim of Stalinism"). With the trams on the Ramblas abandoned by their drivers as the shooting started, and Assault Guards occupying the adjacent **Café Moka** (Ramblas 126), Orwell holed up with a rifle for three days in the rotunda of the **Teatre Poliorama** (Ramblas 115) opposite, in order to defend the POUM HQ if necessary. Breakfasting sparsely on goat's cheese bought from the Boqueria market (its stalls largely empty), concerned about Eileen and caught up in rumour and counter-rumour, Orwell considered it one of the most unbearable periods of his life.

When the fighting subsided, Orwell returned to the front, where he was shot through the throat by a fascist sniper. Yet that was only the start of his troubles. Recuperating in a sanatorium near Tibidabo, he learned that the POUM had been declared illegal, its members rounded up and imprisoned. He avoided arrest by sleeping out in gutted churches and derelict buildings and playing the part of a tourist by day, looking "as bourgeois as possible", while scrawling POUM graffiti in defiance on the walls of fancy restaurants. Eventually, with passports and papers arranged by the British consul, Orwell and Eileen escaped Barcelona by train – back to the "deep, deep sleep of England" and the writing of his passionate war memoir, *Homage to Catalonia*. His presence in the city is commemorated by the small Plaça George Orwell in the Barri Gòtic (see p.55).

Some might protest, but La Boqueria really can claim to be the best market in Spain. Built on the site of a former convent between 1836 and 1840, the cavernous hall stretches back from the high wrought-iron entrance arch that faces the Ramblas. It's a riot of noise and colour, as popular with locals who come here to shop daily as with snap-happy tourists. Everything radiates out from the central fish and seafood stalls – bunches of herbs, pots of spices, baskets of wild mushrooms, mounds of cheese and sausage, racks of bread, hanging hams and overloaded meat counters. Many get waylaid at the entrance by the eye-candy seasonal fruit cartons and squeezed juices, but the flagship fruit and veg stalls here are pricey. It's better value further in, and also in the small outdoor square just beyond the north side of the market where the local allotment-holders and market gardeners gather. Everyone has a favourite market stall, but don't miss Petras and its array of wild mushrooms (stall 867, at the back by the market restaurant, *La Garduña*) or Frutas y Verduras Jesús y Carmen, which is framed with colourful bundles of exotic chillies (it occupies stall 579). And of course, there are some excellent stand-up **tapas bars** in the market as well, open from dawn onwards for the traders – *Bar Pinotxo* is the most famous (see p.177).

Plaça de la Boqueria

Ⓜ Liceu

At the halfway point of the Ramblas, **Plaça de la Boqueria**, a large round **mosaic by Joan Miró** is set in the middle of the pavement. Something of a symbol for the city, it's one of a number of public works in Barcelona by the artist, who was born just a couple of minutes' walk off the Ramblas in the Barri Gòtic; a plaque marks the relevant building on Passatge del Crèdit, off c/de Ferran. Close by, at Ramblas 82, Josep Vilaseca's spectacular **Casa Bruno Quadros** – the lower floor of which is now a bank – was built in the 1890s to house an umbrella store. That explains its delightful facade, decorated with a green dragon and Oriental designs, and scattered with parasols. On the other side of the Ramblas, *modernista* flourishes on a lesser scale adorn the **Antiga Casa Figueras** (1902) at no. 83, an exuberant cascade of stained glass and mosaics that sports a corner relief of a female reaper. It's now home to the renowned bakery-café *Escribà* (see p.177).

Gran Teatre del Liceu

Ramblas 51–59 · 50min tours Mon–Fri 9.30am & 10.30am; 25min tours daily at regular intervals · 50min tour €14, 25min tour €6 · 📞 934 859 900, 🌐 www.liceubarcelona.cat · Ⓜ Liceu

Barcelona's celebrated opera house, the **Gran Teatre del Liceu**, was founded as a private theatre in 1847. It was rebuilt after a fire in 1861 to become Spain's grandest theatre, regarded as a bastion of the city's late nineteenth-century commercial and intellectual classes – in a nod to its bourgeois antecedents, it still has no royal box. The Liceu was devastated again in 1893, when an anarchist, acting in revenge for the recent execution of a fellow anarchist assassin, threw two bombs into the stalls during a production of *William Tell*, killing twenty people. It burned down for the third time in 1994, when a worker's blowtorch set fire to the scenery during last-minute alterations to an opera set. Following a five-year restoration of its lavishly decorated interior, it reopened in 1999.

The traditional meeting place for post-performance refreshments for audience and performers alike, the famous **Cafè de l'Òpera** (see p.177) stands just across the Ramblas.

Liceu tours

Regular **tours** depart from the Liceu's main entrance and conclude in the modern extension, the **Espai Liceu**, which also houses a music and gift shop and café. Consult the website for the current schedule, which varies all year, and for the timing of tours in English. Highlights include the classically inspired **Saló dels Miralls** (Salon of Mirrors), unaffected by any of the fires and thus largely original in decor, and the impressive gilded **auditorium**, which contains 2300 seats and makes this one of the world's largest opera houses.

You'll learn more if you take one of the more expensive fifty-minute morning tours, which also visit the **Cercle del Liceu**, the opera house's private members' club. The burnished rooms here feature tiled floors and painted ceilings, and culminate in an extraordinary *modernista* games room, illuminated by a celebrated series of paintings by Ramon Casas representing Catalan music and dance. For most of its history, membership of the Cercle was restricted to men, until **Montserrat Caballé** – Spain's greatest soprano, born in Barcelona in 1933 – won a court battle to become one of the first women to join.

Teatre Principal and around

Ⓜ Drassanes

Historically a theatre and red-light district, the bottom stretch of the Ramblas, the **Rambla de Santa Mònica**, still has a rough edge or two. Across from the **Teatre Principal**, a statue of **Frederic Soler** (1839–95) – shown seated, with one leg casually crossed over the other – commemorates the playwright, impresario and founder of modern Catalan theatre, better known as Serafí Pitarra.

Back across the Ramblas, street-walkers and theatre-goers alike drank stand-up shots and coffee at **La Cazalla** (Ramblas 25), a famous hole-in-the-wall bar (really just a street

1

UNDER THE ARCH AND INTO THE SHADOWS

One early summer morning in 1945, 10-year-old Daniel Sempere and his father walk under the arch of c/de l'Arc del Teatre, "entering a vault of blue haze…until the glimmer of the Ramblas faded behind us". And behind a large, carved wooden door, Daniel is shown for the first time the "Cemetery of Forgotten Books", where he picks out an obscure book that will change his life. So begins the mega-successful novel **Shadow of the Wind**, by Carlos Ruiz Zafón (2002), a gripping mystery set in postwar Barcelona that uses the city's old town in particular to atmospheric effect. With a copy in hand you can trace Daniel's early progress, from the street where he lives (c/de Santa Anna) to the house of the beautiful, blind Clara Barceló on Plaça Reial, as well as a score of other easily identifiable locations across the city, from the cathedral to Tibidabo – always keeping a wary eye out for a pursuing stranger with "a mask of black scarred skin, consumed by fire".

---

counter), just off the street beneath the arch at the start of c/de l'Arc del Teatre, that's straight out of sleaze-era central casting. This part of the street is also where you'll find the Ramblas' resident **human statues**. The city council confined them to this spot in 2012, to diminish crowding in narrower areas, and also obliged them to audition for slots, meaning those that are chosen are genuinely impressive.

Arts Santa Mònica

Ramblas 7 • Tues–Sat 11am–9pm, Sun 11am–5pm • Free • ⓦ artssantamonica.cat • Ⓜ Drassanes

The Augustinian **convent of Santa Mònica** dates from 1636, making it the oldest building on the Ramblas. Remodelled in the 1980s, with the addition of an extensive glass facade, it's now a contemporary **arts centre**, hosting regularly changing exhibitions in its grand, echoing galleries – there's usually something worth seeing, from an offbeat art installation to a show of archive photographs.

In season, pavement artists, caricaturists and palm readers set up stalls outside the centre on the Ramblas, and they're augmented on weekend afternoons by a **street market** selling jewellery, beads, bags and ornaments.

Museu de Cera

Ramblas 4–6, entrance on Ptge. de Banca • July–Sept daily 10am–10pm; Oct–June Mon–Fri 10am–1.30pm & 4–7.30pm, Sat & Sun 11am–2pm & 4.30–8.30pm • €15, ages 5–11 €9 • ☎ 933 172 649, ⓦ museocerabcn.com • Ⓜ Drassanes

Housed in an impressive nineteenth-century bank building, the city's wax museum, the **Museu de Cera**, stands at the foot of the Ramblas. You'd have to be hard-hearted indeed not to derive some pleasure from the ever more ludicrous series of tableaux presented in its cavernous salons and gloomy corridors, which depict recitals, meetings and parlour gatherings attended by an anachronistic – not to say perverse – collection of personalities, film characters, public figures, heroes, villains, artists and musicians. Thus Yasser Arafat lectures Churchill, Hitler and Bill Clinton, while a concert by Catalan cellist Pau Casals numbers Princess Diana and Mother Teresa among the audience, before the museum culminates in cheesy underwater tunnels, space capsules and an unpleasant "Terror" room. Needless to say, it's extremely ropey and enormously amusing, and you also won't want to miss the museum's extraordinary grotto-bar, the **Bosc de les Fades** (see p.196).

THREE GRACES FOUNTAIN, PLAÇA REIAL

Barri Gòtic

Spreading east from the Ramblas, the Barri Gòtic, or Gothic Quarter, forms the very heart of the old town. Its buildings date principally from the fourteenth and fifteenth centuries, when Barcelona reached the height of her medieval commercial prosperity, and culminate in the extraordinary Gothic cathedral, La Seu. It takes the best part of a day to see everything here; particular highlights are the Roman remains at the Museu d'Història de Barcelona and the frankly unclassifiable collections of the Museu Frederic Marès. Other quirks and diversions range from exploring the old Jewish quarter to touring the grand salons of the Ajuntament. That said, sauntering through the narrow alleys, shopping for antiques, tracing the long-lost Roman walls, or simply sitting at a café table in one of the lovely squares are every bit as enjoyable.

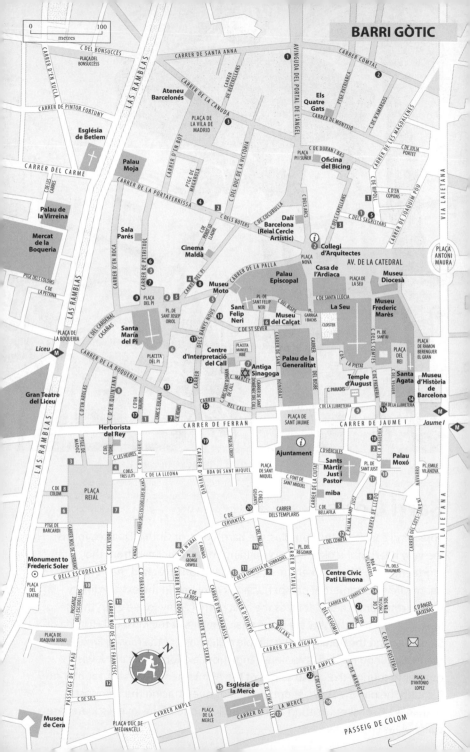

2

The picture-postcard images of the Barri Gòtic are largely based on the streets north of c/de Ferran and c/de Jaume I, where tourists throng the boutiques, bars, restaurants, museums and galleries. Even here, the district is not entirely preserved and prettified, and the occasional modern block sticks out unapologetically amid the medieval splendours. Further south, from Plaça Reial and c/d'Avinyó to the harbour, the Barri Gòtic is less gentrified and sometimes just plain run-down. This section boasts no specific sights or museums, though it does hold great shops, cafés, tapas bars and restaurants – just take care at night in the poorly lit streets.

La Seu

Pl. de la Seu • Mon–Fri 8am–12.45pm, 1–5pm & 5.45–7.30pm, Sat 8am–12.45pm, 1–5pm & 5.15–8pm, Sun 8am–1.45pm, 2–5pm & 5.15–8pm • Free admission to cathedral and cloister, choir €3, roof €3, except Mon–Sat 1–5pm & Sun 2–5pm, when admission is €7, and includes choir, roof and museum • ⓦ catedralbcn.org • ⓜ Jaume I

Barcelona's mighty cathedral, **La Seu**, whose high, intricate facade and soaring towers dominate the core of the Barri Gòtic, ranks among the great Gothic buildings of Spain. Located on a site previously occupied by a Roman temple and then an early Christian basilica, it was begun in 1298 and finished in 1448, save for the neo-Gothic main facade, only completed in the 1880s. The cathedral is dedicated to the city's second patroness, **Santa Eulàlia** (known as Laia in Barcelona), a young girl brutally martyred by the Romans in 304 AD for daring to prefer Christianity. Her remains were initially placed in the original harbourside church of Santa María del Mar in La Ribera, which explains why she's also patron saint of local sailors and seafarers. In 874 Laia was reinterred in the basilica, and her remains later placed in an ornate alabaster tomb that rests in a crypt beneath the high altar.

The cathedral interior

Visit La Seu in the morning or late afternoon, and admission to the cathedral's **interior** and **cloister** is free, though it costs extra to enter the beautifully carved choir. If you want to see everything, come in the afternoon, when the obligatory admission charge includes entry to all sections, including the choir, the **museum**, filled with glittering church treasure, and various chapels not otherwise open to the public.

Beyond the ornate fifteenth-century choir, sealed off in the centre of the nave, which confronts you as you enter the church, all eyes lead to the raised altar. Broad steps descend in front of it to the gated **crypt** that contains the venerated **tomb of Santa Eulàlia**. The tomb itself is always visible through the grating, but on Laia's saint's day, February 12, the crypt is thrown open for visits and a choir sings in her honour.

● SHOPS		■ BARS		● CAFÉS		■ ACCOMMODATION	
Almacenes del Pilar	13	L'Ascensor	5	Bar del Pi	4	Hostal Fernando	7
L'Arca	10	La Cerveteca	12	Caelum	5	Hostal Rembrandt	2
Artesania Catalunya	12	Glaciar	3	Dulcinea	3	Hotel Barcelona Catedral	3
Cereria Subirà	14	Milans Cocktail Bar	13	Mesón del Café	9	Hotel Cantón	12
El Corte Inglés	1	Milk	14			Hotel Do	8
Custo Barcelona	9	Oviso	8	● RESTAURANTS		Hotel El Jardí	5
Decathlon	3	Schilling	1	Bidasoa	15	Hotel Racó del Pi	4
Drap	8	Zim	2	Café de l'Acadèmia	10	Itaca Hostel	1
Espácio de Creadores	2			Can Culleretes	8	Mercer Hotel	9
Espai Drap Art	21			Cometacinc	12	Neri Hotel	6
Formatgeria La Seu	18	■ CLUBS & LIVE MUSIC		El Salón	14	Pensió Alamar	11
Formista	5	Fantástico	10	Shunka	1	Pensión Mari-Luz	10
Ganivetería Roca	7	Harlem Jazz Club	9	Venus Delicatessen	13		
Germanes Garcia	11	Jamboree	6				
Gotham	20	Karma	7				
El Ingenio	17	La Macarena	11	● TAPAS BARS			
Llibreria Quera	6	Sidecar	4	Bar Celta Pulpería	17		
La Manual Alpargatera	19			Bodega La Plata	16		
El Mercadillo	4			Ginger	11		
Obach Sombrería	15	■ FLAMENCO CLUB		Matis Bar	2		
Papabubble	22	Tarantos	6	Taller de Tapas	6		
Papirum	16			La Viñatería del Call	7		

2

BOHO BARCELONA AND THE FOUR CATS

There's not much to see in the shopping zone north of the cathedral, but a century or so ago a tavern called **Els Quatre Gats** (The Four Cats; c/de Montsió 3, ⓦ4gats.com) burned brightly and briefly as the epicentre of Barcelona's bohemian in-crowd. It was opened by Pere Romeu and other *modernista* artists in 1897, and the building itself is gloriously decorated inside and out in exuberant Catalan Art Nouveau style – this was the classy architect Josep Puig i Cadafalch's first commission.

Els Quatre Gats soon thrived as the birthplace of *modernista* magazines, the scene of poetry readings and shadow-puppet theatre, and the venue for cultural debate. A young Picasso designed the menu and, in 1900, the café was the setting for his first public exhibition. *Els Quatre Gats* has always traded on its reputation – a place where "accountants, dreamers and would-be geniuses shared tables with the spectres of Pablo Picasso, Isaac Albéniz, Federico García Lorca and Salvador Dalí" (*The Shadow of the Wind*, Carlos Ruiz Zafón). Today, a modern restoration displays something of its former glory, with the – frankly overpriced – bar-restaurant overseen by a copy of Ramon Casas' famous wall painting of himself and Pere Romeu on a tandem bicycle (the original is in MNAC).

La Seu is also known for the richness of its 29 **side-chapels**, which contain splendidly carved and painted tombs. Perhaps the finest are those that supposedly belong to Ramon Berenguer I (count of Barcelona from 1035 to 1076) and his wife Almodis; in fact, however, the tombs hold the remains of an earlier count and Petronila, the Aragonese princess whose betrothal to Ramon Berenguer IV united the crowns of Aragón and Barcelona.

Ride the elevator up to the **roof terrace**, or *terrats*, and you're rewarded with intimate views of the cathedral towers and surrounding Gothic buildings and spires. It's by no means the highest vantage point in town, but nowhere else do you feel so at the heart of medieval Barcelona.

The cloister

The cathedral's magnificent fourteenth-century **cloister**, entered directly from Plaça Garriger I Bachs on its western side, looks over a lush tropical garden complete with soaring palm trees and – more unusually – a gaggle of plump, honking **geese**. If they disturb the tranquillity of the scene, they do so for a purpose: white geese have been kept here for over five hundred years, either (depending on which story you believe) to reflect the virginity of Santa Eulàlia, or as a reminder of the erstwhile Roman splendour of Barcelona, as geese were kept on the Capitoline Hill in Rome.

Plaça de la Seu

Ⓜ Jaume I

The square immediately in front of the cathedral, **Plaça de la Seu**, is flanked by tourist cafés and generally awash with a milling crowd. It's also a regular weekly venue for the dancing of the *sardana*, the Catalan national dance (usually Sun at noon, plus Easter–Nov every Sat at 6pm) – anyone can join in, though it's not as simple as it looks (see box, p.206). Meanwhile, in front of the cathedral, the wide, pedestrianized Avinguda de la Catedral hosts an **antiques market** every Thursday, and a **Christmas craft fair**.

Museu Diocesà

Av. de la Catedral 4 • Tues–Fri 11am–6pm, Sat 11am–2pm & 2.30–6pm, Sun & hols 11am–2pm • €6 • ☏ 933 152 213, ⓦ www.cultura .arqbcn.cat/museu_cat.php • Ⓜ Jaume I

Stand back to look at the cathedral buildings and it's easy to see the line of fortified Roman towers that stood here until being incorporated into the medieval buildings. One such tower, to the left (east) of the main facade, once formed part of the cathedral almshouse (La Pia Almoina), and now holds the **Museu Diocesà**. Its soaring spaces have been beautifully adapted to show religious art and church treasures including a series of frescoes of the Apocalypse (1122 AD) from Sant Salvador in Polinyà, and several graphic retables, one of which depicts St Bartholomew being skinned alive. The museum was being overhauled as the time of writing, with the intention of expanding its section devoted to the life and work of Antoni Gaudí.

Casa de l'Ardiaca and Palau Episcopal

Two late-medieval buildings closely associated with the cathedral stand on its right, western, flank. The **Casa de l'Ardiaca**, originally the archdeacon's residence, encloses a tiny cloistered and tiled courtyard with a small fountain. Entered around the back, via c/de Santa Llúcia, it's now used for changing temporary exhibitions. Look for the curious, carved swallow-and-tortoise postbox to the right of its badly worn Renaissance gateway.

The **Palau Episcopal**, just beyond at the western end of c/de Santa Llúcia, was the bishop's palace and built on a grander scale altogether. Visitors are not allowed inside, but you can go as far as the gates to see the fine outdoor stairway; there's a patio at the top with Romanesque wall paintings.

Plaça Nova

Ⓜ Jaume I

Plaça Nova, which is effectively the western portion of the main cathedral square, marks one of the medieval entrances to the old town – north of it, you're fast entering the wider streets and more regular contours of the modern city. Designed in 1960 from sketches supplied by Picasso, the frieze that surmounts the modern College of Architects, the **Collegi d'Arquitectes**, on its northern side has a crude, almost graffiti-like quality. Picasso refused to come to Spain to oversee the work, unwilling to return to his home country while Franco was still in power.

Reial Cercle Artístic and Dalí Barcelona

C/dels Arcs 5 • Daily 10am–10pm • €10 • ☎ 933 187 866, Ⓦ reialcercleartistic.cat • Ⓜ Jaume I

A short walk from the cathedral, the handsome Gothic palace housing the **Reial Cercle Artístic** (Royal Artistic Circle) hosts exhibitions and concerts, but its biggest attraction is **Dalí Barcelona**, an astonishing gallery that centres on some wildly original bronze sculptures by Salvador Dalí. Completed in the 1970s as a private commission for a wealthy Catalan businessman, they're significant for having been made by Dalí himself, rather than to his designs, as was far more common. The sculptures, some humungous, others tiny, are theatrically if a little chaotically displayed: surrounded and occasionally dwarfed by hundreds of Dalí's vigorous drawings, sketches, watercolours and photographs; framed in niches beneath Gothic stone arches; hidden away in pitch-black rooms behind red velvet curtains. From the extraordinary *Cosmic Elephant* to the Cubist *Surrealist Angel*, the sculptures, and the artworks (which also include ceramics and glass), obsess on the themes that fascinated Dalí throughout his life: the sea, women, horses, mythology, religion, bullfights, sex and the grotesque.

Museu Frederic Marès

Pl. de Sant Iu 5–6, off c/dels Comtes • **Museu Frederic Marès** Tues–Sat 10am–7pm, Sun & hols 11am–8pm • €4.20, under-16s free, plus Sun after 3pm & first Sun of the month free • ☎ 932 563 500, Ⓦ www.museumares.bcn.cat • **Café d'Estiu** April–Sept Tues–Sun 10am–10pm • Ⓜ Jaume I

Occupying a wing of the old royal palace, and entered off c/dels Comtes on the cathedral's eastern side, the **Museu Frederic Marès** celebrates the diverse passions of sculptor, painter and restorer Frederic Marès (1893–1991). His beautifully presented collection of ancient

2

CORPUS CHRISTI AND THE DANCING EGG

One of Barcelona's biggest annual religious festivals, **Corpus Christi** (late May/early June), is celebrated with the dancing of the *sardana*, parades of *gegants* (festival giants) and a big procession from the cathedral. Unique to Corpus Christi is the *l'ou com balla*, the **dancing egg**, which bubbles atop fountain water-jets across the old town. Records of *l'ou com balla* in Barcelona date back to the seventeenth century, though its origins are obscure; nonetheless, it's possible to see that an egg (a hollowed-out, weighted eggshell) gaily dancing on spurts of water represents not only the Eucharist but rebirth, renewal and even a celebration of spring. The city council's festival programme lists where you can see this oddity for yourself – most old-town courtyard fountains put on a show, including those of La Seu and the Museu Marès.

---

and medieval sculpture does little to prepare visitors for Marès' true obsession – a kaleidoscopic array of curios and collectibles. In addition, the large arcaded courtyard, studded with orange trees, is one of the most romantic spots in the old town, and holds a summer-only café, *Café d'Estiu*, that's a perfect place to take a break from sightseeing.

Sculpture collection

Frederic Marès trained as a sculptor at Barcelona's La Llotja (School of Fine Arts) and became known for his monumental sculpture, including grand works now on display in Plaça de Catalunya. His later focus, however, was on the restoration of Catalunya's decaying medieval treasures, many of which are preserved in the galleries on the **ground and basement floors**. Marès' personal collection of medieval sculpture includes a comprehensive series of polychrome wooden crucifixes showing the stylistic development of the form from the twelfth to the fifteenth century. There are also antiquities, from Roman busts to Hellenistic terracotta lamps, while the intricate craftsmanship of medieval masons is displayed in a stunning series of carved doorways, cloister fragments, sculpted capitals and alabaster tombs. Up on the **first floor**, intriguing Baroque and Mannerist pieces complete a remarkable ensemble.

Collector's Cabinet

The upper floors showcase Frederic Marès' extraordinary **Collector's Cabinet** (Gabinet del Col.leccionista). Convinced that "charming objects that lived their lives well loved" should not simply be thrown away, Marès gathered an incredible array of everyday items during fifty years of travel. Entire rooms are devoted to keys and locks, carved pipes snugly cradled in cases, cigarette cards and snuffboxes, fans, gloves and brooches, playing cards, draughtsmen's tools, walking sticks, Japanese *netsuke*, dolls' houses, toy theatres, old gramophones and archaic bicycles, to list just a sample of what's on show. It's an absolute joy to spend an hour or so here, uncovering your own favourite piece of ephemera. In the **artist's library** on the second floor, Marès' own reclining nudes, penitent saints and bridling stags offer an insight into his more orthodox work.

Plaça del Rei

Ⓜ Jaume I

The harmonious enclosed square of **Plaça del Rei**, behind the cathedral apse, was once the courtyard of the palace of the counts of Barcelona, which later became the residence of the count-kings of Aragón. The palace buildings themselves are steeped in history, and include the romantic Renaissance Torre del Rei Martí, the main hall, known as the Saló del Tinell, and the fourteenth-century **Santa Agata chapel** – there's no public access to the tower, though there's a fine view of it from the square, while you can usually see inside both hall and chapel by visiting the Museu d'Història de Barcelona (see p.50).

CLOCKWISE FROM TOP LEFT BRIDGE OF SIGHS (P.53); MUSEU FREDERIC MARÈS (P.47); PLAÇA REIAL (P.54) >

It was in Plaça del Rei that Ferdinand and Isabella received Christopher Columbus on his triumphant return from the Americas in 1493. With the old-town streets packed, Columbus advanced in procession with the monarchs to the palace, where he presented the queen with booty from the trip – exotic birds, sweet potatoes, and six Indians (actually Haitians), taken on board during Columbus's return.

Museu d'Història de Barcelona (MUHBA)

Pl. del Rei, entrance on c/del Veguer • Tues–Sat 10am–7pm, Sun 10am–8pm, hols 10am–2pm • €7, Sun after 3pm free • ☎ 932 562 100, ⓦ museuhistoria.bcn.cat • ⓜ Jaume I

The excellent **Museu d'Història de Barcelona** (Barcelona History Museum) not only extends through the labyrinth of buildings that surround the Plaça del Rei – known as the "Conjunt Monumental" or monumental ensemble – but also, crucially, burrows beneath them to reveal the extensive remains of the Roman city of Barcino.

Descend in the lift (the floor indicator spins back to "12 BC"), and you're deposited on a network of underground metal walkways laid over excavations that extend for 4000 square metres, and stretch under the streets as far as the cathedral. The archeological remains range from the first century BC up to the sixth century AD. Little now stands above chest height, so you'd never know what you were looking at without the audioguide and display panels, but they reflect the transition from Roman to Visigothic rule and beyond. Thus an almost complete factory where the Romans once manufactured the fish sauce *garum* was topped by a Christian church at the end of the sixth century, itself later replaced by the Episcopal Palace.

The upper levels illuminate Barcelona's subsequent history, exploring the city's medieval growth as a major Mediterranean trading port, though displays lack the

---

WALKING AROUND ROMAN BARCELONA

The Barri Gòtic was once entirely enclosed by **Roman walls and towers**, dating from the fourth century AD. Although most were pulled down during the nineteenth century, to create more space for the expanding city, extensive traces of Roman Barcino do still survive. Much is now preserved in, or rather beneath, the Museu d'Història de Barcelona (see above), while the circuit of walls can easily be followed on an hour-long stroll. Brown information boards show the route at various points.

Outside the cathedral, in Plaça Nova, block metal letters a metre high spell out the word "Barcino", underneath a restored tower and a reconstructed part of the Roman **aqueduct**. There's more of the aqueduct on display north of here, set into the facade of a building on c/de Duran i Bas, while a large area of **Plaça de la Vila de Madrid** nearby has been excavated to reveal a row of sunken Roman tombs, known as the Via Sepulcral, slightly below the modern street level.

The line of the wall itself runs past the cathedral and the Museu Diocesà, with the next surviving section visible at **Plaça de Ramon Berenguer El Gran** (at Via Laietana). Some of the walls and towers here are over 13m high, and back onto the Capella de Santa Agata on Plaça del Rei. There's more wall to see if you cross c/de Jaume I and walk down **c/del Sots-Tinent Navarro**, while the most romantic section is the truncated Roman tower in the sunken **Plaça dels Traginers**, planted with a solitary olive tree. Along nearby **c/del Correu Vell**, part of the wall and defence towers were incorporated into a medieval palace – this section is visible in the courtyard of a civic centre (through a gate, opposite c/d'en Groc).

A right turn after here, up c/del Regomir, leads to the **Centre Cívic Pati Llimona**, constructed atop the remains of a gate that led through the Roman wall into inner Barcino. Assorted ancient stones can be seen through a glass window from c/del Regomir, and on weekdays you can wander inside for a closer look (usually Mon–Fri 10am–1.30pm & 2–5.30pm; free). Then head up c/de Ciutat and cross Plaça de Sant Jaume to reach the **Temple d'August**, where four impressive **Roman columns** and the architrave of a temple make an incongruous spectacle, tucked away in the green-painted interior courtyard of the **Centre Excursionista de Catalunya** (c/Paradís 10; Mon 10am–2pm, Tues–Sat 10am–7pm, Sun 10am–8pm, hols 10am–3pm; free). From here it's just a short walk back to the cathedral, though no Roman enthusiast should miss the nearby **Museu d'Història de Barcelona**, which features the underground excavations of Barcino itself.

visceral impact of actually seeing the ancient city laid out at your feet. It also incorporates the beautiful **Capella de Santa Agata** and the impressive **Saló del Tinell**, though the latter hall occasionally hosts temporary exhibitions, which may incur an extra admission charge. A fine example of secular Gothic architecture, with interior arches that span 17m, the Saló del Tinell was the seat of the Catalan parliament from 1370 onwards, and was also where Christopher Columbus delivered his report to Ferdinand and Isabella. Later on, the Spanish Inquisition met here, taking advantage of the popular belief that the walls of the hall would move if a lie was spoken.

2

Església de Santa María del Pi and around
ⓂLiceu

With the cathedral area and Plaça del Rei sucking in every visitor at some point during the day, the third focus of attraction in the Barri Gòtic is to the west, around the church of Santa María del Pi – five minutes' walk from the cathedral or just two minutes from the Ramblas.

Església de Santa María del Pi
Pl. Sant Josep Oriol • Early April to early Oct Mon–Fri 10am–7pm, Sat 10am–6pm, Sun 5–8pm; early Oct to early April Mon–Sat 10am–6pm, Sun 5–8pm • €4; Church free to worshippers at other times, when admission is free • ☎ 933 184 743, ⓦ basilicadelpi.com • ⓂLiceu

The fourteenth-century **Església de Santa María del Pi** stands at the intersection of three delightful little squares. Burned out during the Civil War fighting in 1936, and restored in the 1960s, the church boasts a Romanesque door but is mainly Catalan-Gothic in style, holding simply a single nave with chapels between the buttresses. The plainness of its interior only serves to set off some marvellous **stained glass**, at its most impressive in a 10m-wide rose window. Its treasure room glitters with chalices and ornate reliquaries, and the adjoining small museum covers the church's thousand-year history.

Plaça Sant Josep Oriol and around
The Santa María del Pi church flanks **Plaça Sant Josep Oriol**, the prettiest of the three adjacent squares, and an ideal place to take an outdoor coffee, listen to buskers or browse the weekend **artists' market** (Sat 11am–8pm, Sun 11am–2pm). The statue here is of Àngel Guimerà, nineteenth-century Catalan playwright and poet, who had a house on the square. Meanwhile, off Plaça Sant Josep Oriol, the old town's **antiques trade** is concentrated in shiny galleries and stores along c/de la Palla and c/dels Banys Nous.

Plaça del Pi and Carrer de Petritxol
The church of Santa María del Pi is named – like the squares on either side, **Plaça del Pi** and Placeta del Pi – after the pine trees that once stood here (a solitary specimen still stands in Plaça del Pi). A **farmers' market** spills across Plaça del Pi on the first and third Friday, Saturday and Sunday of each month, while the characteristic cafés of narrow **Carrer de Petritxol** (off Plaça del Pi) are the places to head to for a cup of hot chocolate – *Dulcinea* at no. 2 is the traditional choice – and a browse around the street's commercial art galleries. The most famous is at c/de Petritxol 5, where the **Sala Pares** was already well established when Picasso and Miró were young.

Plaça Sant Felip Neri
ⓂLiceu

In the narrow streets close to the cathedral, behind the Palau Episcopal, you'll stumble upon the pretty little **Plaça Sant Felip Neri**, scarred by Civil War bombing and now a school playground. Antoni Gaudí would walk here every evening after work at the Sagrada Família to hear Mass at the eighteenth-century **Església de Sant Felip Neri**. Many of the buildings that now hedge in this charming square were brought here from other parts of the city. In summer you can eat outside at candlelit tables, set out by the restaurant of the boutique *Neri Hotel* (see p.168).

Museu del Calçat

Pl. Sant Felip Neri 5 • Tues–Sun & hols 11am–2pm • €2.50 • ☎ 933 014 533 • Ⓜ Liceu

One of the buildings that flanks Plaça Sant Felip Neri – the former headquarters of the city's shoemakers' guild (founded in 1202) – now houses a quirky one-room footwear museum. The **Museu del Calçat** contains footwear dating back to the 1600s, ranging from swaggering Puss-in-Boots-style men's boots to tiny eighteenth-century satin slippers, as well as celebrity cast-offs such as Ronaldinho's football boots. In the anteroom, there's also what claims to be the world's largest shoe – don't tell the delightful guide, but it clearly isn't – made for the city's Columbus statue at the bottom of the Ramblas.

Museu Moto

C/de la Palla 10 • Tues–Sat 10.30am–2.30pm & 3.30–7.30pm, Sun 10.30am–2.30pm • €7 • ☎ 933 186 584, ⓦ museumoto.com • Ⓜ Liceu

Barcelona has an astonishing number of motorbikes per capita, so it makes a fitting home for the **Museu Moto**. Laid out in a concrete-floored, garage-like space, this features more than fifty motorcycles made by some of the 150 manufacturers that have operated in the region. Most are handsome post-World War II models, but there are some lovely 1920s specimens, too, and historical panels trace the changes in the industry. Bultaco bikes feature highly, with several Sherpa T models – the iconic firm returned to making bikes in 2013 after a thirty-year gap.

El Call Major and the Antiga Sinagoga

What was once the medieval **Jewish quarter** of Barcelona lies south of Plaça Sant Felip Neri, centred on c/de Sant Domènec del Call. The city authorities have signposted some of the points of interest in what's known as **El Call Major** (*Call* is the Catalan word for a narrow passage).

Antiga Sinagoga

C/Marlet 5, corner with c/de Sant Domènec del Call • Summer Mon–Fri 10.30am–6.30pm, Sat & Sun 10.30am–2.30pm; winter Mon–Fri 11am–5.30pm, Sat & Sun 11am–3pm; sometimes closed Sat for ceremonies • €2.50 • ☎ 933 170 790, ⓦ calldebarcelona.org • Ⓜ Liceu

The most notable surviving landmark of the Jewish quarter is the main synagogue, the **Antiga Sinagoga**. A synagogue existed here, on the edge of the Roman forum, from the

---

JEWISH BARCELONA

Jews were living in Barcelona well before the ninth century, and a Jewish district was documented in the city by the eleventh. Later, as elsewhere in Spain, Barcelona's **medieval Jewish quarter** lay nestled in the shadow of the cathedral, under the Church's careful scrutiny. In the thirteenth and early fourteenth centuries some of the realm's greatest and most powerful administrators, tax collectors and ambassadors hailed from here, but reactionary trends sparked persecution and led to the closing off of the community in these narrow, dark alleys. Nevertheless, a prosperous settlement persisted until the pogrom and forced conversion of 1391 and exile of 1492 (see box, p.244).

These days little except the street name and the synagogue survive as reminders of the Jewish presence – after their expulsion, most of the buildings used by the Jews were torn down and used for construction elsewhere in the city. With the demise of the Franco regime, a small community was again established in Barcelona, and recent years have seen a revival in interest in Barcelona's Jewish heritage. As well as the synagogue, the sites of the butcher's, baker's, fishmonger's and Jewish baths have all been identified. The Jewish cemetery was located over on the eastern side of Montjuïc – which means Jewish Mountain – where the castle now displays around thirty tombstones that were recovered in the early twentieth century.

third century AD until the pogrom of 1391, but even after that date the building survived in various guises – the sunken dye vats from a family business of fifteenth-century New Christian (forcibly converted Jews) dyers are still visible, alongside some original Roman walling. Not many people stop by the synagogue – if you do, you'll get a personalized tour of the small room, courtesy of a member of the local Jewish community.

Centre d'Interpretació del Call

Pl. Manuel Ribé • Tues–Fri 11am–2pm, Sat & Sun 11am–7pm • Free (exhibit on second floor €2.20) • ☎ 932 562 100, ⓦ www.museuhistoria .bcn.cat • Ⓜ Liceu

Aside from the Antiga Sinagoga, most local Jewish buildings have long since vanished. In Plaçeta Manuel Ribé, however, a house that originally belonged to a veil-maker serves as a small museum, the **Centre d'Interpretació del Call**. Informative storyboards (in English) shed light on Barcelona's fascinating Jewish heritage, while the centre also coordinates historical tours and activities.

Plaça de Sant Jaume

Ⓜ Jaume I

The spacious **Plaça de Sant Jaume**, at the end of the main c/de Ferran, marks the very centre of the Barri Gòtic. Once the site of Barcelona's Roman forum and marketplace, it's now at the heart of city and regional government, containing two of Barcelona's most significant buildings, the **Ajuntament**, or City Hall, and the **Palau de la Generalitat**. Whistle-happy local police try to keep things moving in the *plaça*, while taxis and bike-tour groups weave between the pedestrians. The square is also the traditional site of demonstrations and local festivals.

Ajuntament de Barcelona

Pl. de Sant Jaume • Public admitted Sun 10am–1.30pm, entrance on c/Font de Sant Miquel • Free, English-language leaflet provided • ☎ 934 027 000, ⓦ bcn.cat • Ⓜ Jaume I

Although parts of Barcelona's City Hall, the **Ajuntament** on the south side of Plaça de Sant Jaume, date from as early as 1373, its Neoclassical facade was added when the square was laid out in the nineteenth century. You can get a much better idea of the grandeur of the original structure by nipping around the corner, to see its previous main entrance on c/de la Ciutat. It's a typically exuberant Catalan-Gothic facade, but was badly damaged during nineteenth-century renovations.

Visitors are allowed into the building on Sundays, to take a self-guided tour around the rather splendid marble halls, galleries and staircases. The highlights are the magnificent restored fourteenth-century council chamber, the **Saló de Cent**, and the dramatic historical murals by Josep María Sert in the **Saló de les Cròniques** (Hall of Chronicles), while the courtyard features sculptural works by famous Catalan artists.

Palau de la Generalitat

Pl. de Sant Jaume, entrance on c/de Sant Honorat • 1hr tours on second & fourth weekend of the month (except Aug), every hour, 10am–noon; online advance bookings essential, find the application page by searching for "Palau visites" on the website; public also admitted April 23, and Sept 11 & 24 10am–6pm • Free, ID required • ☎ 934 024 600, ⓦ gencat.cat • Ⓜ Jaume I

It was from the **Palau de la Generalitat**, the traditional home of the Catalan government opposite the Ajuntament, that the short-lived Catalan Republic was proclaimed in April 1931. The oldest part of the building is the fifteenth-century facade on c/del Bisbe, which sports a spirited medallion portraying St George and the Dragon. A beautiful cloister with superb coffered ceilings is located on the first floor inside, opening off which are the chapel and salon of Sant Jordi (St George, patron saint of Catalunya as well as England) and an upper courtyard planted with orange trees and peppered with presidential busts. Incidentally, the enclosed Gothic bridge across the narrow c/del Bisbe – the so-called **Bridge of Sighs** – is an anachronism, added in 1928, though it features on many a postcard of the "Gothic" quarter. It connects the Generalitat with the former canons' houses across the street, now used as the official residence of the president.

Aside from the guided tours on alternate weekends, the Generalitat is also open to the public on **Dia de Sant Jordi**, or Saint George's Day (April 23; expect a 2hr wait), as well as **Diada Nacional de Catalunya** (National Day; Sept 11) and **La Mercè** (Sept 24).

Plaça de Sant Just

2

Ⓜ Jaume I

Near the Ajuntament, down c/d'Hercules, **Plaça de Sant Just** is a handsome little corner of the old town, and a particularly nice spot for an alfresco lunch at the excellent *Café de l'Acadèmia*, which puts out dining tables on the square. The square also boasts a medieval **church** and restored fourteenth-century fountain, while one of the flanking Baroque palaces – the remarkable **Palau Moxó** – is open for guided tours.

Església dels Sants Màrtirs Just i Pastor

Enter from the back, at c/de la Ciutat; the main doors on Pl. de Sant Just are open less often • Mon–Sat 11am–2pm & 5–9pm, Sun 10am–1pm • ☎ 933 017 433, Ⓦ basilicasantjust.cat • Ⓜ Jaume I

The very plain stone facade of the **Església dels Sants Màrtirs Just i Pastor**, whose name commemorates the city's earliest Christian martyrs, belies the rich stained glass and elaborate chapel decoration within. What claims to be the oldest parish church site in Barcelona is held to have first supported a foundation at the start of the ninth century; the restored interior, though, dates from the mid-fourteenth century.

Palau Moxó

Pl. de Sant Just 4 • Guided tours Mon–Fri by reservation only • €13 • ☎ 670 466 260, Ⓦ palaumoxo.com • Ⓜ Jaume I

Built in 1770 for a wealthy land-owning family, the **Palau Moxó** has remained in the hands of the Moxó family ever since. That makes it unique in Barcelona – doubly so, in fact, since most of the city's other palatial Baroque residences were destroyed during the Spanish Civil War. It's still a private residence, but certain rooms are open for guided tours each week, during which you'll see grand salons and intimate chambers that offer a fascinating perspective on city-centre living, Baroque style. The Moxós themselves are an interesting bunch, with links to the Güell family, patrons of Antoni Gaudí.

miba

C/de la Ciutat 7 • Tues–Fri 10am–2pm & 4–7pm, Sat 10am–8pm, Sun & hols 10am–2pm • €8, under-12s €6, under-4s free • ☎ 933 327 930, Ⓦ mibamuseum.com • Ⓜ Jaume I

Many of the Barri Gòtic's impressive buildings have grand entrances – but there's only one where you slide down an enclosed steel chute, water-park style, into its vaulted bowels. A regular entrance also provides access to Catalan inventor Pep Torres' Barcelona Museum of Ideas and Inventions, or **miba**, which presents a mixture of his own inventions and those of creative inventors worldwide. Basically a single room that's more likely to appeal to kids than adults, it holds a diverting array of working models and sketched-out ideas, some of them worthy, world-saving devices like portable water-purifiers and sun-seeking plant-pots, and others frankly bonkers.

Plaça Reial and around

Ⓜ Liceu

Of all the old-town squares, the most popular with visitors is the elegant nineteenth-century **Plaça Reial**, hidden behind an archway, just off the Ramblas. Laid out in around 1850, the Italianate square is studded with tall palm trees and decorated iron lamps (made by the young Antoni Gaudí), bordered by high, pastel-coloured arcaded buildings, and centred on a fountain depicting the Three Graces. Taking in the sun at one of the benches puts you in the company of bikers, buskers, beggars and backpackers, not to mention more affluent tourists drinking a coffee at one of the pavement cafés. Things used to be a bit dodgy in Plaça Reial, but the unsavoury characters have largely been driven away, and predatory, menu-toting waiters tend to be the biggest nuisance these days. The surrounding bars and restaurants are becoming increasingly upmarket, but don't expect to see too many locals until night falls.

On Sunday morning Plaça Reial hosts a long-standing **coin and stamp market** (10am–2pm). Otherwise, the arcaded passageways connecting the square with the surrounding streets throw up a few interesting sights, like the quirky **Herborista del Rei** (c/del Vidre; closed Mon), an early nineteenth-century herbalist's shop.

Carrer dels Escudellers and Plaça de George Orwell

The alleys on the south side of Plaça Reial emerge on c/dels Escudellers, where the turning spits of grilled chicken at **Los Caracoles** restaurant make a good photograph. **Carrer dels Escudellers** itself was once a thriving red-light street, and still has a late-night seediness about it, but it teeters on the edge of respectability. Bars and restaurants around here attract a youthful clientele, nowhere more so than those flanking **Plaça de George Orwell**, at the eastern end of c/dels Escudellers. Named in honour of the English writer in 1996, the wedge-shaped square was created by levelling an old-town block – a favoured tactic in Barcelona to let in a bit of light.

Carrer d'Avinyó

Ⓜ Liceu

Carrer d'Avinyó, running south from c/de Ferran towards the harbour, cuts through the most atmospheric part of the southern Barri Gòtic. It used to be a red-light district of some renown, littered with brothels and bars, and frequented by the young Picasso, whose family moved into the area in 1895. It still looks the part – a narrow thoroughfare lined with dark overhanging buildings – but the cafés, streetwear shops and boutiques tell the story of its creeping gentrification. The locals aren't overly enamoured of the influx of bar-crawling fun-seekers – banners and notices along the length of this and neighbouring streets plead with visitors to keep the noise down.

La Mercè

Ⓜ Drassanes

During the eighteenth century, the harbourside neighbourhood known as **La Mercè** was home to the nobles and merchants enriched by Barcelona's maritime trade. After most took the opportunity to move north to the more fashionable Eixample later in the nineteenth century, the streets of La Mercè took on an earthier hue. Since then, c/de la Mercè and the surrounding streets (particularly Ample, d'en Gignas and Regomir) have been home to a series of old-style **taverns** known as *tascas* or *bodegas* – a glass of wine from the barrel in *Bodega la Plata*, or a similar joint, is one of the old town's more authentic experiences.

Església de la Mercè

Pl. de la Mercè · Mon, Tues, Thurs, Fri & Sun 10am–8pm, Wed & Sat 10am–1pm & 6–8pm · Ⓜ Drassanes

The eighteenth-century **Església de la Mercè** is the focus every September of the city's biggest annual celebration, the Festes de la Mercè. Dedicated to the co-patroness of Barcelona, the Virgin of Mercè, whose image is paraded from here, it's the excuse for a week of intense merrymaking, culminating in spectacular fireworks along the seafront. The church itself was burned out in 1936, but the gilt side-chapels, stained-glass medallions and apse murals have been authentically restored, while the statue of Virgin and Child sits behind glass above the altar – a staircase allows you a closer look.

2

NEIGHBOURHOOD BAR, EL RAVAL

El Raval

Known as El Raval, from the Arabic word for "suburb", the old-town area west of the Ramblas has always formed a world apart from the nobler Barri Gòtic. In medieval times it was the site of hospitals, churches, monasteries and various noxious trades, while later it acquired a reputation as the city's main red-light area, known to all (for obscure reasons) as the Barri Xinès – China Town. In recent decades, however, El Raval has changed markedly, particularly in the "upper Raval" around Barcelona's contemporary art museum, MACBA. Cutting-edge galleries, designer restaurants and fashionable bars are all part of the scene here, while the occasionally edgy "lower Raval" holds the neighbourhood's two other outstanding buildings, namely Gaudí's Palau Güell and the church of Sant Pau del Camp, one of the city's oldest churches.

According to the Barcelona writer Manuel Vázquez Montalbán, El Raval once housed "theatrical homosexuals and anarcho-syndicalist, revolutionary meeting places; women's prisons,..condom shops and brothels which smelled of liquor and gloms". Even today in the backstreets between c/de Sant Pau and c/Nou de la Rambla visitors may run the gauntlet of cat-calling prostitutes and petty drug dealers, while a handful of atmospheric old bars trade on their former reputations as bohemian hangouts. Yet the combination of the Olympics and subsequent European Union funding achieved what Franco never could, and cleaned up large parts of the neighbourhood almost overnight. North of c/de l'Hospital, the development of **MACBA**, the adjacent **CCCB** cultural centre and new university faculty buildings have seen entire city blocks demolished and remodelled. To the south, between c/de l'Hospital and c/de Sant Pau, former tenements and alleys were bulldozed away so an entire boulevard – the **Rambla del Raval** – could be gouged through, creating a huge pedestrianized area where none existed before, while the Josep Lluís Mateo-designed **Filmoteca de Catalunya** has polished away some of Plaça Salvador Seguí's grit. At the same time the area's older, traditional residents have gradually been supplanted by a more affluent, arty population, and there's also been a growing influx of immigrants from the Indian subcontinent and North Africa. Alongside the surviving spit-and-sawdust bars, and the recent crop of restaurants, galleries and boutiques, you'll find specialist grocery stores, curry houses, halal butchers and hole-in-the-wall phone and internet offices.

All that said, you'd hesitate to call El Raval gentrified; it clearly still has its rough edges. You needn't be unduly concerned during the day as you make your way around, but it's as well to keep your wits about you at night, particularly in the southernmost streets.

Museu d'Art Contemporani de Barcelona (MACBA)

Pl. dels Àngels 1 • Mon & Wed–Fri 11am–7.30pm (mid-June till mid-Sept till 8pm), Sat 10am–9pm, Sun & hols 10am–3pm • €10 all exhibitions or €6.50 individual special exhibitions, one-year pass €15, under-14s free • English-language tours Mon 4pm & 6pm, Thurs–Sat 4pm, included in admission fee • ☏ 934 120 810, ⓦ macba.cat • ⓜ Catalunya

The iconic **Museu d'Art Contemporani de Barcelona**, which opened in 1995 and is universally known as **MACBA**, anchors the upper reaches of El Raval. The contrast between this huge, white, almost luminous, structure and the buildings that surround it could hardly be starker. Its American architect, Richard Meier, set out to make as much use of natural light as possible, and to "create a dialogue" between the museum and its neighbours; this is reflected in the front of the building, constructed entirely of glass. Once inside, you go from the ground to the fourth floor up a series of swooping ramps that afford continuous views of the square below – usually full of careering skateboarders.

While the museum's **permanent collection** represents the main movements in contemporary art since 1945, focussing largely but not exclusively on Catalunya and Spain, only a small selection is on show at any one time, in regularly changing themed exhibitions. There are always two or three other temporary exhibitions and installations as well, so, depending on when you visit, you may catch works by major names such as Joan Miró, Antoni Tàpies or Eduardo Chillida. Joan Brossa, leading light of the Catalan Dau al Set group of the 1950s, also has work here, as do contemporary multimedia and installation artists like Antoni Muntadas and Francesc Torres. A good museum **shop** sells everything from designer espresso cups to art books.

Centre de Cultura Contemporània de Barcelona (CCCB)

C/de Montalegre 5 • **CCCB** Tues–Sun 11am–8pm • €6 one exhibition, €8 for two; under-12s free, free on Sun after 3pm • **C3 café-bar** Mon–Fri 9am–9pm, Sat & Sun 11am–9pm • ☏ 933 064 100, ⓦ cccb.org • ⓜ Catalunya

As well as hosting excellent (and often challenging) art and city-related exhibitions ranging from photography to architecture, the **Centre de Cultura Contemporània de**

EL RAVAL

ACCOMMODATION

Barceló Raval	7
Casa Camper	5
Hostal Cèntric	1
Hostal Grau	4
Hotel Curious	6
Hotel España	10
Hotel Onix Liceo	11
Hotel Peninsular	9
Hotel Sant Agustí	8
Market Hotel	3
Mesón Castilla	2

CAFÉS

Café de les Delícies	16
Federal	10
Granja M. Viader	9
El Jardí	13
Kasparo	3

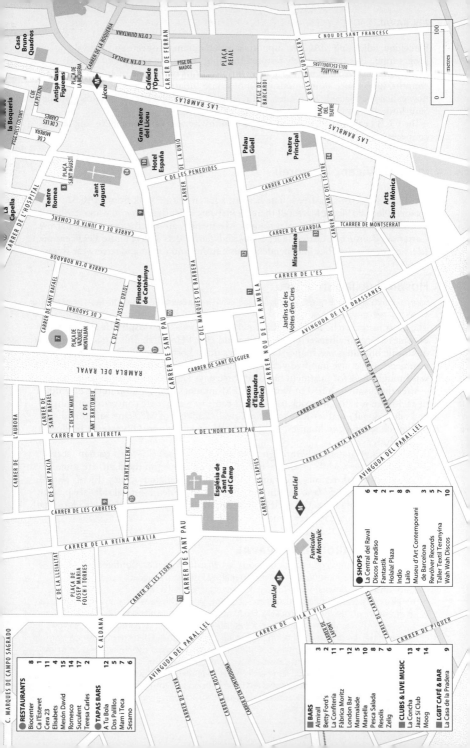

Barcelona, adjoining MACBA, supports a varied cinema, concert and festival programme. This imaginatively restored building is a prime example of the juxtaposition of old and new; originally built in 1714 on the site of an Augustinian convent, it was once an infamous workhouse and lunatic asylum. The main courtyard, now called the Plaça de les Dones, still retains its old tile panels and presiding statue of Sant Jordi, the patron saint of Catalunya.

The CCB's **café-bar**, *C3*, spreads across a sunny *terrassa* on the modern square that connects it to MACBA.

Plaça de Vicenç Martorell

Ⓜ Catalunya

The Raval's nicest traffic-free square lies just a few minutes' walk from MACBA. In the arcaded **Plaça de Vicenç Martorell** there's a first-rate café, the *Kasparo*, whose tables overlook a popular children's playground. Meanwhile, around the corner, the narrow Carrer del Bonsuccés, Carrer de les Sitges and Carrer dels Tallers house a concentrated selection of the city's best independent **music stores** and urban and streetwear shops.

Hospital de la Santa Creu

Entrances on c/del Carme and c/de l'Hospital · **Garden** Daily 8am–dusk · Free · **La Capella** c/de l'Hospital 56 · Tues–Sat noon–8pm, Sun & hols 11am–2pm · Ⓦ lacapella.bcn.cat · Ⓜ Liceu

The most historic relic in the El Raval neighbourhoods, the **Hospital de la Santa Creu** occupies a large site between c/del Carme and c/de l'Hospital. This attractive complex of Gothic buildings was founded as the city's main hospital in 1402, a role that it assumed for over five hundred years. Antoni Gaudí, knocked down by a tram in 1926, was brought here for treatment but died three days later.

After the hospital shifted to Domènech i Montaner's new creation in the Eixample in 1930 (see p.120), the spacious fifteenth-century wards were converted for cultural and educational use; they now hold the Royal Academy of Medicine, an art and design school and two libraries, including the Catalan national library, the Biblioteca de Catalunya.

Visitors can wander freely through a charming, medieval cloistered **garden** (access from either street), while inside the c/del Carme entrance (on the right) are some superb seventeenth-century decorative tiles of various religious scenes. There's also the rather nice open-air *El Jardí* **café** in the garden at the c/de l'Hospital side (see p.180), while the hospital's former chapel, **La Capella** (entered separately from c/de l'Hospital), is an exhibition space for new contemporary artists.

SNOOPING AROUND THE RAVAL

Barcelona-born author, journalist, critic and poet, **Manuel Vázquez Montalbán** (1939–2003) was one of Spain's most popular writers. His shabby, fast-living fictional detective **Pepe Carvalho** – ex-Communist and CIA agent – investigated foul deeds in the city in a series of terrific novels spanning thirty years. By no accident, Montalbán's own passions – for Barcelona itself, and for politics, markets, cooking, food and drink – rubbed off on his detective, and Pepe Carvalho's cases took him around easily identifiable parts of the city, particularly the earthy streets of the Raval. With an office on the Ramblas, the gourmand detective is often picking out groceries in the Boqueria market or grabbing a bite at *Pinotxo*, the classic stand-up market bar, while both Montalbán and Carvalho found their spiritual home in the *Casa Leopoldo* restaurant (c/Sant Rafael 24, off Rambla del Raval; Ⓦ casaleopoldo.com). The remodelled square nearby, by the *Barceló Raval* hotel, was renamed in honour of the author, while an annual crime fiction prize (winners include Henning Mankell, P.D. James and Ian Rankin) bears the name of his celebrated detective.

HIGH SOCIETY AT THE HOTEL ESPAÑA

There's a hidden gem tucked around the back of the Liceu opera house, on the otherwise fairly shabby c/de Sant Pau. Here, in the lower reaches of the Raval, some of the most influential names in Catalan architecture and design came together at the start of the twentieth century to transform the **Hotel España** (c/de Sant Pau 9–11; ⊛ hotelespanya.com; ⓂLiceu) – built as a simple boarding house in 1860 – into one of the city's most lavish addresses (see p.169). With a wonderfully tiled dining room designed by Lluís Domènech i Montaner, a bar with an amazing marble fireplace by Eusebi Arnau, and a bathing area with glass roof (now the breakfast room) whose marine murals were executed by Ramon Casas, the hotel was the fashionable sensation of its day. Over a century later it's back in vogue, since a remarkable restoration has highlighted its classy *modernista* public spaces and brought the rooms up to scratch. Lunch or dinner here is a real in-the-know treat, with the original *modernista* dining room (known as the *Fonda España*) under the helm of Michelin-starred Basque chef Martín Berasategui, while the classy bar welcomes passing visitors.

3

Reial Acadèmia de Medicina

Hospital de la Santa Creu, c/del Carme 47 entrance • Wed only 10am–noon; closed Aug • Free • ☎ 933 171 686, ⓦ ramc.cat • ⓂLiceu

Even on the one day each week that it's open, you may need to ring the bell at the door of the Royal Academy of Medicine to gain admittance to the remarkable eighteenth-century anatomical theatre within. The chamber has been beautifully preserved, with carved wooden seats under a gilded dome, centred on a marble dissecting table.

Rambla del Raval and around

ⓂLiceu

Perhaps the most obvious manifestation of the changing character of El Raval is the **Rambla del Raval**, a palm-lined boulevard driven right through the centre of the district between c/de l'Hospital and c/de Sant Pau. The *rambla* has a distinct character that's all its own, mixing kebab joints and grocery stores with an increasing number of fashionable cafés and bars. The signature building, halfway down, is the glow-in-the-dark designer **Barceló Raval hotel**, while children find it hard to resist a clamber on the massive, bulbous cat sculpture. A weekend **street market** (selling anything from samosas to hammocks) adds a bit more character, while the two extremes of the *rambla* offer a snapshot of the changing neighbourhood. At the bottom end, off **Carrer de Sant Pau**, the *barri*'s remaining prostitutes accost passers-by as they head back towards the Liceu and the Ramblas. The top end, meanwhile, leads you straight into the streets of the "upper Raval", flush with boutiques, bars and galleries.

Carrer de la Riera Baixa

Just off the top of Rambla del Raval, the narrow **Carrer de la Riera Baixa** is at the centre of the city's secondhand and vintage clothing scene. A dozen funky little independent clothes shops provide the scope for an hour's browsing, while the *Resolis* bar (no. 22) makes the best place to take a break in between.

Plaça del Pedró and Carrer d'en Botella

In **Plaça del Pedró** (junction of c/del Carme and c/de l'Hospital) a cherished statue of Santa Eulàlia (co-patron of the city) stands on the site of her supposed crucifixion, facing the surviving apse of a Romanesque chapel. Carrer d'en Botella, just off the square, is unremarkable, save for the plaque at no. 11 that records the **birthplace of Manuel Vázquez Montalbán**, probably the city's most famous writer, whose likes and prejudices found expression in his favourite character, detective Pepe Carvalho (see box opposite).

> **HIDDEN GEMS: EL RAVAL**
>
> Weekend market on Rambla
> del Raval See p.61
> Terrace of Palau Güell See below
> Music shopping See p.234
>
> El Jardí café See p.180
> Art shows at La Capella See p.60
> Summer drinks at Barcelo Raval's 360°
> Terrace See p.168

3

Filmoteca de Catalunya

Pl. Salvador Seguí 1–9 • **Cinema** Tues–Fri 5–10pm, Sat & Sun 4.30–10pm • 4 • **Exhibition Hall** Tues–Sun 4–9pm • Free • ☎ 935 671 070, ⓦ filmoteca.cat • Ⓜ Liceu

A colossus of concrete and glass in Plaça Salvador Seguí – a square long known for its pickpockets and prostitutes – the opening of the Josep Lluís Mateo-designed **Filmoteca de Catalunya** in 2012 marked yet another step in the government's push to revitalize El Raval. As well as two below-ground cinemas, Sala Chomón and Sala Laya, the building holds a film library, a bookshop, and spaces for permanent and temporary cinema-related exhibitions. The programming is thematic, touching on subjects such as Tim Burton's monsters and the silent films of Fritz Lang, with screenings of children's movies on Saturdays and Sundays. All films are shown in their original language, with Spanish or Catalan subtitles.

Palau Güell

C/Nou de la Rambla 3–5 • Tues–Sun & hols: April–Oct 10am–8pm; Nov–March 10am–5.30pm; English guided tour Tues 2pm • €12, ages 10–17 €5; includes audioguide • ☎ 934 725 775, ⓦ palauguell.cat • Ⓜ Liceu

Between 1886 and 1890, the young **Antoni Gaudí** designed the extraordinary **Palau Güell** as a townhouse for the wealthy ship owner and industrialist **Eusebi Güell i Bacigalupi**. Commissioned as an extension of the Güell family's house on the Ramblas, to which it's connected by a corridor, it was the first modern building to be declared a World Heritage Site by UNESCO. Since it reopened in 2012, restored to its original state – complete with remarkable roof terrace – it's gained its rightful status as one of Barcelona's major architectural showpieces.

Steered by a helpful audioguide, visitors explore the Palau Güell from top to bottom, at their own pace. At a time when architects sought to conceal the iron supports within buildings, Gaudí turned them to his advantage, displaying them as decorative features in the grand rooms on the **main floor**. Columns, arches and ceilings are all shaped, carved and twisted in an elaborate style that was to become the hallmark of Gaudí's later works. No expense was spared on the materials used, which ranged from dark marble hewn from the Güell family quarries to the opulent hardwoods seen in the ornate coffered ceilings and marquetry floors. The vast **central hall** is topped with a parabolic dome that's pierced with holes to allow natural light, in emulation of the night sky, and echoes to a thunderous organ that's played throughout the day and is also used for regular recitals.

Even the basement **stables** bear Gaudí's distinct touch, a forest of brick capitals and arches that, with a touch of imagination, become mushrooms and palms. Displays in the supremely light spaces of the attic trace the painstaking twenty-year restoration programme, while tours culminate on the spectacular **roof terrace**, adorned with a fantastical series of chimneys decorated with swirling patterns made from fragments of glazed tile, glass and earthenware. The family rarely ventured up here – it was the servants instead who were exposed to the fullest flight of Gaudí's fantasy as they hung the washing out on lines strung from chimney to chimney.

CLOCKWISE FROM TOP MACBA (P.57); *LA CONFITERÍA* (P.197); LAILO (P.230) >

Església de Sant Pau del Camp

C/de Sant Pau 101 • Daily 10am–1.30pm & 4–7.30pm • Admission to cloister €3 • ☎ 934 410 001 • Ⓜ Paral.lel

Carrer de Sant Pau cuts west through El Raval to the church of **Sant Pau del Camp**, whose name – St Paul of the Field – is a graphic reminder that it once stood in open fields beyond the city walls. A Benedictine foundation of the tenth century, Sant Pau was built after its predecessor was destroyed in a Muslim raid of 985 AD and constructed on a Greek-cross plan. It was renovated again at the end of the thirteenth century; the curious, primitive carvings of fish, birds and faces above the main entrance date from that period, while other animal forms adorn the twin capitals of the charming twelfth-century cloister. Inside, the church is dark and rather plain, enlivened only by tiny arrow-slit windows and small stained-glass circles high up in the central dome.

Mercat de Sant Antoni

3

C/del Comte d'Urgell 1 • Mon–Thurs 7am–2.30pm & 5–8.30pm, Fri & Sat 7am–8.30pm • Ⓦ mercatsbcn.cat • Ⓜ Sant Antoni

The handsome **Mercat de Sant Antoni** – the major produce market for El Raval neighbourhood, dating from 1876 – stands at the neighbourhood's western edge where the Ronda de Sant Pau meets the Ronda de Sant Antoni. Barcelona's old markets have been progressively revamped in recent years, as their nineteenth-century engineering starts to fail, and Sant Antoni is no exception. As of press time, it was being remodelled, while retaining its external character, with its reopening tentatively rescheduled for 2016. For the moment, a temporary market operates on the surrounding streets, while the weekly **book and coin market** still takes place around the perimeter of the original market building (Sun 8.30am–2.30pm), with collectors and enthusiasts arriving early to pick through the best bargains.

Sant Pere, La Ribera and Ciutadella

The two easternmost old-town neighbourhoods of Sant Pere and La Ribera sit one atop the other, divided by Carrer de la Princesa. Both medieval in origin, they are often thought of as a single district, but each has a distinct character. Sant Pere – perhaps the least visited part of the old town – holds two remarkable buildings, the *modernista* concert hall known as the Palau de la Música Catalana and the stylishly designed market, the Mercat Santa Caterina. By way of contrast, the old artisans' quarter of La Ribera is always busy with tourists, thanks to the hugely popular Museu Picasso, and the graceful church of Santa María del Mar, Barcelona's most perfect expression of the Catalan-Gothic style. What's more, if you fancy time out from the old town's labyrinthine alleys, you can always retreat to the city's favourite park, Parc de la Ciutadella, on La Ribera's eastern edge.

Both neighbourhoods have seen a fair amount of regeneration in recent years, particularly Sant Pere, where new boulevards and community projects sit alongside DJ bars and designer shops. La Ribera's cramped, narrow streets, on the other hand, were at the heart of medieval industry and commerce, and it's still the location of choice for many contemporary designers, craftspeople and artists. Galleries and applied art museums occupy the mansions of Carrer de Montcada – the neighbourhood's most handsome street – while the *barri* is at its hippest in the area around the **Passeig del Born**, whose cafés, restaurants and bars make it one of the city's premier nightlife centres.

To walk through both neighbourhoods you can start at Ⓜ Urquinaona, close to the Palau de la Música Catalana, or Ⓜ Arc de Triomf over to the east, while Ⓜ Jaume I marks both the southern end of Sant Pere and the most direct access point to La Ribera.

Palau de la Música Catalana

C/de Sant Pere Més Alt · Guided tours (in English on the hour) daily: Sept–June 10am–3.30pm, Easter week & July 10am–6pm, Aug 9am–8pm · €18 · Tour tickets available by phone, online or at the box office · ☎ 902 475 485, ⓦ palaumusica.cat · Ⓜ Urquinaona

Stumble upon *modernista* architect Lluís Domènech i Montaner's stupendous **Palau de la Música Catalana** from narrow c/de Sant Pere Més Alt, and it barely seems to have enough space to breathe. The extraordinary concert hall was built in 1908 for the Orfeó Català choral group – it's still privately owned, although the Orfeó has moved to L'Auditori in Plaça de las Glòries – and made an immediate statement of nationalistic intent. Smothered in tiles and mosaics typical of *modernisme*, the highly elaborate facade rests on three great columns, resembling elephant legs, while the corner sculpture represents Catalan popular song, its allegorical figures protected by a strident Sant Jordi (St George). Determined to make the interior a veritable "box of light", Domènech i Montaner capped the second-storey auditorium with a mighty, bulbous stained-glass skylight – something contemporary critics claimed to be an engineering impossibility.

To see it at its best, try to come to a performance – the **concert season** runs from September until June (see p.207). Otherwise, it's well worth joining one of the very popular daytime tours of the interior.

Touring the concert hall

Numbers are limited on the hour-long **guided tours** of the Palau de la Música Catalana, so it's best to buy a ticket in advance. The tours start with a short video extolling the virtues of the building, followed by a close-up look at the decorated facade columns and a brief visit to the two floors of the main concert hall. Sculptures of the Muses ring the main stage, while allegorical decoration is everywhere, from the sculpted red and white roses in the colours of the Catalan flag to the representations of music and nature in the glistening stained glass. Successive extensions and interior remodelling have opened up the rest of the original site – the **Petit Palau** offers a smaller auditorium space, while to the side an enveloping glass facade provides the main public access to the box office, terrace restaurant and foyer bar.

Plaça de Sant Pere

Ⓜ Arc de Triomf/Urquinaona

Sant Pere neighbourhood extends around three parallel medieval streets, carrers de Sant Pere de Més Baix (lower), Mitja (middle) and Alt (upper), which contain the bulk of the district's most characteristic buildings and shops – a mixture of boutiques, textile firms, groceries and old family businesses. The three streets converge upon the original neighbourhood square, **Plaça de Sant Pere**, whose foursquare **Església de Sant Pere de les Puelles** flanks one side, overlooking a flamboyant iron drinking fountain and a few cafés that set out outdoor tables. The church is actually one of the oldest in the city, rebuilt in 1147 on tenth-century foundations, though it's been destroyed and burned too many times since to retain any interior interest the high walled façade, although it looks medieval, is a twentieth-century renovation.

Mercat Santa Caterina

Av. de Francesc Cambó 16 • July & Aug Mon–Sat 7.30am–3.30pm; Sept–June Mon–Wed & Sat 7.30am–3.30pm, Thurs & Fri 7.30am–8.30pm • ☎ 933 195 740, Ⓦ mercatsantacaterina.com • Ⓜ Jaume I

At the very heart of Sant Pere is the eye-catching **Mercat Santa Caterina**, whose splendid restoration has retained its original nineteenth-century balustraded market walls and added slatted wooden doors and windows and a dramatic multicoloured wave roof.

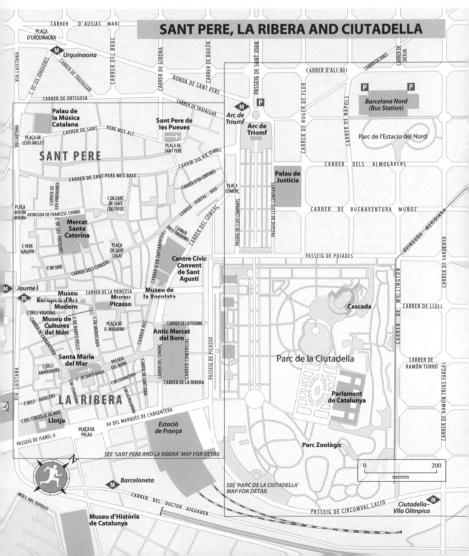

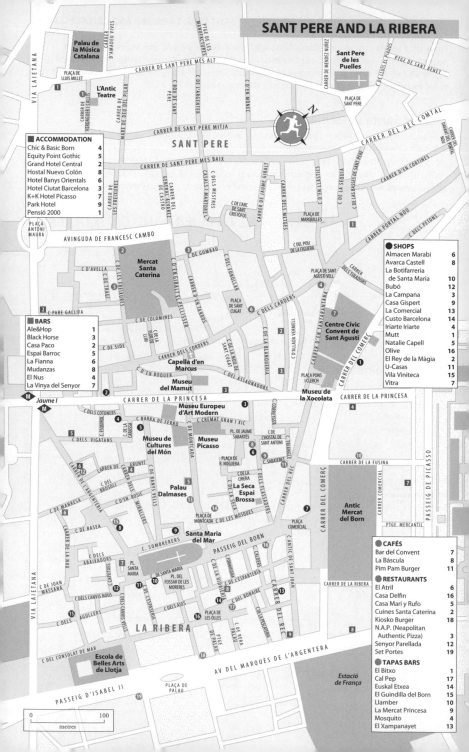

SANT PERE AND LA RIBERA

Palau de la Música Catalana

L'Antic Teatre

SANT PERE

Sant Pere de les Puelles

◼ ACCOMMODATION

Chic & Basic Born	4
Equity Point Gothic	5
Grand Hotel Central	2
Hostal Nuevo Colón	6
Hotel Banys Orientals	8
Hotel Ciutat Barcelona	3
K+K Hotel Picasso	7
Park Hotel	9
Pensió 2000	1

◼ BARS

Ale&Hop	1
Black Horse	3
Casa Paco	2
Espai Barroc	5
La Fianna	6
Mudanzas	8
El Nus	4
La Vinya del Senyor	7

Mercat Santa Caterina

Capella d'en Marcus

Museu del Mamut

Centre Cívic Convent de Sant Agustí

Museu de la Xocolata

● SHOPS

Almacen Marabi	6
Avarca Castell	8
La Botifarreria de Santa Maria	10
Bubó	12
La Campana	3
Casa Gispert	9
La Comercial	13
Custo Barcelona	14
Iriarte Iriarte	4
Mutt	1
Natalie Capell	5
Olive	16
El Rey de la Màgia	2
U-Casas	11
Vila Viniteca	15
Vitra	7

Museu Europeu d'Art Modern

Museu de Cultures del Món

Museu Picasso

Palau Dalmases

La Seca Espai Brossa

Santa Maria del Mar

Antic Mercat del Born

● CAFÉS

Bar del Convent	7
La Báscula	8
Pim Pam Burger	11

● RESTAURANTS

El Atril	6
Casa Delfin	16
Casa Mari y Rufo	5
Cuines Santa Caterina	2
Kiosko Burger	18
N.A.P. (Neapolitan Authentic Pizza)	3
Senyor Parellada	12
Set Portes	19

● TAPAS BARS

El Bitxo	1
Cal Pep	17
Euskal Etxea	14
El Guindilla del Born	15
Llamber	10
La Mercat Princesa	4
Mosquito	13
El Xampanyet	9

LA RIBERA

Escola de Belles Arts de Llotja

Estació de França

0   100
metres

It's one of the best places in the city to shop for food or grab a snack, and its market restaurant and bar are definitely worth a visit in any case. During the renovation work, the foundations of a medieval convent were discovered here – the excavations are visible at the rear of the market.

Plaça de Sant Agusti Vell and around

ⓜ Jaume I

The pretty, tree-shaded **Plaça de Sant Agusti Vell** sits at the centre of Sant Pere's most ambitious regeneration project, which transformed previously crowded alleys into landscaped boulevards. To the north locals tend organic allotments in the middle of the **Pou de la Figuera** *rambla*, while south down **Carrer de l'Allada Vermell** you'll find overarching trees, a children's playground and a series of outdoor cafés and bars. Meanwhile, running down from Plaça de Sant Agusti Vell, **Carrer dels Carders** – once "ropemakers' street" – is now a retail quarter mixing grocery stores and cafés with shops selling streetwear, African and Asian arts and crafts and contemporary jewellery. The little Romanesque chapel at the end of the street, the **Capella d'en Marcus** (usually locked), dates to the twelfth century, but was stripped of interest during the Civil War.

Centre Cívic Convent de Sant Agustí

C/del Comerç 36, entrance on c/d'en Tantarantana • Mon–Fri 9am–10pm, Sat 10am–2pm & 4–9pm • Admission charges vary, some events free • ☎ 932 565 000, ⓦ bcn.cat/centrecivicsantagusti • ⓜ Jaume I/Arc de Triomf

Driving many of the neighbourhood improvements in Sant Pere is the community centre installed inside the revamped **Convent de Sant Agustí**, whose thirteenth-century cloister provides a unique performance space. There's a full cultural programme here, from workshops to concerts, with a particular emphasis on electronic and experimental music and art, and don't miss the excellent convent café, with seats in the cloister, which is a good lunch destination if you're touring the neighbourhood (see p.181).

Museu de la Xocolata

C/del Comerç 36 • Mon–Sat 10am–7pm (mid-June to mid-Sept until 8pm), Sun 10am–3pm • €5, under-7s free • ☎ 932 687 878, ⓦ museuxocolata.cat • ⓜ Jaume I/Arc de Triomf

Perhaps the most exciting thing about the **Museu de la Xocolata**, housed in sections of the Convent de Sant Agustí, is that your entrance ticket is a little bar of chocolate. Inside, the museum does a rudimentary job of tracing the history of chocolate all the way back to its origins as a sacred and medicinal product in ancient Central America (the topic has some local relevance, in that the Bourbon army, which was once quartered in this building, demanded the provision of chocolate for its sweet-toothed troops). Whether you actually go in or not, however, will depend on how keen you are to relish a baffling array of endless chocolate models. Proudly displayed like precious objects are Gaudí buildings and religious icons, Komodo dragons and bullfights – there's even a Lionel Messi, his shorts, boots and stout limbs magnificently gleaming with a cocoa-rich sheen. Some are rather wonderful, while others, like Don Quixote and his dopey horse, are the height of kitsch. The chocolate artistes are individually credited and you can put faces to names at the sculptors' Hall of Fame at the end.

Chocolates are available to buy, of course, and there's a small café serving hot chocolate. At the adjacent Escola de Pastisseria, you can look through huge picture windows to watch the students learning their craft in the kitchens.

Museu Picasso

C/de Montcada 15–23 • Tues, Wed & Fri–Sun 9am–7pm, Thurs 9am–9.30pm • Permanent collection €11, temporary exhibitions extra, under-18s free; free for everyone Thurs 7–9.30pm, Sun 3–7pm & all day on first Sun of month • Free guided tours in English Sun 11am, except Aug; advance bookings essential • ☎ 932 563 022, ⓦ museupicasso.bcn.cat • Ⓜ Jaume I

Although the celebrated **Museu Picasso** ranks among the world's most important collections of Picasso's work, some visitors are disappointed to find it contains none of his best-known pictures, and few in the Cubist style. Nonetheless, the permanent collection holds almost four thousand works, displayed in five adjoining medieval palaces, which provide a fascinating opportunity to trace Picasso's development from his early paintings as a young boy to the major works of later years. The whole place is extremely well laid out, with abundant space and natural light.

It might often seem as if every visitor to Barcelona is trying to get into the museum at the same time, but you can hardly come to the city and not make the effort. Arriving when it opens offers the best chance of beating the crowds. A **café** with a courtyard *terrassa* offers refreshments, and there is of course a **shop**, stuffed full of Picasso-related gifts.

The collection

The museum opened in 1963 with a collection based largely on the donations of Jaume Sabartés, longtime friend and former secretary to the artist – you'll see him pictured as a "poeta decadente" in 1900, in a ruff and hat in 1939, and as a faun in 1946. On Sabartés' death in 1968, Picasso himself added a large number of works – above all, those in the Meninas series – and in 1970 he donated a further vast number of watercolours, drawings, prints and paintings.

The **early drawings**, particularly, are fascinating, in which Picasso – still signing with his full name, Pablo Ruiz Picasso – attempted to copy the nature paintings in which his father specialized. Far from what might be considered juvenilia, they show the experimentation and learning of an emergent genius. Works from his **art school** days in Barcelona (1895–97) offer tantalizing glimpses of the city the young Picasso knew – the Gothic old town, the cloisters of Sant Paul del Camp, Barceloneta beach – and even at the ages of 15 and 16 he was producing serious works, including knowing self-portraits and a closely observed study of his father from 1896. Works in the style of

---

PICASSO IN BARCELONA

Although he was born in Málaga, **Pablo Picasso** (1881–1973) spent much of his youth – from the age of 14 to 23 – in Barcelona. He maintained close links with the city and his Catalan friends even when he left for Paris in 1904, and is said to have always thought of himself as Catalan rather than *andaluz*. The time Picasso spent in Barcelona encompassed the whole of his Blue Period (1901–04) and provided many of the formative influences on his art.

Apart from the Museu Picasso, there are echoes of the great artist at various sites throughout the old town. Not too far from the museum, you can still see many of the buildings in which Picasso lived and worked, notably the **Escola de Belles Arts de Llotja** (c/Consolat del Mar, near Estació de França), where his father taught drawing and where Picasso himself absorbed an academic training. The **apartments** where the family lived when they first arrived in Barcelona – Pg. d'Isabel II 4 and c/Reina Cristina 3, both near the Escola – can also be seen, though only from the outside, while Picasso's first real **studio** (in 1896) was located on c/de la Plata at no. 4. A few years later, many of his Blue Period works were finished at a studio at c/del Comerç 28. His first **public exhibition** was in 1900 at *Els Quatre Gats* tavern (see box, p.46). The other place to retain a link with Picasso is **c/d'Avinyó** in the Barri Gòtic, which cuts south from c/de Ferran to c/Ample. Large houses along here were converted into brothels at the end of the nineteenth century, and Picasso used to haunt the street sketching what he saw. Some accounts of his life – based on Picasso's own testimony, it has to be said – claim that he had his first sexual experience here at the age of 14, and certainly the women at one of the brothels inspired his seminal Cubist work, *Les Demoiselles d'Avignon*.

Toulouse-Lautrec, like the menu Picasso did for *Els Quatre Gats* tavern in 1900, reflect his burgeoning interest in Parisian art, while other sketches, drawings and illustrations (many undertaken for competitions and magazines) demonstrate the development of his unique personal style.

Paintings from the famous **Blue Period** (1901–04) burst upon you – whether its moody Barcelona rooftops or the cold face of *La Dona Morta*. Subsequent galleries only make the barest nods to Picasso's Cubist (1907–20) and Neoclassical (1920–25) stages – though his return to the city with the Ballets Russes in 1917 is commemorated by *Harlequin*. Another large jump brings us to 1957, and the 44 interpretations of **Las Meninas**, brilliantly deconstructing the individual portraits and compositions that make up Velázquez's masterpiece, that Picasso completed between August and December that year. A separate room displays nine gorgeous light-filled Mediterranean scenes, inspired by the pigeons and dovecotes of his Cannes studio, which Picasso painted within a week during that period, and regarded as part of the same set.

Vibrantly decorated dishes and jugs donated by Picasso's wife Jacqueline highlight his work as a **ceramicist**. There are various portraits of Jacqueline here, too, though it's the seventy-year friendship that Picasso shared with Jaume Sabartés, reflected in mature portraits, character studies and jokey sketches by one friend of another, that offers the clearest expression of endearment. Further rooms display changing exhibitions of **prints**, culled from the museum's 1500-plus engravings and lithographs.

Along Carrer de Montcada

Ⓜ Jaume I

The street on which the Museu Picasso stands – **Carrer de Montcada** – is one of the best looking in the city. Laid out in the fourteenth century, it was, until the Eixample was planned almost five hundred years later, home to most of the city's leading citizens. They occupied spacious mansions built around central courtyards, from which external staircases climbed to the living rooms on the first floor; the facades facing the street were all endowed with huge gated doors that could be swung open to allow coaches access to the interior. Today, almost all the mansions and palaces along La Ribera's showpiece street serve instead as museums, private galleries and craft and gift shops, sucking up trade from Picasso-bound visitors.

Museu de Cultures del Món

C/de Montcada 12 • Tues–Sat 10am–7pm, Sun 10am–8pm • €5, ages 16–29 €3.50, under-16s free, free first Sun of month • ☎ 932 562 300, Ⓦ museuculturesmon.bcn.cat • Ⓜ Jaume I

Housed in two medieval palaces directly across from the Picasso museum, the **Museu de Cultures del Món** – Museum of World Cultures – opened in 2015. It showcases objects of phenomenal beauty and power from the world beyond Europe, not necessarily ancient but mostly imbued by their creators with deep spiritual significance. Drawn partly from the closed Museu Etnòlogic in Montjuïc, and partly from two substantial private collections, it's a somewhat haphazard assortment, but there's no disputing its overall quality or impact.

Downstairs, the African section ranges from the Christian art of Ethiopia to reliquary statuettes, helmets and masks, some credited to specific twentieth-century sculptors. On the higher levels, the Oceania segment includes actual remodelled human skulls from New Guinea, belonging both to enemies and to revered ancestors, and carved moai figures from Easter Island, while the extensive Asian galleries hold everything from Japanese Noh theatre masks and Korean ceramics to jewelled knives from Indonesia and bronze Krishna statuettes from India, with touch-screen displays to explain whatever catches your eye. The pre-Columbian artefacts from the Americas on the top floor belong to hotelier Jordi Clos, the collector responsible for the Museu Egipci (see p.105).

Museu Europeu d'Art Modern

C/de la Barra de Ferro 5 • Daily 10am–7pm • €9, €2 guided tour (Sat & Sun noon), under-10s free • ☎ 933 195 693, Ⓦ meam.es • Ⓜ Jaume I

The **Museu Europeu d'Art Modern**, located in a renovated eighteenth-century palace facing the Museu Picasso, is a modern art museum that genuinely lives up to its name – every work in its permanent collection was created by an artist who's alive and active in the twenty-first century. The emphasis here is on figurative rather than abstract art, and it abounds in hyper-photorealistic paintings. They vary so much in quality, if not style, that the museum itself can't be considered a must-see attraction, but it does make a very appealing venue for the blues, swing and classical concerts that take place on Fridays and Saturdays either in its sculpture-peppered courtyard or beneath the high ceiling of the palace's grand, Neoclassical main room.

Museu del Mamut

C/de Montcada 1 • Daily 10am–9pm • €7.50, under-5s free • ☎ 932 688 520, Ⓦ museomamut.com • Ⓜ Jaume I

Though by no means mammoth in size, the gloriously old-school **Museu del Mamut** (Mammoth Museum) is sure to appeal to *Ice Age* film fans. Apart from a shaggy, life-sized mammoth reaching to within an inch of the ceiling, its cave-like spaces hold a genuine baby mammoth found frozen in the permafrost, and there's even film of a genuine (well, almost) mammoth hunt in which the pursuing humans are every bit as shaggy as the beast. Truly bizarre stuffed specimens include a tiger that's supposedly been rendered sabre-toothed by the addition of some crude tusks, while God only knows what lies beneath the rug-like coat of the woolly rhinoceros. The shop sells jewellery carved from actual mammoth ivory.

Església de Santa María del Mar

Pl. de Santa María • Mon–Sat 9am–8.30pm, Sun 10am–8pm • Admission charged Mon–Sat 1–5pm, €3 (church) or €5 (church, terrace & towers); otherwise free • Ⓦ www.santamariadelmarbarcelona.org • Ⓜ Jaume I

La Ribera's flagship church of **Santa María del Mar** is the city's most exquisite example of pure Catalan-Gothic architecture. Much dearer to the heart of the average local than the overpowering cathedral, La Seu, it was conceived as thanks for the Catalan conquest of Sardinia in 1324. Work began in 1329 and was finished in just over half a century, which explains the consistency of style. It's not obvious today, but Santa María del Mar (ie, of the sea) was also built on what was the seashore in the fourteenth century (hence the title of Ildefonso Falcone's medieval blockbuster novel *Cathedral of the Sea*, which relates its construction).

Dedicated to Catalan maritime glories, the church stood foursquare at the heart of Barcelona's trading district, and indeed came to embody the commercial supremacy of the Crown of Aragón, of which the city was capital. Its wide nave, narrow aisles, massive buttresses and octagonal, flat-topped towers are typical Catalan-Gothic features, while it's probably all to the good that its later Baroque trappings were destroyed during the Civil War. Subsequent long-term restoration work has concentrated on showing off the simple bare spaces of the interior, and the stained glass is especially beautiful.

Plaça del Fossar de les Moreres

The modern brick-lined square known as **Plaça del Fossar de les Moreres**, south of Santa María del Mar church, was formally opened in 1989 to mark the spot where, following the defeat of Barcelona on September 11, 1714, Catalan martyrs fighting for independence against the king of Spain, Felipe V, were executed. An enormous red steel scimitar, arching almost to touch the church, is topped by an eternal flame that commemorates the fallen.

Passeig del Born

Ⓜ Jaume I/Barceloneta

Once the site of medieval fairs and tournaments (*born* means tournament), the fashionable **Passeig del Born** fronting the church of Santa María del Mar is now an avenue lined with plane trees shading a host of classy bars, delis and shops. At night the Born becomes one of Barcelona's biggest bar zones, as spirited locals frequent the drinking haunts, from old-style cocktail lounges to thumping music bars. Shoppers and browsers, meanwhile, scour the narrow, vaulted medieval alleys to either side for boutiques and **craft workshops** – carrers Flassaders, Vidreria and Rec in particular are noted for clothes, shoes, jewellery and design galleries.

El Born Centre Cultural

Pl. Comercial 12, at Pg. del Born • Tues–Sun 10am–8pm • Free access to the centre, €6 exhibitions (includes audioguide) • ☎ 932 564 190, Ⓦ elborncentrecultural.cat • Ⓜ Jaume I/Barceloneta

The handsome **Antic Mercat del Born** (built 1873–76), the largest of Barcelona's nineteenth-century market halls, was the city's main wholesale fruit and veg market until 1971. Then due to be demolished, it was saved by local protest and remained empty for decades. It finally reopened in 2013 as **El Born Centre Cultural**, where three centuries of Catalan history – from the siege of 1714 to the present – are remembered inside a renovated structure of sparkling glass and intricate wrought iron. The transformation took so long partly because excavations revealed that the market stood directly on top of the remains of eighteenth-century shops, factories, houses and taverns that predate the Ciutadella fortress and the Barceloneta district – a fascinating discovery that the city has put on full display.

Elevated walkways enable visitors to look down on the painstakingly preserved ruins, which for their size, condition and era are unique in Europe. Display panels and permanent exhibitions provide historical context, while other galleries host changing temporary exhibitions.

Outside the market, a swath of Carrer del Comerç has been turned into a pedestrian zone, creating a channel that – during the centre's opening hours – leads from Passeig del Born, through the market (and directly above the ruins) and toward the Parc de la Ciutadella.

Parc de la Ciutadella

Daily 10am–dusk • Park entrance free • Entrances on Pg. de Picasso (Ⓜ Barceloneta, or a short walk from La Ribera) and Pg. de Pujades (Ⓜ Arc de Triomf); use Ⓜ Ciutadella-Vila Olímpica for direct access to the zoo

While you might escape to Montjuïc or the Collserola hills for the air, there's no beating the spacious **Parc de la Ciutadella** for a quick break from the downtown bustle. Most of its showcase buildings, which include Catalunya's legislative assembly, the **Parlament**, are not open to the public, but it's still a nice place to spend a lazy summer afternoon strolling the garden paths or piloting a rowboat across the ornamental lake.

The park's name refers to the Bourbon citadel that Felipe V erected on this site to quell the local population following Barcelona's spirited resistance during the War of the Spanish Succession. A great part of La Ribera neighbourhood was brutally destroyed to make way for the fortress, and this symbol of authority survived uneasily until 1869, when the military moved base (the only surviving portion of the citadel,

4

HIDDEN GEMS: SANT PERE, LA RIBERA AND CIUTADELLA

Lunch at Bar del Convent See p.181
Picasso's re-creations of Velázquez's
   Las Meninas See p.71
Boutique-lined Carrer dels Flassaders
   See above

Concerts at Museu Europeu d'Art
   Modern See opposite
Row boats in Parc Ciutadella See p.75
Beers at Ale&Hop See p.198
L'Antic Teatre See p.209

the much-altered Arsenal, has since 1980 housed the Catalan parliament building).
The surrounding area subsequently became a park, which was chosen as the site of the
1888 **Universal Exhibition** – hence the eye-catching buildings and monuments erected
by pioneering *modernista* architects.

Arc de Triomf

Pg. de Lluís Companys • Ⓜ Arc de Triomf

The giant brick **Arc de Triomf** at the inland end of the Parc de la Ciutadella announces
the architectural splendours to come in the park itself. Roman in scale, and conceived
as a bold statement of Catalan intent, it's studded with ceramic figures and motifs, and
topped by two pairs of bulbous domes. Reliefs on its main facade show Barcelona
welcoming visitors to the 1888 Universal Exhibition.

Cascada

Parc de la Ciutadella • Ⓜ Arc de Triomf

The first of the major projects undertaken inside the Parc de la Ciutadella, the monumental **Cascada** fountain in its northeast corner was designed by Josep Fontseré i Mestrès, the architect chosen to oversee the conversion of the former citadel grounds into a park. His assistant in the work was Antoni Gaudí, then a young student, and its Baroque extravagance is suggestive of the flamboyant decoration that was to become Gaudí's trademark. Gaudí is also thought to have had a hand in the design of the Ciutadella's iron park gates.

Near the small open-air **café-kiosk** that makes the ideal vantage point from which to contemplate the fountain's tiers and swirls, you can **rent a rowboat** on the lake, and paddle about among the ducks.

Castell dels Tres Dragons and Museu Martorell

Pg. de Picasso • Ⓜ Arc de Triomf

The **Castell dels Tres Dragons** (Three Dragons Castle), a whimsical red-brick confection at the northwest corner of the park, was designed by *modernista* architect Lluís Domènech i Montaner for use as a café-restaurant for the Universal Exhibition. Home for many years to the local zoology museum, it's not currently in use. Along with the similarly defunct, Neoclassical **Museu Martorell**, which opened in 1882 as Barcelona's first public museum and long housed the city's geological collections, it's slated for restoration at some point.

Umbracle and Hivernacle

Pg. de Picasso • Under renovation at time of writing • Ⓜ Arc de Triomf

The two real unsung glories of Ciutadella are its plant houses, arranged either side of the Museu Martorell. Both are currently closed to visitors and looking somewhat dilapidated, though the plants within are sufficiently tended to cling to life. The imposing **Umbracle** (palm house) is a handsome structure with a barrelled wood-slat roof supported by cast-iron pillars, which allows shafts of light to play across the palms and ferns, while the enclosed greenhouses of the larger **Hivernacle** (conservatory) are separated by a soaring glass-roofed terrace.

4

Parc Zoològic

Main entrance on c/de Wellington • Daily: Jan–late March & late Oct–Dec 10am–5.30pm; last admission 5pm; late March till mid-May & mid-Sept till late Oct 10am–7pm, last admission 6pm; mid-May till mid-Sept 10am–8pm, last admission 7pm • €19.60, under-12s €11.80, under-3s free • ☎ 902 457 545, Ⓦ www.zoobarcelona.cat • Signposted from Ⓜ Ciutadella-Vila Olímpica, or tram T4 stops outside

The city zoo, the **Parc Zoològic**, takes up most of the southeastern part of Ciutadella park. Still essentially nineteenth century in character, confined to the formal grounds of a public park, it currently boasts over two thousand animals from over three hundred species, including such endangered animals as the Iberian wolf, the Sri Lankan leopard and the Sumatran tiger. It's widely acknowledged to be due for a major overhaul, but plans have for the moment been stymied by the recession. It remains hugely popular with families, offering mini-train and pony rides, a petting zoo and daily dolphin shows as well as its animal attractions.

PORT VELL

The waterfront

Perhaps the greatest transformation in Barcelona in recent years has taken place along the waterfront, where harbour and ocean have been restored to their rightful role at the heart of the city. Dramatic changes have shifted the cargo and container trade away to the south, opened up the old docksides as promenades and entertainment areas, and landscaped the beaches to the north – it's as if a theatre curtain has been lifted to reveal that, all along, Barcelona had an urban waterfront of which it could be proud. The glistening harbourside merges seamlessly with the old town, with the museums and attractions of Port Vell just steps from the bottom of the Ramblas. No visit to the city is complete without a seafood meal in the eighteenth-century fishing quarter of Barceloneta, followed by a stroll along the beachfront promenade as far as the showpiece Port Olímpic.

Barcelona's **beaches** extend for 5km along the waterfront, from Barceloneta in the centre out to the River Besòs, which defines the northeastern city limits. Locals make use of the sands in a big way – jogging, cycling and skating their length, and descending in force at the weekend for leisurely lunches or late drinks in scores of restaurants and bars. Though the main development is around the Port Olímpic, there are also spruced-up beaches further north, on either side of the old working-class neighbourhood of **Poble Nou**, whose pretty *rambla* makes for an offbeat diversion. Beyond here, the **Diagonal Mar** exhibition district might appear to be a journey too far for most visitors, but its bold urban scale is definitely worth seeing, especially for the **Museu Blau**, the Natural Science Museum's flagship attraction.

Plaça del Portal de la Pau

Ⓜ Drassanes

The Ramblas ends at **Plaça del Portal de la Pau**, coming up hard against the teeming traffic that runs along the harbourside road. The landmark Columbus monument is straight ahead in the middle of the traffic circle, with the quayside square beyond flanked by the **Port de Barcelona** (Port Authority) and **Duana** (Customs House) buildings. An **antiques market**, where you can find dusty treasures like patinated medals, lace-trimmed fans and leather-bound books, fills the square at the weekend (10am–8pm). Away to the south is the **Moll de Barcelona**, a landscaped wharf leading to the Torre de Jaume I **cable-car station** and the **Estació Marítima**, where ferries leave for the Balearics. The large, bulbous building perched in the centre of the wharf is the city's **World Trade Centre**, housing a deluxe hotel, plus offices, convention halls, shops and restaurants.

Mirador de Colom

Pl. del Portal de la Pau • Daily March–Sept 8.30am–8.30pm; Oct–Feb 8.30am–7.30pm • €4.50, under-12s €3, under-4s free • Ⓜ Drassanes

Inaugurated just before the Universal Exhibition of 1888, the striking **Mirador de Colom** commemorates the visit made by Christopher Columbus (known locally as Cristòfol Colom) to Barcelona in June 1493. The explorer tops a grandiose iron column, 52m high, guarded by lions at the base, around which unfold reliefs telling the story of his life and travels – here, if nowhere else, the old mercenary is still the "discoverer of America". A lift whisks you up to the enclosed *mirador* at Columbus's feet for terrific 360-degree city views – the narrow viewing platform, which tilts perceptibly outwards and downwards, is emphatically not for anyone without a head for heights.

Museu Marítim

Av. de les Drassanes • Daily 10am–8pm • €7, under-7s free, plus free on Sun after 3pm • ☎ 933 429 920, Ⓦ mmb.cat • Ⓜ Drassanes

Barcelona's medieval shipyards, or **Drassanes**, at the foot of the Ramblas, date back to the fourteenth century. They remained in continuous use – fitting and arming

---

ANOTHER WRONG TURN FOR COLUMBUS?

When the Italian-born navigator **Christopher Columbus** sailed into Barcelona harbour in 1493, he was received in style by Ferdinand and Isabella. In a bid for new and profitable trading routes, they had financed his voyage of exploration a year earlier, when Columbus had set out to chart a passage west to the Orient. He famously failed in this, as he failed also to reach the North American mainland (instead "discovering" the Bahamas, Cuba and Haiti), but Columbus did enough to enhance his reputation and by 1504 had made three more voyages. Later, nineteenth-century Catalan nationalists took the navigator to their hearts – if he wasn't exactly Catalan, he was the closest they had to a local Vasco da Gama – and so they put him on the pedestal they thought he deserved. The statue is actually pointing in the general direction of Libya, not North America, but as historian Robert Hughes puts it, at least "the sea is Catalan".

5

Catalunya's war fleet or trading vessels – until well into the eighteenth century, when the imposing central cluster of stone-vaulted buildings were taken over for use as military barracks and an arsenal. Now they make a superb location for the **Museu Marítim** (Maritime Museum), which celebrates the city's history as a naval base, trading centre, and port of passage for generations of migrants and visitors.

A major renovation of the museum's displays was still under way at the time of writing, but it has remained open throughout the process. New interactive exhibits are progressively taking their place alongside gems of the permanent collection that include a replica of the magnificent, 60m-long *Royal Galley*, which was built here in 1568 and fought as the Spanish flagship when the Holy League defeated the Ottoman fleet in the Battle of Lepanto three years later. The museum also hosts changing temporary exhibitions, and has a good shop and café, while the admission fee also provides access to the **Santa Eulàlia** schooner across the street.

Santa Eulàlia

April–Oct Tues–Fri, Sun & hols 10am–8.30pm, Sat 2–8.30pm; Nov–March Tues–Fri, Sun & hols 10am–5.30pm, Sat 2–5.30pm; sailing excursions Sat 10am–1pm (reservations essential, by phone or email) • €1, free with Museu Marítim ticket; sailing trips €12, ages 6–16 €6 • ☎ 933 429 929, ✉ reserves@mmb.cat

The pride and joy of the Maritime Museum, the three-masted ocean schooner **Santa Eulàlia**, is moored over on the Moll de la Fusta (beyond the harbour's swing bridge). Built using pine and olive wood in 1918, as the *Carmen Flores*, she originally sped around the Mediterranean, and also made the run between Barcelona and Cuba. She was acquired and fully restored by the museum in 1997, and a short tour lets you walk the deck and view the interior. The *Santa Eulàlia* still sets sail on Saturdays, taking passengers on short harbour and coastal jaunts.

Port Vell

Ⓜ Drassanes/Barceloneta

While Barcelona's remodelled inner harbour, known as **Port Vell** (Old Port), has its local critics – it's undoubtedly touristy and expensive – there's no denying the improvement to what was formerly a decaying harbourside. The city's old timber wharf, for example, the **Moll de la Fusta**, re-emerged as a landscaped promenade with a note of humour injected by the addition of a giant fibreglass crayfish by Catalan designer Xavier Mariscal and, further on, the **Roy Lichtenstein** totem-pole sculpture known as *Barcelona Head*. From the Columbus statue end of the wharf, the wooden **Rambla de Mar** swing bridge strides across to the **Moll d'Espanya**, whose main features are the Maremagnum mall and aquarium. From here, it's only a ten-minute walk around the **marina** to the Palau de Mar and the Catalan history museum.

HARBOURSIDE RIDES BY SKY AND SEA

Barcelona's most thrilling ride has to be the **Transbordador Aeri** cable-car, which sweeps passengers all the way across the inner harbour between the top of the Torre de Sant Sebastiá, near the tip of Barceloneta, and the hill of Montjuïc (departures every 15min; daily: March, April, Sept & Oct 11am–7pm; June–Aug 11am–8pm; Nov–Feb 11am–5.30pm; €11 one-way, €16.50 return; ☎ 934 304 716, ⓦ telefericodebarcelona.com). As you dangle high above the water, you can enjoy superb views over the city. In principle there's an additional stop in the middle, at Torre de Jaume I in front of the World Trade Centre in Port Vell, but that has been closed for some time pending repairs. As the cable-car can only carry nineteen people at a time, you can expect queues – and potential disappointment – in summer and at weekends. Note that strong winds can also close the ride.

From the quayside just beyond the foot of the Mirador de Colom, **Las Golondrinas** sightseeing boats and the *Catamaran Orsom* depart on regular trips throughout the year along the waterfront (see p.25); they're joined on Saturdays by the *Santa Eulàlia* (see above).

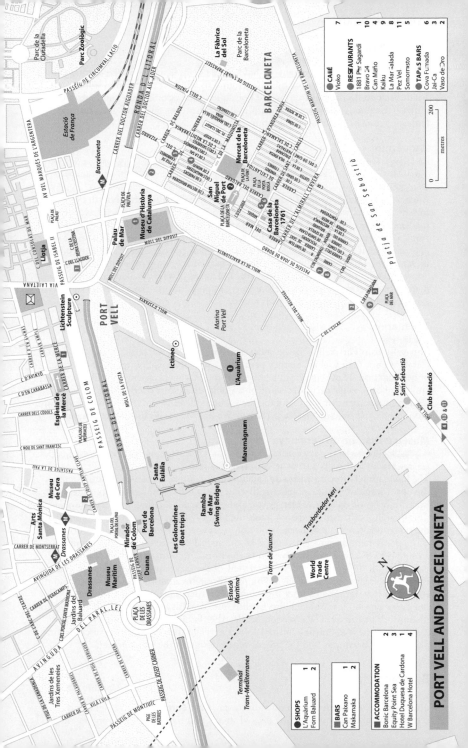

5

Maremagnum

Moll d'Espanya • Daily 10am–10pm • ⓦ maremagnum.es • Ⓜ Drassanes

The **Maremagnum** mall is a typically bold piece of Catalan design, the soaring glass lines of the complex tempered by the surrounding undulating wooden walkways. Inside are two floors of gift shops and boutiques, plus assorted cafés and fast-food outlets (restaurants are open until 1am); outside, benches and park areas provide fantastic views back across the harbour to the city.

L'Aquàrium

Moll d'Espanya • June & Sept daily 9.30am–9.30pm; July & Aug daily 9.30am–11pm; Oct–May Mon–Fri 9.30am–9pm, Sat & Sun 9.30am–9.30pm • €20, ages 5–10 €15, ages 3–4 €7, under-3s free, online discounts available • ☎ 932 217 474, ⓦ aquariumbcn.com • Ⓜ Drassanes/Barceloneta

Anchoring Moll d'Espanya, **L'Aquàrium** drags in families and school parties year-round to see "a magical world, full of mystery". Or, to be more precise, to see eleven thousand fish and sea creatures in 35 themed tanks representing underwater caves, tidal areas, tropical reefs and other maritime habitats. It's vastly overpriced and, despite the claims of excellence, it offers few new experiences, save perhaps the 80m-long walk-through underwater tunnel which brings you face to face with gliding rays and cruising sharks. Some child-centred displays and activities and a nod towards ecology and conservation matters pad out the attractions before you're tipped out into the aquarium shop so they can relieve you of even more of your money.

The marina

Ⓜ Barceloneta

The walk from Port Vell to Barceloneta takes you around the packed **marina**, where Catalans park their yachts like they park their cars – impossibly tightly and with plenty of gesticulation. Hawkers spread blankets on the marina promenade, selling jewellery and sunglasses, while behind is a line of seafood restaurants overlooking the water.

For a sundowner drink overlooking the harbour, head to the *terrassa* bar of rooftop restaurant *1881 per Sagardi* (see p.186), above the Museu d'Història de Catalunya.

Museu d'Història de Catalunya

Pl. de Pau Vila 3 • Tues–Sat 10am–7pm (Wed until 8pm), Sun & hols 10am–2.30pm • €4.50, under-25s €3.50, under-8s free; Oct–June free for everyone last Tues of month • ☎ 932 254 700, ⓦ mhcat.net • Ⓜ Barceloneta

The fascinating **Museu d'Història de Catalunya** (Catalunya History Museum) occupies the upper levels of the one warehouse that survives on the Port Vell harbourside, the beautifully restored **Palau de Mar**, poised above the seafood restaurants in its lower arcade. This (literally) exhaustive museum traces the history of Catalunya from the Stone Age to the present day, with its spacious exhibition areas wrapped around a wide atrium.

The permanent displays get going with the arrival of Greek settlers at Empúries around 600 BC, and swiftly move on to the Romans, with a mock-up of a small Roman grain ship, and a modern aerial view of the city superimposed on the original Roman walls. From there on in, as you pass through Catalunya's golden years and the Industrial Revolution and enter the modern era, there's plenty to get your teeth into; not every caption is translated into English, but English notes are available throughout. There's a dramatic Civil War section, while other fascinating asides shed light on matters as diverse as housing in the 1960s, the rival nineteenth-century architectural plans for the Eixample, and the origins of the design of the Catalan flag.

Barceloneta

Ⓜ Barceloneta

There's no finer place for lunch on a sunny day than **Barceloneta**, an eighteenth-century neighbourhood of tightly packed streets that has the harbour on one side and

5

MONTURIOL AND THE CATALAN SUBMARINE

Barcelona's connection to the sea goes deeper than you think; it was in its harbour waters in 1059 that the first **man-powered submarine** made its maiden voyage. This "fish-boat", the **Ictineo**, was the work of self-taught scientist, engineer and inventor **Narcís Monturiol i Estarriol** (1819–85). Born in Figueres, Monturiol fell in with radicals as a student in Barcelona. He set up a publishing company in 1846, espousing his beliefs in feminism, pacifism and utopian communism – radical ideas that saw him forced briefly into exile during the heady revolutionary days of 1848. This was a period in which scientific progress and social justice appeared as two sides of the same coin to utopians like Monturiol – indeed, his friend, the civil engineer Ildefons Cerdà, would mastermind the building of Barcelona's Eixample on socially useful grounds.

Inspired by the harsh conditions in which Catalan coral fishermen worked, Monturiol conceived the idea of the **Ictineo**. At 7m long, it could carry four or five men, and made more than fifty dives at depths of up to 20m before being destroyed in an accident. Construction began on an improved version in 1862 – the 17m-long *Ictineo II*, which was intended to be propelled by up to sixteen men. When trials showed that human power wasn't sufficient for the job, Monturiol installed a steam engine. The world's first steam-powered submarine was launched on October 22, 1867, diving up to 30m on thirteen separate runs (the longest lasting for over seven hours). However, the sub never managed to pay its way, and when Monturiol's financial backers withdrew their support, the *Ictineo II* was seized by creditors and sold for scrap – the engine ended up in a paper mill.

Undaunted, Monturiol continued to come up with new inventions. With the submarines he had pioneered the use of the double hull, a technique still used today, while he also made advances in the manufacture of glues and gums, copying documents, commercial cigarette production and steam engine efficiency. Even so, he died in relative obscurity in 1885 and was buried in Barcelona, though his remains were later transferred to his home town. There's a memorial to Monturiol on the main *rambla* in Figueres, while he's remembered in Barcelona not only by a simple plaque at the Cementiri de Poble Nou, but by replicas of his two amazing vessels, the **Ictineo I** and the **Ictineo II**, at the Museu Marítim and Port Vell respectively.

a **beach** on the other. Laid out in 1755, where previously there had been only mudflats, it effectively replaced part of the Ribera district that was destroyed to make way for the Ciutadella fortress to the north. The long, narrow streets are broken at intervals by small squares, and lined with abundantly windowed houses, designed to give the sailors and fishing folk who originally lived here plenty of sun and fresh air.

Some original houses feature a decorative flourish, a sculpted balcony or a carved lintel, while in **Plaça de la Barceloneta** survives an eighteenth-century fountain and the Neoclassical church of **Sant Miquel del Port**. A block over in Plaça de la Font is the beautifully refurbished local market, **Mercat de la Barceloneta** (Mon–Thurs & Sat 7am–3pm, Fri 7am–8pm), which boasts a couple of excellent bars and restaurants.

Barceloneta is famous for its **seafood restaurants**, which can be found all over the neighbourhood, and especially lined along the harbourside **Passeig Joan de Borbó**, where for most of the year you can sit outside and enjoy your meal.

La Fàbrica del Sol

Pg. Salvat Papasseit 1 • Sept–July Tues–Fri 10am–2pm & 4.30–8pm, Sat 10am–2pm & 4–7pm; Aug Tues–Fri 10am–2pm • Free • ⊕ 932 564 430, ⓦ bcn.cat/lafabricadelsol • ⓂBarceloneta

Inside the yellow-painted, red-brick building on the edge of the Parc de la Barceloneta – once the city's gas works – the local council has established **La Fàbrica del Sol**, a pioneering sustainable eco-centre that takes a close look at green living in all its guises, from recycling to transport. There's an introductory film (in English) and you can borrow some English notes at the entrance, but the displays, gadgets and exhibits are all fairly self-explanatory – you've got to love the elevator that weighs its passengers so as to use only the exact amount of energy required to lift them up to the roof terrace to see the building's garden and solar thermal system. From here you also get a view of the park's other notable feature, its whimsical *modernista* water tower (1905), rising like a minaret above the palms.

5

Platja de Sant Sebastià and Passeig Marítim
Ⓜ Barceloneta

Barceloneta's beach, **Platja de Sant Sebastià**, is the first in the series of sandy city beaches that stretches northeast along the coast all the way to the River Besòs. It curves out past the indoor and outdoor swimming pools of the *Club Natació* (see p.223) to the landmark, sail-shaped **W Barcelona** hotel, designed by Catalan architect Ricardo Bofill.

Meanwhile, at the Barceloneta end there are beach bars, outdoor cafés and public sculptures, and a double row of palms backs the **Passeig Marítim** esplanade that parallels the beach as far as the Port Olímpic (a 15min walk). There's a surfing break immediately offshore, while itinerant vendors patrol the sands offering snacks and drinks including mojitos and samosas.

Just before the port there rises the dramatic latticed funnel of wood and steel that is the **Parc Recerca Biomèdica de Barcelona** (PRBB), the city's biomedical research centre.

Casa de la Barceloneta 1761
C/de Sant Carles 6 · Tues–Fri 11am–1pm & 4–8pm, Sat 10am–2pm · Free · Ⓦ bcn.cat/ciutatvella · Ⓜ Barceloneta

The two-storey **Casa de la Barceloneta 1761** has seen its fair share of change over the centuries. Constructed, as the name suggests, in 1761, the Baroque-style building, which faces three streets, was home to one of the neighbourhood's maritime families before being chopped into smaller units, turned into a grocery store and then converted into a restaurant. It had fallen into disrepair before being restored and transformed into a cultural and interpretive centre. Inside, you'll find a small yet informative (for those who read Catalan) exhibition about the evolution of the neighbourhood's buildings, as well as an upstairs gallery space.

Port Olímpic
Ⓜ Ciutadella-Vila Olímpica

As you approach the Olympic port along the Passeig Marítim, a shimmering golden mirage above the promenade slowly resolves itself into a **huge copper fish**, courtesy of Frank Gehry, architect of Bilbao's Guggenheim. The emblem of the huge seafront development constructed for the 1992 Olympics – site of many of the Olympic watersports events – it's backed by the city's two tallest buildings, the **Torre Mapfre** and the steel-framed **Hotel Arts Barcelona**, both 154m high. The bulk of the action is contained within two wharves: the **Moll de Mestral** has a lower deck by the marina lined with cafés, bars and *terrasses*, while **Moll de Gregal** sports a double-decker tier of seafood restaurants. The whole zone turns into a full-on resort in summer, backed by a series of class-conscious clubs along Passeig Marítim that appeal to the local rich kids and A-list celebs.

City beaches
From Port Olímpic (Ⓜ Ciutadella-Vila Olímpica) it's a 15min walk along the promenade to Bogatell beach, or around 1hr all the way to Parc del Fòrum

Beyond the Port Olímpic, the city **beaches** continue right the way up to Parc del Fòrum and Diagonal Mar, split into separate named sections **Nova Icària**, **Bogatell**,

---

BEACH BUSINESS
On the boardwalk arcade, in front of the Hospital del Mar, the city council operates a beach visitor centre, the **Centre de la Platja** (March–May Thurs, Sun & hols 11am–2pm, Fri & Sat 11am–2pm & 3–6pm; June–Sept Tues–Sun 10am–7pm; ☎ 932 210 348, Ⓦ bcn.cat/platges), as a kind of one-stop shop for information and activities along the seafront. There's a programme of seafront walks and activities, a small summer lending library for beach reading, and Frisbees, volleyball and beach tennis gear available for pick-up games on the sand.

5

Mar Bella, **Nova Mar Bella** and **Llevant**, each with showers, playgrounds and open-air café-bars (Mar Bella offers an area for nudists). It's a pretty extraordinary leisure facility to find so close to a city centre – the water might not be as clean as it could be, but the sands are regularly swept and replenished, while joggers, cyclists and bladers have one of the Med's best views for company.

Poble Nou

Ⓜ Poble Nou (at the junction of c/Pujades and c/Bilbao, one block east of Rambla del Poble Nou), or bus #36 from Port Olímpic

The next neighbourhood along from the Port Olímpic is **Poble Nou** (New Village), a largely nineteenth-century industrial area that has been in the throes of redevelopment for well over twenty years now, and is still changing year upon year. The authorities have given

PORT OLÍMPIC AND POBLE NOU

● CAFÉ	
El Tío Ché	2

● RESTAURANTS	
Agua	8
Bestial	7
El Cangrejo Loco	4
Dos Cielos	1
Enoteca	5
Els Pescadors	3

● TAPAS BAR	
Arola	6

■ CLUBS	
CDLC	4
Club Catwalk	7
Sala Razzmatazz	1
Sala Rocksound	2

■ ACCOMMODATION	
Hotel Arts Barcelona	1

5

the regeneration area a suitably contemporary epithet, **22@Barcelona** (ⓦ22barcelona.com), and are currently overseeing the transformation of 120 city blocks, straddling 200 hectares of land, into "the innovation district". The redevelopment of old factories and the like has already had a significant effect, as some of the city's hottest clubs, galleries and art spaces are now found here. You can come here directly on the metro, but it's far nicer to walk along the promenade from the Port Olímpic (15min) to Poble Nou's spruced-up **beaches** – Bogatell, Mar Bella and Nova Mar Bella – before crossing the main highway to reach the neighbourhood's main spine, Rambla del Poble Nou.

Rambla del Poble Nou

Ⓜ Poble Nou

Poble Nou may be in the throes of dramatic change, but the main avenue still ticks along largely unaffected. Pretty, tree-lined **Rambla del Poble Nou** remains entirely local in character – no cardsharps or human statues here – with a run of modest shops, cafés and restaurants, including the classic milk and juice bar of *El Tío Ché* (see p.186), which serves orange or lemon *granissat* (crushed ice) and their famous *orxata* (milky tiger-nut drink).

Cementiri de Poble Nou

Av. d'Icaria • Daily 8am–6pm; free guided tours on first and third Sun (Spanish & Catalan) • ☎ 934 841 999, ⓦ cbsa.es • Ⓜ Bogatell or bus #36 from Port Olímpic

The vast nineteenth-century **Cementiri de Poble Nou** has its tombs set in walls 7m high – the families that tend them have to climb great stepladders to reach the uppermost tiers. With traffic noise muted by the high walls, and birdsong accompanying a stroll around the flower-lined pavements, quiet courtyards, sculpted angels and tiny chapels, this village of the dead is a rare haven in contemporary Barcelona.

Diagonal Mar

Ⓜ El Maresme Fòrum, or tram T4 to Fòrum via Glòries and Av. Diagonal

The waterfront district north of Poble Nou, developed in the wake of 2004's Universal Forum of Cultures Expo, is promoted as **Diagonal Mar**. It's anchored by the Diagonal Mar shopping mall, with classy hotels, convention centres and exhibition halls grouped nearby. Everything here is on a grand scale, starting with **Jacques Herzog**'s dazzling blue biscuit tin of a building hovering – seemingly unsupported – above the ground. This houses the main exhibitions of the Natural Science Museum (the **Museu Blau**), while the vast, landscaped area beyond is a showpiece urban leisure project, the **Parc del Fòrum**. The district can still seem a bit soulless at times – hot as Hades in summer, buffeted by biting winter winds – but it's worth the metro ride for anyone interested in heroic-scale public projects. The tram comes down here too, so you could always glide there or back via Avinguda Diagonal and Glòries to see more of Barcelona in transformation.

Museu Blau

Pl. Leonardo da Vinci 4–5, Parc del Fòrum • Tues–Sat 10am–7pm, Sun & hols 10am–8pm • €6, or €7 combined ticket with Jardi Botànic at Montjuïc, under-25s free, plus free first Sun of the month & every Sun after 3pm • ☎ 932 566 002, ⓦ museuciencies.bcn.cat • Ⓜ El Maresme Fòrum, or tram T4 to Fòrum

To unravel the mysteries of life, the universe and everything you need travel no further than the Natural Science Museum's bold reboot of its heritage collections. The million-strong collection of rocks, fossils, plants and animals – from the smallest microbe to a giant whale skeleton – have a state-of-the-art home in the visually stunning **Museu Blau** (Blue Museum), whose permanent Planeta Vida (Planet Life) exhibition plots a journey through nothing less than the history of life on earth. It's heavily focused on evolutionary, whole-earth, Gaia principles, with plenty of

5

entertaining, interactive bells and whistles to guide you through topics as diverse as sex and reproduction and conservation of the environment. There are also special exhibitions, a separate hands-on children's section (the Niu de Ciència, or "science nest", for under-6s) and regular family activities, plus shop, restaurant and a free-access media library, where you can, for example, listen to birdsong, animal and habitat sounds stored in the fascinating Natura Sonora sound library.

Parc del Fòrum

Ⓜ El Maresme Fòrum, or tram T4 to Fòrum via Glòries and Av. Diagonal

The claim of Diagonal Mar's main open space, the **Parc del Fòrum**, that at 150,000 square metres it's the second largest square in the world after Beijing's Tiananmen Square, may not be true – several other squares are actually bigger than both – but it's unquestionably an immense, undulating expanse, spreading towards the sea and culminating in a giant solar-panelled canopy that overlooks the marina, beach and park areas. In summer, temporary bars, dancefloors, open-air cinema and chill-out zones are established, while the city authorities have shifted some of the bigger annual music festivals and events down here to inject a bit of life outside convention time.

DIAGONAL MAR

ROMANESQUE FRESCO, MUSEU NACIONAL D'ART DE CATALUNYA

Montjuïc

You'll need at least a day to see Montjuïc, the steep hill and park that rises over Barcelona to the southwest. It takes its name from the Jewish community that once settled on its slopes, and there's been a castle on the heights since the mid-seventeenth century. These days, though, Montjuïc is essentially a cultural leisure park, anchored around the heavyweight art collections in the Museu Nacional d'Art de Catalunya (MNAC). This unsurpassed national collection of Catalan art is supplemented by works in two other superb galleries, namely international contemporary art in the Caixa Forum and that of Catalan artist Joan Miró in the Fundació Joan Miró. In addition, there are separate archeological, ethnological, military and theatrical museums, quite apart from the buildings and stadiums associated with the 1992 Olympics, which centred on the heights of Montjuïc.

From the Roman era right up until the 1950s, Montjuïc was quarried to provide the stone from which Barcelona was built. As late as the 1890s, the hill was nothing more than a collection of private farms and woodland on the edge of the old town, though some landscaping had already taken place by the time Montjuïc was chosen as the site of the **International Exhibition** of 1929. The slopes were then laid with gardens, terraces and fountains, while monumental Neoclassical buildings were added to the north side, many of them later adapted as museums. The famous **Poble Espanyol** (Spanish Village) – a hybrid park of collected Spanish architecture – is the most extraordinary relic of the Exhibition, while assorted lush **gardens** still provide enjoyment and respite from the crowds. Above all, perhaps, there are the city and ocean views to savour from this most favoured of Barcelona's hills: from the steps in front of the Museu Nacional, from the castle ramparts, from the Olympic terraces or from the cable-cars that zigzag up the steepest slopes of Montjuïc.

6

ARRIVAL AND GETTING AROUND

By metro For easy access to Caixa Forum, Poble Espanyol and the Museu Nacional d'Art de Catalunya (MNAC) use Ⓜ Espanya (follow exit signs for "Fira/Exposició"). The Olympic area can then be reached by escalators behind MNAC.

By funicular The Funicular de Montjuïc departs from inside the metro station at Ⓜ Paral.lel and takes a couple of minutes to ascend the hill (every 10min: April–Oct Mon–Fri 7.30am–10pm, Sat, Sun & hols 9am–10pm;

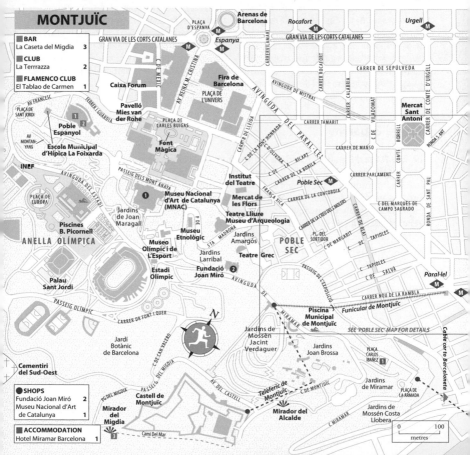

6

Nov–March Mon–Fri 7.30am–8pm, Sat, Sun & hols 9am–8pm; €2.15, transport tickets and passes valid; ⓦ tmb.cat). From the upper station on Av. de Miramar, you can switch to the Montjuïc cable-car or bus services, or walk in around 5min to the Fundació Joan Miró, more like 20min to the MNAC.

Telefèric de Montjuïc The separate Telefèric de Montjuïc cable-car carries passengers in automated eight-seater gondolas up to the castle and back from Av. de Miramar, just across from the upper Funicular de Montjuïc station (daily: March–May & Oct 10am–7pm; June–Sept 10am–9pm; Nov–Feb 10am–6pm; €7.80 one-way/€11.50 return, under-12s €6/8.40, under-4s free; ☎ 933 328 003, ⓦ telefericdemontjuic.cat).

Transbordador Aeri The cross-harbour Transbordador Aeri cable-car crosses high above Barcelona's harbour, all the way from Barceloneta to the Jardins de Miramar (departures every 15min; daily: March, April, Sept & Oct 11am–7pm; June–Aug 11am–8pm; Nov–Feb 11am–5.30pm; €11 one-way/€16.50 return; ☎ 934 304 716, ⓦ telefericodebarcelona.com). From there it's a 10min walk to the Montjuïc cable-car and funicular stations, and another 5min to the Fundació Joan Miró.

By bus City bus #150 (transport tickets and passes valid) covers a circular route around the main Montjuïc attractions, departing from a stop on Av. de la Reina María Cristina, outside ⓜ Espanya. The sightseeing, hop-on-hop-off Bus Turístic follows a similar route.

INFORMATION

Timing your visit Montjuïc covers a wide area, so if you're intent on covering everything it might be better to make two separate visits – MNAC, Poble Espanyol and the Olympic area on one day, and Fundació Joan Miró, the cable-car and the castle on the other. From ⓜ Espanya, it takes a good hour to walk on the road around the hill, past Poble Espanyol, the Olympic area and Fundació Joan Miró to the cross-harbour cable-car station at the far end of Montjuïc. Escalators up the hill between MNAC and the Olympic area cut out the worst of the slog. Walking up the steep hill all the way to the castle is not advised in hot weather (though there are steps through the gardens and between the roads) – use the cable-car.

Tickets The Barcelona Card, Articket and Arqueoticket (see box, p.26) and Bus Turístic pass (see p.25) provide discounted entry into Montjuïc's museums, galleries and attractions.

Eating and drinking Places to eat are thin on the ground, though there are good cafés in Caixa Forum, Fundació Joan Miró and MNAC, outdoor snack bars at the castle and on the slopes below MNAC, and a restaurant with outdoor terrace at the Font del Gat in the Jardins Laribal, below the Fundació Joan Miró. Plenty of decent restaurants and bars can also be found in the neighbouring *barri* of Poble Sec.

Plaça d'Espanya

ⓜ Espanya

The vast **Plaça d'Espanya**, based on plans by noted architect Josep Puig i Cadafalch, served as the gateway to the 1929 International Exhibition. Arranged around a huge Neoclassical fountain, the square is unlike any other in Barcelona, a radical departure from the *modernisme* that was so in vogue elsewhere in the city. It's ringed by landmarks, notably the majestic former bullring, now shopping and leisure centre Arenas de Barcelona (see p.113), and the striking twin towers, 47m high, that stand at the foot of the imposing **Avinguda de la Reina María Cristina**. This avenue spears up towards Montjuïc, and is lined by huge exhibition halls used for trade fairs. From Plaça de Carles Buïgas, at the end of the avenue, monumental steps (and escalators) ascend the hill to the Palau Nacional (home of MNAC), past water cascades and under the flanking walls of two grand Viennese-style pavilions. The higher you climb, the better the views, while a few café-kiosks put out seats on the way up to MNAC.

FLYING THE FLAG

Architect Josep Puig i Cadafalch's simplest idea for the ceremonial gateway to Montjuïc at Plaça d'Espanya were **four 20m-high columns**, erected in 1919 on a raised site below the future Palau Nacional. Who could possibly object? The authoritarian government of General Primo de Rivera, as it happened, which knew perfectly well that as a Catalan nationalist Puig i Cadafalch meant the columns to represent the four stripes of the *senyera*, the Catalan flag. Down they came in 1928, to be replaced by the Magic Fountain. Not until 2010 were the columns seen again in public, reconstructed using the original plans and erected across from the fountain by the city government as both "an act of memory" and a symbol of freedom and democracy.

Font Màgica

Pl. de Carles Buïgas • April–Sept Thurs–Sun 9–11.30pm; Oct–March Fri & Sat only 7–9pm; musical displays every 30min • Free

Things were certainly different in 1929, when mere whooshing water was enough to wow the crowds attending that year's International Exhibition. On several evenings each week, the **Font Màgica** (Magic Fountain) at the foot of the Montjuïc steps still does its stuff, forming the centrepiece of what is now an impressive, if slightly kitsch, sound-and-light show, with sprays and sheets of brightly coloured water dancing to the strains of Holst and Abba. The fountain is also the site of a spectacular firework, music and laser show every September, at the close of the annual Mercè festival.

6

Caixa Forum

Av. de Francesc Ferrer i Guàrdia 6–8 • Daily 10am–8pm; July & Aug Wed open until 11pm • Free • ☎ 934 768 600, ⓦ fundacio.lacaixa.es • Ⓜ Espanya

A terrific arts and cultural centre, located within the old *modernista* Casaramona textile factory, **Caixa Forum** was originally built in 1911 by Josep Puig i Cadafalch. Its renovation and expansion under the auspices of the Fundació La Caixa – following fifty years as a base for police horses – has produced a remarkable building, entered beneath twin iron-and-glass canopies representing spreading trees. The exhibition halls were fashioned from the former factory buildings, whose external structure was left untouched – girders, pillars, brickwork and crenellated walls appear at every turn. The undulating roof (signposted "terrats") offers unique views, while the high Casaramona tower, etched in blue and yellow tiling, is as readily recognizable as the huge Miró starfish logos emblazoned across the building.

A permanent exhibition covers the history and design of the building, while other galleries are given over to rotating selections from the foundation's contemporary international **art collection**, which focuses on the period from the 1980s onwards. In addition, there's an excellent free programme of changing **exhibitions** across all aspects of the arts – recent exhibitions have highlighted subjects as diverse as the Pixar animation studio and the gold of ancient Peru. There's also the Mediateca multimedia space, plus an arts bookshop, children's activities and a 400-seat auditorium for music, art and literary events. The **café** occupies a converted space within the old factory walls, and serves breakfast and light meals.

Pavelló Mies van der Rohe

Av. de Francesc Ferrer i Guàrdia 7, opposite Caixa Forum • Daily 10am–6pm • €5, under-16s free • Guided tours 11am–noon, in English on demand; €7 including admission • ☎ 934 234 016, ⓦ miesbcn.com • Ⓜ Espanya

The German contribution to the 1929 International Exhibition, a pavilion designed by Ludwig Mies van der Rohe, was reconstructed in 1986 by Catalan architects. Used as a reception room during the Exhibition, the **Pavelló Mies van der Rohe** is considered a major example of modern rationalist architecture. The pavilion has a startlingly beautiful conjunction of hard straight lines with watery surfaces, its dark-green polished onyx alternating with shining glass. It's open to visitors but unless one of the occasional temporary exhibitions is in place, there's little to see inside save Mies van der Rohe's iconic, tubular steel *Barcelona Chair*. Still, you can always buy postcards and books from the small shop.

Poble Espanyol

Av. de Francesc Ferrer i Guàrdia 13 • Mon 9am–8pm, Tues–Thurs & Sun 9am–midnight, Fri 9am–3am, Sat 9am–4am, workshops daily 10am–6/8pm, depending on season • €12, ages 4–12 €7, under-4s free, family ticket €33, night ticket €7, combined ticket with MNAC €18 • ☎ 935 086 300, ⓦ poble-espanyol.com • Ⓜ Espanya and 800m walk, or bus #150 or #13 from Av. de la Reina María Cristina

The **Poble Espanyol**, or Spanish Village, was an inspired concept for the International Exhibition of 1929 – a complete village consisting of streets and squares with reconstructions of famous or characteristic buildings from all over Spain, such as the fairy-tale medieval walls of Ávila through which you enter. "Get to know Spain in one hour" is what's promised, and it's nowhere near as cheesy as you might think. The echoing main square is lined with cafés, while the surrounding streets and alleys contain around forty workshops, where you can see engraving, weaving, pottery and other crafts. Inevitably, it's one huge shopping experience – castanets to Lladró porcelain, religious icons to Barcelona soccer shirts – and prices are inflated, but children, who can run free in the absence of traffic, will love it, and there are plenty of family activities.

Get to the village early to enjoy it relatively crowd-free – once the tour groups arrive, it becomes a bit of a scrum. You could always come instead at the other end of the day, to venues like *Tablao de Carmen* for flamenco shows (see p.207) or *La Terrrazza* dance club (see p.201), when the village transforms into a vibrant centre of Barcelona nightlife.

Museu Nacional d'Art de Catalunya (MNAC)

Palau Nacional: May–Sept Tues–Sat 10am–8pm, Sun & hols 10am–3pm; Oct–April Tues–Sat 10am–6pm, Sun & hols 10am–3pm; open Mon when it's a public holiday 10am–3pm • €12, ticket valid for two days within a month, annual pass €18, under-16s & over-65s free; free for everyone Sat 3–8pm & first Sun of the month; charges vary for special exhibitions • ☎ 936 220 360, ⓦ mnac.cat • Ⓜ Espanya/ Poble Sec, or bus #150 from Av. de la Reina María Cristina, or bus #55 from c/de Lleida

The towering, domed **Palau Nacional**, set back on Montjuïc at the top of the long flight of steps from the fountains, was the flagship building of Barcelona's 1929 International Exhibition. Used for the opening ceremony, the palace was due to be demolished once the expo was over, but gained a reprieve and ultimately became home to one of Spain's greatest museums – the **Museu Nacional d'Art de Catalunya** (**MNAC**), showcasing a thousand years of Catalan art in stupendous surroundings.

In such a wide-ranging museum, it can be hard to know where to start. If your time is at all limited, be sure not to miss the medieval collection, which is split into two main sections. One is dedicated to **Romanesque** art, the other to **Gothic**; both were periods during which Catalan artists were pre-eminent in Spain. MNAC also has impressive holdings of European **Renaissance and Baroque** art, as well as an unsurpassed collection of **nineteenth- and twentieth-century Catalan art** (up until the 1950s; subsequent periods are covered by MACBA in the Raval). In addition, there's a changing roster of blockbuster exhibitions and special shows based on the museum's archives. There's also a **café-bar** and gift shop and art **bookshop** in the gloriously restored oval hall, a kiosk on the front terrace, and a separate museum restaurant with more extraordinary views over the city.

The Romanesque collection

From the eleventh century onwards, as the Christian Reconquest spread across the Iberian peninsula, great numbers of sturdy Romanesque churches were built in the high Catalan Pyrenees. Medieval Catalan studios decorated these churches with extraordinary biblical frescoes, and even the most remote Pyrenean valleys boasted lavish masterpieces. By the nineteenth century, however, many of these churches either lay abandoned or had been ruined by renovations. Finally, in 1919, a concerted effort was made to preserve the frescoes for future generations, by removing them to a museum where they could be better displayed.

Today, the frescoes are magnificently presented in reconstructions of the original interiors, enabling you to see exactly where they would have been placed in the church buildings. Most possess a vibrant, raw quality that's best exemplified by those taken from churches in the Boí valley in the Catalan Pyrenees. The highlight of the whole astonishing collection comes in room 7, where the extraordinarily powerful *Christ in Majesty*, painted by the so-called **Master of Taüll** for the apse of the early twelfth-century church of Sant Climent in Taüll, combines a Byzantine hierarchical composition with the imposing colours and strong outlines of contemporary manuscript illuminators.

Look out for details such as the leper, to the left of the Sant Climent altar, patiently allowing a dog to lick his sores. Two large works by Antoni Tàpies are displayed alongside. Frescoes from other churches explore various themes, from heaven to hell, with the displays complemented by sculptures, altar panels, woodcarvings, religious objects and furniture retrieved from the mouldering churches.

The Gothic collection

The evolution from the Romanesque to the Gothic period was marked by a move from murals to painting on wood, and by the depiction of more naturalistic figures in scenes showing the lives of the saints, and later in portraits of kings and patrons of the arts. At first, the Catalan and Valencian schools in particular were influenced by contemporary Italian styles, and you'll see some outstanding altarpieces, tombs and church decoration. Later came the International Gothic or "1400" style, in which the influences became more widespread; the important figures of this movement were the fifteenth-century artists **Jaume Huguet** and **Lluís Dalmau**. Works from the end of this period show the strong influence of contemporary Flemish painting, in the use of denser colours, the depiction of crowd scenes and a concern for perspective. The last Catalan artist of note here, the so-called **Master of La Seu d'Urgell**, is represented by several works, including a fine series of six paintings (Christ, the Virgin Mary, saints Peter, Paul and Sebastian and Mary Magdalene) that once formed the covers of an organ.

The Renaissance and Baroque collections

Many of MNAC's **Renaissance** and **Baroque** works have come from private collections bequeathed to the museum, notably by conservative politician Francesc Cambó and Madrid's Thyssen-Bornemisza. Selections from these bequests are shown in their own rooms within the Renaissance and Baroque galleries, while the other rooms in this section trace artistic development from the early sixteenth to the eighteenth century. Major European artists displayed include Peter Paul Rubens, Giovanni Battista Tiepolo,

---

THE BRILLIANT FLOWERING OF CATALAN ART

Between around 1850 and 1940, Catalan art enjoyed a modern golden age. Break-out artist was **Marià Fortuny i Marsal** – often regarded as the earliest *modernista* artist, and certainly the first Catalan painter known widely abroad, having exhibited to great acclaim in Paris and Rome. He specialized in minutely detailed pictures, often of exotic subjects – his set-piece *Battle of Tetuan*, for example, was based on a visit to Morocco in 1859 to observe the war there. The main name in contemporary Catalan Realism was **Ramon Martí i Alsina**, while the master of nineteenth-century Catalan landscape painting was **Joaquim Veyreda i Vila**, founder of the "Olot School", whose members were influenced both by the work of the early Impressionists and by the distinctive volcanic scenery of the Olot region in northern Catalunya.

However, only with the emergence of **Ramon Casas i Carbó** (whose famous picture of himself and Pere Romeu on a tandem, as displayed at MNAC, once hung on the walls of *Els Quatre Gats*) and **Santiago Rusiñol i Prats** did Catalan art acquire its first contemporary art superstars, taking their cue from the very latest in European styles, whether the symbolism of Whistler or the vibrant social observation of Toulouse-Lautrec. Hot on their heels came a new generation of artists – Josep María Sert, Marià Pidelaserra i Brias, Ricard Canals i Llambí and others – who were strongly influenced by the scene in contemporary Paris. The two brightest stars of the period, though, were **Joaquim Mir i Trinxet**, whose highly charged landscapes tended towards the abstract, and **Isidre Nonell i Monturiol**, who from 1902 until his early death in 1911 painted sombre naturalistic studies of impoverished Gypsy communities.

The other dominant contemporary trend was *noucentisme*, a style at once more classical and less consciously flamboyant than *modernisme* – witness the portraits and landscapes of **Joaquim Sunyer i Miró**, perhaps the best known *noucentista* artist, and the work of sculptors like **Pau Gargallo i Catalán**.

6

TEATRE GREC AND THE BARCELONA FESTIVAL

Montjuïc takes centre-stage each year during Barcelona's annual summer cultural festival (ⓦbarcelonafestival.com), known locally as the Grec, when arias soar from the open-air stage of the **Teatre Grec**, a Greek theatre cut into a former quarry on the Poble Sec side of the hill. Running from late June throughout July and August, the festival incorporates drama, music and dance, with the opening sessions and some of the most atmospheric events staged in the theatre, from Shakespearean productions to shows by avant-garde performance artists. These can be magical nights – a true Barcelona experience – though you'll need to be quick off the mark for tickets, which usually go on sale in May.

Jean Honoré Fragonard, Francisco de Goya, El Greco, Lucas Cranach, Francisco de Zurbarán and Diego Velázquez, though the museum is of course keen to play up Catalan works of the period, by the likes of Barcelona artist Antoni Viladomat (1678–1755). However, more familiar to most will be the masterpieces of the Spanish Golden Age, notably Velázquez's *Saint Paul* and Zurbarán's *Immaculate Conception*.

The modern art collection

MNAC ends on a high note with its unsurpassed **nineteenth- and twentieth-century Catalan art** collection, which is particularly good on *modernista* and *noucentista* painting and sculpture (see box, p.91), the two dominant schools of the period. Rooms highlight individual artists and genres, shedding light on the development of art in an exciting period of Catalunya's history. The works provide a rich, varied experience, ranging from intricate Barcelona street scenes to *modernista* interior design (including furniture by Gaudí), while there are also fascinating diversions into avant-garde sculpture and historical photography. Salvador Dalí is represented by a portrait of his father from 1925, and there's a fascinating array of graphic art from the Civil War era.

Museu Etnològic

Pg. de Santa Madrona 16–22 · Under renovation · ⓦ www.museuetnologic.bcn.cat · ⓜ Espanya/Poble Sec, or bus #55 from c/ de Lleida

The ethnological museum on Montjuïc has been closed for renovations for several years, with much of its extensive collection of art and artefacts from around the globe on display at the Museu de Cultures del Món (see p.71). Precisely what it will hold when it finally reopens remains unclear; check the website for the latest news.

Museu d'Arqueologia de Catalunya

Pg. de Santa Madrona 39–41 · Tues–Sat 9.30am–7pm, Sun & hols 10am–2.30pm · €4.50, under-25s €3.50, under-8s free; Oct–June free for everyone last Thurs of the month · ☎ 934 232 149, ⓦ www.mac.cat · ⓜ Espanya/Poble Sec, or bus #55 from c/de Lleida

No one interested in the early and classical-era history of what's now known as Catalunya should miss the **Museu d'Arqueologia de Catalunya**, whose rich archeological collection spans the centuries from the Stone Age to the time of the Visigoths. Dramatic finds from the region's most famous archeological sites are concentrated here, notably pieces from the Greek site at Empúries on the Costa Brava, including a replica of the renowned marble statue of Asclepius, Greek god of medicine, which dominates the central rotunda. The Second Punic War (218–201 BC) saw the Carthaginians expelled from Iberia by the Romans, who made their provincial capital at Tarragona (Tarraco), with a secondary outpost at Barcelona (Barcino). There's also some fine Roman glassware and mosaic work, while an upper floor interprets life in **Barcino** itself via tombstones, statues, inscriptions and friezes that were found all over the city. The exhibits have been enlivened with modern interactive displays, and some of the stonework is remarkably vivid, depicting the faces of Barcino's original inhabitants as clearly as the day they were carved.

La Ciutat del Teatre

C/de Lleida • Ⓜ Poble Sec

At the foot of Montjuïc, on the eastern slopes, the theatre area known as La Ciutat del Teatre occupies a back corner of the old working-class neighbourhood of Poble Sec. Direct steps descend the hillside, while Passeig de Santa Madrona runs down here from MNAC, passing the archeological museum.

The theatre buildings that make up La Ciutat del Teatre sit in a tight huddle off c/de Lleida. Here you'll find the **Mercat de les Flors** (see p.207) – once a flower market, now a centre for dance and the "movement arts" – and progressive **Teatre Lliure** (see p.209), "Free Theatre", occupying the spaghetti-western-style Palau de l'Agricultura premises built for the 1929 Exhibition.

Walk through the terracotta arch from c/de Lleida, and off to the left is the far sleeker **Institut del Teatre** (see p.209), with its sheer walls contrasting markedly with the neighbourhood's cheap housing, from where laundry is strung just metres away from the gleaming Theatre City. The institute brings together the city's major drama and dance schools, and various conservatories, libraries and study centres.

Poble Sec

Ⓜ Poble Sec/Paral.lel

Lying immediately below Montjuïc, confined by the hill on one side and the busy Avinguda del Paral.lel on the other, the neighbourhood of **Poble Sec**, or "Dry Village", is so called because it had no water supply until the nineteenth century. It's a complete contrast to the landscaped slopes behind it – a grid of contoured narrow streets, down-to-earth grocery stores, bakeries, local shops and good-value restaurants. Asian immigrants have stamped their mark on many of the neighbourhood stores and businesses, while Poble Sec is also emerging as an "off-Raval" nightlife destination, with its fashionable bars and music clubs – pedestrianized **Carrer de Blai** is the focal point of the scene.

Refugi 307

C/Nou de la Rambla 175 • Guided visits Sun at 10.30am (English), 11.30am (Spanish) & 12.30pm (Catalan); otherwise only open to groups with advance reservations • €3.40 • ☎ 932 562 100, Ⓦ www.museuhistoria.bcn.cat • Ⓜ Paral.lel

Many visitors never set foot in Poble Sec, though one of the city's old Civil War air-raid shelters provides a compelling reason to make the short journey across town. **Refugi 307**

A CITY UNDER SIEGE

During the Civil War years, Poble Sec – like many inner-city neighbourhoods – suffered grievously from Nationalist bombing raids, a foretaste of what was to come elsewhere in Europe during World War II. From 1936 onwards, the city authorities oversaw the construction of a system of communal **air-raid shelters**, many of which had been excavated by the time the first raids hit Barcelona early in 1937. Most were constructed in working-class areas like Poble Sec, Barceloneta and Gràcia, where the locals hadn't been able to leave the city or couldn't reach the relative safety of either the metro tunnels or the Collserola hills. Altogether, around 1400 shelters were built in Barcelona (and another two thousand across Catalunya). While some were as simple as reinforced cellars, many, like **Refugi 307**, were larger collaborative efforts that featured vaulted brick-lined tunnels, ventilation, water supplies and even infirmaries and play areas for children. The raids were particularly savage in March 1938, and by the end of the war three thousand inhabitants had died in the bombings, with many more injured and thousands of buildings destroyed. Even so, the shelters undoubtedly saved many lives. In the wake of Republican defeat, after the war, many of the shelters were forgotten, but these days the city authorities are keen to raise their profile in the name of education, and the remembrance of Barcelona's often overlooked wartime history.

was dug into the Montjuïc hillside by local people from 1936 onwards, and the 200m of tunnels could shelter up to two thousand people from Franco's bombing raids. With no radar to protect the city, they had two minutes from the first sound of the sirens to get underground. To take a tour, you can just turn up on the day. Photographic storyboards at the start of the tour provide a bit of background, and then it's hard hat on to follow your guide into the labyrinth to the sound of screaming sirens and droning warplanes.

The Olympic area

Ⓜ Espanya, then either walk via the hillside escalators behind MNAC or take bus #13 from Av. de la Reina María Cristina or #55 from c/Lleida

From Poble Espanyol, the main road through Montjuïc climbs around the hill and up to the city's principal Olympic area, sometimes known as the **Anella Olímpica**

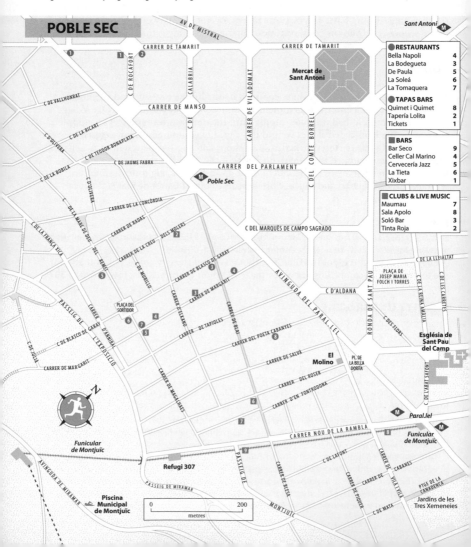

POBLE SEC

RESTAURANTS	
Bella Napoli	4
La Bodegueta	3
De Paula	5
La Soleá	6
La Tomaquera	7

TAPAS BARS	
Quimet i Quimet	8
Tapería Lolita	2
Tickets	1

BARS	
Bar Seco	9
Celler Cal Marino	4
Cervecería Jazz	5
La Tieta	6
Xixbar	1

CLUBS & LIVE MUSIC	
Maumau	7
Sala Apolo	8
Soló Bar	3
Tinta Roja	2

(Olympic Ring). The 1992 Olympics were actually the second planned for Montjuïc. The first, in 1936 – the "People's Olympics" – were organized as an alternative to the Nazis' infamous Berlin games of that year, but the day before the official opening, Franco's army revolt triggered the Civil War and scuppered the Barcelona games. Some of the 25,000 athletes and spectators who had turned up stayed on to join the Republican forces.

The Olympic stadium and other buildings

Estadi Olímpic Lluís Companys, Av. de l'Estadi • No public access, except during events

The stadium at Montjuïc was built for the 1929 Exhibition, but it was refitted entirely for the 1992 Barcelona Olympics, while keeping its original Neoclassical facade. Seventy thousand spectators packed in for the opening and closing ceremonies, though the current stadium capacity is around 54,000. It's used for major sporting events (it hosted the 2010 European Athletics championships) and concerts by the likes of Bruce Springsteen and One Direction. It's also been officially renamed as the **Estadi Olímpic Lluís Companys**, after the Generalitat president who was executed at Montjuïc after the Spanish Civil War.

A vast *terrassa* on the west side of the stadium provides one of the finest vantage points in the city. Long water-fed troughs break up the concrete and marble expanse, while the confident, space-age curve of Santiago Calatrava's **communications tower** dominates the skyline. Rising above the terrace is the steel-and-glass **Palau Sant Jordi**, a 17,000-seat sports and concert hall, while other signature buildings in the Olympic area include Catalan architect Ricardo Bofill's **Institut Nacional d'Educació Física de Catalunya** (**INEF**; a sports university) and – one building you can visit as a general punter – the impressive **Piscines Picornell** (see p.223).

Museu Olímpic i de l'Esport

Av. de l'Estadi 60 • April–Sept Tues–Sat 10am–8pm, Sun & hols 10am–2.30pm; Oct–March Tues–Sat 10am–6pm, Sun & hols 10am–2.30pm • €5.10, under-7s free • ☎ 932 925 379, ⓦ museuolimpicbcn.com • Ⓜ Espanya then 25min walk, or bus #13 or #150 from Av. de la Reina María Cristina

Just across the road from the Olympic stadium, the history of the Games themselves – and Barcelona's successful hosting – are covered in the **Museu Olímpic i de l'Esport**. It's a fully interactive experience, with lots of Olympic memorabilia and sports gear on display, plus sporting videos and an audiovisual presentation, but even so is probably one for hardcore sports fans only.

Fundació Joan Miró

Parc de Montjuïc • July–Sept Tues, Wed, Fri & Sat 10am–8pm, Thurs 10am–9pm, Sun & hols 10am–2.30pm; Oct–June Tues, Wed, Fri & Sat 10am–7pm, Thurs 10am–9pm, Sun & hols 10am–2.30pm; only open on Mon when it's a public holiday • General admission to all areas €11, otherwise exhibitions €7, Espai 13 €2.50 • ☎ 934 439 470, ⓦ fundaciomiro-bcn.org • Ⓜ Paral.lel, then Funicular de Montjuïc and 5min walk, or bus #150 from Av. de la Reina María Cristina, or #55 from c/Llieda

Barcelona's most adventurous art museum, the **Fundació Joan Miró**, houses the life's work of the great Catalan artist Joan Miró (1893–1983), who established an international reputation while always retaining links with his homeland. The stark white modernist museum, designed by Miró's friend, the architect Josep Lluís Sert, and set in lovely gardens overlooking the city, lies just a few minutes' walk from both the Olympic stadium and the Montjuïc funicular and cable-car stations.

Miró showed a childlike delight in colours and shapes and developed a free, highly decorative style – the paintings and drawings, in particular, are instantly recognizable, among the chief links between Surrealism and abstract art. Miró had his first exhibition in 1918; met Picasso in Paris during the 1920s; and subsequently spent his summers in Catalunya and the rest of the time in France, before moving to Mallorca in 1956, where he died.

The museum's huge collection of paintings, graphics, tapestries and sculptures was largely donated by Miró himself, and ranges from 1914 up to 1978. Aside from the permanent displays, the Fundació sponsors excellent temporary exhibitions, film shows, lectures and children's theatre, while summer music nights (usually June and July) are a feature every year. Young experimental artists have their own space in the **Espai 13** gallery, and there's also a contemporary art **library**, a **bookshop** and a **café-restaurant** that's accessible even if you don't pay to get into the museum itself.

The collection

The two-hundred-plus paintings here are disproportionately drawn from Miró's later years – by the time works began to be set aside for the newly proposed museum in the 1960s, he had been painting for almost half a century. However, the collection does include early Realist works that date from before he decided to "assassinate art" and abandon figurative painting in the mid-1920s, like the effervescent *Portrait of a Young Girl* (1919), while other gaps are filled by a collection that was subsequently donated by Miró's widow, Pilar Juncosa, and demonstrates Miró's preoccupations in the 1930s and 1940s. It was during this period that he started his **Constellations** series, introducing the colours, themes and symbols that, eventually pared down to the minimalist basics, came to define his work: reds and blues; women, birds and tears; the sun, moon and stars. That same period also saw the fifty black-and-white lithographs of the **Barcelona Series** (1939–44), executed in the immediate aftermath of the Civil War. They are a dark reflection of the turmoil of the period, all snarling faces and great black shapes and shadows.

For a rapid appraisal of Miró's entire *oeuvre* look in on room 21, holding 23 works on long-term loan from a Japanese collector. They serve as a kind of potted retrospective, in which you can trace Miró's development from his early Impressionist landscapes (1914) to the minimal renderings of the 1970s. Elsewhere you'll find several of Miró's enormous bright **tapestries**; his **pencil drawings**, particularly of misshapen women and gawky ballerinas; and **sketches and notes** including simple doodles on scraps of old newspaper. His **sculptures** are on display outdoors, both in the gardens and on the spacious roof terrace.

Works by other artists

The museum also holds works created in homage to Miró by other artists, including fine pieces by Yves Tanguy, Fernand Léger, Balthus, Antoni Tàpies, Robert Motherwell and Eduardo Chillida. Perhaps the single most compelling exhibit, however, is Alexander Calder's **Mercury Fountain**, which he built for the Republican pavilion at the Paris Universal Exhibition of 1936–37 – the same exhibition for which Picasso painted *Guernica*. Like *Guernica*, it's a tribute to a town, this time the mercury-mining town of

---

ON THE MIRÓ TRAIL

When you've seen one Miró, well, you start to see them everywhere in Barcelona, whether it's T-shirts for tourists or branding for businesses. There's the large ceramic mural on the facade of Terminal B at the **airport**, for a start, or the circular pavement mural at **Plaça de la Boqueria** that catches your attention every time you stroll down the Ramblas. Miró designed the starfish logo for the **Caixa de Pensions** savings bank (there's one splashed across the Caixa Forum arts centre on Montjuïc) and also the **España logo** on Spanish National Tourist Board publications. There's his towering *Dona i Ocell* ("Woman and Bird"') in the **Parc Joan Miró**, near Barcelona Sants train station, while a smaller *Dona* stands with other Catalan works in the courtyard of the **Ajuntament** (city hall). In many ways, Barcelona's a Miró city, whatever Picasso fans might think.

Almáden – its name spelled out in dangling metal letters above the fountain – which saw saturation bombing during the Civil War.

Castell de Montjuïc

Carretera de Montjuïc 66 · **Castle** Daily: April–Sept 10am–8pm; Oct–March 10am–6pm · €5, under-16s free, Sun free for everyone after 3pm · **Grounds** Daily: April–Sept 9am–7pm; Oct–March 9am–9pm · Free · ☎ 932 564 440, ⓦ www.bcn.cat/castelldemontjuic · Direct access by Telefèric de Montjuïc, or bus #150 from Av. de la Reina María Cristina

The best way to reach Barcelona's **castle**, at the very top of Montjuïc, is by the Telefèric de Montjuïc (see p.88). The cable-car tacks up the hillside, offering magnificent views on the way, before depositing you just outside the forbidding red-brick walls of the eighteenth-century fortress itself. It's worth coming up here simply to admire the dramatic location, and to admire the superb views out over the port from the grounds, which are free to enter.

   Paying admission to the castle buys you marginally better views, especially from its surprisingly broad ramparts, but more importantly gives access to fascinating displays on its history and significance. Finally handed over to the city in 2008, the fortress had long been a symbol of the city's occupation by a foreign power – the Spanish state. After all, it had served for decades as a military base and prison, with its mighty cannon trained on the city down below, and it was here that the last president of the prewar Generalitat, **Lluís Companys i Jover**, was executed on Franco's orders on October 15, 1940. Companys had been in exile in Paris after the Civil War, but was handed over to Franco by the Germans upon their capture of the French capital; he's buried in the nearby Cementiri del Sud-Oest. Small wonder, therefore, that the captions in the castle's Montjuïc interpretation centre refer to it as "hated for centuries".

Camí del Mar and Mirador del Migdia

Below the castle ramparts, a panoramic pathway – the **Camí del Mar** – has been cut from the cliff edge, providing further magnificent views, first across to Port Olímpic and the northern beaches, and then southwest as the path swings around the castle. This is an unfamiliar view of the city, of the sprawling docks and container yards, with cruise ships and tankers usually visible negotiating the busy sea lanes.

   The path is just over 1km long and ends at the back of the castle battlements near the **Mirador del Migdia**, where there's a great open-air chill-out bar, *La Caseta del Migdia* (see p.200). Down through the trees is the *mirador* itself, a balcony with extensive views over the Baix Llobregat industrial area. You can see across to the Olympic stadium from here, while in the immediate foreground is the extraordinary **Cementiri del Sud-Oest**, stretching along the ridge below, whose tombs are stacked like apartment blocks on great conifer-lined avenues.

Jardí Botànic de Barcelona

C/Dr Font i Quer 2 · Daily: April–Sept 10am–7pm; Oct–March 10am–5pm · €3.50, or €7 combined ticket with Museu Blau, under-16s free · ☎ 932 564 160, ⓦ www.museuciencies.bcn.cat · ⓜ Espanya, then 20min walk via escalators, or bus #150 from Av. de la Reina María Cristina or #55 from c/Lleida

Principal among Montjuïc's many gardens is the city's botanical garden, the **Jardí Botànic de Barcelona**, laid out on terraced slopes that offer fine views across the city. Montjuïc buses run here directly, while the entrance is just a five-minute walk around the back of the Olympic stadium. It's a beautifully kept contemporary garden, where wide, easy-to-follow paths (fine for buggies, strollers and wheelchairs) wind through landscaped zones representing the flora of the Mediterranean, Canary Islands, California, Chile, South Africa and Australia. Just don't come in the full heat of the summer day, as there's very little shade. Guided tours in Spanish/Catalan every weekend (except Aug) show you the highlights, but you get an English-language printed guide included in the entry fee.

THE GARDENS OF MONTJUÏC

Botanical gardens aside, Montjuïc holds plenty of places where you can roll out a picnic rug or let the children scamper around safely.

Signposted off Avinguda de Miramar, west of (and below) the Fundació Joan Miró, the terraces, clipped hedges and grottoes of the **Jardins Laribal** (daily 10am–dusk; free) date from 1918. They surround the spring of **Font del Gat**, which has been a picnic site since the nineteenth century. Josep Puig i Cadafalch built a restaurant here of the same name for the 1929 International Exhibition, and it's open now for lunch (1–3.45pm; closed Mon), with wonderful views from its terrace.

East of here, the Montjuïc cable-car passes over the **Jardins de Mossèn Jacint Verdaguer** and adjacent **Jardins Joan Brossa** (both daily 10am–dusk; free), which tack up the hillside to the castle. Walking down through the gardens from the castle makes a pleasant way to return to the lower slopes of Montjuïc, through the site of the former Montjuïc amusement park, now fully landscaped with children's play areas – halfway down, there are sweeping city views from the **Mirador de l'Alcalde**.

Outside the upper cross-harbour cable-car station, you'll find the formal **Jardins de Miramar** (always open; free), plus more fine views from the cable-car station café-*terrassa*. Steps lead down from a point close to the cable-car station into the precipitous cactus gardens of the **Jardins de Mossèn Costa i Llobera** (daily 10am–dusk; free), which look out over the port. The flourishing stands of Central and South American, Indian and African cacti, some over 6m high, make a dramatic scene experienced by few visitors to Montjuïc, though the people lounging on the steps and in the shade of the bigger specimens suggest it's something of an open secret among the locals.

Museu de Carrosses Fúnebres

C/Mare de Déu de Port 56–58 • Wed–Sun 10am–2pm • Free • ☎ 934 841 999, ⓦ cbsa.cat/colleccio • Bus #21 from Ⓜ Paral.lel

One of Barcelona's more esoteric attractions, the **Museu de Carrosses Fúnebres** (Funerary Carriage Museum), fittingly stands at the entrance to Montjuïc cemetery. The horse-drawn carriages on display were used for city funeral processions from the 1830s until the service was mechanized in the 1950s, when the silver Buick that's also on show came into use. Most of the carriages and hearses are extravagantly decorated in gilt, black or white, and some, such as the Grand Doumont and the Stove, carried dignitaries, politicians and big-name bullfighters to their final resting places. There are also plenty of old photographs of them in use in the city's streets, alongside antique uniforms, mourning wear and formal riding gear. Guided tours are given for free on Saturdays at noon (Spanish/Catalan).

CASA BATLLÓ

Dreta de l'Eixample

Now Barcelona's main shopping and business district, the nineteenth-century street grid north of Plaça de Catalunya was designed as part of a revolutionary urban plan. Dubbed the Eixample in Catalan – and pronounced *aye-sham-pla*, the "Extension" or "Widening" – the plan divided districts into regular blocks, whose characteristic wide streets and shaved corners survive today. Two parallel avenues, Passeig de Gràcia and Rambla de Catalunya, form its backbone, with everything to the east known as the Dreta de l'Eixample (the right-hand side). It's here, above all, that the bulk of the city's famous *modernista* buildings are found, along with an array of classy galleries and fashionable hotels, shops and boutiques. It's not a neighbourhood as such – and you won't be able to see everything here on a single outing – but the Dreta does contain many of the city's most stylish, show-stopping buildings.

Acting as a sort of open-air museum, Dreta de l'Eixample features the masterworks of a new class of **modernista architects**, who changed the way Barcelona looked from around 1880 onwards. These extraordinary buildings – notably by Antoni Gaudí i Cornet, Lluís Domènech i Montaner and Josep Puig i Cadafalch – were commissioned by status-conscious merchants and businessmen. Built as private houses and apartments, many are now open to the public. Most are found within the triangle formed by the Passeig de Gràcia, Avinguda Diagonal and the Gran Via de les Corts Catalanes, within a few blocks of each other. The standout sights are Gaudí's **La Pedrera** apartment building, and the so-called **Mansana de la Discòrdia**, or "Block of Discord" (Pg. de Gràcia, between carrers del Consell de Cent and d'Aragó), which gets its name because the three adjacent houses, casas **Lleó Morera**, **Amatller** and **Batlló** – built within a decade of each other by three different architects – show off wildly varying manifestations of the *modernista* style and spirit. The Dreta also holds the not-to-miss **gallery** dedicated to Catalunya's most eminent postwar artist Antoni Tàpies, and a great neighbourhood **market**.

7

Casa Lleó Morera

Pg. de Gràcia 35 • Guided tours Mon–Sat 10am–6.30pm; check website for schedule; there's always an hour-long English tour at 11am; reservations essential • €15, ages 13–25 €13.50, under-13s free; Express tour €12 • ☎ 936 762 733, ⓦ casalleomorera.com • ⓟ Passeig de Gràcia

Designed by Lluís Domènech i Montaner and completed in 1905, the six-storey **Casa Lleó Morera** is the least obviously extravagant of the buildings in the "Block of Discord", and its exterior has suffered more than its neighbours from "improvements" wrought by subsequent owners. The original arches and sculptures have long since been removed from its ground floor – Salvador Dalí bought some of them – which is now occupied by the luxury leather goods store Loewe.

The wonderful Art Nouveau interior, however, can be seen on regular guided tours. The sheer scale and opulence of the spaces is quite extraordinary, from the huge see-and-be-seen room at the front, with its floor-to-ceiling windows, marquetry floor and ornate fireplace, to the sumptuous dining room at the back, where light streams in through the exquisite stained glass of the bay window, and the decorated mosaic panels on the walls incorporating ceramic modelled faces of family members. From the paved rear garden terrace, overlooked by an enormous ceramic mulberry tree – echoing a motif seen throughout the house, in reference to the family name, "morera", meaning mulberry – you can see that the semicircular bay climbs another three storeys. All tours

---

DESIGN A CITY...DESIGNER CITY

As Barcelona grew more industrialized throughout the nineteenth century, the old town became overcrowded and unsanitary. In 1851, the Spanish state finally gave permission to knock down the encircling walls and allow the city to expand beyond its medieval limits.

When it came to building what amounted to an entire new town, Barcelona then, as now, didn't do things by halves. The city authorities championed a fan-shaped plan by popular municipal architect **Antoni Rovira i Trias**, whose design radiated out from the existing shape of the old town. (His statue sits on a bench in Gràcia's Pl. Rovira i Trias, with his Eixample plan set in the ground beneath him.) However, much to local chagrin, Rovira's elegant if conventional plan was passed over by the Spanish government in favour of a revolutionary blueprint drawn up by utopian engineer and urban planner **Ildefons Cerdà i Sunyer**. This was defiantly modern in style and scale – a massive grid marching off to the north, intersected by broad avenues cut on the diagonal. Districts would be divided into wide, spacious blocks, with buildings limited in height, and central gardens, schools, markets, hospitals and other services provided for the inhabitants.

Cerdà eventually saw most of his more radical social proposals ignored, as the Eixample rapidly became a fashionable area in which to live and speculators developed buildings on the proposed open spaces. Even today though, the underlying fabric of his plan is always evident, while in certain quiet corners and gardens the original emphasis on social community within grand design lives on.

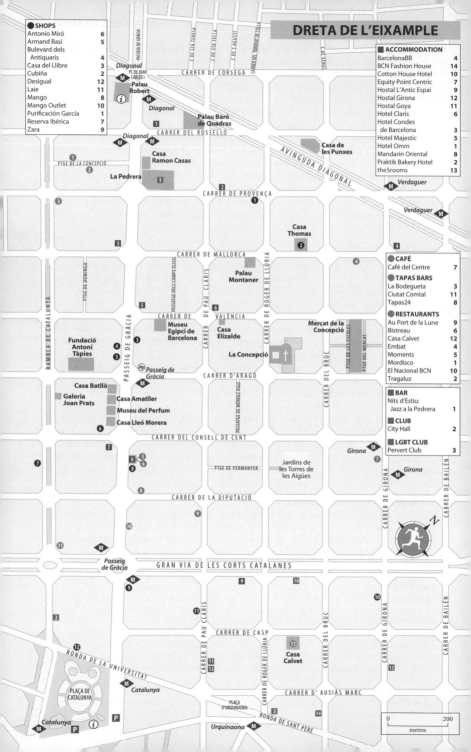

stick to the first level only, but it's still best to coincide with one of the less frequent hour-long versions rather than a half-hour "Express" tour.

Museu del Perfum

Pg. de Gràcia 39 • Mon–Fri 10.30am–8pm, Sat 11am–2pm • €5 • ☎ 932 160 121, ⓦ museodelperfume.com • Ⓜ Passeig de Gràcia

There's no missing the **Museu del Perfum**, which is sited at the back of the Regia perfume store; simply step into the store and you'll be overwhelmed by the cloying pong. They'll probably have to turn the lights on for you to enter the museum itself, though, which is devoted to an exquisite collection of perfume vessels and containers rather than to their contents. These range from tiny ceramic and alabaster jars from ancient Egypt and Carthage, via Roman glass, up to Turkish filigree-and-crystal ware and bronze and silver Indian elephant flasks. Modern times are represented by scents made for Grace Kelly and Elizabeth Taylor, and if you're diligent enough to scan all the shelves you should spot the "Sun King" bottles designed by Salvador Dalí.

7

MODERNISME – WHO'S WHO AND WHAT'S WHAT

Modernisme – the Catalan offshoot of Art Nouveau – was the expression of a renewed upsurge in Catalan nationalism. Catalunya's economic recovery in the early nineteenth century provided the initial impetus, and the subsequent cultural renaissance – the Renaixença – led to fresh stirrings of a Catalan awareness and identity (see box, p.91). Three architects in particular came to prominence in Barcelona and, in doing so, introduced a building style that has given the city a look like no other.

ANTONI GAUDÍ I CORNET

Born in Reus, near Tarragona, to a family of artisans, **Antoni Gaudí i Cornet** (1852–1926) brought much more than *modernisme* to his creations, but the imaginative impetus he provided was incalculable. Fantasy, spiritual symbolism and Catalan pride are evident in every building he designed, while his architectural influences were Moorish and Gothic, embellished with elements from the natural world. These themes are visible in projects as diverse as his extraordinary suburban industrial estate, Colònia Güell, and his masterpiece church, the Sagrada Família. Yet Gaudí rarely wrote a word about the theory of his art, preferring to leave it to the buildings to provoke a reaction– no one stands mute in front of an Antoni Gaudí masterpiece.
Key buildings and works:

Casa Batlló See p.104	**Colònia Güell** See p.150	**Palau Güell** See p.62
Park Güell See p.126	**La Pedrera** See p.106	**Sagrada Família** See p.115

LLUÍS DOMÈNECH I MONTANER

With Gaudí in a class of his own, it was **Lluís Domènech i Montaner** (1850–1923) who was perhaps the greatest pure *modernista* architect. Drawing on the rich Catalan Romanesque and Gothic traditions, his work combined traditional craft methods with modern technological experiments – with spectacularly innovative results.
Key buildings and works:

Casa Lleó Morera See p.101	**Hospital de la Santa Creu i**	**Palau de la Música**
Castell dels Tres	**de Sant Pau** See p.120	**Catalana** See p.66
Dragons See p.75		

JOSEP PUIG I CADAFALCH

Like that of other *modernista* architects, the work of **Josep Puig i Cadafalch** (1867–1957) contains a wildly inventive use of ceramic tiles, ironwork, stained glass and stone carving. His first commission, the **Casa Martí**, housed the famous *Els Quatre Gats* tavern for the city's avant-garde artists and hangers-on, while in uptown mansions built for the newly enriched Barcelona bourgeoisie, Puig i Cadafalch brought to bear distinct Gothic and medieval influences.
Key buildings and works:

Casa Amatller See p.104	**Casa de les Punxes** See p.108	**Els Quatre Gats** See box, p.46

Casa Amatller

Fundació Amatller, Pg. de Gràcia 41 · Daily 10am–7pm; check website for tour schedule; reservations advised · €15, under-13s €7.50 · ☎ 934 617 460, ⓦ www.amatller.org · Ⓜ Passeig de Gràcia

Josep Puig i Cadafalch's striking **Casa Amatller** apartment block (c.1900) was designed for Antoni Amatller, a Catalan chocolate manufacturer, art collector, photographer and traveller. It's a triumph of decorative detail, particularly the facade, which rises in steps to a point, studded with ceramic tiles and heraldic sculptures, while inside the hallway's twisted stone columns are interspersed with dragon lamps. Much of the house is now given over to the library and archive of the Amatller Institute of Hispanic Art, but it's also open for regular **guided tours**, on which you can admire its original Art Nouveau furniture and interior design, and take a peep at Amatller's photographic studio as well as chocolate tasting in the kitchen.

Casa Batlló

7

Pg. de Gràcia 43 · Daily 9am–9pm · €21.50, under-19s €18.50, under-7s free; buy tickets in advance, in person or online · ☎ 932 160 306, ⓦ www.casabatllo.es · Ⓜ Passeig de Gràcia

The most extraordinary creation on the "Block of Discord", Antoni Gaudí's **Casa Batlló** (pronounced *by-o*) was designed for the industrialist Josep Batlló. The original apartment building, built in 1877, was considered dull by contemporaries, so Gaudí was hired to give it a face-lift, and completed the work by 1907. The result was very far from dull, as indicated by nicknames that include "House of Bones", "House That Yawns" and "House That Breathes". Salvador Dalí called it "a house of sea-shapes, representing the waves on a stormy day". Its conspicuous feature is the undulating facade, adorned with balconies that might be carnival masks or the teeth-laden jaws of fish, and pockmarked higher up with circular ceramic buttons laid on a bright mosaic background. The interior, however, is every bit as compelling, meaning that despite the crowds and high prices, the **self-guided audio tours** should absolutely not be missed.

There's barely a straight line in the entire building, which resembles some great organism, threaded through by sinuous polished-wood banisters and complete with snakeskin-patterned walls, plus curving window frames, fireplaces and doorways. Every room is bathed in natural light, while gratings in the doors and elsewhere, modelled perhaps on the gills of fish, allow outside air to circulate.

For once, the audioguides are excellent, pointing out details you might otherwise miss and providing all the necessary context. They steer you up from the main floor, including the gloriously light salon that overlooks Passeig de Gràcia, via the patio and rear terrace, into the attic, supported by Gaudí's trademark catenary arches, and culminate when you emerge on the rooftop to find yourself surrounded by colourful **chimneys**, crusted with mosaics and broken tiles. Commentators have often described this scaly roofscape as representing the spine of the dragon killed by Sant Jordi (St George), and the small tower holding a three-dimensional cross as the knight's lance, plunged into the dragon's back.

Fundació Antoni Tàpies

C/d'Aragó 255 · Tues–Sun 10am–7pm · €7, under-16s €5.60 · ☎ 934 870 315, ⓦ fundaciotapies.org · Ⓜ Passeig de Gràcia

The definitive collection of the work of Catalan abstract artist **Antoni Tàpies** is housed in *modernista* architect Lluís Domènech i Montaner's first important building, the **Casa Montaner i Simon** (1880), which was originally constructed for the publishing firm of Montaner i Simon. Converted in 1990 to house the **Fundació Antoni Tàpies**, the building is capped by Tàpies's own striking sculpture, **Núvol i Cadira** ("Cloud and Chair"; 1990), a tangle of glass, wire and aluminium.

While the building itself is a beauty, with its Moorish-style flourishes, cast-iron columns and lack of dividing walls, Tàpies's art tends to polarize opinion. It's not

ANTONI TÀPIES

Born on C/de la Canuda in the Barri Gòtic, **Antoni Tàpies i Puig** (1923–2012) initially studied law at the University of Barcelona, though he left before completing his degree. Drawn to art from an early age, and largely self-taught (though he did study briefly at Barcelona's Acadèmia Valls), he became in 1948 a founding member of the influential Dau al Set ("Die at Seven"), a group of seven artists that produced a monthly avant-garde magazine of the same name which ran until 1956. His first major paintings date from as early as 1945, by which time he was already interested in collage (using newspaper, cardboard, silver wrapping, string and wire) and engraving techniques.

During the Dau al Set period, after coming into contact with Miró among others, **Tàpies** went through a brief Surrealist phase. However, after a stay in Paris he found his feet with an **abstract style** that matured in the 1950s, when he held his first major exhibitions, including shows in New York and Europe. Tàpies's large works are deceptively simple, though underlying messages and themes are signalled by the collage-like inclusion of everyday objects and a wide use of symbols on the canvas. He also continually experimented with unusual materials, like oil paint mixed with crushed marble, or by employing sand, clay, cloth or straw in his collages.

Tàpies's work became increasingly **political** during the 1960s and '70s: *A la memòria de Salvador Puig Antich, 1974* ("In Memory of Salvador Puig Antich, 1974") commemorates a Catalan anarchist executed by Franco's regime, while slogans splashed across his works, or the frequent use of the red bars of the Catalan flag, leave no doubt about his affiliations. The works preceding his death were more sombre still, featuring recurring images of earth, shrouds and bodies, as echoes of civil war and conflict. Meanwhile, he had left a string of important outdoor works across the city, including the mysterious glass box that is his *Homenatge a Picasso* ("Homage to Picasso"; 1983), on Passeig de Picasso, outside the gates of the Parc de la Ciutadella.

7

immediately accessible (in the way of, say, Miró), and most visitors seem either to love or hate the gallery. A selection of works from the permanent collection is on show, displayed chronologically, while three or four exhibitions each year highlight works and installations by contemporary artists. The foundation also includes a peerless archive on Tàpies's work, held in the gorgeous **library** on the upper floor, fashioned from the original shelves of the publisher's warehouse.

Museu Egipci de Barcelona

C/de València 284 • Jan to late June & early Sept to Nov Mon–Fri 10am–2pm & 4–8pm, Sat 10am–8pm, Sun 10am–2pm; late June to early Sept & Dec Mon–Sat 10am–8pm, Sun 10am–2pm • €11, under-5s free; extra charges sometimes for temporary exhibitions • Guided tours Sat at 11am (Catalan) & 5pm (Spanish) • ☎ 934 880 188, ⓦ museuegipci.com • Ⓜ Passeig de Gràcia

The **Museu Egipci de Barcelona**, half a block east of Passeig de Gràcia, holds an exceptional private collection of artefacts from ancient Egypt – there's nothing else in Spain quite like it. It was founded by hotelier and antiquity collector Jordi Clos – whose deluxe *Hotel Claris*, a block away, still has its own private museum – and displays a remarkable gathering of over a thousand objects, ranging from amulets to sarcophagi. Spreading over three floors, it's all very beautifully presented, with an emphasis on exploring the shape and character of Egyptian society. The real pleasure here is a serendipitous wander, turning up items like a wood-and-leather bed of the First and Second Dynasties (2920–2649 BC); a magnificent pectoral adornment that once belonged to costume designer Natacha Rambova, the second wife of Rudolph Valentino; some remarkable flint knives and bronze axes; and cat mummies from the Late Period (715–332 BC). There's also a good bookshop and a terrace café, plus a full programme of study sessions, children's activities and themed evening events.

Jardins de les Torres de les Aigües

C/de Roger de Llúria 56, between c/del Consell de Cent and c/de la Diputació · Daily 10am–dusk, Aug & Sept Sat & Sun until 3pm · Free · Ⓜ Girona

The original nineteenth-century Eixample urban plan was drawn up with local inhabitants very much in mind. Space, light and social community projects were part of the grand design, and something of the original municipal spirit can be seen in the **Jardins de les Torres de les Aigües**, an enclosed square (reached down a herringbone-brick tunnel) centred on a Moorish-style water tower. Handsomely restored by the city council, it turns it into a backyard family beach every summer, complete with sand and paddling pool.

Another example of the old Eixample lies directly opposite, across c/Roger de Llúria, where the cobbled **Passatge del Permanyer** cuts across an Eixample block, lined by candy-coloured single-storey townhouses.

Mercat de la Concepció and around

7

Between c/de València and c/d'Aragó · Mon & Sat 8am–3pm, Tues–Fri 8am–8pm, July & Aug closes 3pm · Ⓦ laconcepcio.cat · Ⓜ Girona

The Dreta's finest neighbourhood market, the **Mercat de la Concepció**, was inaugurated in 1888, its iron-and-glass tram-shed structure reminiscent of others in the city. Flowers, shrubs, trees and plants are a Concepció speciality, and the florists on c/de València stay open 24 hours a day. As well as a couple of good snack bars inside the market, there are a few outdoor cafés to the side.

La Concepció

C/Aragó 299, entrance on c/de Roger de Llúria · Daily 7.30am–1pm & 5–9pm · Free · Ⓜ Girona

The market takes its name from the church of **La Concepció**, a block west, whose quiet cloister is a surprising haven of slender columns and orange trees. Part of a fifteenth-century Gothic convent that once stood in the old town, the church was abandoned in the early nineteenth century and then transferred here brick by brick in the 1870s, along with the Romanesque belfry from another old-town church.

Palau Montaner

C/de Mallorca 278 · Not open to visitors; check for updates on Ⓦ rutadelmodernisme.com · Ⓜ Passeig de Gràcia

The **Palau Montaner** was built in 1896 for a member of the Montaner i Simon publishing family. After the original architect quit, *modernista* architect Lluís Domènech i Montaner took over halfway through construction, and the top half of the facade is clearly more elaborate than the lower part. Meanwhile, the period's most celebrated craftsmen were set to work on the interior, which sports rich mosaic floors, painted glass, carved woodwork and a monumental staircase. Now the seat of the Madrid government's delegation to Catalunya, the building is not currently open to visitors.

La Pedrera

Pg. de Gràcia 92, entrance on c/de Provença · **Self-guided daytime tours** Daily: March–Oct 9am–8.30pm; Nov–Feb 9am–6.30pm, closed one week in Jan · €20.50, ages 7–12 €10.25, under-7s free; premium tickets €27/€12.50 · **English-language guided tours** Daily noon & 4pm · €25/€14.75 · **Gaudí's Pedrera: The Origins** March to mid-June & mid-Sept to Oct daily 9–11pm; mid-June to mid-Sept Mon–Thurs & Sun 9–11pm, Fri & Sat 10.15–11pm; Nov–Feb Wed–Sat 7–10pm · €34/€17, except Fri & Sat mid-June to mid-Sept €49 · ☎ 902 202 138, Ⓦ lapedrera.com · Ⓜ Diagonal

The weird and wonderful apartment building that was constructed by Antoni Gaudí as the **Casa Milà** between 1905 and 1911, but is universally known as **La Pedrera** – "The Stone Quarry" – deservedly ranks among Barcelona's most popular tourist attractions. It was declared a UNESCO World Heritage Site in 1984. The hulking, rippled facade, curving around the street corner in a single smooth sweep, is said to have been inspired by the mountain of Montserrat just outside the city, while the apartments themselves, whose balconies of tangled metal drip over the facade, resemble eroded cave dwellings. It's all so seamlessly sinuous that Gaudí's contemporaries joked that the new tenants would only be able to keep snakes as pets.

Gaudí himself described as the building as "more luminous than light". This was his final secular commission, and even here he was injecting religious motifs and sculptures until its owners told him to remove them. Alarmed by the anti-religious fervour of the "Tragic Week" in Barcelona in 1909, when anarchist-sponsored rioting destroyed churches and religious foundations, they forbade him to add the sculpture of the Virgin Mary with which he planned to complete the roof. Gaudí, by now working full-time on the Sagrada Família, was appalled, and resolved to use his skills exclusively for religious purposes in future.

La Pedrera is always busy with visitors, so at peak periods it's essential to book in advance. Ordinarily you have to reserve for a specific date and time; if you're not sure of your timings, booking a "premium" ticket means you can visit at any time within a month of whatever date you choose. Those arriving without reservations can jump the queue by paying extra for a premium ticket on the spot. The whole place reopens in the evening for after-dark audiovisual tours under the title of **Gaudí's Pedrera: the Origins**. Check the website for the schedule of tours in different languages. The admission price always includes a glass of cava; on Friday and Saturday in summer it also includes live jazz; all year it can be combined with dinner at the on-site *Pedrera Café* for a total cost of €59.

Note that the building's grand main entrance on Passeig de Gràcia also provides access to an **exhibition hall** run by the Fundació Caixa de Catalunya, which hosts temporary art shows by major international artists, plus a full programme of children's and family activities, concerts and events. For hours, fees and booking details, see ⓦ fundaciocatalunya-lapedrera.com.

Touring La Pedrera

Visitors to La Pedrera only get to see a small proportion of the building, as most of the apartments are still privately occupied. Entering the complex, you step first into the larger of La Pedrera's two oval interior courtyards, from which a closed-off staircase leads up to the lush first-floor home of the building's original owners. You're directed instead into an elevator that climbs straight up to its crowning glory, the extraordinary **terrat** or roof terrace (which may be closed if it's raining). Those among the bizarre structures up here that most resemble chimneys, albeit crusted with broken tiles and/or shattered champagne bottles, tend in fact to stand atop ventilation shafts, while others mark the top of stairwells; by and large it's what look like clusters of helmeted sentinels or warriors that truly are chimneys. As you stroll around the rooftop, taking in the superb views, you'll notice the arches in two of the larger structures perfectly frame such landmarks as the Sagrada Família.

An excellent exhibition on Gaudí's life and work has been installed beneath the 270 curved brick arches of the **attic** immediately below. All his major Barcelona buildings are covered, in displays that illustrate how he drew his inspiration from natural forms like python skeletons, pumpkins and seashells.

A NIGHT ON THE TILES

Gaudí fans can get closer to the great man's work at two unique venues – and enjoy a night out in the process. At **Nits d'estiu: Jazz a la Pedrera** (see p.201), Gaudí's amazing ceramic-tiled rooftop at La Pedrera is the evening backdrop for a complimentary glass of cava and live jazz. For a meal in glam surroundings, **Casa Calvet** (see p.189) – Gaudí's earliest commissioned townhouse building (1899), erected for a prominent local textile family – is now a fancy restaurant. Although fairly conventional in style, the Baroque inspiration on display in the sculpted facade and church-like lobby was to surface again in his later, more elaborate buildings on Passeig de Gràcia.

The one apartment that is included on the tour itineraries, **El Pis** (simply, "the apartment") on the fourth floor, re-creates the design and style of a *modernista*-era bourgeois apartment in a series of extraordinarily light rooms that flow seamlessly from one to the next. They're filled with period furniture and effects, while the moulded door and window frames, and even the brass door handles, bear witness to Gaudí's ergonomic sense of design.

Casa Ramon Casas

Pg. de Gràcia 96 · Mon–Fri 10am–8.30pm, Sat 10.30am–9pm · ☎ 932 156 050, ⓦ vincon.com · Ⓜ Diagonal

Next to La Pedrera, the **Casa Ramon Casas** (1899) was built as a house and studio for the wealthy Barcelona artist Ramon Casas i Carbó (1866–1932). He had found early success in Paris with friends Santiago Rusiñol and Miquel Utrillo, and the trio were later involved in *Els Quatre Gats* tavern, which Casas largely financed.

The **Vinçon** store was established in the building in 1941, and has since the 1960s been renowned as Spain's pre-eminent purveyor of furniture and design. Its amazing furniture floor gives access to a terrace with views of the interior of La Pedrera, while the **Sala Vinçon** gallery in Casas' original studio (same hours; free admission) puts on excellent shows of graphic and industrial design and contemporary furniture.

Palau Robert

Pg. de Gràcia 107 · Mon–Sat 10am–8pm, Sun & hols 10am–2.30pm · Free · ☎ 932 388 091, ⓦ gencat.cat/palaurobert · Ⓜ Diagonal

Catalunya's regional information centre, inside the **Palau Robert** at the top of Passeig de Gràcia, hosts changing **exhibitions** on all matters Catalan, from art to business. Both the main palace – built as a typical aristocratic residence in 1903 – and its former coach house hold exhibition spaces, while the centre is also an important **concert venue** for recitals and orchestras. The pretty gardens around the back make a popular meeting point for local nannies and their charges.

Palau Baró de Quadras

Av. Diagonal 373 · No public access · Ⓜ Diagonal

Neo-Gothic palace or *modernista* apartment building? How you categorize the beautifully detailed **Palau Baró de Quadras** – a Josep Puig i Cadafalch structure from 1904 that's home to the Institut Ramon Llull, promoting the Catalan language – depends on how you approach it. With intricate carvings, an ornate balcony and mansard roof, the Avinguda Diagonal facade takes a cue from northern European palaces. The building's Carrer del Rosselló side is decorated in a more subdued, but very lovely, *modernista style*.

Casa de les Punxes

Av. Diagonal 416–420 · No public access · Ⓜ Verdaguer

Architect Josep Puig i Cadafalch's largest work, the soaring Casa Terrades, is more usually known as the **Casa de les Punxes** (House of Spikes) because of its red-tiled turrets and steep gables. Built in 1903 for three sisters, and converted from three separate houses spreading around an entire corner of a block, the crenellated structure is almost northern European in style, reminiscent of a Gothic castle.

Esquerra de l'Eixample

The long streets of the Esquerra de l'Eixample, west of Rambla de Catalunya and reaching as far as Barcelona Sants train station, characterize the central Barcelona neighbourhood that's probably least visited by sightseers. With the major architectural highlights found on the Eixample's right-hand side, the Esquerra (left-hand side) was intended by its nineteenth-century planners to hold public buildings, institutions and industrial concerns, many of which still stand. However, it does contain some cultural interest – not least two standout art galleries and an eye-catching public park or two – while the former Arenas bullring has been restyled as a leisure and shopping complex. This is also one of Barcelona's hottest night-out destinations, featuring both Michelin-starred restaurants and some of the city's best bars and clubs, particularly in the gay-friendly streets of the so-called Gaixample district, behind the university.

ESQUERRA DE L'EIXAMPLE

BARS	
Belchica	13
BIERCaB	10
Danzarama	15
Dry Martini	4
Velódromo	2

CLUBS	
Antilla BCN Latin Club	6
Luz de Gas	1
Quilombo	3

LGBT CAFÉS & BARS	
Aire	5
Atame	9
Dietrich	8
People Lounge	12
Punto BCN	7

LGBT CLUBS	
Arena Madre	11
Arena Classic	14
Arena VIP/Arena Dandy	16
Metro	

● CAFÉ	
Fast Vinic	8

● RESTAURANTS	
Cinc Sentits	5
Etapes	6
La Flauta	7
Gresca	3
Igueldo	2

● TAPAS BARS	
Cerveseria Catalana	4
La Taverna del Clínic	1

■ ACCOMMODATION	
Alternative Creative Youth Home	7
Casa de Billy	6
Gran Hotel Torre Catalunya	2
Hotel Axel	3
Hotel Inglaterra	8
Praktik Rambla	5
Room Mate Emma	1
Somnio Barcelona	4

● SHOPS	
Altair	5
Arenas de Barcelona	4
Babelia Books	6
Come In	2
Estanc Duaso	3
Jean-Pierre Bua	1

Universitat de Barcelona

Gran Via de les Corts Catalanes 585, at Pl. de la Universitat · Ⓜ Universitat

Built in the 1860s, the grand Neoclassical main building of the **Universitat de Barcelona** is now largely used for ceremonies and administration purposes, but no one minds if you stroll through the doors. There's usually an exhibition in the echoing main hall, while two fine arcaded courtyards beyond, plus extensive gardens, provide a welcome escape from the traffic.

Fundació Francisco Godia

C/de la Diputació 250 · Mon & Wed–Sat 10am–8pm, Sun 10am–3pm · €6 · Free guided tours Sat & Sun at noon · ☎ 932 723 180, Ⓦ fundacionfgodia.org · Ⓜ Passeig de Gràcia

Sited in a handsomely restored *modernista* mansion, the private art collection of the **Fundació Francisco Godia** spans eight centuries, showcasing an exquisite selection of medieval to modern Catalan art. The pieces were amassed by aesthete and 1950s racing

CONTEMPORARY ARCHITECTURE

It's easy to get sidetracked by the *modernista* architecture of the Eixample, and to forget that Barcelona also boasts plenty of contemporary wonders. Following the death of Franco, there was a feeling among architects that Barcelona had a lot of catching up to do, but subsequently the city has taken centre-stage in the matter of urban design and renewal. Now the world looks to Barcelona for inspiration.

Even during the Franco years, exciting work had taken place, particularly among the Rationalist school of architects working from the 1950s to the 1970s, like **José Antonio Coderch**. From the latter part of this period, too, dates the earliest work by the Catalan architects – among them **Oriol Bohigas**, **Carlos Buxadé**, **Joan Margarit**, **Ricardo Bofill** and **Frederic Correa** – who later transformed the very look and feel of the city. The impetus for change on a substantial level came from hosting the **1992 Olympics**. Nothing less than the redesign of entire city neighbourhoods would do, with decaying industrial areas either swept away or transformed. While Correa, Margarit and Buxadé worked on the refit of the **Estadi Olímpic**, Bofill was in charge of **INEF** (the Sports University) and had a hand in the airport refit. Down at the harbour, Bohigas and others were responsible for creating the visionary **Vila Olímpica** development, carving residential, commercial and leisure facilities out of abandoned industrial spots. New city landmarks appeared, like **Norman Foster's Torre de Collserola** tower at Tibidabo, and the twin towers of the *Hotel Arts* and **Torre Mapfre** at the Port Olímpic.

Attention later turned to other neglected areas, with signature buildings announcing a planned transformation of the local environment. Richard Meier's contemporary art museum, **MACBA**, in the Raval, and Helio Piñon and Alberto Viaplana's **Maremagnum** complex at Port Vell anchored those neighbourhoods' respective revivals. Ricardo Bofill's Greek-temple-style **Teatre Nacional de Catalunya** was an early indicator of change on the eastern side of the city, and several major projects have focussed on the area. Anchored by the eye-catching 142m-high **Torre Agbar**, a giant glowing cigar of a building by Jean Nouvel, the **Plaça de les Glòries Catalanes** is undergoing radical restructuring as a public plaza. Work is well under way on a new transport interchange, and it's also home to the **Disseny Hub**, the sleek, zinc-plated "Stapler" that now holds the city's applied arts collections (see p.121).

At the foot of Avinguda Diagonal, down on the shoreline, the former industrial area of Poble Nou was transformed by the works associated with the Universal Forum of Cultures held in 2004. **Diagonal Mar**, as the area is now known, sits at the heart of a new business and commercial district linking Barcelona with the once-desolate environs of the River Besòs. Meanwhile, on the other side of the city, Richard Rogers has revitalized the city's old bullring, at Plaça d'Espanya, now the **Arenas de Barcelona**, incorporating a domed promenade and viewing platform atop a shopping and leisure centre.

Plans to build the city's second AVE (high-speed train) station at **La Sagrera**, however, seem to have stalled; in theory both the station and Frank Gehry's dramatic 34-storey Torre Sagrera are still under construction, but there's been minimal activity since recession hit in 2010.

8

driver, Francisco "Paco" Godia, an avid art collector in later life, and while not all of the collection can be shown at any one time, a representative selection is always on display – whether it's Romanesque carvings or Gothic art, the *modernista* paintings of Isidre Nonell, Santiago Rusiñol and Ramon Casas among others, or the varied selection of ceramics from most of the historically important production centres in Spain. Special exhibitions run in tandem, for which there's seldom an extra charge, and you can also admire trophies and mementoes from Godia's Formula 1 career on the ground floor.

Museu del Modernisme Català

C/de Balmes 48 • Mon–Sat 10.30am–7pm, Sun & hols (except Mon) 10.30am–2pm • €10, under-16s €5, under-6s free • ☎ 932 722 896, ⓦ mmcat.cat • ⓜ Passeig de Gràcia

Barcelona's traditional "gallery district", around c/Consell de Cent, makes a fitting location for the stupendous *modernista* collection housed in the **Museu del Modernisme Català**. The private enterprise of the celebrated local Gothsland antiques gallery, it displays a collection that was forty years in the making. Craftsman Eusebi Arnau's famous marble decorative vase, which served as the symbol of the Gothsland gallery for over thirty years, is just one of 350 works on show across two exhibition floors in a restored building that was once a textile warehouse.

The ground floor is largely devoted to *modernista* furniture, from screens to sofas, with a Univers Gaudí section that includes sinuous mirrors and tables created by Antoni Gaudí for the casas Batlló and Calvet. Downstairs, the grand vaulted basement holds paintings, sculptures and huge stained-glass panels. Above all, this is a rare opportunity to examine extraordinary Art Nouveau fixtures and fittings by artists with whom you may not be familiar: wonderful creations by pioneering cabinet-maker Joan Busquets i Jané (1874–1949), for example; the dramatic carved mahogany headboards of Gaspar Homar i Mezquida (1870–1955); or the expressive terracotta sculptures of Lambert Escaler i Milà (1874–1957), which include several busts of women floating on seas of swirling hair. As a crash course in the varied facets of Catalan *modernisme*, beyond the iconic buildings themselves, it's invaluable.

Mercat del Ninot and around

C/de Mallorca 133 • Usual hours Mon–Fri 8am–9pm, Sat 8am–3pm • ☎ 933 234 909, ⓦ mercatdelninot.com • ⓜ Hospital Clínic

One of the oldest markets in the city, the colossal **Mercat del Ninot** takes up a large area between carrers Villaroel and Casanova. Built in 1892, it has like many Barcelona markets been undergoing a major refurbishment for several years. It's currently a vast and inaccessible construction site, though a small temporary market is operating on c/Casanova, in front of the massive **Hospital Clínic**.

Escola Industrial

Corner of c/del Comte d'Urgell and c/del Rosselló • ⓜ Hospital Clínic

Around the back of the Hospital Clínic, it's worth having a look at the **Escola Industrial**, which was converted in 1908 from buildings of the former Batlló textile mill. It occupies four entire Eixample blocks, with later academic buildings added in the 1920s, including a chapel by Joan Rubió i Bellvér, who worked with Antoni Gaudí. Students usually fill the courtyards, and you're free to take a stroll through to view the highly decorative buildings.

Museu i Centre d'Estudis de l'Esport

C/de Buenos Aires 56–58 • June to mid-Sept Mon–Fri 8am–3pm; mid-Sept to May Mon–Fri 8am–2pm & 3–5pm • Free • ☎ 934 192 232 • ⓜ Hospital Clínic

Built as a private house in 1911 by Josep Puig i Cadafalch, with the incongruous look of an Alpine inn, the quirky **Museu i Centre d'Estudis de l'Esport** contains probably the most unassuming sporting "Hall of Fame" found anywhere in the world. In a couple of quiet, wood-panelled rooms photographs of 1920s Catalan rally drivers and footballers are displayed alongside a motley collection of memorabilia. Local sporting prowess is traced back as far as 129 AD, when a Barcelona youth won a chariot race at the Olympic Games.

Parc de l'Espanya Industrial

C/de Muntades 37 • Daily 10am–dusk • Free • ⓜ Sants Estació

If you have time to kill at Barcelona Sants station, nip around the south side to Basque architect Luis Peña Ganchegui's urban park, the **Parc de l'Espanya Industrial**. Built on the site of an old textile factory, it has a line of red-and-yellow-striped lighthouses at the top of glaring white steps, with an incongruously classical Neptune in the water below. Altogether, six sculptors are represented here – Andrés Nagel was responsible for the enormous dragon – and, along with the boating lake, café-kiosk, playground and sports facilities provided, the park takes a decent stab at reconciling local interests with the mundane nature of the surroundings.

Parc Joan Miró

C/de Tarragona 74 • Daily 10am–dusk • Free • ⓜ Tarragona

Laid out on the site of Barcelona's nineteenth-century municipal slaughterhouse, **Parc Joan Miró** features a raised piazza whose only feature is Joan Miró's gigantic mosaic sculpture **Dona i Ocell** ("Woman and Bird"), towering above a shallow reflecting pool. It's a familiar symbol if you've studied Miró's other works, but the sculpture is known locally by several other names – all of them easy to guess when you consider its erect, helmeted shape. The rear of the park is given over to games areas and landscaped sections of palms and firs, with a kiosk café and some outdoor tables found in among the trees. The children's playground here is among the best in the city, with a climbing frame and aerial runway as well as swings and slides.

8

Arenas de Barcelona

Gran Via de les Corts Catalanes 373–385, at Pl. d'Espanya • Daily 10am–10pm • ☎ 932 890 244, ⓦ arenasdebarcelona.com • ⓜ Espanya

The landmark building on the north side of Plaça d'Espanya is the fabulous Moorish-style bullring, the **Arenas de Barcelona**, originally built in 1900 but reopened as a swish shopping and leisure centre in 2011. Conceived by architect **Richard Rogers** as a gateway to the city centre, and preserving the beautiful brick exterior, the various retail levels at Arenas are hung in sweeping circular galleries, while right on top, outside, a wide walk-around promenade circles the **dome** that offers 360-degree views of the western side of the city. An express elevator whisks you up here from street level, or you can take the glass lifts or escalators inside, through four floors of shopping and entertainment that include a cinema, gym and health centre, and several restaurants, some of which are on the top-floor promenade.

Casa de la Papallona

C/de Llança 20 • No public access • ⓜ Espanya

It's worth walking around the Arenas de Barcelona and craning your neck up to the top of the six-storey Casa Fajol, universally known as the **Casa de la Papallona** (1912). The work of architect Josep Graner i Prat (1844–1930), it's crowned by a huge ceramic butterfly (*papallona*) made using the favoured *modernista* technique of *trencadís*, or broken coloured tiles formed to make a picture.

HOSPITAL DE LA SANTA CREU I DE SANT PAU

Sagrada Família and Glòries

Many visitors simply make the necessary pilgrimage by metro to see Antoni Gaudí's great church of the Sagrada Família, out in the eastern reaches of the Eixample, and then head straight back into the centre. While you're here, though, it's well worth checking out the lesser-known *modernista*-era buildings nearby, and above all the enchanting pavilions of the Hospital de la Santa Creu i de Sant Pau. A few blocks south, the area known as Glòries is home to the city's main concert hall, music and design museums, and the flagship national theatre building. Glòries was originally conceived as the nucleus of the nineteenth-century city expansion plan. That never materialized, but the neighbourhood is destined for dramatic redevelopment, as the city council breathes new life into its peripheral urban areas.

Sagrada Família

C/de Mallorca 401 • Daily: March & Oct 9am–7pm; April–Sept 9am–8pm; Nov–Feb 9am–6pm • €15, under-10s free; guided tour, audioguide and tower ascent each €4.50 extra • 50min guided tours in English (no advance purchase) April–Oct daily 11.15am, 12.30pm, 1.45pm & 3pm; Nov–March Mon–Fri 10.15am, 12.15pm & 3pm, Sat & Sun 11.15am, 12.30pm, 1.45pm & 3pm • ☎ 935 132 060, ⓦ sagradafamilia.cat • Ⓜ Sagrada Família

Nothing – really, nothing – can prepare you for the sheer visceral impact of seeing the **Basilica de la Sagrada Família** for the first time. As work on Gaudí's masterpiece races towards completion, and its extraordinary towers climb ever closer towards the heavens, the glorious, overpowering church of the "Sacred Family" is now more than ever a symbol for the city, speaking volumes about the Catalan urge to embrace uniqueness and endeavour. By no coincidence, the most fantastic expression of the architectural creativity in which Barcelona excels was one of the few churches left

ANTONI GAUDÍ AND THE SAGRADA FAMÍLIA

Begun in 1882 by public subscription, the **Sagrada Família** was originally intended by its progenitor, the Catalan publisher Josep Bocabella, to be an expiatory building that would atone for the increasingly revolutionary ideas then at large in Barcelona. Bocabella appointed the architect Francesc de Paula Villar to the work, and his plan was for a modest church in an orthodox neo-Gothic style. Two years later, however, after arguments between the two men, the 31-year-old **Antoni Gaudí** took over as Architect Director. He changed the direction and scale of the project almost immediately, seeing in the Sagrada Família an opportunity to reflect his own deepening spiritual and nationalist feelings.

Initial work on the church was slow. It took four years to finish the crypt (1901), and the first full plan of the building was only published in 1917. Gaudí himself vowed after finishing Park Güell in 1911 that he'd never work on secular projects again, and he devoted the rest of his life to the Sagrada Família. While his church design displayed apparently lunatic flights of fantasy, it was always rooted in functionality and strict attention to detail. He eventually moved to live in a small studio on site, and carried on adapting the plans ceaselessly right up until his untimely death.

Antoni Gaudí was run over by a tram on the Gran Via on June 7, 1926. Initially unrecognized, as he had become a virtual recluse, he died in hospital three days later. His death was treated as a Catalan national disaster, and all of Barcelona turned out for his funeral procession. Following papal dispensation, he was buried in the Sagrada Família crypt, a fitting resting place for an architect whose masterpiece was designed (he said) to show "the religious realities of present and future life…man's origin, his end". Everything from the Creation to Heaven and Hell, in short, was included in his one magnificent sacred ensemble.

Only one facade of the church was then complete, and work stalled on the Sagrada Família with the coming of the Civil War. Most of Gaudí's plans and models were destroyed amid the turmoil – indeed George Orwell called the Sagrada Família "one of the most hideous buildings in the world", and described the anarchists as showing "bad taste in not blowing it up when they had the chance".

Construction finally restarted, amid great controversy, during the 1950s, and has continued ever since. Some critics argued that the Sagrada Família should be left incomplete as a memorial to Gaudí, though the architect himself always saw the project as requiring centuries. Financed by private funding and ticket sales, rather than government or church, the work has long been overseen by chief architect **Jordi Bonet**, the son of one of Gaudí's assistants. While Gaudí's own plans have been followed wherever possible, both Bonet and sculptor **Josep María Subirachs** (1927–2014), who worked for decades on the Passion facade, have been accused of infringing his original spirit.

Computer-aided design and high-tech construction techniques have so greatly speeded up the processes involved, however, that the debate is effectively over. Even if the builders fail to meet their current target, of finishing the church to mark the centenary of Gaudí's death in 2026 – an anniversary that some hope may also be marked by Gaudí's elevation to nothing less than official sainthood – no doubt now remains that the Sagrada Família will indeed be completed in the near future.

9

untouched during the 1909 "Tragic Week" church-burnings and the 1936 revolution, and even the coldest hearts continue to find the Sagrada Família inspirational in both form and spirit.

The Sagrada Família passed perhaps the most crucial milestone in its history in 2010, when, with the nave finally roofed over, it was consecrated as a **basilica** by Pope Benedict. Contrary to popular belief, it's not, and was never intended to be, a cathedral; that word only applies to the seat of a bishop. It is, however, now a fully functioning church, complete with altar, pews, organ, stained-glass windows and regular Masses. That doesn't mean it's always a peaceful place to visit, though – it's also a **building site**, with all the cacophony of cranes, drills, and general clatter that suggests.

Work is progressing so fast that it's impossible to predict exactly how the building may look when you visit. At the time of writing, out of its planned eighteen spires, only the smallest eight had been completed, in the form of four "Apostles" grouped on each of the Nativity and Passion facades. That leaves four Apostles still to build on the Glory facade; four Evangelists; and one spire each for the Virgin Mary and Jesus Christ. Surmounted by a giant cross, the central Jesus Christ will be the tallest of all, at 170m, thereby making the Sagrada Família the tallest building in Barcelona, and the tallest church in the world.

Visiting the Basilica

All tickets to enter the Sagrada Família are for a specific date and time. Buy yours online as far in advance as possible; in summer, you've very little chance of simply turning up and being able to get in. And if you want to go up one of the towers, book that as well – numbers are even more restricted, and even when tickets to the church itself are available at the gate, you may have to wait several hours for the next available slot for the towers.

Aim to visit as early in the day as possible, to beat the crowds. If you're lucky, you may coincide with an English-language tour. Failing that, you can get substantially the same information on the audioguides. Whether you visit with a guide or by yourself, you'll start by circling the outside of the church. The eastern **Nativity facade**, facing c/de la Marina, was the first to be completed and is alive with fecund detail, its very columns resting on the backs of giant tortoises. Contrast this with the Cubist austerity of Subirachs' work on the western **Passion facade** (c/de Sardenya), where the brutal story of the Crucifixion is played out across the harsh mountain stone.

The interior of the Basilica is an immense space that's every bit as "luminous" as Gaudí hoped. Gaudí envisaged it as essentially a forest, filled with the light that streams through its stained glass windows, with its columns as the trees that bear the weight of the structure down to the foundations.

Separate elevators climb the **towers** on the Passion and Nativity facades. As well as a close-up look at the spires themselves, which have been likened to everything from perforated cigars to celestial billiard cues, you'll be rewarded by partial views of the city through an extraordinary jumble of latticed stonework, ceramic decoration, carved buttresses and sculpture.

The museum

Tickets to the Sagrada Família also offer access to the excellent **museum** that extends through most of its lower level, and trace Gaudí's career, with models and diagrams to explain the construction and symbolism of the church. Some of Gaudí's own original drawings are displayed in dim light, as well as photos of him escorting various dignitaries around the site, and of his funeral. You can also peer down at his actual tomb in the crypt, and watch sculptors and model-makers at work in the plaster workshop.

INTERIOR, SAGRADA FAMÍLIA >

9 # Hospital de la Santa Creu i de Sant Pau

C/de Sant Antoni María Claret 167, at c/de la Independència • April–Oct Mon–Sat 10am–6.30pm, Sun 10am–2.30pm; Nov–March Mon–Sat 10am–4.30pm, Sun 10am–2.30pm; English-language tours daily all year noon & 1pm • Self-guided €8, guided €14; under-16s free; free self-guided tours for everyone on first Sun of month • ☎ 932 682 444, ⓦ santpaubarcelona.org • ⓜ Hospital de Sant Pau

Lluís Domènech i Montaner's *modernista* public hospital, the **Hospital de la Santa Creu i de Sant Pau**, is possibly the one piece of architecture in town that can rival the Sagrada Família for size and invention. A fairy-tale precinct of dazzling Art Nouveau imagination, it has its own metro stop, but it's much better to approach by walking up the four-block Avinguda de Gaudí from the church, which gives terrific views back over the spires of the Sagrada Família.

Domènech i Montaner started work on the project in 1902, with the brief of replacing the medieval Santa Creu hospital in the Raval. He created an astonishing complex of whimsical pavilions, topped by golden-tiled domes, festooned with turrets and towers, and covered with sculpture, mosaics, stained glass and ironwork. They're set just far enough apart not to overshadow each other, in what was originally a botanic garden and is now a single paved precinct that remains replete with orange trees.

The hospital finally closed in 2009, with its patients moving to an adjoining new hospital, and the building reopened for tours in 2014. Of the 48 pavilions that Domènech i Montaner originally envisaged, 23 were completed; twelve now constitute a World Heritage Site, and six of those have reopened to visitors following a €100 million restoration programme. While the whole place is quite stunning in scale and exterior decoration, they're essentially empty shells. The pick of the bunch is what was the main administration building, which has an ornate Gothic-style chapel upstairs, kitted out with Art Nouveau tiles and floral mosaics, and is also used for conferences and concerts.

Palau Macaya

Pg. de Sant Joan 108 • Courtyard access only • Mon–Fri 10am–2pm & 4–8pm • Free • ☎ 934 579 531, ⓦ obrasocial.lacaixa.es • ⓜ Verdaguer

Josep Puig i Cadafalch's palatial **Palau Macaya**, four blocks west of the Sagrada Família, dates from 1898–1900. It's a superbly ornamental building with an attractive Gothic-inspired courtyard and canopied staircase from which griffins spring. Pause as you pass by to view the unusual exterior carvings by *modernista* craftsman **Eusebi Arnau i Mascort**, including the angel with a "box" Brownie camera and the sculptor himself cycling to work, or drop in to see the free exhibition run by the Fundació La Caixa, on Puig i Cadafalch and *modernisme*.

Casa Planells

Av. Diagonal 332 • No public access • ⓜ Monumental

Built in 1923–24, the **Casa Planells** apartment block – a sinuous solution to an acute-corner building – simplifies many of the themes that Gaudí exaggerated in his work. It's actually by **Josep María Jujol i Gilbert**, who was one of Gaudí's early collaborators, responsible not only for La Pedrera's iconic undulating balconies but also much of the famous mosaic work in Park Güell.

Plaça de les Glòries Catalanes

ⓜ Glòries

All Barcelona's major avenues meet at the **Plaça de les Glòries Catalanes**, a glorified roundabout that's dedicated to the "Catalan glories", from architecture to literature. This is the focal point of the city's latest bout of regeneration, with plans to tunnel the traffic underground, and to open up a grand pedestrianized park centring on the new **Museu del Dissney**.

MODERNISME'S CRAFTY COLLABORATORS

Despite the overwhelming noise of the big-gun architects of the time, modernisme was often a true collaborative effort between the architects and their craftsmen and artisans. Lluís Domènech i Montaner, in particular, recognized the importance of ensemble working, and established a pioneering craft workshop in the building he designed initially as a restaurant for Barcelona's Universal Exhibition of 1888 (known as the Castell dels Tres Dragons). Antoni Gaudí, too, always worked with skilled craftsmen, including his longtime collaborator – and a master of mosaic decoration – **Josep María Jujol i Gilbert** (1879–1949).

Another significant figure, **Eusebi Arnau i Mascort** (1864–1933), provided meticulous carvings for all the main *modernista* architects – much loved are his quirky figures adorning Josep Puig i Cadafalch's Casa Macaya and the tour-de-force carved fireplace in the Raval's *Hotel Espanya*.

Some projects brought together the cream of craft talent. Thus the glorious stained glass by Antoni Rigalt and elaborate facade sculpture by Miquel Blay form an integral part of Domènech i Montaner's Palau de la Música Catalana. Meanwhile, the stunning private houses being built across Barcelona for wealthy captains of industry looked as good on the inside as they did on the outside, filled with furniture by *modernista* craftsmen like cabinet-maker extraordinaire **Joan Busquets i Jané** (1874–1949) and artist and interior designer **Gaspar Homar i Mezquida** (1870–1955).

Glòries is already positioned as a gateway to the Diagonal Mar district, with **trams** running there down Avinguda Diagonal. Meanwhile, the roundabout also holds French architect **Jean Nouvel**'s cigar-shaped **Torre Agbar** (142m), the headquarters of the local water company (Aigües de Barcelona). A highly distinctive aluminium-and-glass tower with no fewer than four thousand windows, its shape was inspired by the rocky protuberances of Montserrat.

A huge shopping mall lies across the Diagonal from here, while further across the Gran Via the park and play areas of **Parc del Clot** show what can be done in an urban setting within the remains of a razed factory site. Jean Nouvel also designed the **Parc del Centre del Poble Nou** further down the Diagonal (10min walk from Glòries or tram stop Pere IV), an eye-catching contemporary park set on another former industrial site – a surviving brick chimney stands in the centre, surrounded by willow trees.

Museu del Disseny

Pl. de les Glòries Catalanes 37–38 • **Museu del Disseny** Tues–Sun 10am–8pm **Hub** Mon 4–8.30pm, Tues–Sun 10am–8.30pm • Museum €5, under-16s free, entrance to Hub free; free for everyone Sun 3–8pm & all day on first Sun of month • ☎ 932 566 800, Ⓦ museudeldisseny.cat • Ⓜ Glòries

Barcelona's showpiece **Museu del Disseny** (Design Museum) gathers what used to be the separate collections of the city's decorative arts, ceramics, textile and clothing, and graphic arts museums into a single, stunning new building, the **Disseny Hub**. Nicknamed La Grapadora ("The Stapler") after its shape, the building consists of two parts: a narrow, zinc-plated above-ground section whose topmost floors cantilever over the motorway; and a wide, semi-subterranean base that houses temporary exhibitions, a library, a cafeteria and the headquarters of local design institutions.

As for the exhibits, it's effectively several distinct museums in one. Of the four upper floors, the first most closely corresponds to what you might expect of a design museum, displaying everyday objects, largely of Catalan origin, that range from chairs, tables and bicycles to toilets and, yes, staplers. The second floor holds a rather random but unarguably beautiful assortment of decorative arts from the third century onwards, starting with Coptic textiles from Egypt and winding up with ceramic works by Picasso and Miró. Next comes a floor devoted to fashion, illustrating how clothing has alternately emphasized and hidden various body shapes over the past five centuries, while the top floor traces the history of graphic design in Barcelona.

9

TREASURE-HUNTING AT ELS ENCANTS VELLS

A trove of dusty delights, the city's flea market, **El Encants Vells**, has a shiny new home, adjacent to the Teatre Nacional de Catalunya at Av. Meridiana 69 (Mon, Wed, Fri & Sat 9am–8pm, plus public auctions Mon, Wed & Fri 8–9.30am; ⓦ encantsbcn.com; ⓜ Glòries). Several levels of open-air treasure-hunting action here are protected by a large reflective canopy.

While it's definitely modern looking, the new incarnation hasn't lost its street-bazaar vibe. You name it, you can buy it: old sewing machines, cheese graters, photograph albums, cutlery, lawnmowers, clothes, shoes, CDs, antiques, furniture and out-and-out junk. It's best in the early morning, and haggling for any "old charms" (*encants vells*) you might fancy is de rigueur, but you're up against experts.

Teatre Nacional de Catalunya

Pl. de les Arts 1 • Tues & Thurs tours on the hour 10am–1pm; €5; reservations required • ☎ 933 065 747, ⓦ tnc.cat • ⓜ Glòries or tram T4

Designed by local architect Ricardo Bofill and inaugurated in 1997, the **Teatre Nacional de Catalunya** – Catalunya's national theatre – is a soaring glass box, encased within a Greek temple on a raised dais, to the southwest of Glòries. You can book to go on guided building and backstage **tours**, while its bar and restaurant are open in the evening – a summer evening's drink on the open-air *terrassa* is a nice way to take in the grandiose surroundings.

L'Auditori and the Museu de la Música

L'Auditori c/de Lepant 150 • ⓦ auditori.cat **Museu de la Música** c/de Padilla 155 • Tues–Sat 10am–6pm, Sun 10am–8pm • €5, under-16s free; free for everyone Sun 3–8pm & all day on first Sun of month • ☎ 932 563 650, ⓦ www.museumusica.bcn.cat • ⓜ Glòries/Marina

Forming a sort of cultural enclave with the national theatre, one block over, **L'Auditori** is the city's contemporary concert hall, built in 1999. Housed within it, the **Museu de la Música** displays a remarkable collection of instruments and musical devices, from serpentine seventeenth-century horns to reel-to-reel cassette decks. It's all very impressive, with soaring glass-walled cases letting you view the pieces from all sides, and yet it struggles to engage, partly because of the sheer number and variety of instruments and partly because of the impenetrable commentary, with sections called things like "The humanist spirit and the predominance of polyphony". Still, there's a bit of big-screen Elvis here and African drumming there, and if you've ever wanted to pluck at a harp without anyone shouting at you, this is the place.

PARC DEL LABERINT

Gràcia, Park Güell and Horta

Gràcia – the closest neighbourhood to the Eixample – had long remained a village before it was finally annexed as a city suburb in the late nineteenth century. It still retains a genuine small-town atmosphere, distinct from the old-town neighbourhoods, while its vibrant cultural scene and nightlife counters the notion that Barcelona begins and ends on the Ramblas. The one unmissable attraction lies on the slopes on the neighbourhood's northern flank – the surreal Park Güell, created by architectural genius Antoni Gaudí. Meanwhile, nearby Horta ("garden"), so called after the gardens and country estates that once characterized the area, holds two further distinctive parks – Creueta del Coll, a prime example of the new urban projects that have revitalized forgotten corners of the city, and the eighteenth-century Parc del Laberint, where a renowned maze speaks of a very different era.

Gràcia

Still very much the liberal, almost bohemian, stronghold it was in the nineteenth century, the northern neighbourhood of **Gràcia** feels set apart from the city in many ways. Its traditional annual summer festival, the **Festa Major** every August – a week's worth of concerts, parades, fireworks and parties – has no peer in any other neighbourhood, and although actual sights in Gràcia are few and far between, it's well known for its cinemas, bars and restaurants. Wander the narrow, gridded streets, park yourself on a bench under a plane tree, catch a film, grab a beer or otherwise take time out from the rigours of city-centre life – you'll soon get the feel of a neighbourhood that, unlike some in Barcelona, has a genuine soul.

10

ARRIVAL AND DEPARTURE
GRÀCIA

By bus Buses #22 or #24 from Pl. de Catalunya run to Gràcia, stopping on the main c/Gran de Gràcia.

By metro and train The most convenient metro stations are Ⓜ Diagonal (south), Ⓜ Fontana (north) or Ⓜ Joanic (east), or

take the FGC train from Pl. de Catalunya to Gràcia station.

On foot Gràcia is a 30min walk from Pl. de Catalunya. From any of the neighbourhood stations, it's around a 500m walk to Gràcia's central squares.

Mercat de la Llibertat

Pl. Llibertat 27 • Mon–Fri 8.30am–8.30pm, Sat 8.30am–3pm • ☎ 932 170 995, ⊛ www.mercatsbcn.com • Ⓜ Fontana or FGC Gràcia

It's only logical to start a visit to Gràcia where the locals start, first thing in the morning – shopping for bread and provisions in the **Mercat de la Llibertat**, a block west of c/Gran de Gràcia. The building was first revamped in 1893 by a former pupil of Gaudí, **Francesc Berenguer i Mestrès**, who sheltered its food stalls under a *modernista* wrought-iron roof. It's since been beautifully restored again and is always worth a walk through, especially if you fancy the breakfast of champions – oysters, grilled razor clams and a glass of cava – available from one of the classy stand-up café counters.

10

Casa Vicens

C/les Carolines 24 • No public access • Ⓜ Fontana

Antoni Gaudí's first major private commission, the **Casa Vicens** (1883–85), is on the northern edge of Gràcia. Here he took inspiration from the Moorish style, covering the facade in linear green-and-white tiles with a flower motif. The decorative iron railings are a reminder of Gaudí's early training as a metalsmith and, to further prove his versatility – and how Art Nouveau cuts across art forms – Gaudí also designed much of the mansion's furniture. For the moment, you can't get in to see it, though it was bought in 2014 by new owners who promised to open it to the public at some point in future.

10

THE THREE SQUARES BAR CRAWL

Three squares tucked away in the middle of Gràcia (⑩ Fontana/Diagonal), within a few blocks' walk of each other, contain many of the best neighbourhood cafés and bars. A night out in Gràcia invariably means passing through them at some point. Traditionally, **Plaça del Sol** has been the beating heart of the district's nightlife, though it was redesigned rather soullessly in the 1980s and is not quite so appealing during the day. Far more in keeping with Gràcia's overall village-like tenor is the mouthful that is **Plaça de la Revolució de Setembre de 1886**, just to the east of Plaça del Sol, and especially **Plaça Vila de Gràcia**, to the south across Travessera de Gràcia. The 30m-high clocktower in the latter (known as **Plaça Rius i Taulet** until 2008) was a rallying point for nineteenth-century radicals, whose twenty-first-century counterparts prefer to meet for brunch at the popular café *terrassas*.

Plaça de la Virreina
⑩ Fontana

Pretty **Plaça de la Virreina**, backed by the parish church of Sant Joan, is one of Gràcia's favourite squares, with the *Virreina* bar and others providing drinks and a place to rest and admire the handsome houses, most notably **Casa Rubinat** (1909), c/de l'Or 44, the last major work of Francesc Berenguer. Children and dogs, meanwhile, scamper around the small drinking fountain. Nearby streets, particularly **Carrer de Verdi**, contain many of the neighbourhood's most fashionable boutiques, galleries, cinemas and cafés.

Park Güell

Antoni Gaudí's extraordinary urban park on the hillside above Gràcia, **Park Güell** was his most ambitious project apart from the Sagrada Família. Commissioned by Eusebi Güell (patron of Gaudí's Palau Güell, off the Ramblas), it was originally planned as a private housing estate of sixty dwellings, furnished with ornamental paths, recreational areas and decorative monuments. The idea was to build a "Garden City" of the type popular at the time in England – that's why the official name follows Gaudí in using the English spelling of "Park". Gaudí worked on the project from 1900 until 1914, but in the end only two houses were actually built, and the park was officially opened to the public instead in 1922.

Park Güell ranks among the city's most popular tourist attractions, receiving millions of visitors each year. As a result, you now have to pay for access to the area that holds its most iconic sites, the **Zona Monumental**. A maximum of 400 visitors are allowed in every half-hour, and each ticket is only valid for a specific half-hour time-slot (once inside, you can stay as long as you like). Tickets can be reserved online up to three months in advance. You can also buy them at ticket offices or ATMs in the park itself – in summer, check the website to see whether they're still available for the day you plan to visit – but you may have to wait for the next available time-slot.

Access to the rest of the park remains free. The wooded, landscaped gardens make a nice spot for a picnic, but other than to enjoy the sweeping city views from the very highest point – the **Turó de les Tres Creus**, where three stone crosses atop a stepped tumulus mark the spot where Gaudí had planned to place a chapel – it's unlikely to hold your interest for long. There's a large outdoor **café** immediately above the Zona Monumental, but it's usually filled with visitors killing time before they're allowed to go in.

ARRIVAL AND DEPARTURE   PARK GÜELL

As the park straddles a steep hill, all approaches involve an ascent on foot to reach the main entrance on c/d'Olot. Leaving the park, you'll have to walk back down c/de Larrard to Travessera de Dalt for bus or metro connections back to the city, though taxis do hang about the gates on c/d'Olot.

By bus Bus #24 from Pl. de Catalunya, Pg. de Gràcia or c/Gran de Gràcia, drops passengers on Carretera del Carmel at the eastern side of the park. The Bus Turístic stops at the foot of c/de Larrard.

By metro Marginally the closest station to the Zona Monumental is ⓜ Lesseps in Gràcia; the 15min walk from there heads right along Travessera de Dalt and then left up steep c/de Larrard. Alternatively, get off at ⓜ Vallcarca and walk a few hundred metres down Av. de Vallcarca, to find mechanical escalators on your left that ascend Bxda. de la Glória to the park's western entrance, from where footpaths lead back down to the Zona Monumental.

Zona Monumental

Daily: April, Sept & Oct 8am–8pm; May–Aug 8am–9.30pm; Nov–March 8.30am–6.15pm • €7 online, €8 on site, under-7s free • ☎ 902 200 302, ⓦ parkguell.cat

Spreading across the slopes, looking down across the city to the Mediterranean, the core of Park Güell, sealed off as the **Zona Monumental**, is an almost hallucinatory swirl of ideas and excesses. You can use your timed ticket to enter at any of three points, but it makes sense to approach it via the original main entrance, on c/d'Olot. The porter's lodge to the right hosts an informative exhibit that places the park in the context of its times, but there's usually a long queue to get into its restricted spaces; the corresponding lodge to the left now serves as a gift shop.

Straight ahead, a monumental stairway climbs past a giant mosaic salamander known as **el drac** (the dragon) to reach the vast **Hall of Columns**, where 84 Doric columns soar at disconcertingly irregular angles to enclose a space that Gaudí intended to be the estate's market. Art critic Sacheverell Sitwell (in *Spain*) described it as "at once a fun fair, a petrified forest, and the great temple of Amun at Karnak, itself drunk, and reeling in an eccentric earthquake".

10

Perhaps the most famous element of the park is the long, meandering **ceramic bench** that snakes along the edge of the terrace that forms the roof of the Hall of Columns. Entirely covered with a brightly coloured, broken tile-and-glass mosaic (a method known as *trencadís*), it forms a dizzying sequence of abstract motifs, symbols, words and pictures.

Casa Museu Gaudí

Park Güell, outside Zona Monumental • Daily: April & May 10am–8pm; June–Sept 9am–8pm; Oct–March 10am–6pm • €5.50, combined ticket with Sagrada Família €18.50 • ☎ 932 193 811, ⓦ casamuseugaudi.org

One of Gaudí's collaborators, Francesc Berenguer, designed and built a turreted house for the architect, which is now known as the **Casa Museu Gaudí**, and stands immediately east of the Zona Monumental. Gaudí was persuaded to live here from 1906 until 1925, when he left to camp out at the Sagrada Família for good. The downstairs rooms celebrate his work as a designer, via a diverting collection of furniture he created for other projects – a typical mixture of wild originality and brilliant engineering – while upstairs his ascetic study and bedroom have been kept much as he knew them. Religious texts and images offer some inkling of his personality, and various plans and objects explain more about the park.

Parc de la Creueta del Coll

Pg. de la Mare de Deu del Coll 77 • Daily 10am–dusk • Free • Bus #28 from Pl. de Catalunya, via Pg. de Gràcia, stops 100m from the park, or ⓜ El Coll/La Teixonera

There could be no greater contrast with Park Güell than Horta's **Parc de la Creueta del Coll**, a contemporary urban park that was laid out by Olympic architects Martorell and Mackay on the site of an old quarry. You're greeted at the top of the park steps by an Ellsworth Kelly metal spike, while suspended by steel cables over a reflecting pool is a massive 50-tonne concrete claw, "In Praise of Water", by the Basque artist Eduardo Chillida. There's a stand of palm trees by a small artificial lake, which becomes a summer swimming pool, and concrete promenades and picnic areas under the sheer quarry walls.

Combining the park with a visit to Park Güell is easy, too, though you'll need a keen sense of direction to find it from the rear exit of Park Güell – it helps if you've climbed Güell's three-crosses hill and fixed in mind the quarry walls, which you can see across the valley. It's far easier to visit Parc de la Creueta del Coll first, then walk back down the main Passeig de la Mare de Deu del Coll until you see the signpost pointing down c/Balears (on your left) – from there, signposts guide you into Park Güell the back way.

Parc del Laberint

Pg. dels Castanyers 1–17 • Daily 10am–dusk • €2.17; free Wed & Sun • ⓜ Mundet: use the Pg. Vall d'Hebron (Muntanya) exit, walk up the main road and against the traffic flow for 1min (past the sports pitches) and turn left into the grounds of the Velòdrom (cycle stadium)

Half a dozen metro stops beyond Gràcia, and confronted by the roaring traffic on the Passeig Vall d'Hebron, it seems inconceivable that there's any kind of sanctuary to hand. Just a couple of minutes' walk from Mundet metro, however, puts you at the gates of the **Parc del Laberint**, sited behind the cycle stadium. The former estate mansion is used by the city's parks and gardens department, while the late eighteenth-century gardens (the oldest in the city) are open for visits and make an enchanting spectacle. A series of shady paths, terraces, pavilions and water features embrace the hillside, merging with the pine forest beyond.

The topiary **maze** at the very heart of the park, **El Laberint**, was created for the Marquis de Llupià i Alfarràs in 1792 and designed as an Enlightenment puzzle concerning the forms of love. A statue of Eros serves as the reward for reaching the centre. Near the park entrance are a drinks kiosk, picnic area and children's playground.

Les Corts, Pedralbes and Sarrià-Sant Gervasi

Northwest of Barcelona city centre, what was once the village of Les Corts is now largely indistinguishable from the rest of the modern city, save for the hallowed precincts of Camp Nou, FC Barcelona's stupendous football stadium. Nearby, across Avinguda Diagonal, the Palau de Pedralbes is home to serene public gardens, while a half-day's excursion can be made by walking from the palace, past the Pavellons Güell and Gaudí's dragon gate, up to the calm cloisters of the Gothic monastery of Pedralbes. Complete the day by returning via Sarrià, to the east, with a pretty main street and market to explore. At night the focus shifts to the bars and restaurants of neighbouring Sant Gervasi, in the streets north of Plaça de Francesc Macià.

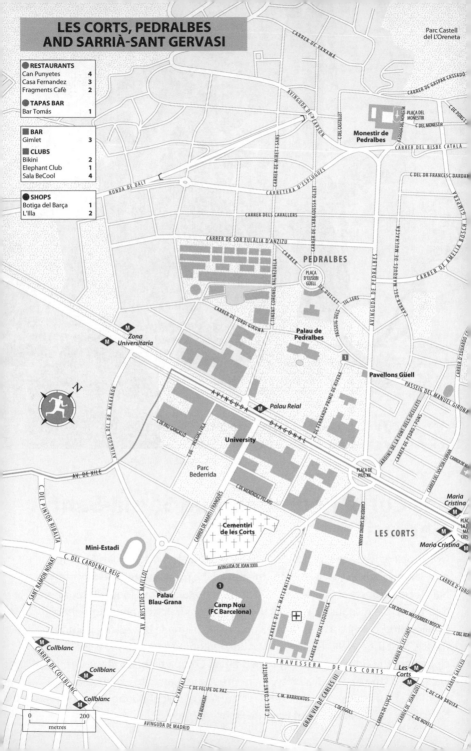

LES CORTS, PEDRALBES AND SARRIÀ-SANT GERVASI

RESTAURANTS
Can Punyetes   **4**
Casa Fernandez   **3**
Fragments Cafè   **2**

TAPAS BAR
Bar Tomás   **1**

BAR
Gimlet   **3**

CLUBS
Bikini   **2**
Elephant Club   **1**
Sala BeCool   **4**

SHOPS
Botiga del Barça   **1**
L'Illa   **2**

Uptown Avinguda Diagonal

Ⓜ María Cristina or tram T1, T2 or T3 from Pl. de Francesc Macià

The uptown section of **Avinguda Diagonal** runs through the heart of Barcelona's flashiest business and shopping district. The giant **L'Illa** shopping centre flanks the avenue – its stepped design is a prone echo of New York's Rockefeller Center. Designer fashion stores are ubiquitous, particularly around **Plaça de Francesc Macià** and Avinguda de Pau Casals – at the top of the latter, **Turó Parc** (daily 8am–dusk) makes a good place to rest weary feet, with a small children's playground and a café-kiosk. For picnic supplies, the traditional neighbourhood market, **Mercat de Galvany** (c/de Santaló 65; Mon–Thurs 7am–2pm, Fri & Sat 7am–2.30pm; Ⓦmercatgalvany.es), is just three blocks to the east. Meanwhile, behind L'Illa, it's worth seeking out **Plaça de la Concordia**, another surprising survivor from the past amid the uptown tower blocks. The pretty little square is dominated by its church belltower and ringed by local businesses (florist, pharmacy, hairdresser). Have a quiet drink at one of the outdoor cafés or head to *Fragments Cafè* (see p.193) for excellent bistro-style food.

11

Camp Nou and FC Barcelona

Av. Aristides Maillol • Ⓦ fcbarcelona.com • Ⓜ Collblanc/Palau Reial, then a 10min walk, or Bus Turístic stops outside the stadium

Football in Barcelona being a genuine obsession, support for the local giants **FC (Futbol Club) Barcelona** has been raised to an art form. *Més que un club* ("More than just a club") is the proud boast, and certainly during the dictatorship years the club stood as a symbol around which Catalans could rally. Arch-rivals Real Madrid, on the other hand, were always seen as Franco's club. In recent years, culminating in Barcelona's fifth coronation as European champions in 2015, the swashbuckling players in the famous "blaugrana" (claret and blue) shirts have won hearts worldwide with their elegant *tiki-taka*, pass-and-move style, to become every football fan's second favourite team.

There's no more invigorating introduction to Catalan passions than to take in a match at the magnificent **Camp Nou** ("New Ground") stadium, sited in the Les Corts neighbourhood, behind the university buildings. Europe's largest stadium was built in 1957, enlarged for the 1982 World Cup semifinal to accommodate 98,000 people, and is

---

IT'S ONLY A GAME?

Some people believe football is a matter of life or death… I can assure you it is much, much more important than that.
Bill Shankly

No Catalan football supporter would disagree with Liverpool legend and quip-meister Bill Shankly. These are fans who boo their own team if they think the performance isn't up to scratch, thousands of white handkerchiefs waving along in disapproval. A disappointing season is seen as a slur on the Catalan nation, and if success goes instead to bitter rivals Real Madrid, then the pain is almost too much to bear. When team figurehead and captain **Luís Figo** was transferred to Madrid in 2000 (one of only a handful to have played for both clubs), the outrage was almost comical in its ferocity – at a later match between the two sides, a pig's head was thrown onto the pitch as Figo prepared to take a corner. In recent years, though, there has been a lot more cheering than booing, as the team has played with a swagger rarely seen in modern club football. Under their former coach **Josep "Pep" Guardiola** – one-time Barça player and all-Catalan hero – Barcelona evolved into a team of scintillating beauty, not only running rings around rivals from home and abroad, but also providing the bulk of the side that won the World Cup for Spain for the first time in 2010. The Barcelona style – don't give the ball away, ever, period – is learned at **La Masia**, the club's own training centre and school for young footballers, most of whom are Catalan or come at an early age from elsewhere. Half the current team are graduates, including the peerless, best-in-the-world, Lionel Messi. Things change quickly in football, but the production line at La Masia is the best guarantee that boos and white hankies will be absent from the Camp Nou for a while longer yet.

about to undergo a face-lift, scheduled for completion in 2021, that will increase its capacity to around 105,000. Camp Nou provides one of the best football-watching experiences in the world, and attending a match here – tickets tend to be readily available for all but the very biggest clashes (see p.222) – serves as an invigorating introduction to Catalan passions. Whether you get to a game or not, the museum and stadium tour is a must, while the entire complex of what claims to be the "World's Top Sports Club", hosting FC Barcelona's sixteen professional and amateur teams, also puts on basketball, handball and hockey games, and holds a public ice rink, souvenir store and café.

Museum and stadium tour

Entrance on Av. Aristides Maillol • Jan–March, Nov & Dec Mon–Sat 10am–6.30pm; April to mid-June & mid-Sept to Oct Mon–Sat 9.30am–7pm; mid-June to mid-Sept daily 9.30am–7.30pm, Sun & hols always until 2.30pm, last tour 1hr before closing; on match days, and also on the day before Champions League matches, the museum is open but there are no tours • €23, under-14s €17, under-6s free; audioguide €5 • Ⓦ fcbarcelona.com • Ⓜ Palau Reial

Hundreds of fans daily make the pilgrimage to Camp Nou, where the combined visit to the club's museum and the stadium itself – billed as the "**Camp Nou Experience**" – provides a magnificent celebration of Spain's national sport. Tracing the history of the club from its foundation in 1899, the **museum** gradually shifts from black-and-white photos and battered old boots and balls to a relentless succession of silverware, including the six cups won in 2009 alone, Barcelona's *annus mirabilis*; a cracking multimedia zone profiles historic games and famous players and relives the match-day atmosphere. Beyond that, the **self-guided tour** winds through the visitors' changing rooms and players' tunnel out onto the pitch, and then leads up to the press gallery and directors' box for stunning views. You can take a selfie alongside a life-size photo of Lionel Messi, or pay for all sorts of official souvenir photos, before you're finally steered into the **FC Botiga** megastore, which sells everything from replica shirts (prices start at €100-plus) to branded bottles of wine.

11

Palau de Pedralbes

Av. Diagonal 686 • Gardens daily 10am–dusk • Free • Ⓜ Palau Reial or tram T1, T2 or T3

Opposite the university on Avinguda Diagonal, formal grounds stretch up to the Italianate **Palau de Pedralbes** – basically a large villa with pretensions. Owner Eusebi Güell donated it to the Spanish royal family in 1918, for use on their visits to Barcelona. The king stayed here for the first time in 1926, but within five years he had abdicated, and the palace somewhat lost its role. Franco kept it on as a presidential residence and it later passed to the city. Until recently it housed the applied art collections now displayed in the Museu del Disseny (see p.121).

Although the palace is now closed to the public, the **gardens** – a breezy oasis of Himalaya cedars, strawberry trees and bougainvillea – are worth a visit. Hidden in a bamboo thicket, to the left-centre of the facade – is the "Hercules fountain" (1884), an early work by Antoni Gaudí. He also designed the parabolic pergola to the right, which is covered in climbing plants and makes a nice place to sit and rest your feet. In June and July each year, the gardens hold a season of big-name concerts known as the **Barcelona Music Festival** (Ⓦ festivalpedralbes.com).

Pavellons Güell

Av. de Pedralbes 7 • Daily 10am–4pm, last entry 3.30pm • €4, under-18s €2 • ☎ 933 177 652, Ⓦ rutadelmodernisme.com • Ⓜ Palau Reial, then a 5min walk

As an early test of his capabilities, Antoni Gaudí was asked by his patron, Eusebi Güell, to rework the entrance, gatehouse and stables of the Güell summer residence, which was sited on a large working estate well away from the filth and unruly mobs of downtown Barcelona. While the summer house itself was later given to the royal family, and rebuilt

---

HERE BE DRAGONS

The slavering beast on Gaudí's dragon gate at the Pavellons Güell is not the vanquished dragon of Sant Jordi (St George), the Catalan patron saint, but the one that appears in the **Labours of Hercules** myth, a familiar Catalan theme in the nineteenth century. Gaudí's design was based on a work by the Catalan renaissance poet **Jacint Verdaguer**, a friend of the Güell family, who had reworked the myth in his epic poem, *L'Atlàntida* – thus, the dragon guarding golden apples in the Gardens of Hesperides is here protecting instead an orange tree (considered a more Catalan fruit). Gaudí's gate indeed can be read as a homage to Verdaguer, with its stencilled roses representing those traditionally given to the winner of the Catalan poetry competition, the Jocs Floral, which the poet won in 1877.

---

as the Palau de Pedralbes, the brick-and-tile stables and outbuildings – known as the **Pavellons Güell** – survive as Gaudí created them. They are frothy, whimsical affairs showing more than a Moorish touch to them, with minaret-like turrets that display Gaudí's first experimentation with *trencadís* (broken tile mosaics), a technique he then used continually on his more famous projects.

However, it's the **gate** that's the most famous element. An extraordinary winged dragon made of twisted iron snarls at the passers-by, its razor-toothed jaws spread wide in a fearsome roar: backing up to pose for a photograph suddenly doesn't seem like such a good idea. You can see the gate for free; paying the entry fee entitles you to peep into the dilapidated gatehouse; walk through Gaudí's innovative, parabolic-arched stables, which now hold assorted tools and equipment used in the construction of La Pedrera; and admire the brickwork from the small gardens.

Monestir de Pedralbes

Bxda. del Monestir 9 • April–Sept Tues–Fri 10am–5pm, Sat 10am–7pm, Sun 10am–8pm; Oct–March Tues–Fri 10am–2pm, Sat & Sun 10am–5pm, hols 10am–2pm • €5, under-16s free, free Sun after 3pm, and all of first Sun of each month • ☎ 932 563 427, ⓦ monestirpedralbes.bcn.cat • Ⓜ Palau Reial and 20min walk, or FGC Reina Elisenda (frequent trains from Pl. de Catalunya) and 10min walk, or bus #64 from Pl. Universitat

Founded in 1326 for the nuns of the Order of St Clare, the Gothic **Monestir de Pedralbes** is, in effect, an entire monastic village preserved on the outskirts of the city, within medieval walls that completely shut out the noise and clamour of the twenty-first century. It took medieval craftsmen a little over a year to prepare Pedralbes (from the Latin *petras albas*, "white stones") for its first community of nuns. The speed of the initial construction and the subsequent uninterrupted habitation by the order helps explain the extreme architectural harmony. After six hundred years of isolation, the monastery was sequestered by the Generalitat during the Civil War and it later opened to the public in 1983 – a new adjacent convent was built as part of the deal, where the Clare nuns still reside.

The cloisters

The triple tiers of the magnificent **cloisters** of the Monestir de Pedralbes are supported by the slenderest of columns, with the only sound the tinkling water from the fountain. Side rooms and chambers give a clear impression of medieval convent life, from the chapter house and austere refectory to a fully equipped kitchen and infirmary. The real highlight here, though, is a small chapel to the right of the entrance, the **Capella de Sant Miquel**, which is adorned with remarkably vivid frescoes painted in 1346 by Catalan artist Ferrer Bassa. High-tech displays in rooms nearby explain their symbolism and restoration, while a small room beside the chapel itself holds the carved marble tomb of the monastery's original sponsor, Elisenda de Montcada, wife of Jaume II. Widowed in 1327, six months after she and her husband laid the first stone, Elisenda retired to an adjacent palace, where she lived until her death in 1364.

HIDDEN GEMS: LES CORTS, PEDRALBES AND SARRIÀ-SANT GERVASI

Pavellons Güell See p.133
Sculpture spotting in the Jardins del
  Palau de Pedralbes See p.133
Plaça de la Concordia See p.132

Ferrer Bassa's stunning murals at
  Monestir de Pedrables See opposite
Bar Tomás See p.192
A stroll through Sarría See below

The nuns' former dormitory – now given a black marble floor and soaring oak-beamed ceiling – houses a selection of the rarer **treasures**. While the nuns themselves eschewed personal trappings, the monastery acquired valuable art and other possessions over the centuries – including pieces of Gothic furniture, paintings by Flemish artists, an impressive series of so-called "factitious" altarpieces from the sixteenth century (made up of sections of different style and provenance), and some outstanding illuminated choirbooks. The monastic **church** alongside, a simple, single-naved structure, retains some of its original fourteenth-century stained glass.

11

Sarrià

FGC Sarrià (take c/Mare de Deu de Núria exit), or bus #64 from Monestir de Pedralbes/Pl. Universitat

Once a small town in its own right, the **Sarrià** district still looks the part, with a narrow, traffic-free main street – c/Major de Sarrià – at the top of which stands the much-restored church of **Sant Vicenç**. The church flanks the main Passeig de la Reina Elisenda de Montcada, across which lies the neighbourhood market, **Mercat Sarrià**, housed in a 1911 *modernista* red-brick building. You'll find a few other surviving old-town squares down the main street, prettiest of which is **Plaça Sant Vicenç de Sarrià** (off c/Mañe i Flaquer), where there's a statue of the saint. If you make it this way, don't miss the *Bar Tomás*, just around the corner on c/Major de Sarrià (see p.192), for the world's best *patatas bravas*.

Tibidabo and Parc de Collserola

The views from the heights of Tibidabo (550m), the peak that signals the northwestern boundary of Barcelona, are legendary. On a clear day you can see across to the Pyrenees and out to sea even as far as Mallorca. However, although many visitors make the tram and funicular ride up to Tibidabo's wonderfully old-fashioned amusement park, few realize that the Parc de Collserola stretches beyond, an area of peaks, wooded river valleys and hiking paths that's one of the city's best-kept secrets. You can walk into the park from Tibidabo, but it's actually better to start from its information centre, across to the west, above the hilltop village of Vallvidrera, which can be reached by another funicular ride. Meanwhile, families won't want to miss the CosmoCaixa science museum, which can easily be seen en route to or from Tibidabo.

CosmoCaixa

C/Isaac Newton 26 • Tues–Sun 10am–8pm • €4; under-16s free, but children's activities €4, planetarium €4 • ☎ 932 126 050, Ⓦ obrasocial.lacaixa.es • FGC Av. del Tibidabo (trains from Pl. de Catalunya) and 10min walk, or Tramvia Blau (see p.138) or Bus Turístic stop close by

For anyone travelling with children in tow, Barcelona's enormous, up-to-the-minute science museum is an absolute must-see attraction, which takes at least two hours to do justice. Originally housed in a converted *modernista* hospice, **CosmoCaixa** was extended in 2005 to include a light-filled public concourse and a huge underground extension that's entered by means of a vast descending staircase that spirals around a desiccated Acariquara tree from the Amazon, and is intended to symbolize a journey back to the origin of life on earth. Hands-on experiments and displays on the lowest of its four subterranean levels range across life, the universe and everything, "from the quark to Shakespeare". Most require a very large thinking cap, so younger children are soon going to be zooming around the open spaces. But there's no denying the overall pull of the two main attractions, namely the hundred tonnes of "sliced" rock in the **Mur Geològic** (Geological Wall) and, best of all, the **Bosc Inundat** – nothing less than a thousand square metres of real Amazonian rainforest, complete with caimans, an anaconda safely ensconced in its own private enclosure, and giant catfish.

Pick up a schedule when you arrive of the programme of children's and family activities, at their most frequent during weekends and school holidays. There are also daily 3D shows in the **planetarium**, plus a great gift shop and a café-restaurant with outdoor seating beneath the restored hospital facade.

12

Torre Bellesguard

C/ de Bellesguard 16 • Tues–Sun 10am–3pm, last entry 2.30pm; check website for schedule of English-language tours • Self-guided tour €9, under-18s €7.20; guided tour €16/€12.50 • ☎ 932 504 093, Ⓦ bellesguardgaudi.com • FGC Av. del Tibidabo (trains from Pl. de Catalunya) and 15min walk, or Tramvia Blau and Bus Turístic stop close by

One of Gaudí's least known works, the **Torre Bellesguard** a few blocks west of CosmoCaixa, has recently opened to visitors. Built between 1900 and 1909, and still a private residence, it's a surprising hybrid of Gothic castle – in reference to the long-vanished castle of Catalunya's King Martin the Humane, which occupied this high eminence in the fifteenth century – and *modernista* manor house, with plenty of Moorish influences in the mix as well, including its smooth white interior spaces and abundant use of tiles. To explore the place thoroughly, it's best to coincide with a guided tour (there's usually one English-language tour each day, at 11am; book ahead if possible), but even if you take the self-guided tour you'll be briefly ushered inside.

Parc d'Atraccions Tibidabo

Pl. del Tibidabo • Days and hours vary, but basically March–May & Oct–Dec Sat, Sun & hols only; June–Sept & hols Wed–Sun: park open noon–7/11pm depending on season; closed Jan & Feb • Skywalk ticket €12.70, full admission €28.50; €7.80/€10.30 for those under 1.2m tall • ☎ 932 117 942, Ⓦ tibidabo.es

Barcelona's self-styled "magic mountain" amusement park, the **Parc d'Atraccions**, has been thrilling its citizens for over a century. It's a mix of traditional rides, plus an influx of high-tech roller-coasters and free-fall drops, laid out around several levels of the mountaintop, connected by landscaped paths and gardens. Some of the most famous historic attractions are grouped under the discounted "**Skywalk**" ticket, like the aeroplane – spinning since 1928 – the carousel and the quirky **Museu d'Autòmates**, a collection of coin-operated antique fairground machines in working order. Summer weekends finish with parades, concerts and a noisy *correfoc*, a theatrical **fireworks** display.

Sagrat Cor

Daily 10am–8pm • €2 • ⓦ templotibidabo.info

There are amazing views from everywhere in Tibidabo park, and they become even more extensive if you climb the shining steps of the neighbouring Templo Expiatorio de España, otherwise known as the **Sagrat Cor** (Sacred Heart), topped by a huge statue of Christ. Inside the church, an elevator (*ascensor*) climbs to a sensational viewing platform, from where the city, surrounding hills and sea shimmer in the distance.

ARRIVAL AND DEPARTURE   PARC D'ATRACCIONS TIBIDABO

Getting to Tibidabo is a convoluted business but it is also half the fun, since you'll need to combine several forms of transport. Expect the trip from the city centre to take up to an hour, all told.

By train, tram and funicular Take the FGC train (Tibidabo line #7) from Pl. de Catalunya station to Av. del Tibidabo (the last stop), where you cross the road to the tram/bus shelter. An antique tram service, the Tramvia Blau (departures every 15–30min: mid-June to mid-Sept daily 10am–7.30pm; Nov–March Sat, Sun & hols 10am–6pm;

TIBIDABO AND PARC DE COLLSEROLA

■ ACCOMMODATION	
ABaC	2
Gran Hotel La Florida	1

● RESTAURANT	
El Asador de Aranda	1

■ BAR	
Mirablau	1

● SHOP	
CosmoCaixa	1

April to mid-June & mid-Sept to Nov Sat, Sun & hols 10am–7.30pm; €5.50 single) then runs you up the hill to Pl. del Doctor Andreu; there's a bus service instead out of season during the week. By the tram and bus stop on Pl. del Doctor Andreu (where there are several café-bars and restaurants), you change to the Funicular del Tibidabo, with connections to Tibidabo at the top (every 15min; operates when the Parc d'Atracions is open; €4.10 with park admission, €7.70 without).

By bus The Bus Turístic stops at Av. del Tibidabo, where you can change for the Tramvia Blau. Alternatively, the special Tibibus (T2A) runs direct to Tibidabo from Pl. de Catalunya (from 10.15am every day that the park is open; €2.95, fare reimbursed with park admission). Local bus #111 runs on a circuit (every 30min; city passes and transport tickets valid) between Tibidabo park and Vallvidrera village.

Torre de Collserola and Vallvidrera

Torre de Collserola: C/de Vallvidrera al Tibidabo • Days and hours vary, but basically: March–June & Sept–Dec Sat & Sun noon–2pm & 3.15–6pm; June–Aug Wed–Sun noon–2pm & 3.30–8pm; closed Jan & Feb • €6, under-14s €4, under-3s free, combined ticket available with Parc d'Atraccions • ☎ 932 117 942, ⓦ torredecollserola.com • Bus #111 from Tibidabo or Vallvidrera village

Follow the road from the Tibidabo car park and it's only a few minutes' walk to Norman Foster's **Torre de Collserola**, a communications tower that soars high above the tree line, with a glass lift that whisks you up ten floors (115m) for yet more stunning views – 70km, they claim, on a good day.

Afterwards, you could just head back to Tibidabo for the funicular-and-tram ride back to the city, but to complete a circular tour it's more interesting to follow the cobbled path near the tower's car park, which brings you out on the pine-clad edges of **Vallvidrera**, a well-to-do suburban village perched on the flank of the Collserola hills – a twenty-minute walk all told from Tibidabo. There's another **funicular** station here (every 6–10min; Mon–Fri 5am–midnight, Sat & Sun 5.36am–2am), connecting to Peu del Funicular, an FGC station on the Sabadell and Terrassa line from Plaça de Catalunya.

Vallvidrera's main square is far from obvious – turn left out of the funicular station and walk down the steep steps, and Plaça de Vallvidrera is the traffic roundabout at the bottom.

Parc de Collserola

Centre d'Informació daily 9.30am–3pm • ☎ 932 803 552, ⓦ www.parcnaturalcollserola.cat • FGC Bxda. de Vallvidrera (on the Sabadell or Terrassa line from Pl. de Catalunya; 15min)

Given a half-decent day, local bikers, hikers and outdoors enthusiasts alike make a beeline for the city's ring of wooded hills beyond Tibidabo. The **park information centre** lies in oak- and pinewoods, an easy, signposted ten-minute walk up through the trees from the FGC Baixada de Vallvidrera train station. There's a bar-restaurant here with an outdoor terrace, plus an exhibition on the park's history, flora and fauna; while the staff hand out English-language leaflets detailing the walks that range from a twenty-minute stroll to the Vallvidrera dam to a couple of hours circling the hills.

Some walks – like the oak-forest hike – swiftly gain height for marvellous views over the tree canopy, while others descend through the valley bottoms to springs and shaded picnic areas. Perhaps the nicest short stroll from the information centre is to the **Font de la Budellera** (1hr 15min return), a landscaped spring deep in the woods. If you follow the signs from the *font* to the Torre de Collserola (another 20min), you can return to Barcelona instead via the funicular from Vallvidrera, or even take in the views from the Collserola tower or Tibidabo before heading back.

12

MONTSERRAT

Out of the city

Catalunya stretches from the Mediterranean coast to the Pyrenees, and its
excellent public transport links mean that even on a short trip out from
Barcelona you can easily see destinations ranging from historic cities to
rolling vineyards, and from ancient churches to seaside resorts. Most lie
within an hour's journey by train – it really isn't worth renting a car unless
you want to see a lot of Catalunya in a short time. These accounts are geared
towards day-trips; to find out about accommodation in the region, contact
the local tourist offices, consult ⓦcatalunya.com, or get hold of the separate
Rough Guide to Spain.

13

Although there are plenty of traditional coastal bolt-holes close to Barcelona, like Castelldefels to the south or the small towns of the Costa Maresme to the north, unquestionably the best local seaside destination is **Sitges**, on the Costa Daurada half an hour south. It's a charming resort with an international reputation, extremely popular with gay visitors and chic city-dwellers. Otherwise, the one essential excursion is to **Montserrat**, the extraordinary mountain and monastery 40km northwest of Barcelona, reached by a precipitous cable-car or mountain railway ride. Besides being a site of great significance for Catalans, it's also a terrific place for a hike in the hills.

If you enjoy Barcelona's varied church architecture, there's more to come, starting with Gaudí's inspired work at the **Colònia Güell**, an idealistic community established by the architect's patron Eusebi Güell. This is a half-day's outing, while a second half-day can be spent visiting the Benedictine monastery at **Sant Cugat del Vallès** and the complex of early medieval churches at **Terrassa**, all largely unsung and utterly fascinating. Another route out of the city, due west, leads through the wine-producing towns of **Sant Sadurní d'Anoia** and **Vilafranca del Penedès**, both of which can be seen in a day's excursion with enough time for a wine-tasting tour.

It's also straightforward to see something of Barcelona's neighbouring cities, all very different from the Catalan capital. South of Barcelona, beyond Sitges, **Tarragona** has a compact old town and an amazing series of Roman remains, while nearby **Reus**, the birthplace of Antoni Gaudí, features an interpretive museum that's the last word on the man and his work. To the north, inland from the coast, sits medieval **Girona**, perhaps

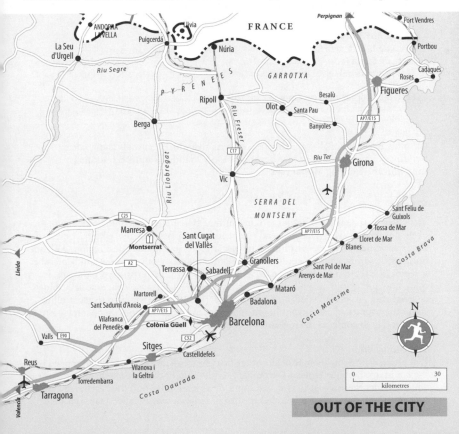

OUT OF THE CITY

13

REGIONAL FESTIVALS

FEBRUARY–MAY

Carnival February or March, dates vary. Sitges has Catalunya's best Carnival celebrations (see p.144).

International Jazz festival Three weeks in March, Terrassa (🌐jazzterrassa.org). Acts playing in clubs and old-town squares.

Fires i Festes de la Santa Creu First week in May, Figueres, with processions and music.

Trapezi Third week in May. International circus fair in Reus, with street performances and spectacle.

Festa de Corpus Christi (moveable feast, sometimes falls in early June). Big processions and streets decorated with flowers in Sitges.

JUNE–AUGUST

Dia de Sant Joan June 24. Celebrated everywhere; watch out for things shutting down for a day on either side.

Festa Major de Sant Cugat del Vallès Last week in June.

Festa Major de Sant Pere Last week in June, in Reus. The town's biggest annual bash.

Gay Pride Sitges Second week in July (sometimes held in June). Several days of events, parties and street parades.

Festa de Sant Magi August 19 in Tarragona.

Festa Major Last week in August. Festival to honour Sitges' patron saint, Sant Bartolomeu.

Festa Major in Vilafranca del Penedès August 29 & 30 (🌐festamajorvilafranca.cat). Dedicated to Sant Felix, with human towers, dancing and processions.

SEPTEMBER–OCTOBER

Festa de la Fil·loxera September 8. Sant Sadurní d'Anoia's big annual festival.

Festa de Santa Tecla September 23, in Tarragona, with processions of *gegants* and human castles.

The Setmana del Cava Second week of October. A sort of cava festival is held in Sant Sadurní d'Anoia.

Festival Internacional de Cinema Fantastic Early October (🌐sitgesfilmfestival.com). Sitges hosts a sci-fi, horror and fantasy fest, complete with film premieres and zombie walks.

the most beautiful of all Catalan cities, with its river, fortified walls and golden buildings, while **Figueres** not far beyond boasts Catalunya's most extraordinary museum, the amazing **Museu Dalí**.

Sitges

The lovely seaside town of **Sitges**, 36km south of Barcelona, is definitely the highlight of the local coast. The great weekend escape for young Barcelonans, who have created a resort very much in their own image, it's also a noted gay holiday destination, with an outrageous carnival and an ebullient nightlife to match – between June and September it seems like there's one nonstop party going on. What may surprise you, though, is quite how pretty and unspoiled the old town remains. Out of season, especially, Sitges is delightful: far less crowded, and with a temperate climate that encourages strolling along the promenade and exploring the narrow central lanes. Note that Monday isn't the best day to come, as the museums and many restaurants are closed.

The old town

Old Sitges centres on a tangle of alleyways that climb up and over the knoll, topped by the landmark Baroque **Església Parroquial** (parish church) dedicated to Sant Bartolomeu, which divides the seafront in two. Sweeping views stretch beyond the beaches to either side and along the coast, while a cluster of late-medieval whitewashed mansions holds assorted museums and galleries.

13

Scores of handsome, more recent townhouses were built in Sitges in the nineteenth century by successful local merchants (known as "Americanos") who returned from Cuba and Puerto Rico. A walk along the seafront promenade reveals the best of them, adorned with wrought-iron balconies, stained-glass windows and ceramic decoration. The pedestrianized shopping street, **Carrer Major**, is the best place for browsing boutiques.

Museu Cau Ferrat and Museu Maricel

C/Fonollar • Tues–Sun: March–June & Oct 10am–7pm; July–Sept 10am–8pm; Nov–Feb 10am–5pm • €10 • ☎ 938 940 364, Ⓦ museusdesitges.cat

The gorgeous renovated mansion, overlooking the sea, which now contains the **Museu Cau Ferrat** served from 1891 onwards as the home and workshop of artist and writer **Santiago Rusiñol i Prats** (1861–1931). Rusiñol organized five *modernista* festivals in Sitges between 1892 and 1899, and the town flourished as a major *modernista* centre under his patronage. Magnificently tiled rooms now display an extraordinary array of paintings, artefacts and decorative ironwork gathered by Rusiñol, including works by Rusiñol himself and contemporaries such as Picasso, and even a couple of minor El Grecos that he bought when the painter's reputation was much less elevated than it is today.

Admission includes access to the nominally distinct but seamlessly connected **Museu Maricel** next door. This holds the bulk of Sitges' municipal art collection,

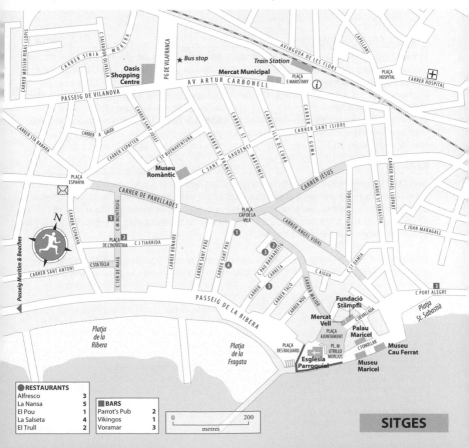

RESTAURANTS				
Alfresco	3			
La Nansa	5	**BARS**		
El Pou	1	Parrot's Pub	2	
La Salseta	4	Vikingos	1	
El Trull	2	Voramar	3	

SITGES

13

which is sizeable enough to be set out as an interesting history of Spanish art from the tenth century onwards.

Fundació Stämpfli

Pl. de l'Ajuntament 13 • March–June & Oct Fri–Sun 10am–7pm; July–Sept Tues–Sun 10am–8pm; Nov–Feb Fri–Sun 10am–5pm • €3.50 • ☎ 938 940 364, ⓦ fundacio-stampfli.org

Housed in Sitges' former fish market and a similarly venerable adjoining building, the **Fundació Stämpfli** is home to the wide-ranging contemporary art collection of Swiss-born artist Peter Stämpfli and his wife, Anna Maria, who have been active members of the local art scene since the 1970s. The works – some eighty paintings, sculptures and more by international artists such as Erró, Gérard Fromanger and Stämpfli himself – offer a sweeping view of various art movements from the past fifty years. The renovated space in which the collection is presented is simple but beautiful, with a vaulted, wood-beamed ceiling and gleaming floors.

The seafront

The clean sand **beaches** located to both east and west of the old-town headland, become extremely crowded in high season. For more space it's best to keep walking west along the promenade, past a series of eight interlinked beaches that runs a couple of kilometres down the coast as far as the *Hotel Terramar*. There are breakwaters, beach bars, restaurants, showers and watersports facilities along the way, with the more notorious gay nudist beaches found at the far end.

ARRIVAL AND INFORMATION

SITGES

By train Trains to Sitges leave Pg. de Gràcia or Barcelona Sants stations roughly every 30min (destination Vilanova or St Vicenç), and take 30–40min depending on the service. The last departure back to Barcelona is at around 10.30pm (starting again at around 5am).

By bus Mon-Bus (ⓦ monbus.cat) runs a direct service to Sitges from Barcelona airport (Mon–Fri once or twice an hour 7.40am–11.40pm, Sat & Sun every 2–3hr), which

takes around 35min and stops two blocks from the train station; the buses actually start from Ronda Universitat in Barcelona itself around 20min earlier. There are also hourly nightbuses year-round between Pg. de Vilafranca in Sitges and Pl. Catalunya and Pl. Espanya in Barcelona.

Oficina de Turisme Pl. Eduard Maristany 2, next to the train station (Mon–Fri 10am–2pm & 4–6.30pm, Sat 10am–2pm & 4–7pm, Sun 10am–2pm; ☎ 938 944 251, ⓦ sitgestur.cat).

EATING

Sitges has a huge array of restaurants, and the quality is largely very good, thanks to a discerning, upmarket tourist crowd and well-heeled locals. Every restaurant along the front does a paella with a promenade view, though some of the more interesting places are hidden away in the backstreets. For picnic supplies visit the **Mercat Municipal** (Mon, Wed & Sat 8.30am–2pm, Tues, Thurs & Fri 8.30am–2pm & 5.30–8.30pm), close to the train station on Av. Artur Carbonell, which is good for cured meats, olives, cheese, fresh bread and fruit.

Alfresco c/d'en Pau Barrabeitg 4 ☎ 938 940 600, ⓦ alfrescorestaurante.es. Romantic old-town restaurant,

tucked away off a stepped alley and boasting its own trellised patio, serving Catalan cuisine with some Asian

---

CARNIVAL TIME

Carnival in Sitges (*Carnestoltes* in Catalan; Feb/March) is a spectacular affair, thanks largely to the strong gay presence. It opens on the so-called Fat Thursday with the arrival of the Carnival King, following which there's a full programme of parades, masked balls, concerts, beach parties and sausage sizzles. The traditional *xatónada* gala dinners are named after the carnival dish, *xató*, a kind of salt-cod salad, which originates in Sitges. There's a **children's procession** on Sunday, while Carnival climaxes in Sunday night's **Debauchery Parade** and the even bigger Tuesday-night **Extermination Parade**, featuring exquisitely dressed drag queens swanning about the streets in high heels. Bar doors stand wide open, bands play and processions and celebrations go on until dawn. Ash Wednesday itself sees the more traditional Burial of the Sardine.

13

influences – fresh scallops with Thai sauce and courgette noodles for €22, steak with ratatouille for €26. Feb–April & Oct–Dec Thurs–Sat 8.30pm–midnight; May–Sept Tues–Sun 0.30pm–midnight.

La Nansa c/Carreta 35 ☎938 941 927, ⊛restaurant lanansa.com. Family-run fish restaurant – *nansa* means fishing net – where the seafood-rich €30 set menu features the local variation on the paella, *arròs a la Sitgetana*, complete with a healthy splash of Sitges' Malvasia wine. Mon & Thurs–Sun 1.30–4pm & 8.30–11pm, Wed 8.30–11pm; closed Jan.

El Pou c/de Sant Pau 5 ☎931 289 921, ⊛elpoudesitges .com. Upscale, only-in-Sitges but nonetheless very welcoming tapas bar, where the Catalan-Japanese fusion menu includes wagyu sliders (two for €6.35), duck

carpaccio (€7.50) and meatballs with squid (€4.50). Mon & Wed 7–11.30pm, Thurs–Sat 1–3.30pm & 8–11,30pm Sun 1 4pm & 8–11.30pm.

La Salseta c/de Sant Pau 35 ☎938 110 419, ⊛lasalseta .com. Classic, unpretentious Catalan dishes (cod with garlic confit, seafood paella, and plenty of vegetarian options), cooked with slow-food attention and using locally sourced ingredients, keep this cosy little dining room filled with tourists and locals alike. Daily 1–4pm & 8–11pm.

El Trull Ptge. Mossén Fèlix Clarà 35 ☎938 944 705, ⊛eltrullsitges.com. Classy French restaurant just off c/Major, where the great-value €22 dinner set menu always includes a range of oven-baked meat and fish main courses. Mon, Tues, Thurs & Fri 7.30–11pm, Sat & Sun 1.30–4.30pm & 7.30–11pm; closed Jan.

DRINKING AND NIGHTLIFE

The focus of local **nightlife** is c/Primer de Maig and c/Montroig, lined with café-*terrassas* that are busy in summer from morning to night. Call in at *Parrot's* for the lowdown on the gay scene and to find out which clubs are in this year.

★**Parrot's Pub** Pl. de l'Industria ☎938 941 350, ⊛parrots-sitges.com. The stalwart of the gay bar scene in Sitges, with seats under lurid shaded parasols. The owners also run a Mediterranean hotel and restaurant (dinner only) next door. Daily 11am–2am.

Vikingos c/del Marqués de Montroig 7–9 ☎938 949 687, ⊛losvikingos.com. Long-standing party-zone bar with an enormous a/c interior and streetside terrace. This and the similar *Montroig* next door serve drinks, snacks

and meals from morning until night to a really mixed crowd. Mon–Wed 1pm–12.30am, Fri 1pm–1am, Sat 11am–1.30am, Sun 11am–12.30am.

Voramar c/de Port Alegre 55 ⊛pub-voramar.com. Charismatic seafront bar, away from the main crowds, just right for an ice-cold beer or sundowner cocktail. It's a bit more pub-like than many in town, and generally attracts an older clientele. Daily except Wed 4.30pm–1am.

Montserrat

The mountain of **Montserrat** stands just 40km northwest of Barcelona, off the road to Lleida. Rock crags, hermitage caves and, above all, a vast **monastery** make it the most popular day-trip from the city, reached in around ninety minutes by train and then cable-car or mountain railway for the final thrilling ride up. Once there, you can visit the basilica and monastery buildings, and complete your day with a **walk** around the woods and crags, using the two funicular railways that depart from the monastery complex. There are cafés and restaurants at the monastery, but they are relatively pricey, none too inspiring and very busy at peak times – there's a lot to be said for taking your own picnic instead and striking off into the hills for an alfresco lunch.

Legends hang easily upon Montserrat. Fifty years after the birth of Christ, St Peter is said to have deposited an image of the Virgin (known as La Moreneta, the Black Virgin), carved by St Luke, in one of the mountain caves. The icon was lost in the early eighth century after being hidden during the Moorish invasion, but reappeared in 880, accompanied by the customary visions and celestial music. The chapel built to house it was in 976 superseded by a Benedictine monastery, set at an altitude of nearly 1000m. Miracles abounded and the Virgin of Montserrat soon became the chief cult-image of Catalunya and a pilgrimage centre second in Spain only to Santiago de Compostela in Galicia, with the main **pilgrimages** to Montserrat taking place on April 27 and September 8. In addition to the tourists, tens of thousands of newly married couples come here to seek La Moreneta's blessing, while Montserrat has also become an important nationalist symbol for Catalans.

13

The monastery

Basilica Daily 7.30am–8pm; access to La Moreneta 8–10.30am & noon–6.30pm; mid-July to Sept also 7.30–8pm • **Boys' choir** Mon–Fri 1pm, Sun at noon & 6.45pm • Free

Of the religious buildings, only the Renaissance **basilica**, dating largely from 1560 to 1592, is open to the public. **La Moreneta** stands above the high altar – reached from behind, by way of an entrance to the right of the basilica's main entrance. The approach to this beautiful icon reveals the enormous wealth of the monastery, as you queue along a corridor leading through the back of the basilica's rich side-chapels. Signs at head height command "SILENCE" in various languages, but nothing quietens the line which waits to kiss the image's hands and feet. The best time to visit the basilica is when Montserrat's world-famous **boys' choir** sings. The boys belong to the Escolania, a choral school established in the fourteenth century and unchanged in musical style since its foundation.

The monastery's various outbuildings – including hotel and restaurant, post office, souvenir shop, self-service cafeteria and bar – fan out around an open square, and there are extraordinary mountain views from the terrace.

Museu de Montserrat

Museu de Montserrat April to mid-June & mid-Sept to Oct Mon–Fri 10am–5.45pm, Sat & Sun 10am–6.45pm; mid-June to mid-Sept daily 10am–6.45pm; Nov–March daily 10am–5.45pm • €7 • ☎ 938 777 745, ⓦ museudemontserrat.com • **Espai Audiovisual** Mon–Fri 9am–5.45pm, Sat & Sun 9am–6.45pm • €2, or €7.50 with Museu de Montserrat

The **Museu de Montserrat** presents a few archeological finds brought back by travelling monks, together with paintings and sculpture dating from as early as the thirteenth century, including works by Old Masters, French Impressionists and Catalan *modernistas*. There's also a collection of Byzantine icons, though other religious items are in short supply, as most of the monastery's valuables were carried off by Napoleon's troops who sacked the complex in 1811. For more on the history, and to learn something of the life of a Benedictine community, visit the stimulating **Espai Audiovisual**, near the information office.

Mountain walks

Funicular departures vary by season, but mostly every 20min, 10am–5pm • Santa Cova €3.50 return, Sant Joan €9 return, combination ticket €10

As you follow the mountain tracks that lead from the monastery to the nearby caves and hermitages, you can contemplate Goethe's observation of 1816: "Nowhere but in

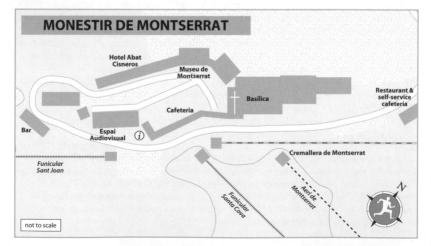

13

his own Montserrat will a man find happiness and peace." The going is pretty good on all the tracks and the signposting is clear, but you do need to remember that you're on a mountain – take a bottle of water and keep away from the edges.

Two separate **funiculars** run from points close to the cable-car station; pick up a map with walking notes from the Montserrat tourist office. One drops to the path for **Santa Cova**, a seventeenth-century chapel built where the Moreneta icon is said to have been found. It's an easy walk there and back, which takes less than an hour.

The other funicular rises steeply to the hermitage of **Sant Joan**, from where it's a tougher 45-minute walk to the **Sant Jeroni** hermitage, and another fifteen minutes to the Sant Jeroni summit at 1236m. This is an excellent place to watch for peregrines, crag martins and black redstarts; in summer you may also spot alpine swifts, while Iberian wall lizards emerge from the crevices to bask on the rockfaces. Several other walks are also possible from the Sant Joan funicular, perhaps the nicest being the 45-minute circuit around the ridge that leads all the way back down to the monastery.

ARRIVAL AND DEPARTURE   MONTSERRAT

There are two ways to reach Montserrat by public transport – cable-car and mountain railway – but in the first instance you need to take the **FGC train** (line R5, direction Manresa), which leaves Barcelona's Pl. d'Espanya (🚇 Espanya) daily (hourly intervals 8.36am–4.36pm; extra departures March–Oct Mon–Fri 11.56am–4.56pm).

By cable-car Get off the train at Montserrat Aeri (1hr) for the connecting cable-car, the Aeri de Montserrat (every 15min: March–Oct daily 9.40am–2pm & 2.35–7pm; Nov–Feb Mon–Fri 10.10am–2pm & 2.35–5.45pm, Sat, Sun & hols 9.40am–2pm & 2.35–6.15pm; €7 one-way, €10 return; ☎ 938 350 005, 🌐 aeridemontserrat.com). Queues are possible at busy times. Returning to Barcelona, the R5 trains depart hourly from Montserrat Aeri (from 9.45am).

By mountain railway The Montserrat mountain railway, the Cremallera de Montserrat (hourly; daily 8.48am–5.48pm; April–June & Oct Sat & Sun until 7.48pm; July–Sept daily until 7.48pm; ☎ 902 312 020, 🌐 cremallera demontserrat.cat), departs from Monistrol de Montserrat (the next stop after Montserrat Aeri, another 4min), and takes 20min. Returning to Barcelona, the R5 trains depart hourly from Monistrol de Montserrat (from 8.15am).

Tickets An information desk at Pl. d'Espanya station and

the FGC shop at El Triangle detail all the fare options, including return through-tickets from Barcelona (around €20) for either train/cable-car or train/mountain railway. Two combination tickets are available, and can also be bought at the Pl. de Catalunya tourist office in Barcelona: the Trans Montserrat (€29.30), which includes all transport services, including unlimited use of the mountain funiculars; and the Tot Montserrat (€46.20), which includes the same plus monastery museum and audiovisual exhibit entry and a cafeteria lunch.

By car Take the A2 motorway as far as the Montserrat exit, and then follow the BP-1103 to the Montserrat turn-off – or park at either the cable-car or the mountain-railway station and take the rides up instead. All-in cable-car/ Cremallera/Montserrat attraction combo tickets are available at the station for drivers who park and ride.

INFORMATION

Visitor centre At the monastery (Mon–Fri 9am–5.45pm, Sat & Sun 9am–6.45pm; ☎ 938 777 701, 🌐 www.mont serratvisita.com). You can pick up maps of the complex and

mountain, and they can also advise about accommodation, from camping to staying at the three-star *Abat Cisneros* hotel.

Sant Cugat and Terrassa

A series of remarkable churches lies on the commuter train line northwest of Barcelona, the first in the dormitory town of **Sant Cugat del Vallès** – just 25 minutes from the city – and the second (actually a group of three) another fifteen minutes beyond in the industrial city of **Terrassa**. You can easily see all the churches in a morning, but throw in lunch and this just about stretches to a day-trip, and it's not a bad ride in any case – after Sarrià, the train emerges from the city tunnels and chugs down the wooded valley into Sant Cugat.

13

Sant Cugat del Vallès

Reial Monestir Mon–Sat 8am–noon & 4–9pm, Sun open for Mass from 9am • Free • **Museu de Sant Cugat** Jardins del Monestir • June–Sept Tues–Sat 10.30am–1.30pm & 5–8pm, Sun & hols 10.30am–2pm; Oct–May Tues–Sat 10.30am–1.30pm & 4–7pm, Sun & hols 10.30am–2pm • €3.50, under-16s free • ☎ 936 759 951, ⓦ museu.santcugat.cat

The Benedictine **Reial Monestir** (Royal Monastery) at **Sant Cugat del Vallès** was founded as far back as the ninth century, though most of the surviving buildings date from three or four hundred years later. Its fawn stone facade and triple-decker bell tower make a lovely sight as you approach from the square outside, through the gate, past the renovated Bishop's Palace and under a splendid rose window. Finest of all, though, is the beautiful twelfth-century Romanesque **cloister**, with noteworthy capital carvings of mythical beasts and biblical scenes. Their unusual homogeneity owes to the fact that all were completed by a single sculptor, Arnau Gatell.

The main church is free to visit, but the cloister, the entrance to which is to one side of the church, forms part of the **Museu de Sant Cugat**, which also includes the restored dormitory, kitchen and refectory of the monastery, and holds exhibitions about its history and monastic life. What were once the monastery's kitchen gardens lie across from the Bishop's Palace, though the formerly lush plots that sustained the brothers are now mere dusty gardens, albeit with views over the low walls to Tibidabo and the Collserola hills. Plaça Octavia, outside the monastery, has a weekly **market** every Thursday.

ARRIVAL AND INFORMATION   SANT CUGAT

By train FGC trains on the S1 line connect Pl. de Catalunya in Barcelona with Sant Cugat, which is in Zone 2, every 10–15min (ⓦ fgc.cat). Once in Sant Cugat, walk straight ahead out of the train station and down the pedestrianized c/Valldoreix, taking the first right and then the first left (it's still c/Valldoreix), and then keep straight along the shopping street (c/Santa María and then c/Santiago Rusiñol) until you see the monastery bell tower (10min walk).

Oficina de Turisme Sant Cugat del Vallès, Pl. Octavia 10, inside the main doorway of the monastery (June–Sept Tues–Fri 10.30am–1.30pm & 5.30–7pm, Sat 10am–2pm & 5–8pm, Sun & hols 10am–2pm; Oct–May Tues–Fri 10.30am–1.15pm & 4.15–5.45pm, Sat 10am–2pm & 4–6pm, Sun & hols 10am–2pm; ☎ 936 759 952, ⓦ turisme .santcugat.cat).

Terrassa

Terrassa, a large city with a population of 200,000 located 25km northwest of Barcelona, was an important textile producer in the nineteenth century, and retains many fine *modernista*-style factories, mills and warehouses that now enjoy protected status. But Terrassa boasts a much longer history, and its true treasures stand on the edge of the city centre, built on the site of the Roman town of Ègara – three pre-Romanesque churches, dating from the fifth to the tenth centuries.

La Seu d'Ègara

La Seu d'Ègara, Pl. del Rector Horns 1 • Tues–Sat 10am–1.30pm & 4–7pm, Sun & hols 11am–2pm • €7, under-6s free • ☎ 937 833 702, ⓦ seudegara.cat

Known as **La Seu d'Ègara**, Terrassa's fully restored ecclesiastical complex centres on its largest church, **Sant Pere**, which sports a badly faded Gothic mural and a tenth-century mosaic fragment within its walls. The church of **Santa María** is far better endowed, boasting a mosaic pavement outside and sunken baptismal font inside, both of which date from the fifth century. Much later Gothic (fourteenth- and fifteenth-century) murals and altarpieces – one by Catalan master Jaume Huguet – are also on display. But it's the fifth-century baptistry of **Sant Miquel** that's the most fascinating – a tiny, square building of rough masonry, steeped in gloom, with eight assorted columns supporting the dome, each with a carved Roman or Visigothic capital. Underneath sits the partially reconstructed baptismal bath, while steps lead down into a simple crypt.

FROM TOP AQÜEDUCTE DE LES FERRERES, TARRAGONA (P.155); GIRONA (P.158); SITGES BEACH (P.144) >

13

By train FGC trains from Barcelona (S1 line from Pl. de Catalunya; ⍟ fgc.cat) depart every 20–30min – get off at Terrassa-Rambla, the last stop, which is in Zone 3. The churches are a 20min walk from the station – turn right from the Rambla d'Ègara exit, then immediately right again into Pl. de Clavé, follow c/Major up to Pl. Vella, cross the square, turn up c/Gavatxons and follow c/Sant Pere, c/ Nou de Sant Pere and c/de la Creu Gran, finally crossing a viaduct to arrive at the entrance. There is a more convenient

Renfe mainline train station in Terrassa (direct trains from Barcelona Sants every 20min; ⍟ renfe.com) – a straight 10min walk down c/del Mas Adel to the churches – but only the FGC line connects both Sant Cugat and Terrassa. **Oficina de Turisme** Raval de Montserrat 14 (Mon–Fri 9am–2pm & 5–7pm, Sat 10am–2pm & 5–8pm, Sun & hols 10am–2pm; Aug open mornings only; ☎ 937 397 019, ⍟ visitaterrassa.cat). Organizes guided tours of the city's industrial heritage.

Colònia Güell

Before work at Barcelona's Park Güell got under way (see p.126), Antoni Gaudí had already been charged with the design of parts of Eusebi Güell's earliest attempts to establish a Utopian industrial estate, or *colònia* (colony), on the western outskirts of the city. The **Colònia Güell** at Santa Coloma de Cervelló was very much of its time – more than seventy similar colonies were established along Catalan rivers in the late nineteenth century, using water power to drive the textile mills. The concept was also familiar in Britain, where enlightened Victorian entrepreneurs had long created idealistic towns (Saltaire, Bournville) to house their workers.

The Colònia Güell was begun in 1890, and by 1920 incorporated over one hundred houses and public buildings, plus the chapel and crypt for which Gaudí was responsible. The Güell company was taken over in 1945 and the whole complex closed as a going concern in 1973, though the buildings have since been restored – and, indeed, many are still lived in today. There are rows of terraced houses, with front gardens tended lovingly by the current inhabitants, while brick towers, ceramic panels and stained glass elevate many of the houses above the ordinary. It's a working village, so you'll also find a bank and pharmacy, as well as two or three cafés and restaurants, and on Saturdays there is a farmers' market.

Gaudí's church

May–Oct Mon–Fri 10am–7pm, Sat & Sun 10am–3pm; Nov–April Mon–Fri 10am–5pm, Sat & Sun 10am–3pm; closed for visits during Mass on Sun (11am & 1pm) • €7

Gaudí's **church** – built into the pine-clad hillside above the colony – is a masterpiece. While you can see the angular exterior from the outside for free, to see the far more dramatic interior you'll have to first buy a ticket at the visitor centre. The **crypt** was designed to carry the weight of the chapel above, its palm-tree-like columns supporting a brick vault, and the whole lot resembling a labyrinth of caves fashioned from a variety of different stone and brick. Several of Gaudí's more extraordinary flights of fancy – like the original scalloped pews, the conch shells used as water stoups, the vivid stained glass and the window that opens up like the wings of a butterfly – presage his later work on the Sagrada Família. Despite appearances, the church was never actually finished, and Gaudí stopped work on it in 1914. Ongoing restoration aims to complete the outer walls, though Gaudí's planned 40m-high central dome is unlikely ever to be realized.

By train Take the FGC train S4, S8 or S33 (direction Martorell; departures every 15–20min; ⍟ fgc.cat) from Pl. d'Espanya to the small Colònia Güell station; the ride takes 20min. From the station, follow the painted blue footprints across the highway and into the *colònia*; they lead directly to the visitor centre (10min).
Centre d'Acollida de Visitants (May–Oct Mon–Fri 10am–7pm, Sat & Sun 10am–3pm; Nov–April Mon–Fri

10am–5pm, Sat & Sun 10am–3pm; ☎ 936 305 807, ⍟ gaudicoloniaguell.org). The visitor centre has an exhibition (with English notes).
Guided tours Tours of the church, of the estate or of both the church and the estate are available daily throughout the year; admission with one tour €9.50, with both €11.50. An audioguide is also offered.

EATING AND DRINKING

13

Ateneu Unió Pl. Joan Güell 5 ☉ 936 613 111. The big, old-fashioned bar-restaurant on the quiet central square is good for sandwiches, tapas and a bargain €9 *menú del dia* (€12 at weekends) served on the sunny *terrassa*. Daily 6am–11pm.

L'Alt Penedès wine region

L'Alt Penedès wine region (@altpenedes.net), roughly halfway between Barcelona and Tarragona, is the largest Catalan producer of still and sparkling wines – as becomes increasingly clear the further the train heads into the region, with vines as far as the eye can see on both sides of the track. Both the two main towns to visit can easily be seen in a single day: **Sant Sadurní d'Anoia**, closer to Barcelona, is the self-styled "Capital del Cava", home to around fifty producers of sparkling wine, while **Vilafranca del Penedès**, ten minutes down the line, is the region's administrative capital and produces mostly still wine, red and white.

If you're serious about **visiting vineyards**, the trip is better done by car, as many of the more interesting boutique producers lie out in the countryside. Either of the towns' tourist offices can provide a good map pinpointing all the local vineyards as well as the rural farmhouse restaurants. However, even by train you'll be able to visit a winery or two, including one of the most famous of Catalan wine names.

Sant Sadurní d'Anoia

The small town of **Sant Sadurní d'Anoia** (population 12,000), built on land watered by the Riu Noya, has been an important centre of wine production since the eighteenth century. When, at the end of the nineteenth century, French vineyards suffered heavily from phylloxera, Sant Sadurní prospered, though later it too succumbed to the same wasting disease – something remembered still in the annual September festival by the parade of a representation of the feared phylloxera parasite. The production of cava, for which the town is now famous, began only in the 1870s – an industry that went hand in hand with the Catalan cork business, established in the forests of the hinterland. Today, a hundred million bottles a year of cava are turned out by dozens of companies, many of which are only too happy to escort you around their premises, show you the fermentation process and let you taste a glass or two.

The wineries

Freixenet Daily tours and tastings, lasting 1hr 30min; usually Mon–Sat 9.30am–4.30pm, Sun 10am–1pm; check website for variations; reservations suggested • €7.50, under-18s €4.50, under-8s free • ☉ 938 917 000, @ freixenet.es • **Codorníu** English tours Mon–Fri 11.30am & 3.30pm, Sat & Sun 10am; reservations suggested • €9, under-18s €6, under-8s free • ☉ 938 913 342, @ www.codorniu.com

Most people never get any further than the most prominent and most famous company, **Freixenet** – producer of those distinctive black bottles – whose building is right outside the train station. Many other companies have similar arrangements,

---

CAVA

Cava is a naturally sparkling wine made using the *méthode champenoise*, the traditional method for making champagne. The basic **grape** varieties of L'Alt Penedès are *macabeu*, *xarel.lo* and *parellada*, which are fermented to produce a wine base and then mixed with sugar and yeast before being bottled: a process known as **tiratge**. The bottles are then sealed hermetically – the **tapat** – and laid flat in cellars – the **criança** – for up to nine months to ferment for a second time. The wine is later decanted to get rid of the sediment before being corked.

The cava is then **classified** according to the amount of sugar used in the fermentation: either Brut (less than 20g a litre), Sec (20–30g), Semisec (30–50g) or Dolç (more than 50g). This is the first thing to take note of before buying or drinking: Brut and Sec are to most people's tastes and are excellent with almost any food, or as an aperitif; Semisec and Dolç are better consumed as dessert wines.

13

including the out-of-town **Codorníu** – the region's earliest cava producer – which has a fine building by *modernista* architect Josep Puig i Cadafalch as an added attraction. There are several dozen other *caves* or cellars in and around town, all shown on a map available at the Sant Sadurní tourist office.

Vilafranca del Penedès

As a town, **Vilafranca del Penedès** is rather more interesting than Sant Sadurní. Founded in the eleventh century in a bid to attract settlers to land retaken from the expelled Moors, it became a prosperous market centre. That character remains evident today, in a compact old town at whose heart lie narrow streets and arcaded squares adorned with restored medieval mansions.

From the train station, walk up to the main Rambla de Nostra Senyora and cut to the right up c/de Sant Joan to the enclosed Plaça de Sant Joan, which has a small daily produce **market**. A rather larger affair takes place every Saturday, when the stalls also stock clothes, household goods, handicrafts and agricultural gear. The **Festa Major**, meanwhile, at the end of August and the first couple of days in September, brings the place to a standstill: dances and parades clog the streets, while the festival is renowned for its display of *castellers* – teams of people competing to build human towers (see box, p.215).

Vinseum

Pl. Jaume I 5 • June–Sept Tues–Sat 10am–7pm, Sun & hols 10am–2pm; Oct–May Tues–Sat 10am–2pm & 4–7pm, Sun & hols 10am–2pm • €7 • ☎ 938 900 582, ⓦ vinseum.cat

Vilafranca's town museum, the **Vinseum**, is housed in a medieval mansion in the centre, and is the best place to get to grips with the region's wine industry. Exhibitions range far and wide, with the emphasis as much on local traditions and culture as wine, and visits culminate with a tasting or two in the museum's own tavern, which is open daily until 11pm on weekdays and until midnight at the weekend.

The wineries

Torres Mon–Sat 9.15am–4.45pm, Sun & hols 9.15am–1pm • Tours of varying lengths, some with food as well, from €6 • ☎ 938 177 487, ⓦ clubtorres.com • **Jean Leon** Mon–Fri 9am–6pm, Sat, Sun & hols 9am–2pm • Tours from €15, reservations required • ☎ 938 995 512, ⓦ jeanleon.com

The vineyards of Vilafranca are all out of town, though the largest and best-known winery, **Torres**, is only a 3km taxi ride northwest, on the Sant Martí de Sarroca road. Also owned by Torres is boutique winemaker **Jean Leon** at Torrelavit, closer to Sant Sadurní, whose American-modernist-inspired visitor centre is set in particularly bucolic surroundings.

ARRIVAL AND DEPARTURE
L'ALT PENEDÈS

By train Renfe services from Pl. de Catalunya or Barcelona Sants (Mon–Fri every 30min, Sat & Sun every 1hr, ⓦ renfe .com) run west into L'Alt Penedès, calling at Sant Sadurní d'Anoia (40min) and Vilafranca del Penedès (50min).

INFORMATION AND TOURS

Spanish Trails Adventures (☎ 935 001 616, ⓦ spanish -trails.com) offers full-day, small-group escorted Penedès wine tours (from €105, transport and lunch included), including a cycling-wine tour option that lets you bike the quiet country lanes while visiting two or three wineries.
Catalunya Bus Turístic (ⓦ catalunyabusturistic.com) stops off at Jean Leon, Miguel Torres and Freixenet for tastings and tours during a half-day circuit (leaves Barcelona Thurs & Sun 8.30am; €69).

SANT SADURNÍ D'ANOIA
Oficina de Turisme c/del Hospital 26 (Tues–Sun 10am–2pm; ☎ 938 913 188, ⓦ turismesantsadurni.com). The office is in the centre of town – a 15min walk from the train station – at the CIC Fassina Cava Welcome Center, which offers visitors an introduction to the bubbly stuff (€6 entry; see website for tour schedule).

VILAFRANCA DEL PENEDÈS
Oficina de Turisme c/Hermenegild Clascar 2 (Mon 3–6pm, Tues–Sat 9.30am–1.30pm & 3–6pm, Sun & hols 10am–1pm; ☎ 938 181 254, ⓦ turismevilafranca .com).

13

EATING AND DRINKING

VILAFRANCA DEL PENEDÈS

la Fàbrica c/Hormonegild Clascar 4 ❶938 171 336, ⓦrestaurantlafabrica.com. This Japanese-Mediterranean fusion spot inside an old pasta factory has an excellent lunchtime menu (€12), as well as à la carte offerings that range from (quite fittingly) home-made pastas to tempura and sushi (mains €8–17). Mon–Sat 1.15– 3.30pm & 8.30–11.30pm.

inzolia c/de la Palma 21, off c/de Sant Joan ❶938 181 938, ⓦinzolia.com. The most agreeable place in town to sample the local wines – a range of cavas and wines is sold by the glass, and there's a good wine shop attached. Mon–Sat 10am–3pm & 5–10pm.

Tarragona

Majestically sited on a rocky hill, perched directly above the sea 100km southwest of Barcelona, **TARRAGONA** is an ancient place: settled originally by Iberians and then Carthaginians, it was later used as the base for the Roman conquest of the peninsula, which began in 218 BC with Scipio's march south against Hannibal. The fortified city became an imperial resort and, under the Emperor Augustus, who lived here for two years, "Tarraco" was the most elegant and cultured city of Roman Spain, boasting at its peak a quarter of a million inhabitants.

Tarragona today is still a very handsome city – especially the upper town, with the sweeping Rambla Nova at its heart, lined with cafés and restaurants. The parallel Rambla Vella marks the start of the old town, while to either side of the *ramblas* are scattered a profusion of relics and monuments from Tarragona's Roman past. In addition to those, the city also holds a wide range of museums, dedicated among other things to modern art, old weapons, the port and harbour, and the noble Castellarnau family, but the only essential visit is to the archeology museum. Note that most of the sights are **closed on Mondays**, though the Catedral, old town and the exterior of certain Roman remains can still be seen.

Catedral

Pl. de la Seu • Mid-March to mid-June & mid-Sept to Oct Mon–Sat 10am–7pm; mid-June to mid-Sept to Oct Mon–Sat 10am–8pm; Nov to mid-March Mon–Fri 10am–5pm, Sat 10am–7pm • €5, under-16s €3, under-7s free, includes entry to Museu Diocesà • ❶977 247 069, ⓦcatedraldetarragona.com

The focal point of the medieval old town, the **Catedral** is a site of great antiquity; the Christian church was built over the provincial Roman forum. Sitting at the top of a broad flight of steps, the main facade presents a soaring Gothic portal framed by Romanesque doors, surmounted by a cross and an elaborate rose window. Other than during services, entrance to the cathedral is through the lovely **cloisters** (*claustre*; signposted up a street to the left of the facade), where among several oddly sculpted capitals is one representing a cat's funeral being directed by rats. The ticket also gives access to the **Museu Diocesà**, piled high with ecclesiastical treasures.

Museu Nacional Arqueològic

Pl. del Rei 5 • June–Sept Tues–Sat 9.30am–8.30pm, Sun 10am–2pm; Oct–May Tues–Sat 9.30am–6pm, Sun 10am–2pm • €4.50 • ❶977 236 209, ⓦmnat.cat

The huge collection of the modern **Museu Nacional Arqueològic**, on the seaward edge of the old town, is largely devoted to the Roman era, and serves as a marvellous reflection of the richness of imperial Tarraco. Thematic displays cover the various remains and buildings around the city, as well as whole rooms devoted to statues, inscriptions, ceramics, jewellery, mosaics – including a colourful floor mosaic depicting dozens of species of fish – and some remarkable glass vessels.

Museum tickets also include admission to Tarraco's ancient **necropolis** – a twenty-minute walk from the centre, down Avinguda Ramon i Cajal, off Rambla Nova – where both pagan and Christian tombs have been uncovered.

13 ## Roman Tarragona: Museu d'Història de Tarragona

April–Sept Tues–Sat 9am–9pm, Sun & hols 9am–3pm; Oct–March Tues–Sat 9am–7pm, Sun & hols 9am–3pm • Each site €3.30, joint ticket to all €7.40, under-16s free • ☎ 977 242 220, ⓦ tarragona.cat

Most of Tarragona's Roman sites are grouped under the umbrella of the **Museu d'Història de Tarragona** (Tarragona History Museum), and share the same opening hours. These start most spectacularly with the **Pretori i Circ Romans** (entered from Pl. del Rei), built at the end of the first century AD to hold chariot races. The vaults and

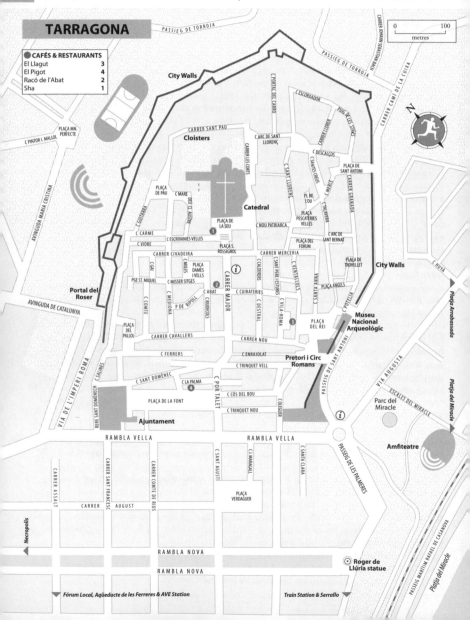

TARRAGONA

● CAFÉS & RESTAURANTS	
El Llagut	3
El Pigot	4
Racó de l'Abat	2
Sha	1

13

chambers have been restored to spectacular effect, while a lift takes you up to the roof of the Pretorium Tower – which chillingly still served as a prison in the post Civil War years – for the best view in Tarragona, looking down over the nearby **Amfiteatre**. There may only be scant remains of the ceremonial provincial forum (Pl. del Fòrum), but the **Fòrum Local** (c/Lleida, a short walk west of Rambla Nova, near the central market) is far more impressive, where the evocative remains of a temple, shops, Roman road and house foundations can still be seen.

Aqüeducte de les Ferreres

Off N240, Lleida road • Open access • Free • Take the bus marked "Sant Salvador" (every 30min; 10min) from the stop outside Av. Prat de la Riba 11 (western end of Rambla Nova and off Av. Ramon i Cajal)

Arguably Tarragona's most remarkable monument, the **Roman aqueduct** that brought water to the city from the Riu Gayo, some 32km distant, stands 4km outside the original city walls. Its most impressive surviving section, nearly 220m long and 26m high, lies in an overgrown valley, off the main road, in the middle of nowhere, and is popularly known as the *Pont del Diable* ("Devil's Bridge").

Local beaches

The rocky coastline below Tarragona conceals a couple of reasonable beaches. The closest to town is the long **Platja del Miracle**, over the rail lines below the amphitheatre, but **Platja Arrabassada**, a couple of kilometres further up the coast, is nicer by far, and holds a smattering of beach bars. Reach it on a pleasant thirty-minute walk by taking Via Augusta off the end of Rambla Vella, then turning right at the *Hotel Astari*.

ARRIVAL AND INFORMATION   TARRAGONA

By train Hourly AVE (high-speed) trains from Barcelona Sants take just 35min, but tickets are expensive and the Camp de Tarragona AVE station is a 10min drive from the centre of town, which adds on the price of a taxi. Otherwise, normal trains from Estació França, Pg. de Gràcia and Barcelona Sants (every 30min; ⓦrenfe.com) take just over an hour: turn right out of the station, climb the steps ahead of you to reach Rambla Nova, by the statue of Roger de Llúria (10min).

Oficina de Turisme c/Major 39 (July–Sept Mon–Sat 10am–8pm, Sun & hols 10am–2pm; Oct–June Mon–Fri 10am–2pm & 3–5pm, Sat 10am–2pm & 3–7pm, Sun & hols 10am–2pm; ❼ 977 250 795, ⓦ tarragonaturisme.cat).

EATING AND DRINKING

The pretty old-town squares, like Pl. del Rei, Pl. del Fòrum and Pl. de la Font are the best places for outdoor drinks and meals. The last in particular features more than a dozen **cafés**, **bars and restaurants** serving everything from *pintxos* to pizzas. Otherwise, for a tasty paella lunch it's worth heading down to Tarragona's so-called fishermen's quarter, **Serrallo**, a 15min walk west along the industrial harbourfront from the train station.

★ **El Llagut** c/de Natzaret 10, at Pl. del Rei ❼ 977 228 938. The best place in the town centre for seafood and rice dishes, with a quiet *terrassa* opposite the archeological museum, and exceptionally welcoming staff. There's a great set-lunch deal for €13; otherwise à la carte meals cost around €25. July & Aug daily 1–4pm & 8.30pm–midnight; Sept–June Mon 1–4pm, Tues–Sat 1–4pm & 8.30pm–midnight.

El Pigot Pl. de la Font 24 ❼ 977 217 766. Lunch menus around the town's nicest square are all similarly priced at around €12.50 but locals plump for the reliably good Catalan food at *El Pigot* – from summer salads to signature rice and *fideuà* dishes. Main dishes otherwise cost around €11–25. Don't miss an ice cream afterwards from *Sirvent*, the well-known parlour just a few doors down the square.

Daily 12.30–4pm & 7.30–11.30pm.

Racó de l'Abat c/de l'Abat 2 ❼ 977 780 371, ⓦ abat restaurant.com. Stone arches, beamed ceilings and crimson plaster walls give this Catalan restaurant – located in a former palace dating from the sixteenth century – an intimate, heritage vibe. The *menú del dia* starts at €15, while most mains (fresh fish, grilled meats) cost around €12–16. June–Sept daily 1–4pm & 8–11pm; Oct–May Mon–Thurs & Sun 1–4pm, Fri 1–4pm & 8–11pm, Sat 8–11pm.

Sha Pl. de la Seu 9 ❼ 634 789 038. Friendly, hippy-tinged café-cum-vintage store right in front of the cathedral, with a great terrace out on the square and a cosy back room filled with splendidly mismatched furniture; a perfect stop-off for drinks and vegetarian food. Tues–Sun noon–midnight.

13 Reus

The charming little city of **Reus**, 100km southwest of Barcelona and 14km northwest of Tarragona, was the birthplace in 1852 of architect Antoni Gaudí, though there was little in his early life to indicate what was to come. He was born to a humble family of boilermakers and coppersmiths, and left for Barcelona when he was 16 years old. Even though there are no Gaudí buildings in Reus, however, it does hold a fascinating interpretive centre dedicated to its most famous son. The Gaudí Centre forms part of the city's **Ruta del Modernisme**, a marked trail around the many buildings and mansions erected in the *modernista* style at the end of the nineteenth century and start of the twentieth, when Reus ranked as Catalunya's second city after Barcelona, and was home to a merchant class made wealthy by the trade in wine and olive oil and, later, textiles, fabrics and ceramics. You can easily see all of Reus's sights in a day out from Barcelona – it's full of pretty squares, good restaurants and handsome pedestrianized shopping streets, with almost everything of note lying within a clearly defined circuit of boulevards.

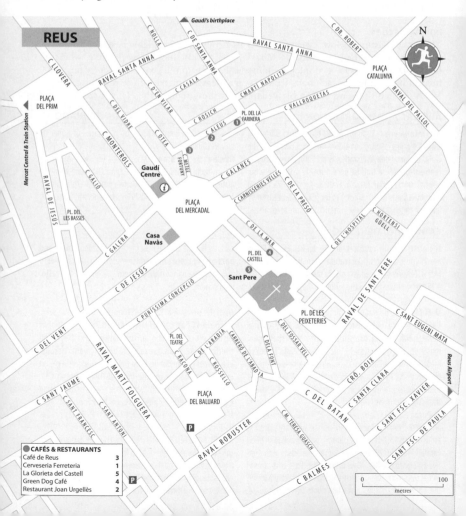

Gaudí Centre

13

Pl. del Mercadal 3 • Mid-June to mid-Sept Mon–Sat 10am–8pm, Sun & hols 11am–2pm; mid-Sept to mid-June Mon–Sat 10am–2pm & 4–7pm, Sun & hols 11am–2pm • €9, under 11s €5, under-8s free • ☎ 977 010 670, ⊕ gaudicentre.com

The **Gaudí Centre**, a gleaming new box of a building on the main square, throws considerable light on the inspiration, methodology and craftsmanship behind Gaudí's work. It's not really a museum as such, though exhibits include copper vessels made by his father; school reports announcing the young Gaudí to be "outstanding" at geometry; his only surviving manuscript notebook; and a reconstruction of his study-workshop at the Sagrada Família. Instead, the centre cleverly investigates the architectural techniques pioneered by Gaudí, with meticulous hands-on models and audiovisual aids that explain, for example, how he created wave roofs and spiral towers. If you ever wondered why none of Gaudí's door frames are straight, or what trees, ferns and snails have to do with architecture, this is undoubtedly the place to find out.

Casa Navàs

Pl. del Mercadal 5 • Tours every Sat at 10.30am, 11.30am & 12.30pm, check with Oficina de Turisme; reservations required • €10, under-7s free, includes Gaudí Centre

Antoni Gaudí may never have built in Reus, but his contemporary, Lluís Domènech i Montaner was responsible for Reus's finest townhouse, the magnificently decorated **Casa Navàs** (1901), across Plaça del Mercadal from the Gaudí Centre. It's still privately owned, but is open for pre-booked tours of the virtually intact period interior, which you shuffle around in overshoes to protect the floor.

Plaça del Mercadal itself used to be the site of the general market – the numbers you can see etched in the square's paving indicated the position of the stalls.

Sant Pere and around

Pl. de Sant Pere • Daily 10.30am–1pm & 4–8pm • Free

Reus's main church, dedicated to its patron saint, **Sant Pere**, is a couple of minutes' walk from the Gaudí Centre. This is where Gaudí was baptized (there's a plaque by the baptismal chapel) and the church also boasts the heart of Reus's number-two son, *modernista* artist Marià Fortuny i Marsal (the plaque here reads "he gave his soul to heaven, his fame to the world, and his heart to his country").

The arcaded square with cafés behind the church, **Plaça de les Peixateries Velles**, was once the local fish market.

Gaudí's birthplace

C/de Sant Vicenç 4

You might as well divert the few minutes from the commercial centre to see **Gaudí's birthplace**. The house is not original, but a plaque marks the site itself, and there's a rather touching sculpture of the young Gaudí playing marbles outside a school just down the street.

ARRIVAL AND INFORMATION

REUS

By air Reus airport, 3km east of town and served by Ryanair flights from the UK, offers connecting buses direct to Barcelona, while local bus #50 runs hourly into town, via the train station.

By train There are hourly Renfe services (⊕ renfe.com) to Reus (via Tarragona) from Pg. de Gràcia and Barcelona Sants; the journey takes 1hr 40min. Taxis wait outside the station, or you can walk to the centre in 15min – head down Pg. Sunyer, turn left at Pl. de les Oques, and follow c/Sant Joan to Pl. del Prim.

Oficina de Turisme Pl. del Mercadal, inside the Gaudí Centre (mid-June to mid-Sept Mon–Sat 10am–8pm, Sun & hols 11am–2pm; mid-Sept to mid-June Mon–Sat 10am–2pm & 4–7pm, Sun & hols 11am–2pm; ☎ 977 010 670, ⊕ reusturisme.cat). You can pick up a good map of town, and ask about guided tours (not always in English).

13

EATING AND DRINKING

Restaurants are plentiful and surprisingly good value for the most part, with a particular concentration around Pl. del Mercadal and along nearby c/de Santa Anna. The daily market (Mon–Sat) takes place at the **Mercat Central** on c/Sant Joan, not far from the train station.

Café de Reus c/del Metge Fortuny ☎ 977 126 266, ⓦ cafedereus.com. This gorgeous nineteenth-century café, just up a lane off the main square, holds an ornate panelled bar and a simpler café, while in summer you can eat outside on the square. Seasonal menus available day and night cost €12–25. Daily 8am–1am.

★ **Cerveseria Ferreteria** Pl. de la Farinera 10 ☎ 977 340 326, ⓦ laferreteriadereus.com. A really lovely setting to enjoy tapas and grills (€3–12, weekday lunch menu €12.50), in a converted historic ironmonger's shop, with tools still in cabinets and bottles stacked on the old wooden shelves. There's also a pretty *terrassa* in the square outside. Daily noon–midnight.

La Glorieta del Castell Pl. del Castell 2 ☎ 977 340 826, ⓦ restaurantlaglorietadelcastell.com. A traditional place, with market-led Catalan cuisine and good-value

menús del dia day and night (€17.60–23.10, otherwise €12–25). Mains include grilled bream with artichokes, *fideuà* or pork in a vermouth sauce. Mon & Wed–Sat 1–4pm & 8.30–11.30pm, Sun 1–4pm.

Green Dog Café Pl. del Castell 5 ☎ 977 370 074. This laidback café/pub, in a small square by the cathedral, is a great spot for an evening or late-night drink, and often puts on live music. Mon–Thurs & Sun 9am–2.30am, Fri & Sat 9am–3am.

Restaurant Joan Urgellès c/d'Aleus 7 ☎ 977 342 178, ⓦ joanurgelles.com. Fancy contemporary cuisine, with inventive dishes like kangaroo steak in bacon-and-shrimp cream or lobster salad with tomato confit, mushrooms and truffle. Dinner menus at €25 and €40, plus a daily lunch menu at €19.50. Mon 8.30–11pm, Tues–Sat 1.30–4pm & 8.30–11pm.

Girona

The ancient walled city of **GIRONA** stands on a fortress-like hill, high above the Riu Onyar, 100km northeast of Barcelona but now barely forty minutes by train. Fought over in almost every century since this site held the Roman fortress of Gerunda, it has been rebuilt and added to many times: following the Moorish conquest of Spain, Girona was an Arab town for over two centuries, and there was also a continuous Jewish presence for six hundred years. The overall impression for the visitor is of an overwhelmingly beautiful medieval city, with old and new towns divided by the river, which is crisscrossed by footbridges, with pastel-coloured houses reflected in the waters below. The compact wedge of land that comprises the old town contains all the sights and monuments, and it takes only half an hour or so to walk from end to end – making historic Girona an easy and very enjoyable day-trip from Barcelona.

Catedral

Pl. de la Catedral • Mon–Sat 10am–7.30pm (Nov–March 10am–6.30pm), Sun 10am–2pm • €7, includes audioguide and visit to nave, treasury and cloister, Sun free & under-7s free • ⓦ catedraldegirona.org

The centrepiece of old Girona, its mighty Gothic **Catedral**, is approached by a magnificent flight of seventeenth-century Baroque steps. Inside, there are no aisles, just one tremendous Gothic nave vault with a span of 22m. Such emphasis on width and height is a defining feature of Catalan-Gothic "hall churches", of which this is the ultimate example. The cathedral treasures include the famous eleventh-century "Creation Tapestry", the finest surviving specimen of Romanesque textile. But it's the exquisite Romanesque **cloisters** (1180–1210) that make the strongest impression, boasting minutely carved figures and scenes on double columns.

Banys Arabs

C/Ferran el Catòlic • April–Sept Mon–Sat 10am–7pm, Sun & hols 10am–2pm; Oct–March Mon–Sat 10am–2pm • €2, under-16s €1 • ☎ 972 190 797, ⓦ banysarabs.cat

The intact remains of Girona's so-called **Banys Arabs**, reached via the twin-towered Portal de Sobreportas below the cathedral, are the best-preserved ancient baths in

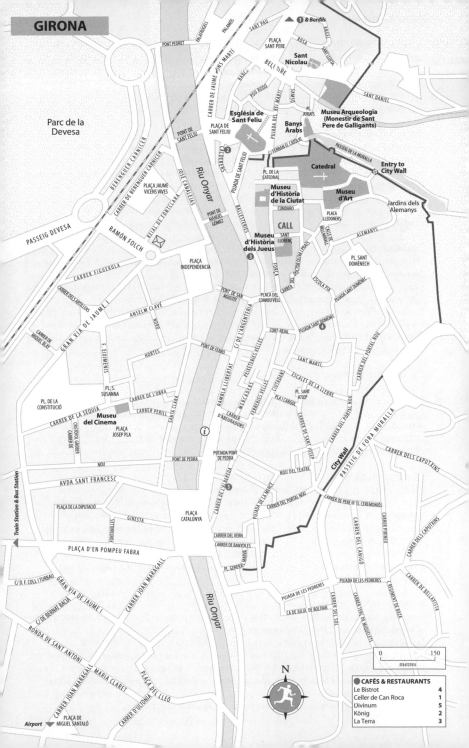

13

Spain after those at Granada. Despite the name, they date from the thirteenth century, a couple of hundred years after the Moors' occupation of Girona had ended, and they're a very graceful blend of Romanesque and Moorish elements, albeit probably built by Moorish craftsmen. It only takes ten minutes or so to explore the three principal rooms, each designed for different temperatures, with an underfloor heating system.

Museu d'Història de Girona

C/de la Força 27 • May–Sept Tues–Sat 10.30am–6.30pm, Sun 10.30am–1.30pm; Oct–April Tues–Sat 10.30am–5.30pm, Sun 10.30am–1.30pm • €4, under-16s free • ☎ 972 222 229, ⓦ www.ajuntament.gi/museuciutat

Girona's excellent history museum, the **Museu d'Història de Girona**, a couple of streets down from the cathedral, traces the city's story from its origins as Parva Gerunda up to the Franco era. Its most beautiful exhibits are unquestionably its well-preserved Roman mosaics, but there's an especially interesting room devoted to the trades practised in the medieval city.

Museu Arqueològic

Monestir de Sant Pere de Galligants, c/de Santa Llúcia 8 • June–Sept Tues–Sat 10.30am–7pm, Sun 10am–2pm; Oct–May Tues–Sat 10am–6pm, Sun 10am–2pm • €4.50, under-8s free • ☎ 972 202 632, ⓦ www.mac.cat

From the cathedral square, the main street, Pujada Rei Martí, leads downhill to the Riu Galligants, a small tributary of the Onyar. The **Museu Arqueològic** stands on the far bank in the former monastic church of Sant Pere de Galligants, a harmonious setting for displays of Roman statuary, sarcophagi and mosaics. The beautiful Romanesque cloisters contain heavier medieval relics, such as inscribed tablets and stones, including some bearing Jewish inscriptions.

Passeig Arqueològic

Daily 8am–10pm • Free

Near the archeological museum, steps up through landscaped grounds lead onto the walls of the old city. You can walk right around their perimeter on the **Passeig Arqueològic**, or archeological route, and enjoy views out over the rooftops and the cathedral. There are endless little diversions along the way, into old watchtowers, down blind dead-ends and around crumpled sections of masonry.

The Jewish quarter

Quite apart from its Roman remains and Arab influences, Girona also contains one of the best-preserved **Jewish quarters** in western Europe, home at its height to around three hundred people who formed a sort of independent town within Girona, protected by the king in return for payment. From the eleventh century onwards, however, the Jewish community suffered systematic persecution and, until the expulsion of the Jews from Spain in 1492, the quarter was effectively a ghetto, its residents restricted to its limits and forced to wear distinguishing clothing if they did leave.

Museu d'Història dels Jueus

C/de la Força 8 • July & Aug Mon–Sat 10am–8pm, Sun & hols 10am–2pm; Sept–June Mon, Sun & hols 10am–2pm, Tues–Sat 10am–6pm • €4, free 1st Sun of month • ☎ 972 216 761, ⓦ girona.cat/call

For an impression of the cultural and social life of Girona's medieval Jewish community, visit the **Museu d'Història dels Jueus**, sited up the skinniest of stepped streets. It's a huge, labyrinthine complex, much of it so heavily restored that you'd never be able to tell exactly which of its many rooms, staircases, courtyards and buildings held the synagogue, the butcher's shop, the baths and other community buildings and services, but everything is very beautifully displayed and explained.

Museu del Cinema

13

c/Sèquia 1 • May, June & Sept Tues–Sat 10am–8pm, Sun & hols 11am–3pm; July & Aug daily 10am–8pm; Oct–April Tues–Fri 10am–6pm, Sat 10am–8pm, Sun & hols 11am–3pm; • €5, under-14s free, free 1st Sun of month • ☎972 412 777, ⓦ www.museudelcinema.cat

If you're visiting Girona on a day-trip from Barcelona, it's well worth giving yourself time as you head back to the station for a visit to the superb **Museu del Cinema**. Based on an extraordinary private collection, this is not so much a museum of cinema as of what it calls "cinema before cinema", with an utterly intriguing array of the gadgets and artefacts that provided popular entertainment before cinema itself came along, from Indonesian shadow puppets to eighteenth- and nineteenth-century devices like phantasmagoria, fantascopes and magic lanterns. It's all rounded up with movie memorabilia including costumes from *Tootsie* and *Hello Dolly*.

ARRIVAL AND INFORMATION   GIRONA

By air Regular bus services run from Girona airport, 12km south of the city, to Girona, Barcelona or the Costa Brava (see p.21).

By train Renfe trains (ⓦrenfe.com) run at least hourly between Sants and Pg. de Gràcia stations in Barcelona, and Girona, with high-speed services taking around 37min and costing around €24 return, and slower trains taking between 1hr 15min and 1hr 40min and costing slightly less. All services arrive at the same station in Girona,

across the river in the modern part of the city; the 10min walk to the old town is well signposted, and you can also take a taxi.

Oficina de Turisme Rambla de la Llibertat 1 (April–Oct Mon–Fri 9am–8pm, Sat 9am–2pm & 4–8pm, Sun & hols 9am–2pm; Nov–March Mon–Fri 9am–7pm, Sat 9am–2pm & 3–7pm, Sun & hols 9am–2pm; ☎972 226 575, ⓦgirona.cat/turisme).

EATING AND DRINKING

Cafés and restaurants abound along Rambla de la Llibertat and the parallel Pl. del Vi, and there's also a group of bars with lovely terraces at the opposite end of the old town, under Sant Feliu church. Another dozen or so restaurants, all with alfresco terraces, stand just over the river in pretty Pl. Independencia.

Le Bistrot Pujada de Sant Domènec ☎972 218 803. Good-value bistro in a pretty and relatively peaceful spot just below St Dominic church, which often puts out tables on the steps. The food is straightforward Catalan, and a decent three-course lunch will cost you €15 during the week and €20 at the weekend. Daily 1pm–1am.

★Celler de Can Roca Can Sunyer 48, off Yaialà road 2.5km northwest of the centre ☎972 222 157, ⓦcellercanroca.com. Hailed as the world's best restaurant by *Restaurant* magazine in 2013, this showcase contemporary-Catalan restaurant has three Michelin stars, and offers delights like caramelized olives served hanging from a small tree, and steak tartare with mustard ice cream. Tasting menus start at €155, and reservations are of course essential. Tues–Sat 1–3.30pm & 9–11pm; closed 3 weeks in Dec and 1 week in Aug.

Divinum c/Albareda 7 ☎872 080 218, ⓦdivinum.cat.

Sleek restaurant near the tourist office, serving top-notch modern Catalan cuisine, with individual dishes like foie gras with vanilla and apple or steak tartare at €14–26, and a wonderful €45 tasting menu. Mon–Sat 1.30–3.45pm & 8.30–11pm.

König c/dels Calderes 16 ☎972 225 782, ⓦkonig.cat. With its pretty *terrassa* under the high walls of Sant Feliu church, this all-day café-bar makes a pleasant stop for a drink. Food (€3–8) is along the lines of salads, tapas, sandwiches and burgers. Daily 8am–midnight.

La Terra c/Ballesteries 23 ☎972 219 254. Friendly, very inexpensive hippy-ish café, where you can savour simple €8 quiche or burger lunches at tables nestled into the glassed-in balconies overlooking the river, or simply call in for carrot cake with coffee or colourful fresh-squeezed fruit juices. Daily 10am–2am.

Figueres

As a provincial town in northern Catalunya that's home to a population of just thirty thousand, **FIGUERES** would pass almost unnoticed were it not for the Museu Dalí, installed by **Salvador Dalí** in a building as surreal as the exhibits within. It's a popular day-trip from Barcelona, as ultra-fast trains now take less than an hour to make the 135km journey northeast of the city.

13

The museum is very much the main event in town, though it's easy to fill in the rest of the day in the handsome centre. Pavement cafés line the tree-shaded *rambla*, while art galleries, clothes stores and gift shops line the pedestrianized streets and squares. On Tuesday, Thursday and Saturday, you'll coincide with the main **fruit, veg and flower market** – Thursday is best, since there's also a huge **clothes market**. As Figueres is a "tourist town", shops in the historic centre are allowed to open on Sundays and holidays.

Museu Dalí

Pl. Gala i Salvador Dalí • March–May Tues–Sun 9.30am–6pm; June daily 9.30am–6pm; July & Sept daily 9am–8pm; Aug daily 9am–8pm & 10pm–1am; Oct Tues–Sun 9.30am–6pm; Nov–Feb Tues–Sun 10.30am–6pm; last admission always 45min before closing • €12, under-8s free • ☎ 972 677 500, ⓦ salvador-dali.org

The **Museu Dalí** appeals to everyone's innate love of fantasy, absurdity and participation. While it's not a collection of Dalí's greatest hits – those are scattered far and wide – what you do get beggars description, and should not be missed.

The building (a former theatre) is an exhibit in itself, topped by a huge metallic dome and decorated with a line of luminous egg shapes. **Outlandish sculptures** and statues adorn the square and facade, and things get even crazier inside, where the walls of the circular courtyard are ringed by stylized mannequins preparing to dive from the heights. Below sits the famous **Rainy Cadillac**, where you can water the snail-encrusted occupants of a steamy Cadillac by feeding it with coins. In the **Mae West Room** an unnerving portrait of the actress is revealed by peering through a mirror at giant nostrils, red lips and hanging tresses, while elsewhere you'll find a complete life-sized orchestra, some of Dalí's extraordinary furniture (like the fish-tail bed) and ranks of **Surrealist paintings** – including one room dominated by the ceiling fresco of the huge feet of Dalí and Gala (his Russian wife and muse).

The museum also contains many of Dalí's own collection of works by other artists, from Catalan contemporaries to El Greco, and there are temporary exhibitions, too, while your ticket also allows admission to see the **Dalí-Joies** – a collection of

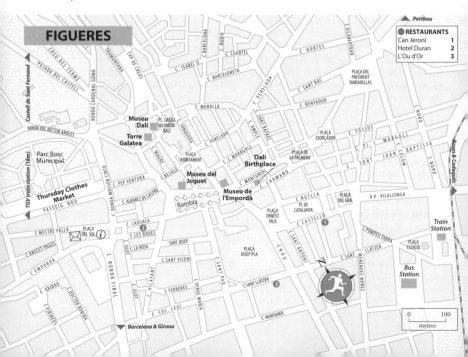

13

SURREAL SALVADOR

Salvador Dalí i Domènech (1904–89) was born in Figueres – you can see the exterior of his **birthplace**, which is marked with a plaque, at c/Monturiol 6, as well as that of the Dalí family's next home, at no. 10. He gave his first exhibition in the town's municipal theatre when he was just 14 and, after a stint at the Royal Academy of Art in Madrid (he was expelled), he made his way to Paris, where he established himself at the forefront of the Surrealist movement. A celebrity artist in the US in the 1940s and 1950s, he returned eventually to Europe where, among other projects, he set about reconstructing the now-defunct theatre. This opened as the Museu Dalí in 1974, which Dalí then fashioned into an inspired repository for his works.

By 1980, Dalí was growing increasingly frail. After suffering severe burns in a fire in 1984, he moved into the **Torre Galatea**, the tower adjacent to the museum, and controversy surrounded his final years. Spanish government officials and friends feared that he was manipulated in his senile condition. Allegations that he signed blank canvases has inevitably led to doubts over the authenticity of some of his later works. Dalí died in Figueres on January 23, 1989. His body now lies behind a simple granite slab inside the museum.

extraordinary jewels, designed in the 1940s for an American millionaire and displayed here with Dalí's original drawings.

ARRIVAL AND INFORMATION   FIGUERES

By train High-speed trains from Barcelona Sants and Pg. de Gràcia take just 53min to reach the Figueres Vilafant TGV station, 1.5km west of the centre; somewhat less frequent slower trains from the same Barcelona stations take up to 2hr and stop at Figueres' original station, 1km east of the centre. Both routes are operated by Renfe (⊛renfe.com). Fares vary for each specific train, but broadly speaking you can expect to pay perhaps €28 round-trip for the slower route, more like €36 for the faster one. All trains call at

Girona, which is around 15min from Figueres on the fast route, 30–40min on the slower. The "Museu Dalí" is signposted from both Figueres stations, and there's also a €2 bus from the TGV station.

Oficina de Turisme Pl. del Sol, in front of the post office building (late June to mid-Sept Mon–Sat 9am–8pm, Sun 10am–3pm; mid-Sept to late June Mon–Sat 10am–2pm & 4–7pm, Sun 10am–2pm; ☎972 503 155, ⊛visitfigueres .cat).

EATING AND DRINKING

A gaggle of largely missable tourist **restaurants** is crowded into the narrow streets around the Dalí museum, while more cafés and restaurants overlook the *rambla*. Lunch menus everywhere go for €10–12, with the sunniest seats to be found at the top of the *rambla*. Elsewhere, there's a better selection of hidden-away restaurants that are more geared to locals, where the food tends to be more interesting and authentic.

Can Jeroni c/Castelló 36 ☎972 500 983, ⊛canjeroni .com. Locals like this tiled tavern opposite the market, where country-style dishes and grills (*torrades*, salads, steaks, chops, sausages) go for €7–17. Mid-Sept to mid-June Mon–Thurs 8am–3.30pm, Fri & Sat 8am–3.30pm & 8.30–10pm; mid-June to mid-Sept Mon, Tues & Sat 8am–3.30pm, Wed–Fri 8am–3.30pm & 8.30–10pm.

★**Hotel Duran** c/Lausaca 5 ☎972 501 250, ⊛hotel duran.com. The top choice in town, known for its excellent regional cuisine, including fresh fish landed daily from the

nearby coast. It's fairly pricey (mains €13–26) though there is a reasonable lunchtime menu for €20 and a more elaborate tasting menu at €47. Daily 12.45–4pm & 8.30–11pm.

L'Ou d'Or c/de Sant Llàtzer 16 ☎972 503 765, ⊛loudor .com. This pretty little restaurant, with courtyard seating, calls itself a *truiteria*, from the Catalan for *tortilla*. An uncomplicated set menu is served day and night, featuring such dishes as hake, or trout with almonds, for around €14. Mon–Sat 1–3.30pm & 8–11pm.

Accommodation

Finding a hotel vacancy in Barcelona at any time of year can be difficult, so it's always best to book in advance. Prices are high for Spain but still pretty reasonable when compared to other big European cities, while stylish rooms on a moderate budget – in this designer style capital – are fairly easy to come by. There's a wide range of overnight options in the city, from youth hostels and budget *pensions* to glam five-star-plus resort hotels, housed in medieval mansions and *modernista* masterpieces alike. If you're looking for the home-from-home experience then Barcelona also has lots of self-contained apartments for rent, not to mention an increasing number of private "bed-and-breakfast" establishments – some simply the traditional room in someone's house, others very stylish and pricey boutique bolt-holes.

Places to stay go under various names – *pensió, residència, hostal,* hotel – though only **hotels and pensions** are recognized as official categories. These are all star-rated (hotels, one- to five-star; *pensions,* one- or two-star), but the rating is not necessarily a guide to cost or ambience. Some of the smaller, boutique-style *pensions* and hotels have services and facilities that belie their star rating; some four- and five-star hotels have disappointingly small rooms and an impersonal feel.

Apartment rentals are an increasingly popular option (see box, p.166). As for **youth hostels**, some traditional backpacker dives survive here and there, but they have largely been superseded by well-equipped, well-run modern hostels with en-suite dorm rooms as well as private rooms. For a more intimate experience there are plenty of **budget pensions** that also have dorms and shared accommodation. A youth hostel, incidentally, is an *albergue*; *hostal* is the word for a *pensió*.

14

ESSENTIALS

ROOM RATES

Prices Rates given in our reviews reflect the usual cost of a double or twin room in high season (basically Easter–Oct, plus Christmas/New Year, major trade fairs, festivals and other events). The cheapest rooms in a simple hotel, sharing a bathroom, cost around €50 (singles from €30), though for private facilities €70–80 a night is more realistic. Places with a bit of boutique styling start at around €100, while for Barcelona's most fashionable hotels, count on €250–400 a night. Studio apartments sleeping two start at around €100, while a hostel dorm bed costs between €15 and €30 a night, depending on the season.

Tax A ten-percent tax, IVA, is added to all accommodation bills, though it's sometimes included in the quoted price. An additional "tourist tax" for stays of up to seven nights is also charged on top of your bill – €0.65 to €2.25 (determined by the type of property) per person per night. Under-17s are exempt, though, and most tourist establishments in Barcelona fall into the lowest tax band.

Discounts Book directly online through hotel websites for the best available rates. Some places offer discounts in the off-season months of January, February and November, while others have special rates in August (when business travel is scarce).

Breakfast While many hotels put on a lavish buffet spread, breakfast can be expensive (around €10–15 per person), so if all you want is coffee and a croissant it's better to go out to a café.

RESERVATIONS

Hotels You can reserve hotel accommodation online with the city tourist board (🌐 barcelonaturisme.com) or make same-day bookings in person only at their tourist offices at Pl. de Catalunya, the airport, Sants train station and elsewhere.

Credit cards Although you may be asked for a credit card number to secure a room, at most hotels your card won't be charged until your stay. However, some smaller *pensions* may take a deposit or charge you in advance. Credit cards are accepted almost everywhere (though American Express isn't always).

WHERE TO STAY

If you hanker after a **Ramblas** view, you'll pay for the privilege – generally speaking, there are much better deals to be had either side of the famous boulevard, often just a minute's walk away. Alongside some classy boutique choices, most of Barcelona's cheapest accommodation is found in the old town, principally the **Barri Gòtic** and **El Raval** neighbourhoods, which can both still have their rough edges – be careful (without being paranoid) when coming and going after dark. East of the Barri Gòtic, in **Sant Pere** and **La Ribera**, there are a number of safely sited budget, mid-range and boutique options, handy for the Picasso museum and the Born nightlife area. North of Plaça de Catalunya, the **Eixample** – split into Right (**Dreta**) and Left (**Esquerra**)– has some of the city's most fashionable hotels, often housed in converted palaces and mansions and located just a few minutes' walk from the *modernista* architectural masterpieces. Hotels near Sants station are convenient for **Montjuïc** and the metro system, and those further north in **Les Corts** for the Avinguda Diagonal shopping district. For waterfront views look at **Port Vell** at the end of the Ramblas, and at the **Port Olímpic** southeast of the old town – while new four- and five-stars abound much further out on the metro at the **Diagonal Mar** conference and events site. If you prefer neighbourhood living, then the northern district of **Gràcia** is the best base, as you're only ever a short walk away from its excellent bars, restaurants and clubs.

14

APARTMENT RENTALS

Available by the night or week, prices for apartment rentals can compare well with mid-range hotels, but make sure you're happy with the location (some are out in the suburbs) and understand all the costs – cleaning charges, utility bills and taxes can all push up the attractive quoted figure. Try **Barcelona On-Line** (Ⓦbarcelona-on-line.com) or **Inside-BCN** (Ⓦinsidebarcelona.com), while Barcelona-based **My Favourite Things** (Ⓦmyft.net) has an eye for offbeat rooms and apartments in private houses. **Izaka** (Ⓣ934 122 779, Ⓦizaka.com) offer a cluster of spacious and very classy city-centre apartments, particularly suited for business travellers, with high-season rates starting at around €160 per day.

With the advent of online community marketplaces such as **Airbnb** (Ⓦairbnb.com) and **9flats** (Ⓦ9flats.com), designed to connect travellers with locals who have spaces to rent, a new pool of competitively priced – and sometimes unique – lodging has entered the where-to-stay game. Take your pick: from a sailboat in Port Olímpic to a private penthouse overlooking Park Güell. But be aware: the legal status of private-let online services is under constant threat, and Airbnb was recently fined €30,000 by the Catalan government.

INTERNET AND WI-FI

While you get cheap or free internet and wi-fi in most hotels and hostels, a few of the swankier hotels still tend to charge like a wounded bull for internet access after an initial free period. Always check the small print before you sign up.

THE RAMBLAS

★**Hostal Benidorm** Ramblas 37 Ⓣ933 022 054, Ⓦhostalbenidorm.com; ⓂDrassanes; map p.38. Refurbished *pensió* opposite Pl. Reial that offers real value for money, hence the tribes of young tourists. Plain rooms are available for one to five people, all with satellite TV and a/c, bathtubs or showers, and a balcony and Ramblas view if you're lucky. **€75**

Hostal Mare Nostrum Ramblas 67, entrance on c/de Sant Pau 2 Ⓣ933 185 340, Ⓦhostalmarenostrum.com; ⓂLiceu; map p.38. A cheery Ramblas *pensió* whose English-speaking management offers comfortable double, triple and family rooms with satellite TV and a/c. The rooms – all are en suite – are modern and double-glazed against the noise, and some come with balconies and street views. **€110**

Hotel Eurostars Ramblas Boquería Ramblas 91–93 Ⓣ933 435 461, Ⓦeurostarsramblasboqueria.com; ⓂLiceu; map p.38. Snappy little boutique rooms in a small three-star hotel right outside the Boqueria market. There's not much space, but all you need is on the doorstep, and the soundproofing is good so you get a street view without the racket. **€165**

★**Hotel H1898** Ramblas 109, entrance on c/de Pintor Fortuny Ⓣ935 529 552, Ⓦhotel1898.com; ⓂCatalunya; map p.38. The former headquarters of the Philippines Tobacco Company has four grades of room (the standard is "Classic") in deep red, green or black, plus sumptuous suites, some with their own private pool, jacuzzi and garden. Public areas are similarly dramatic, such as the neocolonial hall, lounge and bar, and the tropics-kissed terrace restaurant *La Isabela* (open April–Oct), while other facilities include both outdoor and indoor pools, and a glam spa. **€335**

Hotel Husa Oriente Ramblas 45 Ⓣ933 022 558, Ⓦhotelhusaoriente.com; ⓂLiceu; map p.38. For somewhere on the Ramblas that's traditional but not too pricey, this historic three-star is your best bet. Converted from a former convent, its grand public rooms and taste-fully updated bedrooms display nineteenth-century style; some of the latter have Ramblas views (though the quieter ones face inwards). Special rates from €85. **€160**

Hotel Sehrs Rivoli Ramblas Ramblas 128 Ⓣ934 817 676, Ⓦhotelrivoliramblas.com; ⓂCatalunya; map p.38. The elegant rooms in this stylish four-star hotel near the top of the avenue are imaginatively furnished (Art Deco to avant-garde), and all come with spacious bathrooms, while the front ones have floor-to-ceiling windows with classic Ramblas views. There's also a lovely rooftop terrace and bar open during the summer months. **€150**

Le Méridien Barcelona Ramblas 111 Ⓣ933 186 200, Ⓦlemeridienbarcelona.com; ⓂCatalunya; map p.38. The five-star *Méridien*, one of the high-end Ramblas stalwarts, offers "deluxe" as the norm; you can expect your bedroom to feature designer leather furniture, an iPod-dock and splash-proof TVs in the natural-toned marble bathroom. You pay a lot more for a Ramblas view or any kind of extra space (another €200 for example gets you a "Mediterranean" suite with terrace and outdoor rain shower), though things are surprisingly democratically priced in the flash *CentOnze* restaurant, which opens right onto the Ramblas. **€236**

BARRI GÒTIC

Hostal Fernando c/de Ferran 31 ☎933 017 993, ⓦhfernando.com; ⓜLiceu; map p.44. Rooms at these prices fill quickly around here (low-season dorms from just €19 and rooms from €72); that they're also light, modern and well kept by friendly people is a real bonus. All come with a/c and private bathrooms, while straightforward dorm accommodation is available in en-suite rooms that sleep four to eight. Dorms €27, rooms €90

★**Hostal Rembrandt** c/de la Portaferrissa 23 ☎933 181 011, ⓦhostalrembrandt.com; ⓜLiceu; map p.44. A clean, safe, old-town budget *pensió* that has been smartened up over the years by friendly English-speaking owners, who request "pin-drop silence" after 11pm. Simple tile-floored rooms (a bit cheaper without private bathroom) have a street-side balcony or little patio, while larger rooms are more versatile and can sleep up to four. €65

Hotel Barcelona Catedral c/dels Capellans 4 ☎933 042 255, ⓦbarcelonacatedral.com; ⓜJaume I; map p.44. Exceptionally friendly modern hotel in an unbeatable location, just a few metres north of the main cathedral square, offering comfortable and stylish contemporary rooms and substantial buffet breakfasts plus a gym, restaurant, bar and rooftop pool. €149

Hotel Cantón c/Nou de Sant Francesc 40 ☎933 173 019, ⓦhotelcanton-bcn.com; ⓜDrassanes; map p.44. A modest one-star hotel that's only two blocks off the Ramblas and close to the harbour and Port Vell. The 47 rooms feature uniform blue-and-white trim curtains and bedspreads, central heating and a/c, fridge and wardrobe. A few rooms have balconies (though they don't have much of a view) – all are well insulated against street noise. A buffet continental breakfast is available, served in a stone-walled dining room, and room prices drop a good bit out of season. €72

★**Hotel Do** Pl. Reial 1 ☎934 813 666, ⓦhoteldoreial.com; ⓜLiceu; map p.44. Renowned Catalan architect Oriol Bohigas led the renovation of this nineteenth-century Neoclassical building on the city's emblematic Pl. Reial. The result is a gastronomic boutique hotel with eighteen impeccably appointed rooms, most overlooking the square, which seamlessly blends the contemporary with the timeless. On top of this, quite literally, is the rooftop lounge and blue-tiled plunge pool, plus spa with sauna, steam bath and heated bench. It's not cheap, but the finer things in life rarely are. €230

Hotel El Jardí Pl. Sant Josep Oriol 1 ☎933 015 900, ⓦeljardi-barcelona.com; ⓜLiceu; map p.44. The hotel's location, overlooking the charming Pl. del Pi, is what sells this place – and explains the steep-ish prices for quarters that can seem a bit bare and poky. But some rooms (the top ones have terraces or balconies, from €15 extra) look directly onto the square, and there's a range of cheaper internal rooms too. You can have breakfast at the hotel, but the *Bar del Pi* in the square below is nice. €90

Hotel Racó del Pi c/del Pi 7 ☎933 426 190, ⓦh10hotels .com; ⓜLiceu; map p.44. A stylish little three-star hotel in a great location. Appealing rooms – some with balconies over the street – have wood floors and granite-and-mosaic bathrooms. There's a glass of cava on check-in, and free coffee and snacks during the day in the bar. €214

Itaca Hostel c/de Ripoll 21 ☎933 019 751, ⓦitacahostel .com; ⓜJaume I; map p.44. Bright and breezy converted house close to the cathedral, offering spacious hostel rooms (sleeping six, eight or ten) with balconies. Dorms are mixed, though you can also reserve a private room or even an apartment (sleeps up to six; €120), and with a hostel capacity of only thirty it rarely feels overcrowded. There's a kitchen and book-exchange service, coffee and breakfast available and decent discounts in the low season. Dorms €19, rooms €60

Mercer Hotel c/dels Lledó 7 ☎933 102 387, ⓦmercer barcelona.com; ⓜJaume I; map p.44. When it comes to Old World charm, the beautiful Mercer is about as old as it gets. Though the luxurious hotel itself is just a few years old,

14

BALCONIES, VIEWS AND NOISE

Almost all hotels and *pensions* in Barcelona have at least some rooms with a **balcony** over the street or square. These tend to be the brightest rooms in the building and, because of the obvious inherent attraction, they usually cost more than other rooms. However, it can't be stressed enough that rooms facing onto Barcelona's streets are often noisy. Traffic is a constant presence (including the dawn street-cleaners) and, in a city where people are just getting ready to go out at 10pm, you can be assured of a fair amount of pedestrian noise too, particularly in the old town, and especially at weekends. Soundproofed windows and double-glazing deal partly with the problem, but you tend not to have this luxury in cheaper *pensions* – where throwing open the windows may be the only way to get some air in the height of summer anyway. Bring earplugs if you're at all concerned about having a sleepless night.

Alternatively, ask for an **internal room** (*habitació interior*). It's true that most buildings are built around a central air or lift shaft, and your view could simply be a lime-green wall 1m away and someone's washing line. However, some places are built instead around an internal patio, so your room might overlook a pot-plant terrace or garden – and you shouldn't get any street noise.

14

---

parts of the building are ancient (the Roman wall that surrounded the ancient city of Barcino makes up the rear facade). Architect Rafael Moneo highlighted a huge mix of architectural styles when restoring the building: medieval arches, wooden coffered ceilings and ornate Gothic columns found in the rooms and public areas marry with contemporary designer furnishings. Rooms are elegant, spacious and silent. Two restaurants, a rooftop bar and pool, a vertical garden of aromatics such as lavender and rosemary and a lovely interior patio offer options for relaxation. €425

★**Neri Hotel** c/de Sant Sever 5 ☎933 040 655, Ⓦhotelneri.com; Ⓜ Liceu/Jaume I; map p.44. Close to the cathedral, a delightful eighteenth-century palace houses this stunning boutique hotel of just 22 rooms and suites, featuring swags of flowing material, rescued timber, granite-toned bathrooms and lofty proportions. Designers have

created eye-catching effects, like a tapestry that falls four floors through the central atrium, while a beamed library and stylish roof terrace provide a tranquil escape. Guests can take their breakfast, which is served as a buffet, either out in the courtyard in summer or in chef Benito Iranzo's fine contemporary Mediterranean restaurant. €360

Pensió Alamar c/de la Comtessa de Sobradiel 1 ☎933 025 012, Ⓦpensioalamar.com; Ⓜ Liceu/Jaume I; map p.44. If you don't mind sharing a bathroom then this simply furnished *pensió* makes a convenient base. There are twelve rooms (singles, doubles and triples), most with little balconies, and while space is tight, there's a friendly welcome, laundry service and use of a kitchen. Requests no noise after midnight, so it suits early-birds and sightseers rather than partygoers. No credit cards. €45

★**Pensión Mari-Luz** c/del Palau 4, 2° ☎933 173 463, Ⓦpensionmariluz.com; Ⓜ Jaume I/Liceu; map p.44. This old mansion, on a quieter-than-usual Barri Gòtic street, offers inexpensive rooms (most share bathrooms), plus a more personal welcome than in many other places of its kind. Someone's been to IKEA for furniture and there are contemporary art prints on the walls, central heating and a/c, laundry facilities and a small kitchen. It can be a tight squeeze when full. Rates drop in low season. €69

EL RAVAL

★**Barceló Raval** Rambla del Raval 17–21 ☎933 201 490, Ⓦwww.barceloraval.com; Ⓜ Liceu/Sant Antoni; map pp.58–59. This glow-in-the-dark tower is the landmark of the neighbourhood; its USP is the 360-degree top-floor terrace with plunge pool and sensational city views. Sophisticated, open-plan rooms have a crisp, space-station-style sheen, plus iPod docks, espresso machines and other cool comforts, while the slinky lobby *B-lounge* is the place for everything from tapas to cocktails. €136

Casa Camper c/d'Elisabets 11 ☎933 426 280, Ⓦcasacamper.com; Ⓜ Universitat/Liceu; map pp.58–59. Synonymous with creative, comfy shoes, Barcelona-based *Camper* has taken a bold step into the hospitality business with this sleek, minimalist hotel. Each of the twenty rooms are divided by a corridor: the "sleeping" side (a red-coloured bedroom with bathroom) faces a six-storey-tall vertical garden; the other part is a "mini-lounge" with a flat-screen TV, hammock and street-facing balcony. Breakfast is included, as are the drinks and savoury and sweet treats (salads, sandwiches, cakes) available around the clock in

the lobby, and adjacent to the hotel is the Michelin-starred *Dos Palillos* (see p.180). To burn off all this good food, there's also a 24hr gym, free for all guests. €217

Hostal Cèntric c/de Casanova 13 ☎934 267 573, Ⓦwww.hostalcentric.com; Ⓜ Universitat; map pp.58–59. A good upper-budget choice, a couple of minutes' walk from the Raval. The bright, modern rooms are decorated in a soothing, neutral palette, have private bathrooms, a/c, safes and flat-screen TVs, and some come with a balcony. There's a sunny terrace at the rear. €104

★**Hostal Grau** c/de les Ramelleres 27 ☎933 018 135, Ⓦhostalgrau.com; Ⓜ Catalunya; map pp.58–59. A really friendly and very attractive *pensió* that's been updated and adapted over the years. Private bathrooms in the rooms and ecofriendly touches such as handmade, all-natural mattresses. You'll pay €15 more for superior rooms with balconies, while two small private apartments in the same building (sleeping two to four, available by the night; €150) offer a bit more independence. The kitchen has recently been renovated and there's a café next door. €70

Hotel Curious c/del Carme 25 ☎933 014 484, Ⓦhotelcurious.com; Ⓜ Liceu; map pp.58–59. Stylish budget digs that offer coordinated, elemental room colours and a huge Barcelona photo backdrop behind each bed. Aside from a free buffet breakfast and helpful staff, services are on the light side, but you're only a few steps from the Ramblas or from the Raval's restaurants and nightlife. €130

★**Hotel España** c/de Sant Pau 9–11 ☎935 500 000, ⓦhotelespanya.com; ⓜLiceu; map pp.58–59. The revamp of the classic *Hotel España* (see box, p.61) as a four-star-plus has been a remarkable success. The sumptuously restored *modernista* icon with its gem-like interior – colourful tiles, bright mosaics, sculpted marble, iron swirls and marine motifs – has no equal in the city. While public areas reboot the *modernista* era, guest rooms are a perfectly judged boutique blend of earth tones and designer style, with rain-showers, iPod docks and the like. There's a plunge pool and chill-out deck on the roof terrace, while the handsome house restaurant – known as *Fonda España* – offers contemporary Catalan bistro dishes by top chef Martín Berasategui. **€154**

Hotel Onix Liceo c/Nou de la Rambla 36 ☎934 816 441, ⓦonixliceohotel.com; ⓜLiceu/Drassanes; map pp.58–59. Steps from Palau Güell, this four-star hotel features minimalist decor that melds nicely with the building's older architectural elements, such as the grand marble staircase that curves up from the lobby to the second floor. There's a tropical patio and big-for-Barcelona pool on the ground floor and an airy Mozarab-influenced lounge area, plus free refreshments are available throughout the day. In-room amenities include a/c, flat-screen TVs and minibars. **€129**

Hotel Peninsular c/de Sant Pau 34 ☎933 023 138, ⓦhotelpeninsular.net; ⓜLiceu; map pp.58–59. This interesting old building originally belonged to a priestly order, which explains the slightly cell-like quality of the rooms. However, there's nothing spartan about the galleried inner courtyard (around which the rooms are ranged), hung with dozens of tumbling houseplants, while breakfast is served in the arcaded dining room. **€80**

Hotel Sant Agustí Pl. Sant Agustí 3 ☎933 181 658, ⓦhotelsa.com; ⓜLiceu; map pp.58–59. Barcelona's

TOP 5 STYLE ON A BUDGET

Casa Gracia See p.174
Chic & Basic Born See below
Hostal Goya See p.171
Hotel Banys Orientals See p.170
Market Hotel See below

14

oldest hotel occupies a former seventeenth-century convent building, with balconies overlooking a restored square and church. It's of three-star standard, with the best rooms located in the attic, from where there are rooftop views. **€125**

★**Market Hotel** c/del Comte Borrell 68, at Ptge. Sant Antoni Abat ☎933 251 205, ⓦmarkethotel.com.es; ⓜSant Antoni; map pp.58–59. The designer-budget *Market* makes a definite splash with its part-Japanese, part neocolonial look – think jet-black rooms with hardwood floors and shutters, and boxy wardrobes topped with travel trunks. It's a feel that flows through the building and down into the impressive restaurant, where the food is exceptionally good value, while the hotel's vintage Asian-style *Bar Rosso* has become a bit of a local hipsters' haunt. **€100**

Mesón Castilla c/de Valldonzella 5 ☎933 182 182, ⓦwww.mesoncastilla.com; ⓜUniversitat; map pp.58–59. A curious throwback to 1950s rural Spain, every inch of this two-star hotel is carved, painted and stencilled, from the grandfather clock in reception to the wardrobe in your room. The large rooms (some with terraces; €22 extra) feature country-style furniture, there's a vast rustic dining room (buffet breakfast included) and – best of all – a lovely tiled rear patio on which to read in the sun. **€105**

SANT PERE AND LA RIBERA

★**Chic & Basic Born** c/de la Princesa 50 ☎932 954 652, ⓦchicandbasic.com; ⓜJaume I; map p.68. From the babbling blurb ("it's fresh, it's cool, it's fusion") to the open-plan, all-in-white decor, everything here is punchily boutique and in-your-face. The 31 rooms mix glamour and comfort with laugh-aloud conceits like adjustable mood-lighting, sashaying plastic curtains and mirrored walls; larger rooms cost €25 more. Chic, certainly; basic, not at all, though the concept eschews room service, minibars and hordes of staff at your beck and call. There are other *Chic & Basic* outlets in the Raval, one on c/Tallers (near Pl. Universitat), one near the zoo and the other off the bottom of the Ramblas, and some Barri Gòtic apartments too (details on the website). **€110**

Equity Point Gothic c/dels Vigatans 5 ☎932 312 045, ⓦequity-point.com; ⓜJaume I; map p.68. Of Barcelona's three *Equity Point* hostels, this is the most backpacker-orientated, which might or might not be a good thing, depending on your view, age and capacity for company. Multi-bunk rooms have an en-suite shower-bathroom, each

bed has its own bedside cabinet and reading light, and there are lockers, left-luggage and tour services, and an old-town roof terrace. Winter prices go as low as €15. Open 24hr. Includes breakfast. Dorms **€25**

★**Grand Hotel Central** Via Laietana 30 ☎932 957 900, ⓦgrandhotelcentral.com; ⓜJaume I; map p.68. It might be on one of the city's noisiest thoroughfares, but the soundproofing does its job handsomely in this wham-glam designer hotel beloved of all the style mags. Spacious, ever-so-lovely rooms hit all the right buttons – hardwood floors, Egyptian cotton sheets, high-end toiletries – and up on the roof there are amazing views from the sundeck and infinity pool. Meanwhile, the fabulous hotel restaurant and café, *Ávalon*, showcases the new-wave Catalan cooking of chef Ramón Freixa. **€248**

★**Hostal Nuevo Colón** Av. del Marquès de l'Argentera 19, 1° ☎933 195 077, ⓦhostalnuevocolon.com; ⓜBarceloneta; map p.68. In the hands of the same friendly family for decades, this well-kept *pensió* sports 24

14

TOP 5 VIEWS

Barceló Raval See p.168
Gran Hotel La Florida See p.174
Hotel Casa Fuster See p.174
Hotel Majestic See p.172
Hotel Miramar Barcelona See opposite

spacious rooms, painted yellow and kitted out with directors' chairs and double-glazing. Sunny front rooms, lounge and terrace all have side views to Ciutadella park. You'll save around €20 in a room with shared facilities; there are also three self-catering apartments available (by the night; €155) in the same building, which sleep up to six. **€70**
Hotel Banys Orientals c/de l'Argenteria 37 ☎ 932 688 460, ⓦ hotelbanysorientals.com; Ⓜ Jaume I; map p.68. Cool boutique hotel with 43 minimalist rooms, plus some more spacious duplex suites (€150) in a nearby building. Hardwood floors, crisp white sheets, sharp marble bathrooms and urban-chic decor – not to mention bargain prices for this sort of style – make it a hugely popular choice. The attached restaurant, *Senyor Parellada*, is a great find too. **€120**
Hotel Ciutat Barcelona c/de la Princesa 33–35 ☎ 932 697 475, ⓦ ciutatbarcelona.com; Ⓜ Jaume 1; map p.68. Contemporary elegance at three-star prices in a hotel that's well sited for old-town sightseeing and the Picasso museum. The stylish, colour-coordinated rooms are soundproofed against street noise, if a bit tight on space. Up top there's a cute deck and small pool for lounging

about, and a handsome restaurant below. **€120**
K+K Hotel Picasso Pg. de Picasso 26 ☎ 935 478 600, ⓦ kkhotels.com; Ⓜ Jaume I/Barceloneta; map p.68. A sophisticated four-star hotel offering bright, contemporary rooms with spacious granite bathrooms, a/c, soundproofing and tea- and coffee-making facilities. On the roof, there's a swimming pool and terrace overlooking the verdant Parc de la Ciutadella. A bar and bistro serves cocktails and tapas, which you can enjoy out on the interior patio. Breakfast included; secure underground parking available. **€222**
Park Hotel Av. del Marquès de l'Argentera 11 ☎ 933 196 000, ⓦ parkhotelbarcelona.com; Ⓜ Barceloneta; map p.68. The classy update for this elegant, modernist 1950s building starts with the chic bar and lounge, and runs up the feature period stairway to rooms in fawn and chocolate-brown with parquet floors, marble bathrooms and beds with angular reading lights. It's a bit on the pricey side for a three-star, but there's real retro style here. **€130**
★ **Pensió 2000** c/de Sant Pere Més Alt 6, 1º ☎ 933 107 466, ⓦ pensio2000.com; Ⓜ Urquinaona; map p.68. As close to a traditional, family-style B&B as Barcelona gets – seven en-suite rooms (some overlooking the Palau de la Música Catalana, across the street) in a welcoming mansion apartment strewn with books, plants and pictures. A third person could easily share most rooms (€20 supplement), and kids are welcome at knock-down prices. A choice of breakfasts (not included) is served either in your room or on the internal patio. Laundry service available. **€80**

PORT VELL AND BARCELONETA

★ **Bonic Barcelona** c/de Josep Anselm Clavé 9 ☎ 626 053 434, ⓦ bonic-barcelona.com; Ⓜ Drassanes; map p.79. Chic and charming "urban guesthouse", just a few steps from the port and Ramblas, with Gothic-Moorish decor and gorgeous tile floors. The eight rooms are simply furnished, and the three bathrooms are shared. Advance reservations essential; minimum two-night stay. **€90**
Equity Point Sea Pl. del Mar 1–4, ☎ 932 312 045, ⓦ equity-point.com; Ⓜ Barceloneta; map p.79. The budget beachside choice: neat little modern bunk rooms sleep six or seven, with an en-suite shower-bathroom in each one. The attached café, where you have breakfast (included), looks right out onto the boardwalk and palm trees. In low season prices fall steeply. Open 24hr. Dorms **€26**
Hotel Duquesa de Cardona Pg. de Colom 12 ☎ 932 689 090, ⓦ hduquesadecardona.com; Ⓜ Drassanes; map p.79. Step off the busy harbourfront highway into this soothing four-star haven, set in a remodelled sixteenth-century mansion. The rooms are calm and quiet, decorated

in earth tones and immaculately appointed. Although not all of them have harbour views, everyone has access to the stylish roof-deck overlooking the harbour. It's great for sundowner drinks and has what is probably the city's smallest outdoor pool. **€165**
★ **W Barcelona** Pl. de la Rosa dels Vents 1 ☎ 932 952 800, ⓦ w-barcelona.com; Ⓜ Barceloneta; map p.79. This signature building on the Barceloneta seafront is one of the city's most iconic structures. No-one calls it the "W", though – to locals it is the "Vela" (sail) because of its shape. Open-plan designer rooms have fantastic views through floor-to-ceiling windows, and facilities are first-rate: infinity pool, state-of-the-art spa, and "whatever-you-want" concierge service. There's a hip, resort feel, with direct beach access, and famous guest DJs on the see-and-be-seen rooftop lounge. Standout restaurant *Bravo 24* (see p.186) is courtesy of star Barcelona chef Carles Abellan but you can also chill out with cocktails and high-class burgers on the terrace of *Salt Beach Club*. **€320**

PORT OLÍMPIC

Hotel Arts Barcelona c/Marina 19–21, Port Olímpic ☎ 932 211 000, ⓦ ritzcarlton.com/hotels/barcelona; Ⓜ Ciutadella-Vila Olímpica; map p.83. Still the city

benchmark for five-star designer luxury, service and standards: effortlessly classy rooms feature enormous marble bathrooms and fabulous views, while stunning duplex apartments have their own perks (like 24hr butler service and a personal Mini Cooper). The upper floors belong to *The Club* – an exclusive hotel-within-a hotel with a luxurious lounge and concierge service. You're only a hop from the beach, but seafront gardens encompass a swimming pool and hot tub. The jaw-dropping Six Senses spa occupies the top two floors, while dining options include the two-Michelin-starred *Enoteca* by Paco Perez (see p.187), and the open-air terrace of *Arola* by Michelin-starred chef Sergi Arola (see p.187). **€425**

MONTJUÏC

Hotel Miramar Barcelona Pl. Carlos Ibañez 3 ☎ 932 811 600, ⓦ hotelmiramarbarcelona.com; ⓜ Paral.lel or Funicular de Montjuïc; map p.87. The remodelled *Miramar* – first built for the 1929 International Exhibition – has 75 super-stylish rooms wrapped around the kernel of the original building, all with views to knock your socks off. From the architecture books in the soaring lobby to the terrace or balcony that comes with nearly every room, it's clearly designer heaven; the room gadgets and stunning pool, garden and deck come as no surprise. True, you're not in the city centre, but it's only a 10min taxi ride from most downtown destinations. **€220**

DRETA DE L'EIXAMPLE

★ BarcelonaBB c/de Mallorca ☎ 637 977 263, ⓦ barcelonabb.com; ⓜ Verdaguer/Girona; map p.102. Lovely rooms, amiable hosts and a tasty breakfast shared with other happy travellers – what's not to love about this cheery B&B? Four rooms (Blue is the smallest; Wooden is the biggest) share two large (and very nice) bathrooms, while the master suite has its own private bathroom. "Chimney" (located a block away in another building) is en suite and offers some more privacy, as do the two apartments available. Advanced reservations essential (contact for directions). **€80**

BCN Fashion House c/del Bruc 13 ☎ 637 904 044, ⓦ bcnfashionhouse.com; ⓜ Urquinaona; map p.102. Italian owners have added a touch of chic flair to what was formerly an *atelier* in Barcelona's "garment district", and the seven spacious, high-ceilinged rooms (some with veranda) are lightened with prints, sculptures and artefacts from their travels. The rooms share three bathrooms and a plant-strewn internal terrace, though a studio-suite (€145) has its own facilities, private terrace area and kitchenette. The buffet breakfast is optional, and off-season deals are good value. **€119**

Cotton House Hotel Gran Vía de les Corts Catalanes 670, 5º ☎ 934 505 045, ⓦ hotelcottonhouse.com; ⓜ Passeig de Gràcia; map p.102. Located in the nineteenth-century former headquarters of the Fundación Textil Algodonera (Cotton Textile Foundation), the latest addition to Barcelona's luxury hotel scene is a designer masterpiece of mirrors, marble and mahogany, creating an atmosphere of old-fashioned elegance. Guests can live out their *Downton Abbey* fantasies as they swish down spiral staircases, peruse leather-bound books in the library or take tea on the terrace. Bed linen is, as you'd expect from the name, as good as it gets, and an artisanal tailoring service is available to create made-to-measure garments. **€300**

★ Equity Point Centric Pg. de Gràcia 33, ☎ 932 312 045 ⓦ equity-point.com; ⓜ Passeig de Gràcia; map p.102. Bills itself as "one of the most spectacular hostels in Europe" and it's hard to disagree, with around 450 beds spread across several floors of a refurbished *modernista* building in a swish midtown location. Dorms sleep up to twelve, while private rooms are also available (sleeping two to four, low-season rates from €80) all with lockers and en-suite shower room, and many with balcony and views. Facilities are first-rate, with bar, kitchen and laundry, and a roof terrace with yet more spectacular city views. Prices include continental breakfast. Dorms **€22**, rooms **€90**

Hostal L'Antic Espai Gran Via de les Corts Catalanes 660 ☎ 933 041 945, ⓦ anticespai.com. ⓜ Passeig de Gràcia; map p.102. Camp and cosy, this beautifully ornate period piece springs a surprise in every room, from mosaic tile floors to antique pendants, with candles and flowers at every turn. Room 102 has an original glassed-in balcony, and 107 opens onto an internal terrace with a candelabra-topped table. Modern bathrooms and DVD players keep comforts up-to-date. **€120**

Hostal Girona c/de Girona 24, 1º ☎ 932 650 259, ⓦ hostalgirona.com; ⓜ Urquinaona; map p.102. Delightful, family-run *pensió* with cosy, traditional rooms, plus corridors laid with rugs, polished wooden doors, antique paintings and restored furniture. There's a whole range of rooms (from as low as €40, all with a/c) – some share a bathroom, others have a shower or full bath, while the biggest and best rooms (€60) have balconies, though you can expect some noise. **€45**

★ Hostal Goya c/de Pau Claris 74, 1º ☎ 933 022 565, ⓦ hostalgoya.com; ⓜ Urquinaona; map p.102. Boutique-style *pensió* that offers nineteen crisply furnished, fabulous rooms on two floors of a mansion building. There's

14

> **TOP 5 MONEY NO OBJECT**
> **Hotel Arts Barcelona** See opposite
> **Hotel Omm** See p.172
> **Mandarin Oriental** See p.172
> **Mercer Hotel** See p.167
> **W Barcelona** See opposite

14

TOP 5 B&BS

BarcelonaBB See p.171
Bonic Barcelona See p.170
Casa de Billy See opposite
Pensió 2000 See p.170
the5rooms See below

a fair range of options, with the best rooms opening onto a balcony or a terrace (€15 extra). Comfortable sitting areas, and free coffee and tea, are available on both floors, while an apartment (sleeping two to six; from €180 for two people) offers more space for groups and families. €110

Hotel Claris c/de Pau Claris 150 ☎ 934 876 262, ⓦ www.derbyhotels.com; ⓜ Passeig de Gràcia; map p.102. Very select five-star-deluxe hotel, from the incense-scented marble lobby complete with authentic Roman mosaics to the hugely appealing rooms ranged around a soaring, water-washed atrium. It even has its own private antiquities museum. If there's a gripe, it's that there's not a lot of room space for your euro, but the staff couldn't be more accommodating and there's a swish rooftop terrace pool. The bar is a cool hangout in its own right, while the hotel restaurant, *East 47*, offers creative Mediterranean cuisine under the gaze of a line of Warhol portraits. €299

★ **Hotel Condes de Barcelona** Pg. de Gràcia 73–75 ☎ 934 450 000, ⓦ condesdebarcelona.com; ⓜ Passeig de Gràcia; map p.102. Straddling two sides of c/de Mallorca, the four-star *Condes* is fashioned from two former palaces; the north side has kept its interior marblework and wrought-iron balconies, but there's little difference between the rooms in either building. All 235 are classily turned out in contemporary style, while some have a balcony or a private terrace with views of Gaudí's La Pedrera. There's also a pretty hotel roof-terrace with a plunge pool, plus *Alaire*, a hip rooftop cocktail bar. Multi-Michelin-starred Basque chef Martín Berasategui offers upmarket bistro dining in *Loidi* restaurant and a more informal menu in *Loidi Bar & Tapas* (both closed Sun). €140

Hotel Majestic Pg. de Gràcia 68 ☎ 934 881 717, ⓦ hotelmajestic.es; ⓜ Passeig de Gràcia; map p.102. This traditional *grand-dame* hotel, first opened in 1918, has been refitted in contemporary style and muted colours to provide a tranquil city-centre base. Big-ticket original art adorns the public areas (it's known for its art collection), and the rooms – larger than many in this price range – have been pleasantly refurbished. The absolute clincher is

the rooftop spa, pool and deck, with amazing views over to the Sagrada Família. €299

Hotel Omm c/del Rosselló 265 ☎ 934 454 000, ⓦ hotelomm.es; ⓜ Diagonal; map p.102. The glam designer experience that is *Omm* means stark but sensational rooms, fearsomely handsome staff, and the Spaciomm "relaxation centre". The Roca brothers serve Michelin-starred fine dining at *Moo* restaurant (closed Sun & Aug), plus slightly less far-out fare at its baby brother, *Roca Bar*. Expect live jazz on the roof terrace, where beautiful people gather to sip cocktails in the moonlight. €250

Mandarin Oriental Pg. de Gràcia 38–40 ☎ 931 518 888, ⓦ mandarinoriental.com/Barcelona; ⓜ Passeig de Gràcia; map p.102. The latest designer addition to Barcelona's most prestigious avenue is the super-sleek *Mandarin Oriental*, which fills the premises of a former bank building with a soaring white atrium and a serene selection of gorgeously light but extremely thick-walled rooms made from old vaults. The suites, with their stunning bathrooms and private terraces, are among the finest in Barcelona. There are the obligatory super-star restaurants, *Moments* and *Bistreau* (see p.189) and a super-cool bar, *Banker's Bar*, which has live music and some of the best cocktails in town. The spa, mimosa garden and rooftop "dipping pool" combine oriental tranquillity and Euro cool. €435

Praktik Bakery c/ Provença 279 ☎ 934 880 061, ⓦ hotelpraktikbakery.com; ⓜ Diagonal; map p.102. Minimalist, all-white designer rooms and a great location aren't the reason for the queue that constantly stretches out of the hotel's door and on to the street. That would be the in-hotel bakery run by Baluard, makers of some of Barcelona's best bread. Breakfast doesn't get much better than the buffet of butter croissants, cakes, buns and pastries that await you here each morning, though it's not the best choice for anyone on a low-carb diet. €140

★ **the5Rooms** c/de Pau Claris 72, 2 ☎ 933 427 880, ⓦ www.thefiverooms.com; ⓜ Urquinaona; map p.102. The impeccable taste and fashion background of owner Jessica is evident at *the5rooms*: gorgeous contemporary-styled B&B rooms are spacious and light-filled, with original artwork above each bed, exposed brick walls and terrific bathrooms. Despite the high-spec surroundings, the feel is house party rather than hotel – breakfast is served whenever you like, drinks are always available, and Jessica is happy to sit down and talk you through her favourite bars, restaurants and galleries. Suites and apartments are also available (from €205 for two). €170

ESQUERRA DE L'EIXAMPLE

★ **Alternative Creative Youth Home** Ronda de la Universitat 17 ☎ 635 669 021, ⓦ alternative-barcelona .com; ⓜ Universitat/Catalunya; map p.110. The hostel hangout for a self-selecting art crowd, who love the laidback vibe, projection lounge, cool music and city-savvy

staff. The regular hostel stuff is well designed too, with a walk-in kitchen, lockers and laundry, and a maximum of 24 people spread across three small dorms. For much of the year rates fall to around €20, though peak summer sees them rise to €36. Dorms €30

Casa de Billy Gran Via de les Corts Catalanes ☎ 934 263 048, ⓦ casabillybarcelona.com; Ⓜ Rocafort; map p.110. A welcoming guesthouse in a restored nineteenth-century building near Pl. d'Espanya with sixteen spotless rooms (singles and doubles; some en suite) elegantly decorated by Billy himself with antique mirrors, armoires and crystal chandeliers. Guests have use of the kitchens (there's one on each floor), while those staying in the "superior rooms" (€20–30 more per night) have access to the penthouse terrace. Small breakfast included, two-night minimum, advance reservations essential (contact for directions), over-18s only. No credit cards. **€90**

★**Gran Hotel Torre Catalunya** Av. de Roma 2–4 ☎ 936 006 966, ⓦ torrecatalunya.com; Ⓜ Sants Estació; map p.110. The landmark four-star-deluxe hotel outside Sants station towers over the surrounding buildings, which means that the large, light, elegant rooms have sweeping views from all sides (the pricier rooms – from €150 – above the twelfth floor are considered "superior"). Breakfast on the 23rd floor is a buzz; there's a panoramic restaurant, too, plus spa with indoor pool, while during the warmer months guests can also use the nearby *Expo* hotel's outdoor pool. **€120**

Hotel Axel c/d'Aribau 33 ☎ 933 239 393, ⓦ axelhotels .com; Ⓜ Universitat; map p.110. Central to the self-image of the city's gay quarter, the Gaixample, the *Axel*'s snazzy "heterofriendly" boutique stylings are a real hit with gay visitors. It's a hip but relaxed space with designer rooms (featuring complimentary beauty products), suites with private terraces, a bar and restaurant that are part of the local scene, plus a fabulous terrace pool and "Skybar", excellent spa and fitness facilities, and a full range of massage and other treatments available. **€170**

Hotel Inglaterra c/de Pelai 14 ☎ 934 922 244, ⓦ hotel-inglaterra.com; Ⓜ Universitat; map p.110. The boutique little three-star sister to the Dreta's *Majestic*

has an excellent location, harmoniously toned rooms and snazzy bathrooms. Space is at a premium, but some rooms have cute private terraces, others street-side balconies, while best of all is the romantic roof terrace, where you can take a dip in the pool and sip on a cocktail. **€199**

Praktik Rambla Rambla de Catalunya 27 ☎ 933 436 690, ⓦ hotelpraktikrambla.com; Ⓜ Passeig de Gràcia; map p.110. This new boutique hotel in a converted *modernista* mansion makes the most of its glorious inheritance by keeping the design touches toned down and letting the architecture do the talking. Big, high-ceilinged rooms (especially the deluxe doubles, about €30 extra) look out onto a tranquil terrace, complete with burbling fountain, where you can enjoy the sunshine in peace just yards from the bustling Rambla de Catalunya. **€124**

Room Mate Emma c/del Rosselló 205 ☎ 932 385 606, ⓦ emma.room-matehotels.com; Ⓜ Diagonal; map p.110. Get beyond the *Battlestar Galactica*-style lobby, and you're left with *Emma*'s undeniably appealing barebones-chic rooms and suites at realistic uptown prices. It's part of a Spanish chain with a fresh, fun vibe and an accommodating air, from free fruit at reception to breakfast until noon. **€117**

★**Somnio Barcelona** c/de la Diputació 251 ☎ 932 725 308, ⓦ somniohostels.com. Ⓜ Passeig de Gràcia; map p.110. Sisters Lauren and Lee from Chicago bring their passion for Barcelona right into their upscale *pensió*, with handy "tips for the day" left in the common room each morning. Simple but smart rooms with wood-block floors cater for singles, couples and friends (it's especially welcoming for women visitors), and there are two six-bed, single-sex dorms. You'll pay another €10 for an en-suite room, while there's slightly more inexpensive shared budget accommodation at their sister hostel, *Duo*, in the same district. Dorms **€22**, rooms **€78**

SAGRADA FAMÍLIA AND GLÒRIES

★**Barcelona Urbany** Av. Meridiana 97 ☎ 932 458 414, ⓦ barcelonaurbany.com; Ⓜ Clot; map pp.116–117. This huge steel-and-glass four hundred-bed hostel might be a bit off the beaten track, but it's handy for the metro (it's an easy ride in to Pl. de Catalunya) and airport train, and has terrific views of the landmark Torre Agbar. The rooms are like space-shuttle pods – boxy en suites with pull-down beds (sleeping two to eight), power-showers and key-card lockers – that are just as viable for couples on a budget as backpackers. Rates vary according to season, but go as low as €13 for dorms and €50 for rooms. There's a bar and terrace, all sorts of tours and offers available, plus free health club and pool entry in the same building. Breakfast included. Dorms **€20**, private rooms **€70**

Hotel Eurostars Monumental c/del Consell de Cent

498–500 ☎ 932 320 288, ⓦ eurostarsmonumental .com; Ⓜ Monumental; map pp.116–117. A good four-star choice within walking distance of the Sagrada Família; sharply styled, well-equipped standard rooms are real value for money, while the top-floor suites (from €170) boast a terrace with loungers and views of the Gaudí basilica and distant hills. **€128**

TOP 5 DORMS AND HOSTELS
Alternative Creative Youth Home See opposite
Barcelona Urbany See above
Equity Point Centric See p.171
Pensión Mari-Luz See p.168
Somnio Barcelona See above

14

GRÀCIA

★**Casa Gracia** Pg. de Gràcia 116 ☎931 874 497, ⓦcasagraciabcn.com; ⓜDiagonal; map p.125. A vibrant and stylish space spread over six floors in a *modernista* building, with comfy leather chairs and large beanbags in the common areas, a huge kitchen in tile and stainless steel, plus bonuses like a concierge, themed dinners and evening concerts. The crisply decorated rooms (from dorms to doubles to six-bed private rooms) have a/c and are en suite, while the deluxe suite pampers with a spa bath, slippers and bathrobes. Though *Casa Gracia* is technically a hostel, you'll feel like you're staying in a (pretty good) hotel. Breakfast included. Dorms **€25**, rooms **€132**

Generator Hostel and Hotel c/ de Corsega 373 ☎932 200 377, ⓦgeneratorhostels.com; ⓜDiagonal; map p.125. Big, bright and abuzz with people having fun, the *Generator* lounge frequently features live music, DJ sets and art performances, as well as a pool table and big-screen TV. The clean, modern rooms range from budget dorms from €9 (including female-only) up to a penthouse costing over €200. There's 24hr reception and free, fast wi-fi. **€40**

Hotel Casa Fuster Pg. de Gràcia 132 ☎932 553 000, ⓦhotelescenter.es/casafuster; ⓜDiagonal; map p.125. *Modernista* architect Lluís Domènech i Montaner's magnificent *Casa Fuster* (1908) is the backdrop for five-star-deluxe luxury with service to match. Rooms are in natural tones, with huge beds and gorgeous bathrooms, while public areas make full use of the architectural heritage, from the magnificent pillared lobby bar, *Café Vienés*, to the wonderful panoramic roof terrace and pool – summer nights see the terrace turned over to chill-out lounge bar *Blue View*. There's also a contemporary restaurant, *Galaxó*, plus fitness centre and 24hr room service. **€275**

PARK GÜELL

Alberg Mare de Déu de Montserrat Pg. de la Mare de Déu del Coll 41–51 ☎932 105 151, reservations on ☎934 838 363, ⓦxanascat.cat; ⓜVallcarca (follow Av. de la República d'Argentina, c/Viaducte de Vallcarca and then signs) or bus #28 from Pl. de Catalunya, plus night buses, stop just across the street; map p.127. This popular hostel, owned by the regional government, is set in a converted mansion, with a tiled and stained-glass interior, gardens, terrace and great city views – it's a long way out, but close to Park Güell. Dorms sleep six, eight or twelve, and there are all the usual facilities plus meals are provided (or there's a local restaurant just around the corner). Guests without an IYHF membership charged an additional €2.05 per night; six-night maximum stay; reception open 8am–11pm; main door closes at midnight, but opens every 30min thereafter. Includes breakfast. Dorms **€24**

TIBIDABO

★**ABaC** Av. Tibidabo 1 ☎933 196 600, ⓦabac barcelona.com; FGC Av. del Tibidabo; map p.138. *The* chic address for intimate, uptown boutique style, the five-star-plus *ABaC* showcases the Michelin-starred talents of celebrity Spanish *Masterchef* presenter Jordi Cruz in a gorgeous designer, glass-and-wood revamp of an old Tibidabo mansion. There are just fifteen rooms – cream and white decor, swishing drapes, sumptuous bathrooms with whirlpool baths and Hermès cosmetics – and services include a spa and lounge bar, though perhaps the measure of the place is the personal-shopper service available for guests. **€300**

Gran Hotel La Florida Carreterra Vallviderera a Tibidabo 83–93, 7km from the centre ☎932 593 000, ⓦhotellaflorida.com; map p.138. Describing itself as an "urban resort", the five-star, hillside *Gran Hotel La Florida* re-creates the glory days of the 1950s, when it was at the centre of Barcelona high society. Its terraces and garden areas have amazing views, while some of the seventy rooms and suites have private gardens or terraces and jacuzzis. Jazz sessions in the club are not to be missed. There's also an achingly lovely spa and pool, and Sunday brunch on the terrace at *L'Orangerie* restaurant is one of the city's great secrets. Special offers can slash the rate by half. **€250**

Cafés, tapas bars and restaurants

If you step no further than the Ramblas or the streets of the Barri Gòtic, you are not going to experience the best of the city's cuisine – in the main tourist areas food and service can be indifferent and prices high. For the finest food the city has to offer, it pays to be a bit more adventurous and explore the backstreets of neighbourhoods like Sant Pere, La Ribera, El Raval and Poble Sec, where you'll find excellent restaurants, some little more than hole-in-the-wall taverns, others surprisingly chic. Most, but not all, of the big-ticket, destination-dining restaurants are found in the Eixample. Gràcia, further out, is a nice village-like place to spend the evening, with plenty of good mid-range restaurants, while for fish and seafood you're best off in the harbourside Barceloneta district or at the Port Olímpic.

Barcelona's thousands of **cafés** keep the city fuelled from morning to night, and you're rarely more than a step away from a coffee fix or a quick sandwich. Many are classics of their kind – century-old establishments or unique neighbourhood haunts – while others specialize in certain types of food and drink. A **forn** is a bakery, a **pastisseria** a cake and pastry shop, a **xocolateria** specializes in chocolate, while a **granja** (milk bar) offers traditional delights like *orxata* (*horchata*, tiger-nut drink) and *granissat* (*granizado*, a flavoured crushed-ice drink).

The **tapas** boom, meanwhile, shows no sign of abating, with increasing numbers of bars and restaurants figuring that small is beautiful when it comes to designing new menus. Little dishes are all the rage, and while there are still plenty of old-style, hanging-ham and counter-display tapas bars in town, there's also a real sense of adventure in new-wave places that are deadly serious about their food. You're as likely to get shrimp tempura, a samosa or a yucca chip as a garlic mushroom these days, while a few standout places offer classy, restaurant-standard experiences that are still truly tapas at heart.

15

Traditional **Catalan and regional Spanish food** remains at the core of many **restaurant** menus, while the city has the usual range of pizza places, curry houses, fast-food joints and the like. But these are exciting times for foodies in Barcelona, as **contemporary Spanish cooking** continues to be a big deal. The minimalist, food-as-chemistry approach, pioneered by best-chef-in-the-world Ferran Adrià (of *El Bulli* fame), has spawned a thousand followers, many with restaurants in Barcelona (and a fair few now with Michelin stars). The best are reinterpreting classic Catalan dishes in innovative ways, and while prices in these gastro-temples are high there's a trend towards more economic, bistro-style dining even by the hottest chefs. Meanwhile, the current fad obsessing city restaurateurs is the fusion of Mediterranean and Asian flavours – a so-called **"Mediterrasian" cuisine** – that combines local, market-fresh ingredients with more exotic tastes. Sometimes this works, sometimes this doesn't, but eating out in Barcelona has never been more interesting.

ESSENTIALS

COSTS AND RESERVATIONS

Prices Overall, eating out in Barcelona is still pretty good value, and you'll be able to dine in a huge variety of restaurants for around €25–30 a head, and around the same if you jump from tapas bar to tapas bar. In fancier, fashionable places you can double this, while "tasting menus" at the current dining hotspots run from €70–120 a head, excluding drinks (still a lot cheaper than equivalents in, say, New York or London).

Getting a good deal Nearly all restaurants offer a weekday (Mon–Fri) three-course *menú del dia* (menu of the day) at lunchtime, with the cheapest starting at about €9, rising to €18–25 in fancier places. In many restaurants the price also includes a drink, so this can be a real bargain (at night, you might pay three or four times as much to eat dinner in the same restaurant).

Reservations and payment If there's somewhere you'd particularly like to eat – certainly at the more fashionable end of the market – you should reserve a table. Some places are booked solid for days, or weeks, in advance. Credit and debit cards are widely accepted in restaurants, though not necessarily in cheaper places, traditional tapas bars and the like. Finally, all restaurant menus should make it clear whether the eight-percent IVA tax is included in the prices or not (it usually is).

STARTING THE DAY

Unless you're staying somewhere with a decent buffet spread, you may as well pass up the overpriced coffee-and-croissant option in your hotel and join the locals for **breakfast** in one of the city's bars, cafés or patisseries. A few euros will get you a hot drink and a brioche, croissant or sandwich just about anywhere – *ensaimadas* (pastry spirals) are a popular choice, while *xocolata amb xurros* (*chocolate con churros* – long, fried, tubular doughnuts with thick drinking chocolate) is a good cold-weather starter. The traditional country breakfast is *pa amb tomàquet* (*pan con tomate*) – bread rubbed with tomato, olive oil and garlic, perhaps topped with some cured ham or sliced cheese. Otherwise, breakfast sandwiches are whatever can be stuffed inside a *flauta* (thin baguette), from cured ham to a slice of *tortilla*.

OPENING HOURS AND CLOSING DAYS

Opening hours Most cafés are open from 7 or 8am until midnight, or much later – so whether it's coffee first thing or à late-night nibble, you'll find somewhere to cater for you. Restaurants are generally open 1 to 4pm and 8.30 to 11pm, though most locals don't eat lunch until at least 2pm and dinner after 9 or even 10pm. However, in tourist zones like the Ramblas and Port Olímpic, restaurants tend to stay open all day and serve on request, while many tapas bars are also open all day from morning until night.

Closing days and holidays Many restaurants close on Sunday or Monday, and on public holidays, and lots close over Easter and throughout August – check the listings for specific details but expect changes, since many places imaginatively reinterpret their own posted opening days and times.

MENUS

Dishes and specialities To ask for a menu, request *la carta*, though be warned that some cheaper places might not have a written menu, with the waiter merely reeling off the day's dishes at bewildering speed.

A warning Budget meals sometimes come in the form of a garishly photographed *plat combinat* (*plato combinado*, combined plate) of things like eggs, steak or calamari with fries and salad, but generally speaking, pictures of dishes on a menu is not an indicator of great cuisine – especially so in the case of the pre-prepared paellas advertised on boards outside tourist restaurants.

THE RAMBLAS

CAFÉS

★ **Cafè de l'Òpera** Ramblas 74 ☎ 933 177 585, ⓦ cafe operabcn.com; Ⓜ Liceu; map p.38. If you're going to pay through the nose for a Ramblas seat, it may as well be at one of the bank of sought-after pavement tables at this famous old café-bar opposite the opera house, which retains its *fin-de-siècle* feel. Surprisingly, it's not a complete tourist-fest, and locals pop in day and night for drinks, cakes and tapas. Daily 8.30am–2.30am.

Cafe Zurich Pl. Catalunya 1 ☎ 933 179 153; Ⓜ Catalunya; map p.38 The most famous meet-and-greet café in town, right at the top of the Ramblas underneath El Triangle shopping centre. It's good for croissants and breakfast sandwiches and there's a huge pavement terrace, but sit inside if you don't want to be bothered by endless rounds of buskers and beggars. Mon–Fri 8am–11pm, Sat & Sun 9am–11pm.

Escribà Ramblas 83 ☎ 933 016 027, ⓦ escriba.es; Ⓜ Liceu; map p.38. "We don't just make pastries, we create illusions", claims the renowned Escribà family business. Visit their classy, historic *modernista*-designed pastry shop in the Antiga Casa Figueras near the Boqueria market and find out why many rate this as the best bakery in Barcelona. Daily 9am–9pm.

TAPAS BARS

Bar Central La Boqueria Mercat de la Boqueria, Ramblas 91 ☎ 933 011 098; Ⓜ Liceu; map p.38. This gleaming, chrome stand-up bar in the market's central aisle is the venue for ultra-fresh market produce, served by snazzy staff who work at a fair lick. Breakfast, snack or lunch, it's all the same to them – salmon cutlets, sardines, calamari, razor clams, hake fillets, sausages, pork steaks, asparagus spears and the rest, plunked on the griddle and sprinkled with salt. Breakfast costs just a few euros or it's €5–15 for some tapas or a main dish and a drink. Mon–Sat 6.30am–4pm.

★ **Bar Pinotxo** Mercat de la Boqueria, Ramblas 91 ☎ 933 171 731, ⓦ pinotxobar.com; Ⓜ Liceu; map p.38. The market's most renowned refuelling stop – just inside the main entrance on the right – attracts traders, chefs, tourists and celebs, who stand three deep at busy times. A coffee, a grilled sandwich and a glass of cava (no, really) is the local breakfast of choice, or let the cheery staff steer you towards the tapas and daily specials (€5–15) – anything from a slice of tortilla to fried baby squid. Daily 7am–11pm.

RESTAURANTS

CentOnze Ramblas 111 ☎ 933 186 200, ⓦ centonze restaurant.com; Ⓜ Liceu; map p.38. Located in the sleek *Le Méridien*, this restaurant boasts great street-level views of Las Ramblas, and is a perfect place to escape the hustle-and-bustle while dining on Boqueria-sourced dishes such as salmon and monkfish carpaccio, strawberry gazpacho and *arròs negre* with fresh clams and aioli (€17.50 lunch menu, €7–22 à la carte). Daily 1.30–4pm & 7–11.30pm.

BARRI GÒTIC

CAFÉS

Bar del Pi Pl. de Sant Josep Oriol 1 ☎ 933 022 123, ⓦ bardelpi.com; Ⓜ Liceu; map p.44. Located on one of Barcelona's prettiest squares, *Bar del Pi* is best known for its terrace tables. Linger over drinks and sandwiches and let the old town reveal its charms, especially during the weekend artists' market. Tues–Fri 9am–11pm, Sat 9.30am–11pm, Sun 10am–10pm.

★ **Caelum** c/de la Palla 8 ☎ 933 026 993, ⓦ caelum barcelona.com; Ⓜ Liceu; map p.44. The lovingly packaged confections in this upscale café-cum-deli (the name is Latin for "heaven") are made in convents and monasteries across Spain. Choose from *frutas de almendra* (marzipan sweeties) from Seville, Benedictine preserves or Cistercian cookies – or hunker down for cakes and coffee in the atmospheric basement crypt. Mon–Thurs

15

10.30am–8.30pm, Fri & Sat 10.30am–11pm, Sun 10.30am–9pm.

Dulcinea c/de Petritxol 2 ☎ 932 311 756; Ⓜ Liceu; map p.44. One of the old town's age-old treats is to come here for a thick hot chocolate, slathered in cream. Then if you've still got room, try one of their pastries or perhaps a dish of *mel i mato* (curd cheese with honey). It's a bygone-era kind of place, with dickie-bow-wearing waiters patrolling the beamed and panelled room bearing silver trays. Daily 9am–1pm & 5–9pm.

Mesón del Café c/de la Llibreteria 16 ☎ 933 150 754; Ⓜ Jaume I; map p.44. Offbeat locals' café, great for quick coffees, pastries and pick-me-ups. You'll probably have to stand, though there is a sort of cubbyhole at the back with a few tables. Mon–Fri 7.30am–9.30pm, Sat & Sun 9am–10.30pm.

TAPAS BARS

Bar Celta Pulpería c/de la Mercè 16 ☎ 933 150 006; Ⓜ Drassanes; map p.44. This brightly lit, no-nonsense Galician tapas bar specializes in typical dishes like octopus (*pop gallego*) and fried green *pimientos* (peppers), washed down with heady regional wine (dishes €3–16). You eat at the U-shaped bar or at tables in the back room, and while it's not one for a long, lazy meal, it's just right to kick off a bout of bar-hopping. Tues–Sun noon–midnight.

★**Bodega La Plata** c/de la Mercè 28 ☎ 933 151 009, Ⓦ barlaplata.com; Ⓜ Drassanes; map p.44. A classic taste of the old town, with a marble counter open to the street and dirt-cheap wine served straight from the barrel. It attracts an enthusiastic local crowd, from businessmen to pre-clubbers, and for €5 or so you can get a couple of drinks and a dish of the speciality anchovies, either marinated or deep-fried like whitebait. Daily 9am–3.30pm & 6.30–11pm.

Ginger c/Palma Sant Just 1 ☎ 933 105 309, Ⓦ ginger .cat; Ⓜ Jaume I; map p.44. Wine, cocktails and creative tapas in a slickly updated 1970s-style setting. It's a world away from *patatas bravas* and battered squid – think apple tartlet with foie gras, tuna tartare and pork ribs with ginger marinade for around €7–12 a pop. Tues–Sat 7.30pm–3am, kitchen open until 12.30am; closed 1 week in Aug.

Matis Bar Pl. Nova 1 ☎ 630 455 043, Ⓦ matisbar.com; Ⓜ Jaume I; map p.44. Half-hidden in the basement of Barcelona's college of architecture, *Matis* boasts a genuine Picasso mural and a cocktail bar with great views of the cathedral. This new venture by Michelin-starred chef Artur

TOP 5 CLASSY CAFÉS

Bar del Convent See p.181
Café de les Delícies See opposite
Cafè de l'Òpera See p.177
Caelum See p.177
Dulcinea See above

Martínez offers informal bar-food instead of fine dining, but keeps standards sky-high with "km-0" local ingredients. Excellent hams and cheeses and a selection of classic tapas are matched by a good wine list. The €25 *pim-pam* tasting menu is superb value. Daily 9am–midnight.

Taller de Tapas Pl. de Sant Josep Oriol 9 ☎ 933 018 020, Ⓦ tallerdetapas.com; Ⓜ Liceu; map p.44. The fashionable "tapas workshop" sucks in tourists with its year-round outdoor terrace and pretty location by the church of Santa María del Pi. The open kitchen turns out reliable market-fresh tapas, with fish a speciality at dinner, from grilled langoustine to seared tuna (most tapas €4–12). There are several other branches around town, though this was the first and has the nicest location. Mon–Thurs & Sun noon–midnight, Fri & Sat noon–1am.

★**La Viñatería del Call** c/de Sant Domènec del Call 9 ☎ 933 026 092, Ⓦ lavinateriadelcall.com; Ⓜ Jaume I; map p.44. The wood-table tavern is principally an eating place – with a long menu of cheese and ham platters, smoked fish, fried peppers and much more – but it's also a great late-night bar, with a serious wine list and jazz and flamenco sounds as a backdrop. If you want to eat, especially at weekends, it's best to reserve a table. Daily 7.30pm–1am.

RESTAURANTS

Bidasoa c/d'en Serra 21 ☎ 933 818 063; Ⓜ Drassanes; map p.44. Tucked away on a narrow street in La Mercè, this third generation-owned restaurant offers simple and fresh Catalan and Basque-Navarre fare at a good price (€5–9). Dishes include tapas, soups, salads and tortillas, as well as hearty mains such as garlic chicken and the house speciality (and sure-fire hangover cure) *cocido Bidasoa*, a medley of sausage, tender beef and chickpeas in a savoury broth – all of which are served by jocular staff in a bright, rustic dining room. Tues–Thurs 1–4pm & 8–11pm, Fri & Sat 1–4pm & 8pm–midnight, Sun 1–4pm.

★**Café de l'Acadèmia** c/de Lledó 1 ☎ 933 198 253; Ⓜ Jaume I; map p.44. Great for a date or a lazy lunch, with creative Catalan cooking served in a romantic stone-flagged restaurant or outside in the medieval square, lit by candles at night. Expect succulent meat grills, fresh fish, rice dishes and a taste of local favourites like *bacallà* (salt cod), wild mushrooms or grilled vegetables. Prices are pretty reasonable (mains €11–18) and it's always busy, so dinner reservations are essential. A no-choice *menú del dia* is a bargain for the quality (and it's even cheaper eaten at the bar). Mon–Fri 1.30–4pm & 8.30–11.30pm; closed 2 weeks in Aug.

Can Culleretes c/d'en Quintana 5 ☎ 933 173 022, Ⓦ culleretes.com; Ⓜ Liceu; map p.44. Supposedly Barcelona's oldest restaurant (founded in 1786), serving straight-up Catalan food (*botifarra* sausage and beans, salt cod, spinach and pine nuts, wild boar stew) in cosy, traditional surroundings. Local families come in droves, especially for

NO SUCH THING AS A FREE LUNCH...

... except, once upon a time, in southern Spain. **Tapas** (from *tapar*, to cover) originated as free snacks given away as covers for drinks' glasses, perhaps to keep the flies off in the baking sun. It's still a much more southern, Andalucian thing, though the Basques, Gallegos and other northerners, all with their own tapas traditions, might disagree. In some parts of Spain, tapas still comes for free with drinks – a dish of olives, a bite of omelette, some fried peppers. But in Barcelona you can expect to pay for every mouthful…unless you count the restaurants which kick off proceedings with an *amuse-gueule* shot glass of soup or designer canapé – free to anyone just about to pay €100 for dinner. The classic old-town tapas bars tend to concentrate on specialities from the Spanish regions, like octopus, peppers and seafood from Galicia; cider, cured meats and cheese from Asturias; or the ubiquitous Basque-style *pintxos*, which are bite-sized concoctions on a slice of bread, held together with a cocktail stick (you're charged by the number of sticks on your plate when you've finished). But contemporary tapas bars in Barcelona think nothing of mixing and matching cuisines, so you could just as easily be munching on a cold soba-noodle salad or a pint-sized lamb kebab.

TOP 5 TRADITIONAL TAPAS

Bar Pinotxo See p.177
Bodega La Plata See opposite
Cal Pep See p.182
Cova Fumada See p.184
Tapería Lolita See p.187

TOP 5 CONTEMPORARY TAPAS

Dos Palillos See p.180
Roca Bar *Hotel Omm*. See p.172
Tapas24 See p.188
La Taverna del Clínic See p.190
Tickets See p.188

15

celebrations or for Sun lunch, and there are good-value set meals available at both lunch and dinner (around €30, otherwise mains €7–15). Tues–Sat 1.30–4pm & 9–11pm, Sun 1.30–4pm; closed 4 weeks in July/Aug.

Cometacinc c/Cometa 5 ☎ 933 101 558, ⓦ cometacinc .com; Ⓜ Liceu; map p.44. Vast wooden shutters frame the entrance to *Cometacinc*, but the two-level restaurant itself is of more modest proportions. Exposed brick walls and wooden ceiling beams give this Barri Gòtic bistro a stylishly old-fashioned air, while the food is mainly modern twists on classic dishes. Mains are around €12 but it's worth going at lunchtime for the excellent €11 *menú del día*. Spend an extra €1.85 and try the roast chicken croquette – you won't regret it. Mon–Fri & Sun 1pm–1am, Sat 4pm–1am.

El Salón c/de L'Hostal d'en Sol 6–8 ☎ 933 152 159, ⓦ elsalon.es; Ⓜ Jaume I; map p.44. It's easy to fall for the cosy charms of *El Salón*, with its candlelit tables in a Gothic dining room and summer terrace in the nearby square. The menu changes every few months, with inventive salads giving way to things like a confit of cod with spinach,

pine nuts and raisins, or lamb with mustard-and-honey sauce. Most mains are in the range €10–16. Mon–Sat 8.30pm–midnight.

★ **Shunka** c/dels Sagristans 5 ☎ 934 124 991; Ⓜ Jaume I; map p.44. Locals figure this to be the best Japanese restaurant in the city – advance reservations are essential, though you might strike lucky if you're prepared to eat early or late. The open kitchen and the bustling staff are half the show, while the food – sushi to udon noodles, Japanese fried chicken to grilled prawns – is really good. You can eat for around €40, though it's easy to spend more. Mon–Sat 1.30–4pm & 8.30–11.30pm, Sat & Sun 2–4pm & 8.30–11.30pm; closed Aug.

Venus Delicatessen c/d'Avinyó 25 ☎ 933 011 585; Ⓜ Liceu/Jaume I; map p.44. Not a deli, despite the name, but a handy place serving Mediterranean bistro cuisine throughout the day and night. It's also good for vegetarians, with dishes like lasagne, couscous, moussaka and salads mostly meat-free and costing around €7–10. Mon–Fri 8.30am–1am, Sat & Sun 10am–2am.

EL RAVAL

CAFÉS

Café de les Delícies Rambla del Raval 47 ☎ 934 415 714; Ⓜ Liceu; map pp.58–59. One of the first off the blocks in this revamped part of the neighbourhood, and still perhaps the best, plonking thrift-shop chairs and tables beneath exposed pipes and girders and coming up with something cute, cosy, mellow and arty. There's breakfast, sandwiches and tapas to share. Mon–Thurs 8.30am–11pm, Fri 8.30am–2am, Sat 11am–2am, Sun 11am–11.45pm.

★ **Federal** c/del Parlament 39 ☎ 931 873 607, ⓦ federalcafe.es; Ⓜ Sant Antoni; map pp.58–59. Sunday brunch is the hottest ticket in town at this effortlessly cool café, squished into a corner townhouse with a great little roof garden on top. Australian owners have imported their own cool vibe, so whether you're looking for a flat white and French toast, a bacon butty and a glass of New Zealand Sauvignon Blanc or a dandelion soy latte, you can guarantee that there's nowhere else quite

THE CUP THAT CHEERS

Coffee in Barcelona is invariably espresso – a *café sol* (*café solo*) or simply *un café*. For decaff (*descafeinat*, *descafeinado*), make sure you ask for it *de màquina* ("from the machine") to avoid an instant sachet. A slightly weaker large black coffee is a *café americano*. A *tallat* (*cortado*) is like a *macchiato*, ie a small strong black coffee with a dash of steamed milk; a larger cup with more hot milk is a *café amb llet* (*café con leche*). Chuck brandy, cognac or whisky into a black coffee and it's a *cigaló* (*carajillo*), or add them to a *tallat* to make a *trifàsic*.

Tea comes without milk unless you ask for it, and is often just a teabag in a cup of hot water. If you do ask for milk, chances are it'll be hot and UHT. Better to try an infusion, like mint (*menta*), camomile (*camomila*) or lime (*tila*).

15

like this in Barcelona. Tues–Thurs 8am–midnight, Fri 8am–1am, Sat 9am–1am, Sun 9am–5.30pm.

Granja M. Viader c/d'en Xuclà 4–6 ☎933 183 486, ⊛granjaviader.cat; ⓜLiceu; map pp.58–59. The oldest traditional *granja* (milk bar) in town is tucked away down a narrow alley just off c/del Carme, with a pavement plaque outside for services to the city. The original owner, Sr Viader, was the proud inventor of "Cacaolat" (a popular chocolate drink), but for a taste of the old days you could also try *mel i mató* (curd cheese and honey) or *llet Mallorquina* (fresh milk with cinnamon and lemon rind). Mon–Sat 9am–1.15pm & 5–9.15pm.

★El Jardí c/de l'Hospital 56 ☎933 291 550, ⊛eljardibarcelona.es; ⓜLiceu; map pp.58–59. The "garden bar", hidden in the elegant courtyard of the Gothic Hospital de la Santa Creu is a real away-from-the-bustle find. There's a year-round covered deck offering drinks, snacks, salads and sandwiches during the day, plus tasting menus and a changing list of tapas. Mon–Fri 10am–midnight, Sat & Sun 10am–12.30am.

Kasparo Pl. de Vicenç Martorell 4 ☎933 022 072; ⓜCatalunya; map pp.58–59. Sited in the arcaded corner of a quiet square, this tiny café and *terrassa* is popular with parents who come to let their kids play in the adjacent playground. There's muesli, Greek yoghurt and toast and jam for early birds, while later in the day sandwiches, tapas and assorted *platos del dia* are on offer – hummus and bread, vegetable quiche, couscous or pasta, for example. Daily 9am–midnight; closed two weeks Dec/Jan.

TAPAS BARS

A Tu Bola c/de Hospital 78 ☎933 153 244, ⊛atubolarest.com; ⓜLiceu; map pp.58–59. Israeli chef Shira whips up falafel-like balls of fresh ingredients, to order, in unexpected but delightful flavour combinations. Home-made harissa, sauces and soft drinks bear hallmarks of the obsessive attention to detail that lifts this far above typical "street food" standard. There aren't many seats so expect a wait at busy times, as the bargain prices (about €12 a head) keep people coming back for more. Mon & Wed 5pm–midnight, Thurs 1pm–midnight, Fri–Sun 1pm–1am.

★Dos Palillos c/d'Elisabets 9 ☎933 040 513, ⊛dos palillos.com; ⓜCatalunya; map pp.58–59. Albert Raurich, former *chef de cuisine* at "world's best restaurant" *El Bulli*, swapped Catalan food for Asian fusion after falling in love with Japan. Attached to the *Casa Camper* (see p.168), his own Michelin-starred two-room restaurant offers à la carte *dim sum* in the front galley bar (steamed dumplings to grilled oysters and stir-fried prawns, mostly €5–7) and a back-room, counter-style Asian bar where tasting menus (€ €75 and €90) wade their way through the highlights. The front bar is a playful take on traditional Spanish tapas bars (cushions on upturned beer-crates, dusty liqueur bottles and steamer baskets); there are no reservations taken for this, though you do have to book for the Asian bar. Tues & Wed 7.30–11.30pm, Thurs–Sat 1.30–3.30pm & 7.30–11.30pm; closed 2 weeks in Dec/Jan & 3 weeks in Aug.

★Mam i Teca c/de la Lluna 4 ☎934 413 335; ⓜSant Antoni; map pp.58–59. An intimate (code for very small) place for superior tapas and fine wines, run by local Slow Food champion Alfons Bach. All the meat is organic, the regional cheeses are well chosen, and market-fresh ingredients go to make up things like daily pasta dishes, a platter of grilled vegetables or a simple serving of lamb cutlets (most dishes €6–22). Finish with chocolate truffles or home-made ice cream. There are only three or four tables, or you can perch at the bar. Mon, Wed–Fri & Sun 1–4pm & 8pm–midnight, Sat 8pm–midnight; closed 2 weeks in Jan.

Sesamo c/de Sant Antoni Abat 52 ☎934 416 411; ⓜSant Antoni; map pp.58–59. This classy tapas place (with bar at the front and restaurant tables at the back) offers up a chalkboard menu of innovative organic dishes that are either vegetarian or vegan. Small and not-so-small dishes roll out of the open kitchen – think Catalan mushroom croquettes, gnocchi with beetroot and hazel-nuts or grilled vegetables with goat cheese and rosemary, all in the range €7–22. The Catalan wines and cheeses are a high point too. Tues–Sun 8pm–midnight.

RESTAURANTS

Biocenter c/de Pintor Fortuny 25 ☎933 014 583, ⊛restaurantebiocenter.es; ⓜLiceu; map pp.58–59. One of the longest-running veggie places in town, with a

TOP 5 VEGGIE-FRIENDLY RESTAURANTS

La Báscula See p.182
Biocenter See opposite
Sesamo See opposite
Teresa Carles See below
Venus Delicatessen See p.179

restaurant-bar across the road from the original health-food store. The fixed-price lunch menu (€10.20, weekends €12.35) starts with soup and a trawl through the salad bar for a first course, followed by a daily changing choice of mains. For dinner, they dim the lights, add candles and sounds and turn out a few more exotic dishes, from *seitan* in a white wine sauce to cheese and mushroom *mezzelune* (mains around €12). Mon–Sat 1–11pm, Sun 1–4pm.

★**Ca l'Estevet** c/Valldonzella 46 ☎933 024 186, ⓦrestaurantestevet.com; ⓜUniversitat; map pp.58–59. An unshifting rock in the fickle seas of foodie fashions, *Ca l'Estevet* has been serving up old-school Catalan cuisine to loyal local customers since 1940 (and, under a different name, for fifty years before that). The practice has made perfect; get a bellyful of the €18 lunch menu or tuck into the likes of grilled *botifarra* sausages, roasted kid or *escudella i carn d'olla* (meat stew), all for €10–20, under the guidance of a white-tux-wearing waiter. Mon & Sun 7–11pm, Tues–Sat 1–4pm & 7–11pm.

Cera 23 c/de la Cera 23 ☎934 420 808, ⓦcera23.com; ⓜSant Antoni; map pp.58–59. It's always 5 o'clock somewhere, so go ahead and start your meal at this charming Galicia-meets-the-Mediterranean bistro with an effervescent blackberry mojito, and then tuck into market-fresh dishes like grilled duck with apples, a black-rice-and-seafood "volcano" or almond-flavoured beetroot gnocchi in balsamic cream (mains €12–18). Mon & Sun 7–11pm, Tues–Sat 1–4pm & 7–11pm.

Elisabets c/d'Elisabets 2 ☎933 175 826; ⓜCatalunya; map pp.58–59. Catalan home-cooking served at cramped tables in a jovial brick-walled dining room. Locals breakfast on a sandwich and a glass of wine, the hearty lunchtime *menú del día* is hard to beat for price (€10.85) or you can just have tapas, sandwiches and drinks at the bar. Meals Mon–Sat 1–4pm, bar open Mon–Sat 7.30am–11pm; closed Aug.

Mesón David c/de les Carretes 63 ☎934 415 934, ⓦmesondavid.com; ⓜParal·lel; map pp.58–59. This down-to-earth Galician bar-restaurant is a firm favourite with neighbourhood families who bring their kids before they can even walk. The weekday *menú* is a steal – maybe lentil broth followed by grilled trout and home-made *flan* – while traditional Galician dishes like octopus or the *combinado Gallego* ("ham, salami, ear") go down well with the regulars. Lunch is around €12, otherwise most dishes €5–16, and there's a good-natured bang on the clog-gong for anyone who leaves a tip. Daily noon–4pm & 8pm–midnight.

★**Romesco** c/de Sant Pau ☎933 189 381; ⓜLiceu; map pp.58–59. Old Barcelona hands talk lovingly of the *Romesco* – and as long as you accept its limitations (dining under strip-lights, gruff waiters) you can hardly go wrong, as the most expensive thing on the menu is a €10 grilled steak and most dishes go for €6 or less. It's basic but good, with big salads, country broths and grilled veg to start, followed by *bacalao a la llauna*, or lamb chops or grilled prawns from the market, scattered with parsley and chopped garlic. If you spend more than €15 each you've probably eaten someone else's dinner as well. Mon–Fri 1–11.30pm, Sat 1–4.30pm & 8–11.30pm; closed Aug.

★**Suculent** Rambla de Raval 43 ☎934 436 579, ⓦsuculent.com; ⓜLiceu; map pp.58–59. Star chef Carles Abellan and talented 27-year-old newcomer Toni Romero have teamed up to refine classic rustic dishes at this bistro. As well as meaning "succulent", the name is a play on the Catalan words "sucar lent" – to dip slowly – and you'll do just that, using the fresh, warm bread to mop up the sauces from dish after lip-smacking dish. The steak tartare on a split, grilled marrowbone (€15) will put hairs on your chest and bring tears of joy to your eyes. Wed–Sun 1–4pm & 8.30–11.30pm.

Teresa Carles c/de Jovellanos 2 ☎933 171 829, ⓦteresacarles.com; ⓜCatalunya; map pp.58–59. Stylish vegetarian and vegan cuisine served in a hip – but most certainly not "hippie" – space with soaring ceilings, exposed bricks walls and soft, white lighting. The lunch menu (€9.50) is a great bargain, while à la carte offerings like artisanal pastas, a hearty *seitan* burger and vegan *ceviche* cost €9–12.50. Brunch served until 2pm. Daily 9am–11.30pm.

SANT PERE AND LA RIBERA

CAFÉS

★**Bar del Convent** Centre Cívic Convent de Sant Agustí, Pl. de l'Acadèmia, c/del Comerç 36, Sant Pere ☎932 103 732, ⓦbardelconvent.com; ⓜJaume I; map p.68. The cloister café-bar in the converted old convent, now cultural centre, is good for drinks at any time and a bargain for lunch and light meals. At night it's more of a bar, with a range of live shows, DJs

15

TOP 5 CHEAP EATS

Can Maño See p.186
Casa Mari y Rufo See p.183
Elisabets See above
Fast Vínic See p.190
Romesco See above

15

CATALAN FOOD AND DISHES

Traditional Catalan food places heavy emphasis on meat, olive oil, garlic, fruit and salad. The cuisine is typified by a willingness to mix flavours, so savoury dishes cooked with nuts or fruit are common, as are salads using both cooked and raw ingredients.

Meat is usually grilled and served with a few fried potatoes or salad, though Catalan sausage served with a pool of haricot beans is a classic menu item. Stewed veal and other casseroles are common, while poultry is sometimes mixed with seafood (known as *mar i muntanya* – "sea and mountain") or fruit for tastes very definitely out of the Spanish mainstream. In season, **game** is also available, especially partridge, hare, rabbit and boar.

As for **fish and seafood**, you'll be offered hake, tuna, squid or cuttlefish, while the local anchovies are superb. Cod is often salted and turns up in *esquixada*, a summer salad of salt cod, tomatoes, onions and olives. Fish stews are a local speciality, though the mainstays of seafood restaurants are the rice- and noodle-based dishes. **Paella** comes originally from Valencia, but as that region was historically part of Catalunya, the dish has been enthusiastically adopted as Catalunya's own. More certainly Catalan is **fideuà**, thin noodles served with seafood – you stir in the fiery *all i olli* (garlic mayonnaise) provided. **Arròs negre** (black rice, cooked with squid ink) is another local delicacy.

Vegetables rarely amount to more than a few French fries or boiled potatoes, though there are some authentic Catalan vegetable dishes, like spinach tossed with raisins and pine nuts, or *samfaina*, a ratatouille-like stew. Spring is the season for **calçots**, huge spring onions, which are roasted whole and eaten with a spicy *romesco* dipping sauce. Autumn sees the arrival of **wild mushrooms**, mixed with rice, omelettes, salads or scrambled eggs. In winter, a dish of **stewed beans or lentils** is also a popular starter, almost always flavoured with bits of sausage, meat and fat.

For **dessert**, apart from fresh fruit, there's always crème caramel (*flan* in Catalan) – fantastic when home-made – though *crema Catalana* is the local choice, more like a crème brûlée, with a caramelized sugar coating. Or you might be offered *músic*, nuts and dried fruit served with a glass of sweet *moscatel* wine.

and concerts. Tues–Thurs 10am–9pm, Fri & Sat 10am–10pm, Sun 11am–5pm.

★**La Báscula** c/dels Flassaders 30, La Ribera ☎933 199 866; Ⓜ Jaume I; map p.68. An old chocolate factory in the backstreets has been given a hippy-chic makeover by a local cooperative and serves up veggie pasta dishes, turnovers, couscous, quiches and salads (around €8.50). Drinks are great too – dozens of teas, coffees, organic wines, juices and shakes – and it's a cool break-from-the-shops spot. Wed–Sat 1pm–midnight, Sun 1–5pm.

Pim Pam Burger c/Sabateret 4, La Ribera ☎933 152 093, ⓦ pimpamburger.com; Ⓜ Jaume I; map p.68. The go-to-choice for a quick bite, *Pim Pam Burger* is the place for burgers, fries, franks and sandwiches (€2.50–6). There are a few stools and tables if you'd rather not eat on the hoof, while *Pim Pam Plats* (ⓦ pimpamplats.com), just around the corner on c/del Rec is their outlet for budget-beating take-home meals. Daily 1pm–12.30am (Pim Pam Plats opens at 11am).

TAPAS BARS

El Bitxo c/de Verdaguer i Callis 9, Sant Pere ☎932 681 708; Ⓜ Urquinaona; map p.68. This is a great find for drinks and tapas, very close to the Palau de la Música Catalana. It's tiny (four small wooden tables and a line of bar stools) but there's a friendly welcome, and the food is good, especially the cured and smoked meats and sausages and regional cheeses (dishes up to €10). Daily 1pm–midnight.

★**Cal Pep** Pl. de les Olles 8, La Ribera ☎933 107 961, ⓦ calpep.com; Ⓜ Barceloneta; map p.68. There's no equal in town for fresh-off-the-boat and out-of-the-market tapas. You will have to queue (there are no reservations), and prices are high for what's effectively a bar meal (up to €50 a head) but it's definitely worth it for the likes of impeccably fried shrimp, grilled sea bass, Catalan sausage and beans, and baby squid and chickpeas – the whole show overseen by Pep himself bustling up and down the counter. Mon 7.30–11.30pm, Tues–Fri 1–3.45pm & 7.30–11.30pm, Sat 1–3.45pm; closed Easter week & last 3 weeks in Aug.

Euskal Etxea Pl. de Montcada 1–3, La Ribera ☎902 520 522, ⓦ euskaletxeataberna.com; Ⓜ Jaume I; map p.68. The bar at the front of the local Basque community centre is great for *pintxos* – pint-sized tapas, held together by a stick. Just point to what you want (and keep the sticks so that the bill can be tallied at the end – most things are a couple of euros each). There's a pricier restaurant out back with more good Basque specialities. Bar Mon–Thurs & Sun 10am–12.30am, Fri & Sat 10am–1am; restaurant 1–4pm & 8pm–midnight.

El Guindilla del Born c/de l'Argenteria 53, La Ribera ☎ 932 215 548; Ⓜ Jaume I; map p.68. A reliable respite from the tourist trail, this big, bright tapas restaurant also offers burgers, salads and takeaway *pollastre a l'ast* (rotisserie chicken). Despite the tourist-trap trappings, the food is very good, with fish (sourced from Barceloneta market) a particular strength. Try the mussels, the seafood salad and the grilled squid with Iberian ham (all €7–11). There's a large terrace but even with the extra seats it gets full at busy periods and you can't book. Daily 10am–1am.

Llamber c/de la Fusina 5, La Ribera ☎ 933 196 250; Ⓜ Jaume I; map p.68. In a former industrial warehouse facing the Mercat del Born cultural centre, renowned Asturian chef Francisco Heras has created a modern factory of first-rate tapas. Open 365 days a year, *Llamber* is a stylish "gastronomic tavern" with a wood-and-brick aesthetic that makes the most of the building's heritage. There are full dishes for around €10–14 each, but the emphasis is very much on eating and drinking in groups. The wine list is full of bargains and the €15.50 lunch menu is one of the best in the area. Mon–Fri noon–1am, Sat & Sun noon–2.30am.

La Mercat Princesa c/dels Flassaders 21, La Ribera ☎ 932 681 518, Ⓦ mercatprincesa.com; Ⓜ Jaume I; map p.68. Enjoy food from more than a dozen gourmet stalls (think plump Chinese dumplings, grilled artisan sausages and artfully mounded *montaditos*) at communal tables inside a restored fourteenth-century palace's interior courtyard. It's a great option, especially if your taste buds are pulling you in multiple directions. From €2.50 a dish depending on what you order. Mon–Wed & Sun 9am–midnight, Thurs–Sat 9am–1am.

Mosquito c/dels Carders 46, Sant Pere ☎ 932 687 569, Ⓦ mosquitotapas.com; Ⓜ Jaume 1; map p.68. Happy indeed are the locals for whom this is their neighbourhood drink-and-chow joint. The Asian tapas bar, festooned with hanging paper lanterns, pours artisan beers and offers an authentic, made-to-order dim sum menu (dishes €3–5), from shrimp dumplings to tofu rolls. Mon 7.30pm–1am, Tues–Sun 1pm–1am.

El Xampanyet c/de Montcada 22, La Ribera ☎ 933 197 003; Ⓜ Jaume I; map p.68. Traditional blue-tiled bar doing a roaring trade in sparkling cava, cider and tapas – anchovies are the speciality, but there's also marinated tuna, spicy mussels, sun-dried tomatoes, sliced meats and cheese. As is often the way, the drinks are cheap and the tapas turn out to be rather pricey (€5–8 each, and portions aren't generous) but there's usually a good buzz about the place. Tues–Sat noon–3.30pm & 7–11pm, Sun noon–3.30pm; closed Aug.

RESTAURANTS

El Atril c/dels Carders 23, Sant Pere ☎ 933 101 220, Ⓦ atrilbarcelona.com; Ⓜ Jaume I; map p.68. Chill out in this fine Aussie-owned bistro-bar, which has a popular

terrassa in a revamped neighbourhood square. Lunch is always a steal, with tapas served at other times, and dinner from 7pm, from a menu that ranges from *moules frites* to lamb skewers with spicy peanut sauce (mains €10–15). The long (11.30am–5pm), lazy Sunday brunch is good, too, while there's a great selection of wines available at the owner's Vino wine store opposite (c/dels Carders 22; Mon–Wed opens 5pm, Thurs–Sun 4pm), which you can take as BYO into the restaurant for a small corkage charge. On Friday and Saturday, there is live music and wine tastings by the glass. Daily noon–midnight.

★**Casa Delfín** Pg. del Born 36, La Ribera ☎ 933 195 088; Ⓜ Jaume I; map p.68. There are many reasons to like this bubbly, updated taverna, not least its sunny *terrassa* outside the old market. It's a slick operation, inside and out, with a long menu that takes a loving look at traditional Catalan dishes, from grilled farmhouse sausage and white beans to crispy artichoke hearts with *romesco* sauce. It's served tapas-style, so you don't have to come for a full meal (dishes €5–20), but if you've got room don't miss English owner Kate's signature pudding, Eton Mess. Mon–Wed 8am–midnight, Thurs & Fri 8am–1am, Sat 10am–1am, Sun 10am–midnight.

Casa Mari y Rufo c/de les Freixures 11, Sant Pere ☎ 933 197 302; Ⓜ Jaume I; map p.68. A great place for no-frills market cooking, with a busy family at a smoky range turning out quick-fried sardines, grilled Catalan sausage, stewed oxtail, steak and chips and the like – or ask what's good from the Mercat Santa Caterina fish stalls that day. Expect whitewashed walls, bare light bulbs and chipped tiles, but with lunch for an unbeatable €12 and dinner for around €30, the locals know a good deal when they see one. Mon–Wed 8am–6pm, Thurs & Fri 8am–2am, Sat noon–2am.

Cuines Santa Caterina Mercat Santa Caterina, Av. de Francesc Cambó 16, Sant Pere ☎ 932 689 918, Ⓦ grupotragaluz.com/en/restaurante/cuines-caterina; Ⓜ Jaume I; map p.68. The handsome neighbourhood market has a ravishing open-plan restaurant, with tables set under soaring wooden rafters. Food in the restaurant touches all bases – pasta to sushi, Catalan rice to Thai chicken – with most things costing €9–12. Or, you can just drink and munch superior tapas at the horseshoe bar. Bar Mon–Wed & Sun 9am–11.30pm, Thurs–Sat 9am–12.30am; restaurant Mon–Wed & Sun 1–4pm & 8–11.30pm, Thurs–Sat 1–4pm & 8pm–12.30am.

15

TOP 5 PLACES FOR BRUNCH

Agua See p.187
El Atril See p.183
Bistreau See p.189
Federal See p.179
La Soleá See p.188

BARCELONA'S BEST BURGERS

Take one financial crisis, add locals looking for value-for-money dining and the current rage for burger bars becomes more understandable. Of course, being Barcelona, we're talking stylish, gourmet burger places, like the crowd-pleasing **Kiosko Burger** (see below), where artisan-made bread, organic beef, hand-cut fries and perky, home-made sauces keep the punters happy. Others swear by the long-standing **Pim Pam Burger** (see p.182), a hole-in-the-wall place in La Ribera that's well placed for the late-night munchies. A couple of great bars also get honourable burger bravos, namely **Betty Ford's** (see p.197) and **Cervecería Jazz** (see p.201), while **Makamaka** (see p.200) in La Barceloneta earns top marks for its juicy burgers and ample outdoor seating. Newcomer **De Paula** (see p.188) makes a strong case to be considered the king of them all, with a winning combo of top quality, charm and relative cheapness.

15

Kiosko Burger Av. del Marquès de l'Argentera 1, La Ribera ☎ 933 107 313, ⓦ kioskoburger.com; Ⓜ Barceloneta; map p.68. Aussie chef Brad Ainsworth runs Barcelona's best gourmet burger outlet here. Great-tasting artisan bread rolls and home-made sauces set the tone, while a dozen superb burgers (€5–9) come any way you like, from Catalan (with a roast garlic alioli) to Japanese (teriyaki sauce). Daily 1pm–1am.

★**N.A.P. (Neapolitan Authentic Pizza)** c/de Gombao 5, Sant Pere ☎ 686 192 690; Ⓜ Jaume I; map p.68. Italian staff. Italian ingredients. Italian pizza. Specifically, Neapolitan thin-base pizza. Like the best pizza places in Naples itself, *N.A.P.* is loud, chaotic, crowded and cheap (€4–7 per pizza). You'll have to queue, then wait as the small wood-fired oven struggles to deal with the workload. But the result is probably the best pizza in town, with the possible exception of *N.A.P.*'s second, less-crowded branch on c/ Baluard, in Barceloneta. Daily 1.30pm–4.30pm & 8pm–midnight.

★**Senyor Parellada** c/de l'Argenteria 37, La Ribera ☎ 933 105 094, ⓦ senyorparellada.com; Ⓜ Jaume I; map p.68. An utterly gorgeous renovation of an eighteenth-century building is the mellow backdrop for genuine home-style Catalan cuisine – octopus braised with potato hash, sautéed vegetables and pork belly, duck with figs, garlicky roasted lamb. Most dishes cost between €8 and €15, while more than a dozen puds await those who struggle through. Daily 1–3.45pm & 8.30–11.30pm.

Set Portes Pg. d'Isabel II 14, La Ribera ☎ 933 192 950, ⓦ 7portes.com; Ⓜ Barceloneta; map p.68. A wood-panelled classic with the names of its famous clientele much to the fore – they've all eaten here, from Errol Flynn to Yoko Ono. The decor in the "Seven Doors" has barely changed in almost two hundred years and, while very elegant, it's not exclusive – you should book ahead, though, as the queues can be horrendous. The renowned rice dishes are fairly reasonably priced (€16–22), but for a full meal you're looking at around €60 a head. Daily 1pm–1am.

PORT VELL AND BARCELONETA

CAFÉS

Vioko Pg. de Joan de Borbó 74, Barceloneta ☎ 932 210 652, ⓦ vioko.es; Ⓜ Barceloneta; map p.79. Quite simply, the slinkiest, swishiest ice cream and chocolate shop in town – *Vioko*'s minimalist white curves serve as the backdrop for artisan *gelati* in flavours such as banana split or pomelo and jasmine, gourmet chocolates and coffee, rainbows of airy macaroons, ready to take away on a stroll along the marina. Mon–Thurs & Sun 10am–1am Fri & Sat 10am–2am.

TAPAS BARS

★**Cova Fumada** c/del Baluard 56, Barceloneta ☎ 932 214 061; Ⓜ Barceloneta; map p.79. Behind brown wooden doors on Barceloneta's market square (there's no sign) is this rough-and-ready tavern with battered marble tables and antique barrels. It might not look like much but the food's great, with ingredients straight from the market (tapas €2–10) – from griddled prawns to fried artichokes.

Mon–Wed 9am–3.20pm, Thurs & Fri 9am–3.20pm & 6–8.20pm, Sat 9am–1.20pm; closed Aug.

Jai-Ca c/de Ginebra 9 & 13, Barceloneta ☎ 932 683 265; Ⓜ Barceloneta; map p.79. Always a winning choice for seafood tapas, with bundles of razor clams, plump anchovies, stuffed mussels and other platters piled high on the bar. Meanwhile, the fryers in the kitchen work overtime, turning out crisp baby squid, fried shrimp and little green peppers scattered with rock salt. Take your haul to a tile-topped cane table, or outside onto the tiny street-corner patio. The second location at no. 9 also has a patio and serves the same menu. Dishes up to €10. No. 13 Tues–Sat 9am–11.30pm; no. 9 daily noon–midnight.

Vaso de Oro c/de Balboa 6, Barceloneta ☎ 933 193 098, ⓦ vasodeoro.com; Ⓜ Barceloneta; map p.79. If you can get in this corridor of a bar you're doing well – Sunday lunch is particularly busy – and there's no menu, but standard bites include *patatas bravas*, fried sausage and tuna salad, with fancier shellfish dishes and meat grills

available too (most tapas €4–15). Unusually, they also brew their own beer – light, dark and IPA – which comes in tall schooners. Daily 9am–midnight.

RESTAURANTS

1881 Per Sagardi Pl. de Pau Vila 3, Barceloneta ☏ 932 210 050, ☷ sagardi.com; ⓂBarceloneta; map p.79. Ride the escalators to the roof of the waterfront Museu d'Història de Catalunya and you'll be met with the smell of woodsmoke. A huge grill dominates the glass-walled *1881 per Sagardi*, churning out Basque dishes like magnificent *txuletón* steaks and Catalan dishes like artichokes with *romesco* sauce. Main courses are about €22–30 each but it's worth paying just to sit on the terrace, which also serves a mean Martini, and watch the yachts sailing in and out of the harbour. Daily 1–4pm & 8pm–midnight; terrace Mon–Fri 1pm–1am, Sat & Sun 1pm–3am.

Bravo 24 Hotel W, Pl. Rosa dels Venta 1 ☏ 932 952 636, ☷ carlesabellan.com; ⓂBarceloneta; map p.79. Within the high-glam hotel W hides an unexpectedly old-fashioned treat for foodies. *Bravo 24*, overseen by star chef Carles Abellan, tempts guests in with its world-class tapas but also offers a menu full of old-school Barcelona dishes like *fricandó* (beef stew), complete with historical descriptions of their origins. The combination of a drop-dead-gorgeous terrace overlooking the beach and next-level comfort food is a winner. Tapas ranges from €2.50 to €16 each and mains are €24–60. Open 365 days/year. Daily 1.30–4pm & 8–11.30pm; tapas 1.30–11.30pm.

★Can Maño c/del Baluard 12, Barceloneta ☏ 933 193 082; ⓂBarceloneta; map p.79. This old-fashioned diner is packed with noisy locals around formica tables. Basically, your choice is fried or grilled fish, such as sardines, mullet or calamari, supplemented by a few daily seafood specials and basic meat dishes. Expect rough house wine and absolutely no frills, but it's an authentic experience, which is likely to cost you less than €15 a head. Mon 8–11pm, Tues–Fri 8–11am, 12.15–4pm & 8–11pm, Sat 8–11am & 12.15–4pm; closed Aug.

PORT OLÍMPIC AND POBLE NOU

CAFÉS

El Tío Ché Rambla del Poble Nou 44–46, Poble Nou ☏ 933 091 872, ☷ eltioche.es; ⓂPoblenou, or bus #36

Kaiku Pg. de Joan de Borbó 74, Barceloneta ☏ 932 219 082, ☷ restaurantkaiku.cat; ⓂBarceloneta; map p.79. You really need to book for this place because the secret is out – a prime location on the seafront terrace for fantastic, Basque-influenced seafood meals (dishes €8–17, cheaper lunch menu served Tues–Fri). The ingredients are first-rate, from fresh fish to rice from the famous growing area of Delta de l'Ebre, and tastes are out of the ordinary – think smoked vegetable rice with mushrooms and rocket, or steamed mussels with thyme. Tues–Sun 1–3.30pm; June–Aug Tues–Sun 1–3.30pm & 7–10.30pm.

★La Mar Salada Pg. de Joan de Borbó 58, Barceloneta, ☏ 932 212 127, ☷ lamarsalada.cat; ⓂBarceloneta; map p.79. While many of the classic fish restaurants in Barceloneta have let standards slip under the groaning weight of tourist numbers, the young team at *La Mar Salada* have instead raised the bar. Buying freshly landed fish straight from the dock directly opposite, they offer refined, creative variations of great seafood dishes at bargain prices. The €17.50 lunchtime *menú del dia* is outrageously good value, and there's even a sunny terrace to eat it on. Mon–Fri 1–4pm & 8–11pm, Sat & Sun 1–11pm.

Pez Vela Pg. del Mare Nostrum 19/21 ☏ 932 216 317, ☷ grupotragaluz.com; ⓂBarceloneta; map p.79. At the base of the towering W hotel this restaurant styled on a "*chiringuito*" (beach bar) serves excellent paella and rice dishes, plus seafood such as clams and Galician-style octopus, from its sunny terrace. It's hard to beat for simple waterfront dining and main courses for €16–24 are reasonable given the swish location. There's also a €35 set lunch. Daily 1pm–midnight.

Somorrosto c/de Sant Carles 11, Barceloneta ☏ 932 250 010, ☷ restaurantesomorrostro.com; ⓂBarceloneta; map p.79. Creative "boat-to-table" Mediterranean cuisine with a mission: preserving and promoting the livelihood and traditions of this fishing community. The three-course evening menu (from €17) is excellent value, and it's great fun to watch the open kitchen in action. Daily 1pm–midnight.

from ⓂBarceloneta; map p.83. A down-to-earth café in a down-to-earth neighbourhood, run by the same family for four generations. The specialities are orange or lemon

---

IT TAKES TWO

You want a seafood paella or an *arròs negre* (black rice, with squid ink), or maybe a garlicky *fideuà* (noodles with seafood). Of course you do. Problem is, you're on your own and virtually every restaurant that offers these classic Barcelona dishes does so for a minimum of two people (often you don't find out until you examine the menu small print). Solution? Ask the waiter upfront, as sometimes the kitchen will oblige single diners, or look for the dishes on a *menú del dia* (especially on Thursdays, traditionally rice day), when there should be no minimum. Probably best not to grab a stranger off the street to share a paella, however desperate you are.

granissat (crushed ice) and their famous *orxata* (tiger-nut drink), but there are also *torrons* (almond fudge), hot chocolate, coffee, croissants and sandwiches. It's a bit off the beaten track, though you can stroll up easily enough from Bogatell beach (15min) or down the *rambla* from Poble Nou metro (10min). Daily 10am–10pm/midnight; reduced hours in winter.

TAPAS BARS

Arola Hotel Arts Barcelona, c/Marina 19–21, Port Olímpic ☎ 932 211 000, ⊛ hotelartsbarcelona.com; ⓂCiutadella-Vila Olímpica; map p.83. Imaginative tapas by Michelin-starred chef Sergi Arola are served on a stunning terrace overlooking Frank Gehry's "Fish" statue, with live music and DJs playing in the evenings. It's a classy, relaxed vibe and the food emphasizes fun not formality. It's not cheap – about €35 for a simple lunch and double that for a full tasting menu – but quality like this always comes at a price. Wed–Fri 1.30–3.30pm & 8–11pm, Sat 2–4pm & 8–11pm, Sun 1–3.30pm & 8–11pm.

RESTAURANTS

Agua Pg. Marítim 30, Port Olímpic ☎ 932 251 272, ⊛ grupotragaluz.com; Ⓜ Ciutadella-Vila Olímpica; map p.83. Much the nicest boardwalk restaurant on the beach-front strip, perfect for brunch, though if the weather's iffy you can opt for the sleek, split-level dining room. The menu is contemporary Mediterranean – grills, *risotti*, pasta, salads and tapas – and the prices are pretty fair for such a prime spot (most dishes €9–23), so it's usually busy. Mon–Thurs & Sun 1–3.45pm & 8–11.30pm, Fri & Sat 1–4.30pm & 8pm–12.30am.

★**Bestial** c/Ramon Trias Fargas 2–4, Port Olímpic ☎ 932 240 407, ⊛ grupotragaluz.com; Ⓜ Ciutadella-Vila Olímpica; map p.83. Right beside Frank Gehry's "Fish" (under the wooden bridge) you'll find a stylish terrace-garden in front of the beach, great for an alfresco lunch. Inside the feel is sharp and minimalist, while the cooking is Mediterranean, with an emphasis on seafood. Tapas and starters are in the €4–15 ranges, with other dishes up to €25. Don't miss the baked fish. At weekends there's DJ music and drinks until 5am. Daily 1–4pm & 8–11.30pm (Fri & Sat until 12.30am).

El Cangrejo Loco Moll de Gregal 29–30, upper level, Port Olímpic ☎ 932 210 533, ⊛ www.elcangrejoloco .com; Ⓜ Ciutadella-Vila Olímpica; map p.83. The terrace at the "Crazy Crab" offers ocean views, and the food is excellent. A salt-cod salad or small fried fish are typically Catalan starters, and the rice dishes are thoroughly recommended. A meal costs from around €40. Daily 1pm–1am.

Dos Cielos c/de Pere IV 272–286, Poble Nou ☎ 933 672 070, ⊛ doscielos.com; Ⓜ Poble Nou or tram T4 to Pere IV via Glòries and Av. Diagonal; map p.83. For a superb meal and unparalleled views of the city's skyline, head to the Torres twins' Michelin-starred restaurant on the 24th floor of the *Meliá Sky* hotel. The impeccably prepared ten-course tasting menu (€100) is seasonal, with the restaurant's vegetables coming from a "bio-garden" five floors up. The sophisticated dining room never feels stuffy, thanks to an amiable staff and 360-degree views of Barcelona. Tues–Sat 1–4pm & 8–11pm (Fri & Sat until 11.30pm).

★**Enoteca** Hotel Arts Barcelona c/Marina 19–21, Port Olímpic ☎ 932 211 000, ⊛ hotelartsbarcelona.com; Ⓜ Ciutadella-Vila Olímpica; map p.83. A contender for the crown of Barcelona's best fine-dining restaurant, *Enoteca* contributes two Michelin stars to the five-star constellation of chef Paco Perez. Everything here from the all-white dining room to the wine list and service is appropriately stellar. The food? A creative tour-de-force of modern Catalan cooking that will put a smile on your face – and a hole in your bank account. Tasting menu €145. Mon & Tues 1–3.30pm & 7.30–11pm, Wed–Sat 7.30–11pm.

★**Els Pescadors** Pl. de Prim 1, Poble Nou ☎ 932 252 018, ⊛ elspescadors.com; Ⓜ Poble Nou; map p.83. The best top-class fish restaurant in Barcelona? It's a tough call, but many would choose this hideaway place in a pretty square with gnarled trees in the back alleys of Rambla de Poble Nou. Lunch outside on a sunny day just can't be beaten (reservations advised). The menu offers daily changing fresh fish dishes, and plenty more involving rice, noodles or salt cod (try the latter with *samfaina*, like a Catalan ratatouille). Most dishes cost €15–40 and if you don't go mad with the wine list you'll escape for around €70 a head. Daily 1–3.45pm & 8–11.30pm; closed 2 weeks Dec/Jan.

POBLE SEC

TAPAS BARS

★**Quimet i Quimet** c/del Poeta Cabanyes 25 ☎ 934 423 142; Ⓜ Paral.lel; map p.94. Poble Sec's cosiest tapas bar is a foodie place of pilgrimage and at busy times everyone has to breathe in to squeeze another punter through the door. The wine bottles are stacked five shelves high (there's a chalkboard menu of wines by the glass), while little plates of classy finger food (mostly €3–10)

are served reverently from the minuscule counter – things like roast onions, marinated mushrooms, stuffed cherry tomatoes, grilled aubergine, anchovy-wrapped olives and a terrific range of regional cheeses. Mon–Fri noon–4pm & 7–10.30pm, Sat noon–4pm; closed Aug.

★**Tapería Lolita** c/de Tamarit 104 ☎ 934 245 231, ⊛ lolitataperia.com; Ⓜ Poble Sec; map p.94. You might have to wait in line to see what all the fuss is about at Joan

15

Martínez's hip bar, which serves cocktails and classic tapas – or "small portions of happiness" – to tuned-in city folk and in-the-know tourists. You can eat and drink for around €25 – don't miss the signature-dish *patatas bravas* or the creamy *ensaladilla Rusa*. Tues & Wed 7pm–midnight, Thurs 7pm–2am, Fri 1–6pm & 7pm–2.30am, Sat 1–4pm & 7pm–2.30am; Aug closes afternoons and at midnight.

Tickets Av. Paral.lel 164, no phone, online reservations only on ⓦes.bcn50.org; ⓜPoble Sec; map p.94. The hullaballoo shows no sign of abating at *Tickets*, the swanky tapas bar under the star-studded helm of pastry-chef supremo Albert Adrià, his *El Bulli*-famed brother Ferran Adrià and the Iglesias brothers of the renowned *Rías de Galicia* seafood restaurant. It's divided into half-a-dozen quirky seating areas that make a play on fairground and theatrical themes, and the terrifically inventive dishes (€5– 20 each, expect to spend €70) mix impeccably sourced ingredients with the flights of fancy expected from the Adrià brothers. With only a hundred covers a night, and online reservations taken up to three months in advance, you can't guarantee a table. Tues–Fri 7–11pm, Sat 1–3.30pm & 7–10.30pm; closed 3 weeks in Aug.

RESTAURANTS

Bella Napoli c/de Margarit 14 ☎934 425 056; ⓜPoble Sec; map p.94. Authentic Neapolitan pizzeria, right down to the cheery waiters and cheesy pop music. The pizzas come straight from the depths of a beehive-shaped oven, or there's a big range of pastas, *risotti* and veal *scaloppine*, with almost everything priced between €9 and €15. Daily 1.30–4.30pm & 8.30pm–midnight.

La Bodegueta c/de Blai 47 ☎934 420 846, ⓦlabodeguetabcn.com; ⓜPoble Sec; map p.94. A true Catalan taverna with food like mother used to make – a relaxed Sunday lunch here brings local families out in force.

DRETA DE L'EIXAMPLE

CAFÉS

Café del Centre c/de Girona 69 ☎934 881 101; ⓜGirona; map p.102. This quiet coffee stop is only four blocks from the tourist sights on the Pg. de Gràcia, but it's well off the beaten track as far as most visitors are concerned. It's well worth the walk for a café that's been here since 1873 and that retains its elegant *modernista* decor, plus the lunch menu is a bargain at €9.90. Mon–Sat 9am–11pm; closed Aug.

TAPAS BARS

La Bodegueta Rambla de Catalunya 100 ☎932 154 894, ⓦrambla.labodegueta.cat; ⓜDiagonal; map p.102. This long-established basement *bodega* serves cava by the glass, a serious range of other wines and good ham, cheese, anchovies and other tapas (€3–15) to soak it all up.

It's a good-natured, red-check-tablecloth-and-barrels kind of place, specializing in *torrades* (cold cuts on toasted country bread), salads and grills (most dishes €7–16) – the excellent grilled veg platter is a good place to start. Daily 1–4pm & 8pm–midnight.

★**De Paula** c/de la Creu dels Molers 65 ☎931 646 980, ⓦdepaula.cat; ⓜPoble Sec; map p.94. The new kid on the burger block might just be the best in town. Charcoal grill? Check. Hand-chopped, quality meat? Check. Artisanal bread? Check. The burgers are posh but the prices (€6–9) and serving sizes will suit everyone. The only downside is the small size, despite a recent expansion. Try the local beers when you're in there – if you can get a table. Mon, Tues & Thurs–Sat 1–4.15pm & 8pm–midnight, Wed 1–4.15pm.

La Soleá Pl. del Sortidor 14 ☎934 410 124, ⓦbarlasolea.com; ⓜPoble Sec; map p.94. This place's *terrassa*, on a down-to-earth square, is a great place for sunny days, while in the cheery if cramped interior there's a backdrop of vibrant colours and young guns behind the counter singing along lustily to *flamenco nuevo* sounds. It's a bistro menu (lunch from 1.30pm, dinner from 8.30pm, dishes €5–12) and all pretty good value – salads and dips to start, followed by proper hamburgers, stir-fries, pasta or a reassuringly old-fashioned Sunday brunch plate of *fideuà* (Catalan noodles). Tues–Sat noon–midnight, Sun noon–5pm (summer Sun open until midnight).

★**La Tomaquera** c/de Margarit 58, no phone; ⓜPoble Sec; map p.94. Sit down in this chatter-filled tavern to a dish of olives and two quails' eggs – and any delicacy ends there as the chefs set to hacking steaks and chops from great hunks of meat. It's not for the faint-hearted, but the grilled chicken is sensational and the *entrecôtes* enormous (most mains €8–15). Locals limber up with an appetizer of pan-fried snails with chorizo and tomato. Tues–Sat 1.30– 3.45pm & 8.30–10.45pm; closed Aug.

In summer you can sit outside at tables on the pretty uptown *rambla*. Mon–Fri 7am–1.45am, Sat 8am–1.45am, Sun & hols 6.30pm–1.45am.

Ciutat Comtal Rambla de Catalunya 18 ☎933 181 997; ⓜPasseig de Gràcia; map p.102. The best of the large uptown tapas-hall-style places is a handy city-centre pitstop that caters for all needs. Breakfast sees the bar groan under the weight of a dozen types of crispy baguette sandwich, plus croissants and pastries, while the daily changing tapas selection (€3–10) ranges far and wide, from *patatas bravas* to octopus. It can be standing room only at lunchtime (and not much of that either), so get there early. Daily 8am–1.30am.

★**Tapas24** c/de la Diputació 269 ☎934 880 977, ⓦcarlesabellan.com; ⓜPasseig de Gràcia; map p.102. Carles Abellan, king of pared-down designer cuisine at his

WHAT'S COOKING?

The man behind the reimagining of modern cuisine – the foams, the essences, the vapours, the taste explosions, the deconstructed, laboratory-tested dishes – is Catalan chef **Ferran Adrià**, whose world-famous, triple-Michelin-starred restaurant *El Bulli*, on the Costa Brava, set the benchmark for creative contemporary cooking. *El Bulli* closed as a restaurant in 2011 – with plans under way to turn it into a cookery foundation (ⓦ elbullifoundation.com) and "centre for creativity" – though Adrià and his brother Albert also have a high-profile presence on the Barcelona dining scene with their new-wave tapas bar, *Tickets* (see opposite), and modern takes on Japanese cuisine (*Pakta*) and Mexican (*Hoja Santa* and *Niño Viejo*). A mysterious new restaurant, enigmatically titled, erm, *Enigma*, is due to open at some point in 2016. Meanwhile, the Adrià effect has spawned a generation of regional chefs – many of them alumni of the *El Bulli* kitchens – who have helped put contemporary Spanish cuisine on the map. Talents like Jordi Vilà, Carles Abellan, Ramón Freixa and Fermí Puig are cooking right now in Barcelona, so it's time to brush up on your chemistry and educate your tastebuds.

15

famed restaurant *Comerç 24*, offers a simpler tapas menu at this retro basement bar-diner. There's a reassuringly traditional feel that's echoed in the menu – *patatas bravas*, Andalucian-style fried fish, meatballs, chorizo sausage and fried eggs. But the kitchen updates the classics too, so there's also *calamares romana* (fried squid) dyed black with squid ink or a burger with foie gras. Most tapas cost €4–16. There's always a rush and a bustle at meal times, and you might well have to queue. Mon–Sat 9am–midnight.

RESTAURANTS

★**Au Port de la Lune** c/de Pau Claris 103 ☏ 934 122 224, ⓦ auportdelalune.es; Ⓜ Passeig de Gràcia; map p.102. This no-nonsense French bistro has been a favourite of local foodies for years. The decor of French books and Serge Gainsbourg photos has one foot over the border of cliché, but the cooking is the real deal: oysters, excellent cheese and a cassoulet so good you'll order more. Fussy eaters should look elsewhere: a sign reading "there's no ketchup, no Coca-Cola, no Coca-Cola light, and there never will be" sets the tone. Lunch menus of €11.50–15 and an evening four-course menu for €25 are unbeatable value. Mon–Fri 8am–5pm & 6.30–11.30pm, Sat 10am–5pm & 6.30pm–midnight, Sun 11am–5pm.

Bistreau Hotel Mandarin Oriental, Pg. de Gràcia 38–40 ☏ 931 518 783, ⓦ mandarinoriental.com/Barcelona; Ⓜ Passeig de Gràcia; map p.102. Occupying the light, impossibly pretty atrium of Barcelona's most stylish hotel, *Bistreau* by Michelin-starred chef Ángel León is, unsurprisingly, a pleasant place to sit and eat. The food doesn't try to match the fine-dining majesty of *Moments* upstairs in the same building, but instead offers a short menu based around original seafood dishes. The €35 set lunch menu is a great way to give it a try. Otherwise expect to pay €15–30 for a main course. Daily 1–3.30pm & 8–10.30pm.

Casa Calvet c/de Casp 48 ☏ 934 124 012, ⓦ casacalvet .es; Ⓜ Catalunya/Urquinaona; map p.102. The wonderfully decorated townhouse built by a young Antoni Gaudí for a Catalan industrialist makes for a truly glam night out. The restaurant offers a seasonally changing, modern Catalan menu, with desserts that are artworks in themselves, though with mains around the €30 mark, lunch at €34 or tasting menus from €50 to €70, expect it to be a purse-emptying experience. Mon–Sat 1–3.30pm & 8.30–11pm; closed 1 week in Aug.

★**Embat** c/de Mallorca 304 ☏ 934 580 855, ⓦ restaurantembat.com; Ⓜ Verdaguer; map p.102. Hidden a few streets away from the tourist traffic, this modern Catalan bistro has won the loyalty of locals over the past ten years by serving refined, first-class food at affordable prices – expect to pay €20–25 for a three-course lunch and double that for a slap-up evening meal. It's a small, white, minimalist space where the money is spent on ingredients not interior designers. Many of the dishes are close to Michelin-star standard, especially the desserts. Mon–Sat 8.30am–3.45pm & 8.30–11pm.

★**Moments** Hotel Mandarin Oriental, Pg. de Gràcia 38–40 ☏ 931 518 787, ⓦ mandarinoriental.com /Barcelona; Ⓜ Passeig de Gràcia; map p.102. Catalan chef Carme Ruscalleda is the only woman in the world to have seven Michelin stars. Her main restaurant, *Sant Pau*, up the coast in Sant Pol de Mar, is a three-star thing of wonder but the two-star *Moments*, run by her son, Raul Balam, isn't far behind. You'll pay €143 for a mind- and budget-blowing tasting menu of exquisite beauty and refinement, set in an appropriately luxurious gold dining room. Tues–Sat 1–3.30pm & 8.30–11pm.

Mordisco Pg. de la Concepció 10 ☏ 934 879 656, ⓦ grupotragaluz.com; Ⓜ Diagonal; map p.102. With less of a look-at-me atmosphere than its sister restaurant *Tragaluz* (see p.190), *Mordisco* turns your attention to the food instead. It's fresh, rustic stuff straight from the charcoal grill, with excellent steak and seasonal mushroom dishes. You can even shop for fresh vegetables and deli ingredients here. That's not to say that style takes a

15

TOP 5 MONEY NO OBJECT

Cinc Sentits See below
Enoteca See p.187
Manairó See opposite
Moments See p.189
Els Pescadors See p.187

---

backseat: this former high-end jeweller's is a palace of white columns with a gorgeous glass-covered courtyard, and the upper floor has been converted into a relaxed cocktail bar. Expect to pay €12–18 for main courses. Daily 12.30pm–midnight, Thurs–Sat drinks until 2am.

★**El Nacional BCN** Pg. de Gràcia, 24 Bis ☎935 185 053, ⓦelnacionalbcn.com; ⓜPassseig de Gràcia; map p.102. It took years to plan and build but the new *El Nacional* lives up to the hype. This massive 2600-square-metre food court offers a one-stop-shop for Spanish cuisine. In its gorgeous, high-ceilinged space you find a fish

restaurant, grill, tapas bar, snack bar, oyster bar, wine bar, cocktail bar and most other bars you can think of. Quality across the board is very high; prices aren't low either, but not bad by Pg. de Gràcia standards. Check it out on the cheap with a quick snack for a few euros or go for broke with a massive €185/kg extra-aged rib-steak cooked on a wood grill. There are no bookings, so be prepared to wait or pick a different section at busy times. Daily noon–1am, Thurs–Sat until 3am.

Tragaluz Ptge. de la Concepció 5 ☎934 870 621, ⓦgrupotragaluz.com/; ⓜDiagonal; map p.102. This place attracts beautiful people by the score, and the classy Mediterranean-with-knobs-on cooking, served under a glass roof (*tragaluz* means "skylight"), doesn't disappoint. Mains include steak tartare, slow-roasted pork with pineapple and pasta with truffles, and cost €15–24. It's a relaxing stop for those fresh off the *modernista* trail (La Pedrera is just across the way). Daily 1.30–4pm & 8.30–11.30pm.

ESQUERRA DE L'EIXAMPLE

CAFÉ

★**Fast Vínic** c/de la Diputació 251 ☎934 873 241, ⓦwww.fastvinic.com; ⓜPasseig de Gràcia; map p.110. *Fast Vínic* is a designer sandwich bar – but not just any sandwiches and not just any bar. The emphasis is on top-of-the-range ingredients from sustainable sources (sandwiches mostly €5–10), while at the same time you get to sample from a range of more than twenty Catalan wines by the glass, starting at pocket-money prices. It's the more democratic outpost of the hallowed wine-and-foodie temple next door that is *Monvínic* (ⓦwww.monvinic.com). Mon–Sat noon–midnight.

TAPAS BARS

Cerveseria Catalana c/de Mallorca 236 ☎932 160 368; ⓜPasseig de Gràcia; map p.110. An uptown beer-and-tapas joint where the counters are piled high with elaborately assembled dishes, supplemented by a blackboard list of daily specials like bacon, cheese and date skewers and mushroom risotto (most tapas €2–10). It gets busy after work and at meal times, and you might have to wait for a table. Daily 9am–1am.

La Taverna del Clínic c/del Rosselló 155 ☎934 104 221, ⓦlatavernadelclinic.com; ⓜHospital Clínic; map p.110. This sleek taverna, so called after the hospital over the road, is a gourmet tapas spot that concentrates on rigorously sourced regional produce. Snacks at the solid marble bar come in at just a few euros, but the serious food, accompanied by artisan-made olive oil and a high-class wine list, is served at one of the ten tables (book in advance) and runs to more like €10–30 a dish, from crispy suckling pig to sea urchins artfully arranged atop mounds of sea salt. Mon–Sat 1–4pm & 8–11.30pm.

RESTAURANTS

Cinc Sentits c/d'Aribau 58 ☎933 239 490, ⓦcincsentits .com; ⓜUniversitat; map p.110. Jordi Artal's "Five Senses" wows diners with his contemporary Catalan cuisine – and it has a Michelin star to boot, so you'll need to book. Three "tasting menus" (€55, €95 and €125, wines pairings available) use rigorously sourced ingredients – wild fish, mountain lamb, seasonal vegetables, farmhouse cheeses – in elegant, pared-down dishes that are all about flavour. Tues–Sat 1.30–3pm & 8.30–10pm; closed 2 weeks in Aug.

Etapes c/d'Enric Granados 10 ☎933 236 914, ⓦwww .restaurantetapes.com; ⓜUniversitat; map p.110. This family-owned restaurant is fuelled by an unusual combination of simplicity and sophistication. The food is refined enough to be called fine dining but steers clear of anything too esoteric. Instead, you'll get things like scallops and pork belly, and prawn tartare followed by home-cooked cakes from *yaya* (grandma). The service is simply excellent and the lunch menu (€15.50) is a steal. In the evenings, there are tasting menus at €35 and €60. Mon–Fri 1–3.30pm & 8–11pm, Sat & Sun 8–11pm.

★**La Flauta** c/d'Aribau 23 ☎933 237 038; ⓜUniversitat; map p.110. One of the city's best-value lunch menus sees diners queuing for tables early – get there before 2pm to avoid the rush. It's a handsome bar-restaurant of dark wood and deep colours, and while the name is a nod to the house speciality gourmet sandwiches (a *flauta* is a thin baguette), there are also meals served tapas-style, day and night (dishes €4–10), based on local market produce, wild mushrooms to locally landed fish. Mon–Sat 7am–1.15am; closed 3 weeks in Aug.

★**Gresca** c/Provença 230 ☎934 516 193, ⓦgresca .net; ⓜDiagonal; map p.110. It is a long-running source of bemusement among food writers that *Gresca's* Rafa Penya does not have a Michelin star. But what's bad news for him is good news for diners: you get to keep eating his superb food in a tiny restaurant that's much cheaper than it really ought to be. The €19 lunchtime *menú del dia* is the best bargain in fine dining that you'll find in Barcelona but, if funds permit, the €38–70 tasting menus are even more spectacular, and showcase creative, technical cooking of the highest standard. Mon–Fri 1.30–4pm & 8.30–11.30pm, Sat 8.30–11.30pm.

Igueldo c/Rosselló 186 ☎ 934 522 555, ✇ restaurante igueldo.com; ⓜ Diagonal; map p.110. Basque co-owners Ana and Gonzalo have imported their regional cuisine, polished by years of practice in some of Spain's finest restaurants. There's a focus on excellent ingredients and an effort to keep prices accessible (mains €17–20, three-course tasting menu €36). Don't miss the steak tartare with beer yoghurt. Mon–Sat 1.30–4.30pm & 8–11.30pm, Sat & Sun 8–11pm.

SAGRADA FAMÍLIA AND GLÒRIES

TAPAS BARS
★ **Bardeni** c/Valencia 454 ☎ 932 314 511, ✇ caldeni.com/bardeni; ⓜ Sagrada Família; map pp.116–117. This "meat bar" is a new extension to the excellent *Caldeni* restaurant next door. It swaps tablecloths and tasting menus for bar-stools and a selection of carnivore-centric snacks, such as oxtail canneloni and hamburgers (all priced around €7) made with specific kinds of beef, such as Nebraska Black Angus and Charolais. Chef/owner Dani Lechuga (whose surname ironically means "lettuce") is from a family of butchers and meat experts so the (sometimes literally) raw materials here are first rate. No reservations. Tues–Sat 1.30–3.30pm & 8.30–10.30pm.

RESTAURANTS
Gorria c/de la Diputació 421 ☎ 932 451 164, ✇ restaurantegorria.com; ⓜ Monumental; map pp.116–117. This elegant family-owned restaurant serves the finest Basque cuisine, like *pochas de Sanguesa* (a sort of white-bean stew), wood-grilled lamb, clams in salsa verde or monkfish stuffed with smoked salmon. Prices are on the high side (€50 a head and upwards), but this is regional Spanish cooking of the highest order. Mon 1–3.30pm, Tues–Sat 1–3.30pm & 9–11.30pm; closed Easter week & Aug.

★ **Manairó** c/de la Diputació 424 ☎ 932 310 057, ✇ manairo.com; ⓜ Sagrada Família; map pp.116–117. Jordi Herrera doesn't look like the kind of guy who cooks delicate, Michelin-starred food. But looks are deceiving; the bearded, motorbike-riding former rugby player has

carved out a reputation as one of the city's top chefs by combining technical wizardry with big, bold flavours. The resulting dishes pack a punch – the signature steak, cooked on a patented beartrap-like system of spikes over a stove-top bonfire (€32), is one of the best you'll ever eat. Tasting menus cost €70 and €90. Mon–Sat 1.30–3.30pm & 8.30–10.30pm.

★ **La Paradeta Sagrada Família** Ptge. Simó 18 ☎ 934 500 191, ✇ laparadeta.com; ⓜ Sagrada Família; map pp.116–117. One of a chain of similar *Paradetas* across the city, "the market stall" looks like its name suggests. Join the queue and you'll arrive at a display of fish and shellfish on ice, priced by weight. Point out the prawns, cockles, mussels, clams, crabs and lobsters that you want and they'll be cooked for you there and then. Listen for your number being called, collect the food from the hatch and tuck into some of the best-priced fresh seafood in town. Expect to pay about €20–25 for a slap-up lunch. No reservations. Daily 1–4pm & 8–11.30pm.

La Taquería Ptge. del Font 5 ☎ 931 261 359, ✇ lataqueria.eu; ⓜ Sagrada Família; map pp.116–117. When it comes to Mexican food in Europe, throwing the word "authentic" around can get you in trouble with the purists but in this case, it's an apt description for this fun little restaurant's offerings: the tangy *tacos al pastor*, savoury *sopa Azteca* and fresh-made guacamole are all hits (€5–10). Tues–Sun 1–4.30pm & 8.30–11.30pm, Fri & Sat until midnight.

GRÀCIA

CAFÉS
Gelateria Caffetteria Italiana Pl. de la Revolució 2 ☎ 932 102 339; ⓜ Fontana; map p.125. The place to go for real handmade Italian ice cream, and a stroll around a pretty square in the sun – expect queues at peak times and then more waiting as you struggle to choose from the twenty-odd flavours. Daily 2pm–1am (Fri & Sat until 2am); opens at 4pm Nov–April.

★ **La Nena** c/de Ramon y Cajal 36 ☎ 932 851 476, ✇ chocolaterialanena.com; ⓜ Fontana; map p.125. First and foremost, it's the food at "the little girl" that's the

main attraction – lovely home-made cakes, plus waffles, quiches, organic ice cream, squeezed juices and the like. But parents love it too, as it's very child friendly, from the

TOP 5 DATE NIGHTS

Café de l'Acadèmia See p.178
Casa Calvet See p.189
El Salón See p.179
La Singular See p.192
Senyor Parellada See p.184

15

changing mats in the loos to the little seats, games and puzzles. Mon–Wed 9am–2pm & 4–10pm, Thurs–Sat 9am–10pm, Sun 10am–10pm; closed Aug.

TAPAS BARS

La Pepita c/de Còrsega 343 ☎ 932 384 893, ⓦ lapepitabcn.com; ⓜ Diagonal/Verdaguer; map p.125. There's usually a queue out the door, and deservedly so. The tapas, like roasted chicken croquettes with *romesco* sauce (€4) or aubergine fritters with goat's cheese, honey and apples (€8), are fantastic, and the atmosphere is chatty and convivial. Hundreds of "love notes" scrawled by customers on the white-tiled walls hint at its popularity. Mon 7.30pm–1am, Tues–Thurs 9am–1am, Fri 9am–2.30am, Sat 10am–2.30am.

RESTAURANTS

L'Arrosseria Xàtiva c/Torrent d'en Vidalet 26 ☎ 932 848 502, ⓦ www.grupxativa.com; ⓜ Joanic; map p.125. Rice done right is hard to find. The microwaved and burnt offerings that pass for paella in most city restaurants enrage proud Valencians, who hate to see their heritage abused in the name of profit margins. For the real thing, try one of the two *Xàtiva* restaurants (the other is in Les Corts). There's also the full range of Catalan rice dishes including creamy *arròs melós*, all made with fresh stock and organic vegetables. The *menú del dia* (€14.50) is a great way to fill up before exploring the area. Daily 1–4pm & 7.30pm–midnight.

★ **Cal Boter** c/Tordera 62 ☎ 934 588 462, ⓦ restaurant calboter.com; ⓜ Verdaguer; map p.125. This old-school neighbourhood bistro is perpetually packed with everyone from hipsters to those in need of hip replacements. Survive the queue (or arrive when it opens) and you'll be rewarded with rib-sticking stews, meatballs, snails and other classic dishes at knockdown prices. The lunch menu is €11.20 and à la carte main courses range from €8 to €16. Decades of customers' letters on the walls are evidence of *Cal Boter's* beloved local status. Tues–Sat 1–4pm & 9pm–midnight, Mon & Sun 1–4pm.

Flash, Flash c/de la Granada del Penedès 25 ☎ 932 370

990, ⓦ flashflashbarcelona.com; ⓜ Diagonal; map p.125. A classic 1970s survivor, *Flash, Flash* does *tortillas* (€6–9) served any time you like, any way you like, from plain and simple to elaborately stuffed, with sweet ones for dessert. If that doesn't grab you, there's a menu of salads, steaks, burgers and fish. Either way, you'll love the original white leatherette booths and monotone "models-with-cameras" cutouts – very Austin Powers. Restaurant daily 1pm–1.30am, bar 11am–2am.

Goliard c/del Progrés ☎ 932 073 175; ⓜ Diagonal; map p.125. Smart but casual *Goliard* offers a pared-down dining experience in a contemporary foodie bistro that looks like it should cost three times as much. Dishes are of-the-moment – octopus and sweet potato in an almond sauce, tuna sashimi on a chive and tomato salsa – and although the menu is divided into starters and mains (most things €7–15), there are smaller portions available if you want to mix and match. The weekday lunch is a really good deal too. Mon–Fri 1–3.30pm & 9–11.30pm, Sat 9–11.30pm; closed 3 weeks in Aug.

Nou Candanchu Pl. Vila de Gràcia 9 ☎ 932 377 362; ⓜ Fontana; map p.125. Good for lunch on a sunny day or a leisurely night out on a budget, when you can sit beneath the clocktower in the ever-entertaining local square. There's a wide menu – tapas and hot sandwiches, but also steak and eggs, steamed clams and mussels, or cod and hake cooked plenty of different ways. It's managed by an affable bunch of young guys, and there's lots of choice for €8–12. Daily 9am–3am.

La Singular c/de Francesc Giner 50 ☎ 932 375 098, ⓦ lasingular-barcelona.com; ⓜ Diagonal; map p.125. The tiniest of kitchens turns out refined Mediterranean food – say, Lebanese-style couscous, or sweet potato gnocchi in arrabiata sauce – at moderate prices, with most dishes costing €9–15. There's always something appealing on the menu for veggies too. It's a cornerstone of the neighbourhood, with a friendly – even romantic – atmosphere, but there are only nine tables, so go early or reserve. Mon–Fri 1.30–4pm & 9pm–midnight (Fri until 1am), Sat 9pm–1am; closed 2 weeks in Aug/Sept.

LES CORTS, PEDRALBES AND SARRIÀ-SANT GERVASI

TAPAS BARS

★ **Bar Tomás** c/Major de Sarrià 49, Sarrià ☎ 932 031 077; FGC Sarrià; map pp.130–131. The best *patatas bravas* in the city? Everyone points you here, to this utterly unassuming, white-formica-table bar in the 'burbs (12min by train from Pl. Catalunya FGC station) for a taste of their unrivalled spicy fried potatoes with garlic mayo and *salsa picante*. Daily noon–4pm & 6–8pm; closed Aug.

RESTAURANTS

Can Punyetes c/de Marià Cubí 189, Sant Gervasi ☎ 932 009 159, ⓦ canpunyetes.com; FGC Muntaner; map

pp.130–131. Traditional grillhouse-tavern – well, since 1981 anyway – that offers slick city diners a taste of older times. There are simple salads and tapas, and open grills turning out sausage, lamb chops, chicken and pork, accompanied by grilled country bread, white beans and char-grilled potato halves. Prices are very reasonable (almost everything is under €10) and locals love it. Daily noon–3.45pm & 8pm–midnight.

Casa Fernández c/de Santaló 46, Sant Gervasi ☎ 932 019 308, ⓦ www.casafernandez.com; FGC Muntaner; map pp.130–131. The long kitchen hours are a boon for the bar-crawlers in this neck of the woods. It's a

15

contemporary place featuring market cuisine, though they are specialists in – of all things – fried eggs, either served straight with chips or with Catalan sausage, fried aubergine and honey or other variations. Most dishes are in the range €6–15. Mon–Sat 1–5pm & 8pm–midnight, Sun & hols noon–4.30pm.

★**Fragments Cafè** Pl. de la Concórdia 12 ☎934 199 613, ⓦfragmentscafe.com; Ⓜ Les Corts; map

pp.130–131. A classy yet casual bistro popular with locals for its fresh, classic food (*patatas bravas* are a speciality) that's served in the charming dining room or in the shaded garden. The lunch menu is a steal (€12), with the rest of the dishes, from tapas to fresh pasta, around €5–14. Tues–Fri 12.30pm–1am (Thurs & Fri until 2.30am), Sat 11.30am–2.30am, Sun 11.30am–1am; closed 2 weeks in Aug.

TIBIDABO

RESTAURANTS

★**El Asador de Aranda** Av. del Tibidabo 31 ☎934 170 115, ⓦasadordearanda.com; FGC Av. Tibidabo; map p.138. There are a number of *Asadors* in town but this is the crown jewel. A multilevel *modernista* mansion with an

opulent interior is the setting for simple but succulent rare-breed lamb (€22) roasted in clay ovens. Wash it down with a bottle of good red wine then have a coffee on the rooftop terrace with views over the city. Daily 1–4pm & 8–11pm, closed Sun eve.

15

COCKTAILS AT *MILK*

Bars, clubs and live music

Whatever you're looking for from a night out, you'll find it somewhere in
Barcelona – bohemian boozer, underground club, cocktail bar, summer
dance palace, techno temple, Irish pub or designer bar, you name it. Some of
the finest places for a drink are cafés and tapas bars (see p.175), and
undoubtedly one of the city's greatest pleasures is to pull up a pavement
seat and watch the world go by. However, the bar scene proper operates at a
different pace, and with a different set of rules. Specialist bars in Barcelona
include *cellers/bodegas* (specializing in wine), *cerveseries* (beer), *xampanyeries*
(champagne and cava) and *cocteleries* (cocktails). Best known of the city's
nightlife haunts are its hip designer bars, while there's a stylish club and
music scene that goes from strength to strength fuelled by a potent mix of
resident and guest DJs, local bands and visiting superstars.

Generally, the bars and clubs in the old town are a mixture of traditional tourist haunts, party-time Irish bars, local drinking places and fashionista hangouts. In the **Barri Gòtic**, it's the streets around Plaça Reial and Plaça George Orwell that see most of the action, while in **La Ribera**, Passeig del Born is the main focus, though a hip scene is developing up in the neighbouring *barri* of **Sant Pere** too. For a slightly edgier bunch of bars, cross over to **El Raval**, where the coolest places are found in the upper part of the neighbourhood near MACBA (especially along c/de Joaquín Costa). You can still find tradition (and sleaze) further south, closer to the port, in the surviving bars of the old Barri Xinès, while over in the unsung neighbourhood of **Poble Sec** there's an increasing number of mellow bars, music venues and late-night haunts and clubs. **Port Olímpic** is more of a mainstream summer-night playground for locals and tourists alike, with scores of bars, all either themed or otherwise fairly mundane, but with the advantage that you can simply hop from one to another if you don't like your first choice. Up in **Gràcia**, there's a lively bar scene and several offbeat music joints. Meanwhile, the bulk of the big-name warehouse and designer venues are in peripheral areas like **Poble Nou** and **Les Corts**, while also high on the list of any seasoned clubber is the tourist fantasy village of **Poble Espanyol** in Montjuïc.

As for music, major bands include Barcelona on their tours, playing either at sports stadium venues or at the city's bigger clubs. The city's pretty hot on **jazz**, **Latin** and **blues**, while **folk**, **roots** and **world music** aficionados need to scour the club gig lists for home-grown and touring talent alike. All sorts of city venues, museums, galleries and institutions have **live music programmes** too – Caixa Forum is particularly well regarded, while the books-and-music chain **FNAC** (ⓦclubcultura.com) sponsors gigs and events at the concert halls at its stores at Plaça de Catalunya, L'Illa Diagonal and L'Illa Diagonal Mar.

16

ESSENTIALS

What's on Local listings magazines *Guía del Ocio* (ⓦguia delociobcn.com) and *Time Out Barcelona* (ⓦtimeout.cat) cover current openings, hours and club nights, and most bars, cafés, boutiques and music stores carry flyers and free magazines containing news and reviews. For the Barcelona music scene, check out the websites ⓦatiza.com and ⓦconciertosbarcelona.es.

Tickets Tickets for major gigs are available from the main ticket agencies (see p.206); in addition, there's a concert ticket desk in the Pl. Catalunya FNAC store (ⓜCatalunya), while the music shops along c/dels Tallers (just off the Ramblas; ⓜCatalunya) also sell gig tickets.

Opening hours Most bars stay open until 2am, or 3am at weekends, while clubs tend not to open much before midnight, only barely getting started by 3am and staying open until 5am, or even later at weekends. Unlike restaurants, bars and clubs generally stay open throughout August.

Admission charges Some clubs are free before a certain time, usually around midnight. Otherwise, expect to pay €10–20 for club admission, though this usually includes your first drink (if there is free entry, don't be surprised to find that there's a minimum drinks charge of anything up to €10). Tickets for gigs run from €20 to €50, depending on the act, though there are cheaper gigs (€5–20) almost every night of the year at a variety of smaller clubs and bars.

THE RAMBLAS

BARS

Boadas Cocktails c/dels Tallers 1 ☎933 189 592, ⓦboadascocktails.com; ⓜCatalunya; map p.38. Inside

Barcelona's oldest cocktail bar, tuxedoed bartenders shake, stir and pour classic drinks for a well-dressed crowd against an Art Deco background. It's a timeless place that's a

---

MUSIC FESTIVALS

Barcelona's festival calendar (see p.214) features several big live music events. Aside from headline concerts during the Generalitat's summer-long **Festival de Barcelona Grec**, the biggest annual music festivals are the techno, rock and indie showcase that is **Primavera Sound** (May) and the **Sónar** (June) electro bleep-fest. Singer-songwriters are showcased every year at **BarnaSants** (Jan–March), while for jazz fans the main event is the **Festival de Jazz** (Nov–Dec), as well as the jazz, blues and Latin-tinged **Festival de Guitarra** (April–May). There's also Gràcia's experimental and electronic music festival, known as **LEM** (Oct).

perfect start for a sophisticated night on the town. Mon–Thurs noon–2am, Fri & Sat noon–3am; closed 3 weeks in Aug.

Bosc de les Fades Ptge. de la Banca 5 ☎933 172 649, ⓦmuseocerabcn.com; ⓜDrassanes; map p.38. Tucked away in an alley off the Ramblas, beside the entrance to the wax museum, the "Forest of the Fairies" is festooned with gnarled plaster tree trunks, hanging branches, fountains and stalactites. It's a bit cheesy and the service isn't the best, but tourists love to huddle in the grottoes with a

cocktail or two. Mon–Thurs 10am–1am, Fri 10am–1.30am, Sat & Sun 11am–1.30am.

La Cazalla Ramblas 25 ⓦlacazalla.com; ⓜDrassanes; map p.38. A historic remnant of the old days, the hole-in-the-wall *Cazalla* (under the arch, at the beginning of c/de l'Arc del Teatre) first opened its hatch in 1912. It was closed for some years, but it's now back in business offering stand-up coffees, beers and shots to an assorted clientele of locals, cops, streetwalkers, and the occasional stray tourist. Daily 7pm–2.30am.

BARRI GÒTIC

BARS

★**L'Ascensor** c/de Bellafila 3 ☎933 185 347; ⓜJaume I; map p.44. Sliding, antique wooden elevator doors announce the entrance to "The Lift", but it's no theme bar – just an easy-going local hangout, great for a late-night drink. Daily 7pm–3am.

La Cerveteca c/d'en Gignàs 25 ☎933 150 407, ⓦlacerveteca.com; ⓜJaume I; map p.44. The city's biggest and best world-beer bar is hardly a beard-and-sandals place, more a cool tasting-bar for ale enthusiasts of all kinds. Mon–Thurs & Sun 6–11pm, Fri & Sat 6pm–midnight.

Glaciar Pl. Reial 3 ☎933 021 163, ⓦlareial.com; ⓜLiceu; map p.44. At this traditional Barcelona meeting point the terrace seating is packed most sunny evenings and at weekends, and the comings and goings in the old town's liveliest square are half the entertainment. Mon–Thurs & Sun 11am–2am, Fri & Sat 11am–3am.

Milans Cocktail Bar c/de Milans 7 ☎932 689 932, ⓦmilanscocktailbar.com; ⓜDrassanes; map p.44. Hidden down a bendy alley, this isn't much more than a hacked-out room in an old Gothic Quarter building, cocktail bar inside, couple of sofas outside, but it works – helped by some wacky art displays, a great soundtrack (Siouxsie to Roxy Music) and one-offs like pop-up vintage clothes sales. Mon–Thurs & Sun 6.30pm–2.30am, Fri & Sat 7pm–3am.

★**Milk** c/d'en Gignàs 21 ☎932 680 922, ⓦmilkbarcelona.com; ⓜJaume I; map p.44. Irish-owned bar and bistro that's carved a real niche as a welcoming neighbourhood hangout. Decor, they say, is that of a "millionaire's drawing room", with its sofas, cushions and antique chandeliers. Get there early for the famously relaxed "recovery" brunch (10am–4pm), or there's dinner (6.30–11.30pm) and cocktails every night to a cool soundtrack. Daily 10am–2.30am.

Oviso c/de N'Arai 5, Pl. George Orwell ☎933 043 726, ⓦrestaurantes-bares-barcelona.com; ⓜDrassanes; map p.44. Holding a mirror onto the neighbourhood, the *Oviso* fits right in with the scruffy urban square outside – a shabby-chic mural-clad café-bar, popular with a hip young crowd. There's a sunny *terrassa*, and the salads and sandwiches are good too, available from breakfast onwards. Mon–Thurs & Sun 10am–2.30am, Fri & Sat 10am–3am.

Schilling c/de Ferran 23 ☎933 176 787, ⓦcafeschilling.com; ⓜLiceu; map p.44. Something of a haven on this heavily touristy drag, *Schilling* has a certain European "grand-café" style, with its high ceilings, big windows and upmarket feel. It's a mixed, chilled place to meet up, grab a *copa* and move on. Mon–Sat 10am–3am, Sun noon–3am.

★**Zim** c/de Dagueria 20 ☎934 126 548; ⓜJaume I; map p.44. Katherine (of the adjacent *Formatgeria La Seu* cheese shop) and co-owner Francesc offer up this tiny, hole-in-the-wall tasting bar for selected wines from boutique Spanish producers. For a soothing glass or two accompanied by farmhouse cheese, wonderful cured meats from the Pyrenees and artisan-made bread, you really can't beat it – and closing time is often somewhat flexible if you're in the mood for more wine. Tues–Sat 6–11pm; closed 2 weeks in Aug.

CLUBS AND LIVE MUSIC

Fantástico Ptge. dels Escudellers 3 ☎933 175 411; ⓜDrassanes; map p.44. A cheery music bar for the pop, indie, new-folk and shoe-gazer crowd, bopping to The Killers, The Pigeon Detectives, Get Cape and the like. Admission usually free. Mon–Sat 11pm–2.30am.

★**Harlem Jazz Club** c/de la Comtessa de Sobradiel 8 ☎933 100 755, ⓦharlemjazzclub.es; ⓜJaume I; map p.44. For many years *the* hot place for jazz, where every style gets an airing, from African and gypsy to flamenco and fusion. There are two shows a night; it's best to get advance tickets for the second spot. Entry €5–10, depending on the night and the act. No credit cards. Gigs twice nightly, around 10pm & midnight (check website for details); closed Aug.

TOP 5 HISTORIC BARS

Almirall See opposite
La Confitería See opposite
Dry Martini See p.202
Marsella See p.198
Velódromo See p.202

HERE FOR THE BEER?

Until recently, **beer** (*cervesa* in Catalan, *cerveza* in Spanish) in Barcelona meant lager, and only lager, but a growing interest in artisan beers, craft brews and foreign imports means many bars now offer a wider choice. Specialist beer-bars **La Cerveteca** (see opposite) in the Barri Gòtic and Sant Pere's **Ale&Hop** (see p.198) are good places to try local brews, while there are artisan beers made on the premises in Gràcia at **La Cervesera Artesana** (see p.203), Barcelona's original brew-pub. Another top spot is the relatively new – and absolutely stunning – microbrewery **La Fàbrica Moritz** (see below) in Raval. For thirty taps of local and international beers plus quality tapas and burgers, try **BIERcaB** (see p.202). There are also a few pioneering bars serving a decent handcrafted beer – standouts are the Asian tapas joint **Mosquito** in Sant Pere (see p.183) and Poble Sec's beer-and-music bar **Cervecería Jazz** (see p.201). The city is also home to some excellent artisan beer festivals, including the **Barcelona Beer Festival** (wbarcelonabeerfestival .com), held over three days each March (the venue varies from year to year), which has proved wildly popular and now attracts thousands of visitors and brewers from across the globe, and **La Fira del Poblenou** (wlafiradelpoblenou.com) in July.

Jamboree Pl. Reial 17 ☎933 191 789, wmasimas.com /jamboree; ⓜLiceu; map p.44. They don't get the big jazz names here that they used to, but the nightly gigs (from €10) still pull in the crowds, while the wild Monday night WTF jazz, funk and hip-hop jam session (from 8pm; €5) is a city fixture. Stay on for the club, which kicks in after midnight (entry €10) and you get funky sounds until the small hours. Gigs daily at 8pm & 10pm, club daily midnight–5am.

Karma Pl. Reial 10 ☎933 025 680, wkarmadisco.com; ⓜLiceu; map p.44. A stalwart of the scene, this old-school studenty basement place can get claustrophobic at times. Sounds are indie, Britpop and US college, while a lively crowd gathers at the square-side bar and *terrassa* which is open from 6pm. Club admission around €10.

Tues–Sun midnight–5am.

La Macarena c/de Nou de Sant Francesc 5 wmacarena club.com; ⓜDrassanes; map p.44. Once a place where flamenco tunes were offered up to La Macarena, the Virgin of Seville – now a heaving temple to all things electro. Entry free until around 1am, then from €5. Mon–Thurs & Sun midnight–4.30am, Fri, Sat & hols midnight–5am.
★**Sidecar** Pl. Reial 7 ☎933 177 666, wsidecarfactory club.com; ⓜLiceu; map p.44. The hippest concert space in the old town – pronounced "See-day-car" – has nightly gigs and DJs that champion rock, indie, roots, electronica and fusion acts. Entry €5–12, though some gigs up to €20. Mon–Thurs 8pm–5am, Fri & Sat 8pm–6am, gigs usually at 10.30pm, DJs at 12.30am.

EL RAVAL

BARS

★**Almirall** c/de Joaquín Costa 33 ☎933 189 917; ⓜUniversitat; map pp.58–59. Dating from 1860, Barcelona's oldest bar is a *modernista* design classic – check out the doors, counter and stupendous glittering bar. Not too young, not too loud, and always good for a late-night drink. Mon–Thurs 6pm–2.30am, Fri & Sat 6pm–3am, Sun noon–2.30am.

Betty Ford's c/de Joaquín Costa 56 ☎933 041 368; ⓜUniversitat; map pp.58–59. With a vibe somewhere between a student lounge and a beach bar, *Betty's* is a bouncy place full of bouncy young things, sipping colourful cocktails and cold Australian beer. Deal with the late-night munchies by getting to grips with their famed burger menu. Daily 5pm–3am.

La Confitería c/de Sant Pau 128 ☎934 430 458; ⓜParal.lel; map pp.58–59. This one-time bakery and confectioner's – featuring a carved wood bar, faded tile floor, murals, antique chandeliers and mirrored cabinets – is now a popular bar and meeting point. It's a handy stop-off on the way to a night out in Poble Sec. Daily 7pm–3am.

Fàbrica Moritz Ronda de Sant Antoni 41 ☎934 260 050, wmoritz.cat; ⓜSant Antoni/Universitat; map pp.58–59. Cultural centre, *cervesería*, museum and more all come together in French architect Jean Nouvel's gorgeous revamp of the Catalan brewer's nineteenth-century factory. An on-site microbrewery supplies the beer, while star chef Jordi Vilà directs the various gastronomic spaces here. Daily 6pm–3am.

London Bar c/Nou de la Rambla 34 ☎933 185 261; ⓜLiceu; map pp.58–59. Opened in 1910, the well-known *London Bar* attracts a mostly tourist clientele these days, but it's still worth looking in as time has not dulled the exuberant *modernista* decor (nor the authentic old-town sleaze just up the street). Mon–Thurs 10am–3am, Fri 10am–4am, Sat 6pm–4am, Sun 6pm–3.30am; closed mornings in July.

Marmalade c/de la Riera Alta 4–6 ☎934 423 966, wmarmaladebarcelona.com; ⓜSant Antoni; map pp.58–59. A hugely glam face-lift for the old Muebles Navarro furniture store has gone for big, church-like spaces and a backlit Art Deco bar that resembles a high altar. Cocktails, bistro meals and gourmet burgers pull in a relaxed dine-and-lounge crowd, and there's a popular weekend

16

16

TOP 5 MUSIC BARS
Belchica See p.202
Casa Paco See below
Cervecería Jazz See p.201
Soló Bar See p.201
Vinilo See p.203

brunch too. If you like the style, give the more informal Barri Gòtic sister bar, *Milk* (see p.196) a whirl as well. Mon–Wed 6.30pm–2.30am, Thurs–Sun 10am–2.30am.

★**Marsella** c/de Sant Pau 65 ☎ 934 427 263; Ⓜ Liceu; map pp.58–59. Authentic, atmospheric 1930s bar – named after the French port of Marseilles – where absinthe is the drink of choice. It featured in Woody Allen's *Vicky Cristina Barcelona*, so expect a spirited mix of film fans, oddball locals and young dudes, all looking for a slice of the old Barri Xinès. Mon–Sat 10pm–3am; closed 2 weeks in Aug.

★**Pesca Salada** c/de la Cera 32 ☎ 686 265 309; Ⓜ Sant Antoni; map pp.58–59. This former fish market turned gin haven turns up the charm with a cleverly executed (and just subtle enough) under-the-sea theme. It's an intimate corner spot with good music, lovingly crafted cocktails and nibbles like *montaditos* (helpful for maintaining one's sea legs as the night goes on). Mon–Sat 7.30pm–3am.

Resolis c/de la Riera Baixa 22 ☎ 934 412 948; Ⓜ Sant Antoni; map pp.58–59. A decaying, century-old bar turned into a cool hangout with decent tapas. The owners didn't do much – a lick of paint, polish the panelling, patch up the brickwork – but now punters spill out of the door onto "secondhand clothes street" and a good time is had by all. Mon–Sat 6pm–midnight.

Zelig c/del Carme 116 ☎ 934 415 622, Ⓦ zelig

SANT PERE AND LA RIBERA

BARS

★**Ale&Hop** c/de les Basses de Sant Pere 10, Sant Pere Ⓦ facebook.com/aleandhop; Ⓜ Urquinaona; map p.68. Consider yourself a beer geek? Then *Ale&Hop* (pronounced "Al-eh-UP") is your kind of bar. Ten rotating taps pour artisanal beers in all styles (porters, stouts, lagers, gluten free) with names like "Dark Alliance" and "Sex-A-Pils". There's also a large selection of bottled beer, a crowd-pleasing vegetarian bar menu and a Sunday brunch (11am to 5pm). Mon–Thurs 6pm–2.30am, Fri & Sat 6pm–3am, Sun 11am–2am.

Black Horse c/d'Allada Vermell 16, Sant Pere ☎ 933 152 053, Ⓦ pubblackhorse.com; Ⓜ Jaume I; map p.68. Barcelona has embraced the "English" pub and "Irish" bar with a vengeance, and every *barri* has a place where the stag and hen groups can feel right at home. On the whole, there's little to choose between them, though by common consent, the *Black Horse* is among the best, with an off-the-beaten-track feel, despite being just a few minutes

-barcelona.com; Ⓜ Sant Antoni; map pp.58–59. The photo-frieze on granite walls and a fully stocked cocktail bar make it very much of its *barri* but *Zelig* stands out from the crowd – two Dutch owners offer a chatty welcome, a tendency towards 1980s sounds and a slight whiff of camp. Tues–Thurs & Sun 11am–2am, Fri & Sat 11am–3am.

CLUBS AND LIVE MUSIC

La Concha c/de Guàrdia 14 ☎ 933 024 118, Ⓦ laconcha delraval.com; Ⓜ Drassanes; map pp.58–59. The Arab-flamenco fusion throws up a great atmosphere, worth braving the slightly dodgy area for. It's a kitsch, gay-friendly joint, dedicated to the "incandescent presence" of Sara Montiel, Queen of Song and Cinema (and icon of the Spanish gay community), with uninhibited dancing by tourists and locals alike. Admission free. Daily 5pm–3am.

★**Jazz Sí Club** c/de Requesens 2 ☎ 933 290 020, Ⓦ tallerdemusics.com; Ⓜ Sant Antoni; map pp.58–59. This is a great place for inexpensive (€5–8) gigs in a tiny sweatbox of a club associated with the Taller de Músics (Music School). Every night from around 8.30 or 9pm there's something different, from exuberant rock, blues, jazz and jam sessions to the popular weekly Cuban (Thurs) and flamenco (Fri) nights. There are usually a couple of sessions a night, with an interval in between. Your first drink is included in the price, and the bar is as cheap as chips. Daily 8–11.30pm.

★**Moog** c/de l'Arc del Teatre 3 ☎ 933 191 789, Ⓦ masimas.com/moog; Ⓜ Drassanes; map pp.58–59. One of the most influential clubs around for electronic sounds, playing techno, electro, drum'n'bass and trance to a cool but up-for-it crowd. The bigger-name international DJs tend to play Wednesday nights. Admission €5–10. Daily midnight–5am.

from the Picasso museum. Mon–Thurs 6pm–2am, Fri 6pm–3am, Sat 1pm–3am, Sun 1pm–2am.

★**Casa Paco** c/d'Allada Vermell 10, Sant Pere ☎ 935 073 719; Ⓜ Jaume I; map p.68. Sant Pere's signature bar is this cool music joint that's a hit on the weekend DJ scene – the tagline "not a disco, just a bar with good music" says it all. There's a great *terrassa* under the trees, and if you can't get a table here try one of several other alfresco bars down the traffic-free boulevard. Meanwhile, the associated *Pizza Paco* across the way (also with its own terrace) means you don't have to go anywhere else for dinner. April–Sept Mon–Thurs & Sun 9am–2am, Fri & Sat 9am–3am; Oct–March Mon–Thurs & Sun 6pm–2am, Fri & Sat 6pm–3am.

Espai Barroc c/de Montcada 20, La Ribera ☎ 933 100 673, Ⓦ palaudalmases.com; Ⓜ Jaume I; map p.68. Every evening the doors are thrown open at the Palau Dalmases for drinks and cocktails in a remodelled medieval mansion known as the *Espai Barroc*, or "Baroque Space".

CLOCKWISE FROM TOP LEFT *CAFÉ DEL SOL* (P.202); *SALA RAZZMATAZZ* (P.200); *DRY MARTINI* (P.202); *SALA BECOOL* (P.204) >

The rather grand and pricey candlelit bar (minimum charge €7) certainly looks the part – it's your opportunity to dress to the nines – and if you come on Thursday evening you'll catch singers belting out arias as you sip fine wines under the chandeliers (recital at 11pm, €20, first drink included). Tues–Sat 8pm–2am, Sun 6–10pm.

La Fianna c/Manresa 4, La Ribera ☎933 151 810, ⓦlafianna.com; ⓜJaume I; map p.68. Flickering candelabras, parchment lampshades, rough plaster walls and deep colours set the Gothic mood in this stylish lounge-bar that's "putting the beat in the Born". Relax on the chill-out beds and velvet sofas, or book ahead to eat – the fusion-food restaurant is open from 8.30pm. Mon–Wed & Sun 6pm–2am, Thurs–Sat 6pm–3am.

Mudanzas c/de la Vidrería 15, La Ribera ☎933 191 137; ⓜBarceloneta; map p.68. Locals like the relaxed feel (especially if you can hide yourself away in the cosy upper room) at *Mudanzas*, while those in the know come for the wide selection of rums, whiskies and vodkas from around the world. Mon–Thurs & Sun noon–2.30am, Fri & Sat noon–3am; Aug opens at 5pm, closed Sun.

★El Nus c/dels Mirallers 5, La Ribera ☎933 195 355; ⓜJaume I; map p.68. *El Nus* still has the feel of the shop it once was, down to the antique cash register, though it's now a kind of jazz bar-cum-gallery – a quiet, faintly old-fashioned, late-night place. Mon–Thurs & Sun 7.30pm–2.30am, Fri & Sat 7.30pm–3am.

La Vinya del Senyor Pl. de Santa María 5, La Ribera ☎933 103 379; ⓜJaume I; map p.68. A great wine bar with front-row seats onto the lovely church of Santa María del Mar. The wine list is really good – with a score available by the glass – and there are oysters, smoked salmon and other classy tapas available. Mon–Thurs noon–1am, Fri & Sat noon–2am, Sun noon–midnight.

PORT VELL AND BARCELONETA

BARS

★Can Paixano c/de la Reina Cristina 7, Port Vell ☎933 100 839, ⓦcanpaixano.com; ⓜBarceloneta; map p.79. A must on everyone's itinerary is this back-street joint with attached shop where the drink of choice – all right, the only drink – is cava (Catalan champagne). Don't go thinking sophistication – it might come in traditional champagne saucers (the sort of thing Dean Martin used to stack in a pyramid and then pour wine over), but this is a counter-only joint where there's fizz, tapas and tapas-in-sandwiches and that's your lot. And who could want more? Mon–Sat 9am–10.30pm; closed 3 weeks in Aug.

★Makamaka Beach Burger Cafe Pg. de Joan de Borbó 76, Barceloneta ☎932 213 520, ⓦmakamaka.es; ⓜBarceloneta; map p.79. You really can't ask for more: creative cocktails and some of the city's finest burgers served on a large *terrassa* steps from the beach. It's Hawaii-meets-Barcelona – laidback, late night and lots of fun. Mon–Thurs & Sun noon–2am, Fri & Sat noon–2.30am.

PORT OLÍMPIC AND POBLE NOU

CLUBS AND LIVE MUSIC

CDLC Pg. Marítim 32, Port Olímpic ☎932 240 470, ⓦcdlcbarcelona.com; ⓜCiutadella-Vila Olímpica; map p.83. With a clientele of A-list celebs, football players, well-heeled tourists and local kids, this beautiful-person lounge-club hangout is for those who want to dine, dance and kick back in like-minded company. Daily: restaurant from noon, club midnight–3am.

Club Catwalk c/de Ramon Trias Fargas 2–4, Port Olímpic ☎932 240 740, ⓦclubcatwalk.net; ⓜCiutadella-Vila Olímpica; map p.83. The sleek, chic portside club of choice for the beautiful of Barcelona, playing house, funk, soul and r'n'b to well-heeled locals and visitors. It's under the landmark *Hotel Arts Barcelona*. Admission €12–15. Daily 10.30pm–6am.

Sala Razzmatazz c/de Pamplona 88, Poble Nou ☎933 208 200, ⓦsalarazzmatazz.com; ⓜBogatell; map p.83. *Razzmatazz* hosts the biggest in-town rock gigs (the concert hall capacity is 3000), while at weekends the former warehouse turns into "five clubs in one", spinning indie, rock, pop, techno, electro, retro and more in variously named music bars like "The Loft", "Pop Bar" or "Lolita". Admission (€12 advance, €17 box office) gets you entrance to all the bars. Daily 1–6am.

Sala Rocksound c/ Almogàvers 116, Poble Nou ☎659 057 339, ⓦsalarocksound.com; ⓜBogatell; map p.83. As you might have guessed from its name, *Rocksound* usually hosts local bands from the heavier side of the musical tracks. It's also the preferred Barcelona venue for a host of touring blues and Americana musicians who love its intimate atmosphere, good sound and cheap drinks. Admission to most gigs is €12–15. Daily 10pm–late.

MONTJUÏC

BARS

La Caseta del Migdia Mirador del Migdia ⓦlacaseta .org; cable car (Telefèric de Montjuïc) or bus #150 to Castell de Montjuïc, then follow signs to "Mirador" (15min walk); map p.87. It's cooler in every sense up on the heights of Montjuïc, as a welcome summer breeze and chill-out sounds entice visitors to the panoramic, open-air bar of *La Caseta*, around the back of the castle. Usually weekends noon–sunset, plus summer weekend DJ nights.

16

CLUBS AND LIVE MUSIC

La Terrrazza Poble Espanyol, Av. Francesc Ferrer i Guàrdia ❶ 607 969 823, ⓦ laterrrazza.com; ⓜ Espanya; map p.87. Open-air summer club that's *the* place to be in Barcelona. Nonstop dance, house and techno, though don't get there until at least 3am, and be prepared for the style police. May–Oct Thurs–Sat 12.30–6am.

POBLE SEC

BARS

★**Bar Seco** Pg. de Montjuïc 74 ❶ 933 296 374, ⓦ barseco.blogspot.com.es; ⓜ Paral.lel; map p.94. The "Dry Bar" is a local hit, with its mellow vibe, freshly squeezed juices, Free Trade drinks and artisan beers. Standout dish from the Slow Food-inspired, veggie-friendly menu is *patatas salvajes* ("wild potatoes") – fried organic skin-on spuds with a fiery *alioli*. Big picture windows look out onto the corner plot, and there's *terrassa* seating over the road. Mon–Wed 8am–8pm, Thurs 8am–1am, Fri 8am–2am, Sat 10am–2am, Sun 10am–8pm.

Celler Cal Marino c/de Margarit 54 ❶ 933 294 592, ⓦ calmarino.com; ⓜ Poble Sec; map p.94. The wines in the barrels are to take away at knockdown prices, and you can drink a *copa* for under two euros, but there's also a more sophisticated wine selection available in this cavernous, stone-walled tavern. Add cheap tapas and a jolly neighbourhood crowd, and there are more than enough reasons to stop by. Tues–Fri noon–3.30pm & 7.30–11.30pm, Sat 11.30am–3pm & 7.30–11.30pm, Sun 11.30am–3pm.

Cervecería Jazz c/de Margarit 43 ❶ 934 433 259, ⓦ cerveceriajazz.com; ⓜ Poble Sec; map p.94. Grab a stool at the carved bar and shoot the breeze over a Catalan craft beer. It's an amiable joint with great music, jazz to reggae, and locals swear that the burgers are the best in town. Tues–Sat 7pm–3am.

La Tieta c/de Blai 1 ❶ 600 742 532; ⓜ Paral.lel; map p.94. Small but perfectly formed, "The Aunt" is a cool drinks and tapas place, with selected wines served by the glass, an open window onto the street and just enough room inside for a dozen or so good friends. Mon–Thurs & Sun 6–11.30pm, Fri & Sat 6pm–midnight.

★**Xixbar** c/de Rocafort 19 ❶ 934 234 314; ⓜ Poble Sec; map p.94. "Chicks" is an old *granja* (milk bar) – which explains the milk pail and big cow photos – turned candlelit, but completely unstuffy, cocktail bar. Gin's the big drink here (they claim over one hundred varieties), and they mix stonking gin cocktails and even have their own specialist gin

DRETA DE L'EIXAMPLE

BARS

★**Nits d'estiu: Jazz a la Pedrera** La Pedrera, Pg. de Gràcia 92 ❶ 902 202 138, ⓦ lapedrera.com; ⓜ Diagonal; map p.102. The city's most exciting pop-up bar has a regular summer season on the extraordinary

shop on site, with tasting courses and other activities. Mon 6.30pm–2.30am, Tues–Sat 5pm–2.30am.

CLUBS AND LIVE MUSIC

★**Maumau** c/d'en Fontrodona 33 ❶ 934 418 015, ⓦ maumaunderground.com; ⓜ Paral.lel; map p.94. If you're really in the know, then *Maumau* is one of your first weekend ports of call – a great underground lounge-club, cultural centre and chill-out space with comfy sofas, nightly film and video projections, exhibitions and a roster of guest DJs playing deep, soulful grooves. Strictly speaking it's a private club, but they tend to let foreign visitors in for free – if you do join, the "Carnet Maumau" (Maumau Card, currently €12) gives you all sorts of discounts and access to hot venues right across the city. Thurs–Sat 9pm–2.30am.

Sala Apolo c/Nou de la Rambla 113 ❶ 934 414 001, ⓦ sala-apolo.com; ⓜ Paral.lel; map p.94. Old-time ballroom turned hip concert venue with gigs on two stages (local acts to big names) and an eclectic series of club nights with names to reckon with (Nasty Mondays, Crappy Tuesdays etc). Sounds range far and wide, from punk or Catalan rumba to the weekend's long-running techno/electro Nitsa Club (ⓦ nitsa.com). "CupCake Night" on Thursdays is highly camp, with an Abba- and Village People-heavy playlist. Gigs €10–35, club nights €10–15. Daily midnight–5am.

Soló Bar c/de Margarit 18 ❶ 933 297 618; ⓜ Poble Sec; map p.94. Bare-bones boho music bar with free live gigs most nights around 9pm, from Latin American beats to alt-rock. Daily 10pm–2am.

Tinta Roja c/de la Creu dels Molers 17 ❶ 934 433 243, ⓦ www.tintaroja.cat; ⓜ Poble Sec; map p.94. More of an experience than most bars, this highly theatrical tango bar features a succession of over-the-top crimson rooms leading to a stage at the back. There's cabaret and live music (tango, rumba, Cuban, flamenco, African) – often free – a couple of nights a week, though special shows are €5–8. Wed 8.30pm–1am, Thurs 8.30pm–2am, Fri & Sat 8.30pm–3am.

Gaudí roof terrace at La Pedrera (see p.106). Performers range from jazz trios to chamber ensembles. Tickets cost €27; advance booking essential, either at the Pedrera ticket office or from the website. June–Aug Thurs–Sat 8.30–11pm.

16

TOP 5 WINE BARS

La Baignoire See below
Can Paixano See p.200
La Tieta See p.201
La Vinya del Senyor See p.200
Zim See p.196

ESQUERRA DE L'EIXAMPLE

BARS

Belchica c/du Villaroel 60 ☎934 511 355; ⓜUrgell; map p.110. Barcelona's first Belgian beer bar guarantees a range of decent brews (including hard-to-find Trappist ales). It's also a muso's joint, playing electronica, new jazz, lounge, reggae and other left-field sounds, and there are live acts once or twice a week. Tues–Thurs & Sun 7pm–2.30am, Fri & Sat 7pm–3am.

BIERCaB c/ Muntaner 55 ☎644 689 045, ⓦwww .biercab.com; ⓜUniversitat; map p.110. Thirty international craft beers on tap, updated constantly, means that there's an ale to slake all thirsts here. The staff are all enthusiastic and well informed, and happy to let you try before you buy. Soak it all up with some of the hearty Wagyu beef burgers or tapas and pick up a bottle of your favourite to take home from the adjoining shop. Mon–Thurs noon–midnight, Fri & Sat noon–2am, Sun 5pm–midnight.

Danzarama Gran Via de les Corts Catalanes 604 ☎933 019 743, ⓦwww.danzarama.com; ⓜUniversitat; map p.110. Stalwart of the uptown gastro-club scene, with a flashy fusion restaurant (open day and night), summer *terrassa* and cool bar and lounge, great for starting the night before some serious dancing elsewhere. Daily 8am–2am (kitchen closed 1–2pm).

★**Dry Martini** c/d'Aribau 162–166 ☎932 175 072, ⓦwww.drymartinibcn.com; ⓜProvença; map p.110. White-jacketed bartenders, dark wood and brass fittings, a self-satisfied air – it could only be the city's legendary uptown cocktail bar, regularly ranked among the best in the world. To be fair, though, no one mixes drinks better and the regulars aren't the one-dimensional business types you might expect. There's also a mysterious hideaway back-room restaurant, *Speakeasy*, where you can play at being Al Capone. Mon–Fri 1pm–2.30am, Sat & Sun 6.30pm–3am.

★**Velódromo** c/de Muntaner 213 ☎934 306 022; ⓜHospital Clínic; map p.110.This Art Deco gem, with a lofty, *Parisien* feel, a swooping staircase and a gleaming bar, is ideal for swish drinks and cocktails. The addition of star chef Carles Abellan to the management team has resulted in an almost round-the-clock menu of excellent tapas and bistro dishes, making it a favourite of early risers – and late-to-bedders – in search of quality snacks. Daily 6am–3am.

CLUBS AND LIVE MUSIC

City Hall Rambla de Catalunya 2–4 ☎932 333 333, ⓦcityhallbarcelona.com; ⓜCatalunya; map p.102. Very popular mainstream dance joint – the handy location helps – which hosts some of the most varied club nights around, from 1980s revival to electro. Admission €12, though usually free before 2am. Daily midnight–6am.

CLUBS AND LIVE MUSIC

Antilla BCN Latin Club c/d'Aragó 141 ☎934 514 564, ⓦantillasalsa.com; ⓜHospital Clínic/Urgell; map p.110. Latin and Caribbean tunes galore – rumba, son, salsa, merengue, mambo, you name it – for out-and-out good-time dancing. There are live bands, killer cocktails and dance classes most nights. Wed 11pm–2am, Thurs 11pm–5am, Fri & Sat 11pm–6am, Sun 7pm–1am.

Luz de Gas c/de Muntaner 246 ☎932 097 711, ⓦluzdegas.com; ⓜDiagonal; map p.110. Former ballroom venue popular with a slightly older crowd, with live music (rock, blues, soul, jazz and covers) every night around midnight. Foreign acts appear regularly, too, mainly jazz-blues types but also old soul acts and up-and-coming rockers. Admission up to €20. Daily 11.30pm–5am, also occasional gigs from 9.30pm.

Quilombo c/d'Aribau 149 ☎934 395 406, ⓜDiagonal; map p.110. Unpretentious music bar – just a bare box of a room really – that's rolled with the years since 1971, featuring live guitarists, Latin American bands and a clientele that joins in enthusiastically, maracas in hand. Mon–Thurs & Sun 9pm–3am, Fri & Sat 7.30pm–3.30am.

GRÀCIA

BARS

La Baignoire c/de Verdi 6 ☎932 843 967; ⓜFontana; map p.125. A small corner of sophistication on an otherwise rowdy street – Ella Fitzgerald warbling away in the background, a dozen good wines by the glass and cheesy nibbles. Mon–Thurs & Sun 7pm–2.30am, Fri & Sat 7pm–3am.

Bobby Gin c/de Francisco Giner 47 ☎933 681 892, ⓦbobbygin.com; ⓜDiagonal; map p.125. The sign near the bar says "*El gintonic perfecto no existe*" (the perfect gin and tonic does not exist). Perhaps. But the sizeable G&Ts (from €8) here come very, very close. Mon–Wed & Sun 7pm–2am, Thurs–Sat 7pm–3am.

Café del Sol Pl. del Sol 16 ☎934 155 663; ⓜFontana; map p.125. The grandaddy of the Pl. del Sol scene sees action day and night. On summer evenings, when the square is packed, there's not an outdoor table to be had, but even in winter this is a popular drinking den – the pub-like interior has a backroom and gallery, often rammed to the rafters. Tues–Thurs 1pm–2.30am, Fri & Sat 1pm–3am.

A Canigó Pl. de la Revolució 10 ☎932 133 049, Ⓦbarcanigo.com; ⓂFontana; map p.125. Family-run neighbourhood bar now entering its third generation. It's not much to look at, but the drinks are cheap and it's a real Gràcia institution, packed out at weekends with a young, hip and largely local crowd. Mon–Thurs 10am–2am, Fri 10am–3am, Sat 8pm–3am.

La Cervesera Artesana c/de Sant Agustí 14 ☎932 379 594, Ⓦlacervesera.net; ⓂDiagonal; map p.125. A score of identikit Irish pubs in town serve Guinness and other imported beers, but for real ale, Catalan style – including an own-brew stout – the city's original microbrewery is well worth a visit. Mon–Thurs & Sun 6pm–2am, Fri & Sat 6pm–3am.

Elephanta c/del Torrent d'En Vidalet 37 ☎932 376 906, Ⓦelephanta.cat; ⓂJoanic; map p.125. This relaxed hideout with flea-market chairs and menus made from old album covers serves crisp mixed drinks (gin is the main attraction) in a chilled-out space that feels just like home. Mon–Wed 6pm–1am, Thurs 6pm–2am, Fri & Sat 6pm–3am, Sun 5–11pm.

★**Vinilo** c/Matilde 2 ☎ 669 177 945; ⓂDiagonal; map p.125. A 1912 gramophone greets you at the entrance of this dimly lit music bar, but the playlist – all on vinyl as the name suggests – is a little more contemporary. Expect to hear anything from Massive Attack to Edith Piaf as you rub shoulders with local musicians, touring indie stars and local hipsters. Daily 8pm–2.30am.

Virreina Pl. de la Virreina 1 ☎932 379 880, Ⓦvirreina bar.com; ⓂFontana; map p.125. Another real Gràcia favourite, on one of the neighbourhood's prettiest squares, with a very popular summer *terrassa*. It's one of those places where you drop by for a quick drink and find yourself staying for hours. Mon–Thurs & Sun 10am–1am, Fri & Sat 10am–2am.

CLUBS AND LIVE MUSIC

★**Centre Artesà Tradicionàrius (CAT)** Trav. de Sant Antoni 6–8 ☎932 184 485, Ⓦtradicionarius.cat; ⓂFontana; map p.125. The best place in town for folk, traditional and world music by Catalan, Spanish and

> ### TOP 5 GOOD-TIME DANCE CLUBS
> **Antilla BCN Latin Club** See opposite
> **La Macarena** See p.197
> **Moog** See p.198
> **Sala Razzmatazz** See p.200
> **La Terrrazza** See p.201

visiting performers, including some occasional big names. Admission is usually €5–15 and you can expect anything from Basque bagpipes to Brazilian singers. There are also music and instrument workshops, while *CAT* sponsors all sorts of outreach concerts and festivals, including an annual international folk and traditional dance festival (Jan–April). Concerts usually at 9.30 or 10pm.

Elèctric Bar Trav. de Gràcia 233 Ⓦelectricbarcelona .com; ⓂJoanic; map p.125. The bar of choice for Gràcia's counterculture crowd, who come for the wildly varied live programming, with something on every night, from poetry slams to electro-folk gigs. It's free if you just want to drink in the grungy bar – performances in the space out back start at 10pm (weekends at 11pm), with admission usually €3–5. Mon–Thurs & Sun 7pm–2am, Fri & Sat 7pm–3am.

★**Heliogàbal** c/Ramon y Cajal 80 Ⓦheliogabal.com; ⓂJoanic; map p.125. Not much more than a boiler room given a lick of paint, but filled with a cool, twenty-something crowd here for the live poetry and music – expect something different every night (Catalan versifying, jazz jam sessions and earnest singer-songwriters), starting at 10pm. Admission is usually €3–10, depending on the act, and drinks aren't expensive. Wed, Thurs & Sun 9pm–2am, Fri & Sat 9pm–3am.

Otto Zutz c/de Lincoln 15 ☎932 380 722, Ⓦottozutz .com; FGC Gràcia; map p.125. It first opened as a club in 1985 and has since lost some of its glam cachet, but this three-storey former textile factory still has a shed-load of pretensions. The sounds are basically hip-hop, r'n'b and house, and with the right clothes and face, you're in (you may or may not have to pay, depending on how impressive you are, the day of the week, the mood of the door staff). Admission €15. Tues–Thurs 11pm–3am, Fri & Sat midnight–6am.

16

LES CORTS, PEDRALBES AND SARRIÀ-SANT GERVASI

BARS

Gimlet c/de Santaló 46, Sant Gervasi ☎932 015 306, Ⓦjavierdelasmuelas.com; FGC Muntaner; map pp.130–131. This favoured cocktail joint is especially popular in summertime, when the street-side tables offer a great vantage point for watching the party unfold. There are also two or three other late-opening bars on the same stretch. Daily 7pm–3am.

CLUBS AND LIVE MUSIC

★**Bikini** Av. Diagonal 547, Les Corts ☎933 220 800, Ⓦbikinibcn.com; ⓂLes Corts/María Cristina; map pp.130–131. This traditional landmark of Barcelona nightlife (behind L'Illa shopping centre) offers a regular diet of great indie, rock, roots and world gigs, followed by club sounds from house to Brazilian, according to the night. Admission €15, though some big-name gigs cost up to €40. Wed, Thurs, Sat & Sun midnight–5am, Fri midnight–5.30am.

THE GIN AND TONIC CRAZE

In Barcelona, they don't let anything come between their gin and their tonic – not even the word "and". The *gintonic*, as it's known, has always been a favourite drink, but in recent years there's been a surge in bars specializing in the classic cocktail and its star ingredient, ginebra. **Bobby Gin** in Gràcia has some sixty varieties, **Pesca Salada** in El Raval stocks 54 kinds and **Xixbar**, which claims to be the first Barcelona bar specializing in gin, mixes it up with more than a hundred types. And the tonic component has not been forgotten, with bars pouring a dizzying array of premium varieties, from the regionally produced Tònica Catalana to those from Argentina, the UK and beyond. It's a refreshing trend worthy of glass-clinking *¡salut!*

TOP 5 GIN BARS

Bobby Gin See p.202
Dry Martini See p.202
Elephanta See p.203

Pesca Salada See p.198
Xixbar See p.201

Elephant Club Pg. dels Til.lers 1, Pedralbes ☎ 933 340 258, ⓦ elephantbcn.com; ⓜ Palau Reial; map pp.130–131. A gorgeous designer stage-set for gorgeous designer people. There's dancing, but mostly there's preening in a series of ornamental, Oriental-style gardens that spill out from a fancy uptown mansion. Admission €15. Thurs 11.30pm–4am, Fri & Sat 11.30pm–5am.

Sala BeCool Pl. Joan Llongueras 5, Sant Gervasi ☎ 933 620 413, ⓦ salabecool.com; ⓜ Hospital Clinic/FGC Muntaner; map pp.130–131. Thumping uptown club venue for local and national rock, indie and electro/techno bands and DJs. Gigs run Thursday to Saturday nights, followed by DJ sessions, with admission for €10 to €20, depending on who's appearing. They also sponsor free Friday-night acoustic nights at the next-door Irish bar, *Dublin*. Thurs–Sat club midnight or 1am until 4am, Thurs–Sun gigs at 10pm.

TIBIDABO

BARS

Mirablau Pl. del Dr Andreu, Av. Tibidabo ☎ 934 340 035, ⓦ mirablaubcn.com; FGC Av. del Tibidabo then Tramvia Blau, or taxi; map p.138. This chic bar by the tram and funicular terminus has unbelievable city views. By day it's a great place for drinks, while at night it's more of an upmarket tapas and music joint. Daily 11am–5am.

16

CONCERT HALL, PALAU DE LA MUSICA CATALANA

Arts and culture

As you would expect from a city of its size, Barcelona has a busy arts and culture calendar – there will always be something worth catching, whether it's a contemporary dance performance, cabaret show or night at the opera. Classical and contemporary music, in particular, gets an airing in some stunning auditoriums, and while local theatre is less accessible for non-Catalan or -Spanish speakers, many cinemas at least show films in their original language. Local performers have always steered away from the classics and gone for the innovative, so the city boasts a long tradition of street and performance art, right down to the human statues plying their trade on the Ramblas. Barcelona excels in the visual arts, too – from traditional exhibitions of paintings to contemporary photography or installation works – and dozens of arts centres and galleries put on varied shows throughout the year.

17

ESSENTIALS

Tickets and information A useful first stop for tickets and information is the Palau de la Virreina, Ramblas 99 (daily 10am–8.30pm; ☎933 161 000; ⓜLiceu). Ticketmaster (☎902 150 025, ⓦticketmaster.es), BCN Shop (☎932 853 832, ⓦbcnshop.barcelonaturisme.com) and Ticketea (☎902 044 226, ⓦticketea.com) are the main advance booking agencies for music, theatre, cinema and exhibition tickets.

What's on The city council's Institute of Culture website, ⓦbcn.cat/cultura, is invaluable – it covers every aspect of art and culture in the city, with links to daily updated arts stories and a comprehensive calendar of events. Otherwise, the best listings magazines are the weekly *Guía del Ocio* (ⓦguiadelociobcn.com) and *Time Out Barcelona* (ⓦtimeout.cat), online or from any newsstand.

CLASSICAL, CONTEMPORARY AND OPERA

Most of Barcelona's **classical** music concerts take place in the *modernista* Palau de la Música Catalana or at the purpose-built, contemporary L'Auditori, while **opera** is performed at its traditional home, the Gran Teatre del Liceu on the Ramblas. Many of the city's churches, including the cathedral and Santa María del Mar, also host concerts and recitals, while other interesting venues holding concerts include the historic Saló del Tinell in the Ajuntament, Palau Robert, FNAC Triangle at Pl. de Catalunya, CaixaForum, the Fundació Joan Miró and CCCB (these last two particularly for **contemporary** music). Notable **festivals** include the Festival de Barcelona Grec (July) and the Festa de la Música (June 21), while there are free concerts in Barcelona's parks each summer, the so-called Música als Parcs.

VENUES

★**Ateneu Barcelonès** c/de la Canuda 6, Barri Gòtic ☎933 426 121, ⓦateneubcn.org; ⓜCatalunya; map p.44. The 150-year-old Ateneu cultural association presents a variety of intellectually stimulating fare throughout the year, including conferences, film screenings and workshops, as well as concerts and recitals (from baroque to contemporary), some of which take place in its verdant garden. Many events are for members only but the building itself, especially the library, is well worth visiting.

L'Auditori c/de Lepant 150, Glòries ☎932 479 300, ⓦwww.auditori.org; ⓜMarina/Glòries; map pp.116–117. The city's main contemporary concert hall is home

to the Orquestra Simfònica de Barcelona i Nacional de Catalunya (OBC), whose weekend concert season runs Oct–June. L'Auditori also puts on other orchestral and chamber works, jazz and world gigs and music for children and families, while it's the main venue for the annual Early Music festival. Under-26s with ID are eligible for discounts of up to fifty percent on tickets. Box office Mon–Sat 3–9pm, Sun 1hr before performance.

Casa Elizalde c/de València 302, Dreta de l'Eixample ☎934 880 590, ⓦcasaelizalde.com; ⓜPasseig de Gràcia; map p.102. Small-scale classical concerts and recitals, plus more offbeat contemporary performances, are held at the cultural centre, usually with free entry.

THE SARDANA – DANCING WITH CATALANS

If you're intrigued by what looks like a mass dance flash mob outside the cathedral, La Seu, chances are you've stumbled upon a performance of the Catalan national dance – the **sardana**. Its origins are obscure, though similar folk dances in the Mediterranean date back hundreds if not thousands of years. It was established in its present form during the mid-nineteenth-century Renaixença (Renaissance), when Catalan arts and culture flourished, and was so identified with expressions of national identity that public dancing of *sardanes* was banned under the Franco regime. Sometimes mocked elsewhere in Spain, Catalans claim it to be truly democratic – a circle-dance open to all, danced in ordinary clothes (though some wear espadrilles) with no restriction in age or number. The dancers join hands, heads held high, arms raised, and though it looks deceptively simple and sedate it follows a precise pattern of steps, with shifts in pace and rhythm signalled by the accompanying *cobla* (band) of brass and wind instruments. This features typically Catalan instruments like the *flabiol* (a type of flute), and both tenor and soprano oboes, providing the characteristic high-pitched music. A strict etiquette applies to prevent the circle being broken in the wrong place, or a breakdown in the steps, and some of the more serious adherents may not welcome an intrusion into their circle by well-meaning first-timers. But usually visitors are encouraged to join the dance, especially at festival times, when the *sardana* breaks out spontaneously in the city's squares and parks.

There are regular *sardana* dances held outside La Seu, in Plaça de la Seu (ⓜJaume I), every Sunday at noon, plus every Saturday at 6pm from Easter until the end of November. The **Federació Sardanista de Catalunya** (ⓦfed.sardanista.cat) also publishes a calendar of dances and events on its website.

Gran Teatre del Liceu Ramblas 51–59 ☎934 859 900; box office c/de Sant Pau 1 ☎934 859 913, ⓦwww.liceubarcelona.cat; ⓜLiceu, map p.38. One of Europe's finest opera houses hosts a wide-ranging programme of opera and dance productions, plus other concerts and recitals. The season runs Sept–June. Make bookings well in advance by phone or online – sales for the next season go on general sale in mid-July. Box office Mon–Fri 1.30–8pm, Sat & Sun 30min before performance.

★**Palau de la Música Catalana** c/del Palau de la Música 4-6, off c/Sant Pere Més Alt, Sant Pere ☎932 957 200 or ☎902 442 882, ⓦpalaumusica.org; ⓜUrquinaona; map p.68. The extravagantly decorated Catalan concert hall is home to the Orfeó Català choral group and venue for concerts by the Orquestra Ciutat de Barcelona among others, though there's a broad remit here – over a season you can catch anything, from *sardanes* to pop concerts. Concert season Sept–June. Box office Mon–Fri 9am–9pm, Sat & Sun 9.30am–9pm.

17

DANCE

Barcelona is very much a contemporary dance city, with its own dedicated dance venue, Mercat de les Flors, as well as regular performances by regional, national and international artists and companies at theatre venues (see p.209) like the TNC, Teatre Lliure and Institut del Teatre – the latter, the city's theatre and dance school, has its own youth dance company, IT Dansa. Although its home is indisputably Andalucía, flamenco also has deep roots in and around Barcelona, courtesy of its *andaluz* immigrants – unless you're looking for a showy night out, the pricey, tourist-oriented *tablaos* (flamenco and dinner shows) are best passed up in favour of the smaller clubs and restaurants that put on performances. If you're here at the end of April, don't miss the wild flamenco shows and parties of the Feria de Abril de Catalunya, a ten-day **festival** held down at the Fòrum site, and there are also two other flamenco festivals each year, De Cajón in winter (Jan–March) and the old town's Festival de Flamenco in May.

DANCE VENUE

Mercat de les Flors c/de Lleida 59, Montjuïc ☎932 562 600, ⓦmercatflors.cat; ⓜPoble Sec; map p.87. The city's old flower market serves as the "national centre for movement arts", with dance the central focus of its varied programme – from Asian performance art to European contemporary dance.

FLAMENCO CLUBS

El Tablao de Carmen Poble Espanyol, Montjuïc ☎933 256 895, ⓦtablaodecarmen.com; ⓜEspanya; map p.87. The long-standing *tablao* in the Poble Espanyol at least looks the real deal, sited in a replica Andalucian street and

featuring a variety of flamenco styles from both seasoned performers and new talent. From €41 for the show and a drink, rising to €85 for the show plus "VIP Menu" dinner. Advance reservations essential. Tues–Sun, shows at 7pm & 9.30pm; free entrance to Poble Espanyol from 4pm.

★**Tarantos** Pl. Reial 17, Barri Gòtic ☎933 191 789, ⓦmasimas.com; ⓜLiceu; map p.44. Some purists are sniffy about the experience, but for a cheap flamenco taster you can't beat *Tarantos* – a couple of rows of seats and a small bar in front of a stage where young singers, dancers and guitarists perform nightly. It's the sister club to jazz/dance club *Jamboree*, at the same address. Tickets from €8. Performances at 8.30pm, 9.30pm & 10.30pm.

FILM

At most of the larger cinemas and multiplexes films are usually shown dubbed into Spanish or Catalan. However, several cinemas do show mostly **original-language** (*versión original* or V.O.) foreign films; the best are listed below. Tickets cost around €8, and most cinemas have one night (usually Mon or Wed) when entry is **discounted**, usually to around €6. Many cinemas also feature **late-night** screenings (*matinades o sessions golfo*) on Friday and Saturday nights, which begin at 12.30 or 1am. The city hosts several small film **festivals** throughout the year, including an international festival of independent short films, plus festivals devoted specifically to children, gastronomy, sports, animation, women, and gay and lesbian film. The Generalitat's FilmoTeca is often the venue for festival screenings. The sci-fi, horror and fantasy fest that is the Festival Internacional de Cinema de Fantàstic (ⓦsitgesfilmfestival.com) is held down the coast in nearby Sitges in October.

CINEMAS

★**Cinema Maldà** c/del Pi 5, Barri Gòtic ☎933 019 350, ⓦcinemamalda.com, ⓜLiceu; map p.44. Hidden away in a little shopping centre just up from Pl. del Pi, the Maldà is a great place for independent movies and festival winners, all in V.O. Discount days: Mon & Thurs €5, Wed €4.

> ### TOP 5 CULTURE ON A BUDGET
> **L'Antic Teatre** See p.209
> **Casa Elizalde** See opposite
> **FilmoTeca** See p.208
> **Sala Montjuïc** See p.208
> **Tarantos** See above

17

FilmoTeca Pl. Salvador Seguí 1–9, El Raval ☎ 935 671 070, ⓦ filmoteca.cat; ⓜ Liceu; map p.110. Run by the Catalan government, the FilmoTeca (now in its new location in El Raval) shows three to five different films (often foreign language, and usually in V.O.) every day – the programme changes every couple of weeks, and themed seasons, classic films, retrospectives and obscure world cinema releases are its stock-in-trade. Tickets are just €4 per film, or there's a €50 pass allowing entry to twenty films.

Méliès Cinemes c/de Villaroel 102, Esquerra de l'Eixample ☎ 934 510 051, ⓦ cinesmelies.net; ⓜ Urgell; map p.110. A repertory cinema specializing in V.O. showings (classics, indie and art-house), with three to five different films daily in its two salas. Discount night is Mon.

★**Phenomena Experience** c/ Sant Antoni María Claret ☎ 932 527 743, ⓦ phenomena-experience.com; ⓜ Sant Pau/Dos de Maig; map pp.116–117. This independent cinema run by and for fans puts the magic back into watching movies. Fall in love again with the great movies of the 1970s, '80s and '90s (in V.O.) and occasional recent favourites, or catch a "beer and pizza night" and watch a genre classic in the company of avid movie geeks, with state-of-the art sound and one of the biggest screens in the country. Tickets €6 (€3 for members).

Verdi/Verdi Park Verdi c/de Verdi 32, Gràcia; Verdi Park, c/de Torrijos 49, Gràcia ☎ 932 387 990, ⓦ cines-verdi.com;

ⓜ Fontana; map p.125. Gràcia's popular sister cinemas are in adjacent streets, showing independent, art-house and V.O. movies from around the world on nine screens. Daily discount for first screening; reduced price Mon–Thurs last screening.

Yelmo-Icaria c/de Salvador Espriu 61, Centre de la Vila, Port Olímpic ☎ 932 217 585, ⓦ www.yelmocines.es; ⓜ Ciutadella-Vila Olímpica; map p.83. Fifteen screens showing mainstream Hollywood V.O. movies at a shopping centre multiplex, a few minutes' walk from the Port Olímpic. Late-night screenings Fri & Sat; discount night Wed.

OPEN-AIR CINEMA

Sala Montjuïc Castell de Montjuïc ☎ 933 023 553, ⓦ salamontjuic.org; cable car (Telefèric de Montjuïc) or cinema bus (normal tickets and passes valid) from Pl. d'Espanya (ⓜ Espanya), departures from 8.30pm, returns when film finishes; map p.87. Every July there's a giant-screen open-air cinema established on the grass under the walls at Montjuïc castle (Mon, Wed & Fri night; tickets €6, deckchair rental €3) – you're encouraged to bring a picnic. Screenings are in the original language, with Spanish subtitles, and range from current art-house hits to film-club stalwarts like *Some Like it Hot*. The films usually start at 10pm, with live music first from 8.45pm, but with space limited to 2000 it's best to get there at opening time (8.30pm) or buy in advance through the cinema's website.

THEATRE AND CABARET

The **Teatre Nacional de Catalunya** (Catalan National Theatre) was specifically conceived as a venue to promote Catalan productions, and features a repertory programme of translated classics (such as Shakespeare in Catalan), original works and productions by guest companies from Europe. The other big local theatrical project is the **Ciutat del Teatre** (Theatre City) on Montjuïc, which incorporates the fringe-style Mercat de les Flors, the progressive Teatre Lliure and the Institut del Teatre theatre and dance school. The centre for commercial theatre is on and off the Ramblas and along Av. Paral.lel and the nearby streets. There are a few options for **children's theatre** (see p.236). Some theatres draw on the city's strong **cabaret** tradition – particularly burlesque, music-hall entertainment – which is far more accessible to non-Catalan or -Spanish speakers than straight theatre. **Tickets** are available from theatre box offices, or the usual agency outlets, while for

ON LOCATION

You can fall in love with Barcelona all over again with a stack of DVDs and a giant bucket of popcorn. Major movie event of recent years for the city was Woody Allen's extended homage to its photogenic landmarks in **Vicky Cristina Barcelona** (2008), a frothy love triangle – partly financed by the city administration, who definitely got their money's worth – that bounced from the Barri Gòtic to the Sagrada Família. However, film buffs point back to 1975 and Michelangelo Antonioni's **The Passenger** as the first major film to showcase the city's attractions, as Jack Nicholson negotiates Gaudí rooftops and cable cars in a cryptic case of stolen identity. Madrid's inimitable Pedro Almodóvar gave his own seedy, oddball take on Barcelona in **All About My Mother** (1999) – an Oscar winner for Best Foreign Language Film – while in Tom Tykwer's **Perfume** (2006), the city's atmospheric old town stood in for eighteenth-century Paris in the adaptation of Patrick Süskind's cult novel. However, the two most arresting Barcelona movies to date show not a single colourful landmark or famous sight, being set entirely within the confines of a Rambla de Catalunya mansion block. All you glean of the city from Jaume Balagueró and Paco Plaza's zombie-virus-shockers **Rec** (2007) and **Rec 2** (2009) is never to join the Barcelona fire brigade, and never to take a hand-held camera (*rec* = record) into a locked-down apartment building...

CATALAN THEATRE COMPANIES

17

Els Comediants (Wcomediants.com) a travelling collective of actors, musicians and artists, established in 1971, who use any open space as a stage to celebrate "the festive spirit of human existence".

La Cubana (Wlacubana.es) is a highly original company that started life as a street theatre group, though it has since moved into television and theatre proper. It still hits the streets occasionally, taking on the role of market traders in the Boqueria or cleaning cars in the street in full evening dress.

Dagoll Dagom (Wdagolldagom.com) specializes in hugely theatrical, over-the-top musicals.

La Fura del Baus ("Vermin of the Sewer"; Wlafura.com) are performance artists who aim to shock and lend a new meaning to audience participation. They've subsequently taken on opera, cabaret, film and installations, lending each a wild, challenging perspective.

last-minute tickets visit the counter at the Palau de la Virreina (Ramblas 99; Mon–Sat 10am–8.30pm), which offers same-day half-price tickets from three hours before the start of the show. The summer **Festival de Barcelona Grec** always has a strong theatre and dance programme; many performances are at the open-air Teatre Grec on Montjuïc (see p.92).

THEATRES

Institut del Teatre Pl. de Margarida Xirgu, Montjuïc ☎ 932 273 900, Wwww.institutdelteatre.org; MPoble Sec; map p.87. The school for dramatic arts and dance has a regular programme of events scheduled at its two theatres, where you can catch performances by the current crop of students.

Teatre Lliure Pl. de Margarida Xirgu 1, Montjuïc ☎ 932 892 770, Wwww.teatrelliure.com; MPoble Sec; map p.87. The "Free Theatre" performs the work of contemporary Catalan and Spanish playwrights, as well as reworkings of the classics, from Shakespeare to Samuel Beckett (some productions have English surtitles). It also hosts visiting dance companies, concerts and recitals. The original theatre, a smaller auditorium in Gràcia, also has a full programme.

Teatre Nacional de Catalunya (TNC) Pl. de les Arts 1, Glòries ☎ 933 065 700, Wtnc.cat; MGlòries; map pp.116–117. Intended to foster Catalan works, the national theatre – built as a modern emulation of an ancient Greek temple – features major productions by Catalan, Spanish and European companies, as well as smaller-scale plays, experimental works and dance productions.

Teatre Poliorama Ramblas 115, El Raval ☎ 933 177 599, Wteatrepoliorama.com; MCatalunya; map p.38. Specializes in modern drama (Catalan and translation) and musicals, often utilizing the talents of offbeat companies like Dagoll Dagom (see box above).

Teatre Romea c/de l'Hospital 51, El Raval ☎ 933 015 504, Wteatreromea.com; MLiceu; map pp.58–59. Has an emphasis on contemporary Catalan and Spanish playwrights and pan-European productions, and gives space to new theatre groups and radical directors.

CABARET AND OTHER VENUES

L'Antic Teatre c/de Verdaguer i Callís 12, Sant Pere ☎ 933 152 354, Wlanticteatre.com; MUrquinaona; map p.68. A small, independent theatre with a wildly original programme of events, many free, from video shows and art exhibitions to offbeat cabaret performances, modern dance and left-field music. In the end though, the best bit may just be the bar (daily 4pm–midnight) and the summer garden *terrassa*.

★**Café Teatre Llantiol** c/de la Riereta 7, El Raval ☎ 933 299 009, Wllantiol.com; MSant Antoni; map pp.58–59. Idiosyncratic cabaret café-theatre whose varied shows feature a mix of mime, song, clowning, magic and dance, and sometimes there's English-language stand-up comedy by local and visiting acts. Shows (€10–15) normally begin at 9pm & 11.30pm (Sat & Sun 6.30pm & 9pm), with an additional late-night Saturday special.

El Molino c/Vila i Vilà 99, Av. Paral.lel, Poble Sec ☎ 932 055 111, Welmolinobcn.com; MParal.lel; map p.94. One of Barcelona's most famous old cabaret theatres reopened in 2010 after many years in mothballs, and the self-styled "Little Moulin Rouge" has a classy new look for its traditional burlesque and music stage shows. There are big-production lunch and dinner shows – signature show is "Made in Paral.lel", an all-singing, all-dancing tribute to the city of Barcelona – with performances daily from Wednesday to Sunday (lunch show from €45, evening show and drink from €40, show plus dinner from €80), plus Monday tango and Tuesday flamenco nights (varied prices). Closed Aug.

TOP 5 BIG NIGHTS OUT

L'Auditori See p.206
Gran Teatre del Liceu See p.207
El Molino See above
Palau de la Música Catalana See p.207
Teatre Nacional de Catalunya See above

17

VISUAL ARTS

Barcelona has dozens of **private art galleries** and exhibition halls in addition to the temporary displays on show in its art centres, museums and galleries. Major venues with regularly changing art exhibitions include CaixaForum, CCCB, MACBA and Fundació Antoni Tàpies for contemporary art; Espai 13 at Fundacío Joan Miró for young experimental artists; MNAC and La Pedrera for blockbuster international art shows; Disseny Hub for industrial and graphic art, design, craft and architecture; and Arts Santa Mònica for contemporary Catalan art and photography. **Commercial galleries** cluster together in the Barri Gòtic on c/de la Palla and c/de Petritxol near the church of Santa María del Pi; in La Ribera on c/de Montcada and Pg. del Born; in El Raval on c/dels Àngels and c/del Doctor Dou near the MACBA; and in the Eixample on Pg. de Gràcia, c/del Consell de Cent and Rambla Catalunya. Note that most commercial galleries are closed on Sundays, Mondays and in August. The weekly *Guía del Ocio* and the Associació de Galeries d'Art Contemporani (@ www.artbarcelona .es) have gallery listings and exhibition news. In spring **photography** fans should look out for the Primavera Fotogràfica, when photography exhibitions are held at various venues around the city. A map showing some of Barcelona's best-known art galleries is available at tourist information centres.

ART AND CULTURAL CENTRES

La Capella c/de l'Hospital 56, El Raval ☎ 934 427 171, @ lacapella.bcn.cat; Ⓜ Liceu; map pp.58–59. This space in the medieval Hospital de la Santa Creu promotes contemporary art of all kinds, though is often a platform for work by young Barcelona artists.

Fundació Foto Colectania c/de Julian Romea 6, Gràcia ☎ 932 171 626, @ colectania.es; Ⓜ Fontana; map p.125. A private foundation that puts on exhibitions culled from the work of more than sixty Spanish and Portuguese photographers, with works from the 1950s onwards.

Miscelänea c/Guardia 10, El Raval ☎ 933 179 398, @ miscelanea.info; Ⓜ Drassanes; map pp.58–59. This nonprofit cultural association promotes the work of up-and-coming artists, mounting ten to fifteen shows a year that have included collections of collages, Polaroid photographs and illustrated skateboard decks. Closed Aug.

Palau Robert Pg. de Gràcia 107, Dreta de l'Eixample ☎ 932 388 091, @ gencat.cat/palaurobert; Ⓜ Diagonal; map p.102. The Catalan government's information office and gallery space sponsors a wide range of shows, all with a Catalan connection.

Palau de la Virreina Ramblas 99, Barri Gòtic ☎ 933 161 000, @ lavirreina.bcn.cat; Ⓜ Liceu; map p.38. Changing shows at the city council's cultural headquarters concentrate on contemporary culture, social studies and photography.

Sala d'Art Jove de la Generalitat c/Calàbria 147, Esquerra de l'Eixample ☎ 934 838 361; Ⓜ Rocafort; map p.110. The Generalitat's youth art space is for artists under 30 – expect anything from formal portraiture to one-off installations. Closed Aug.

COMMERCIAL GALLERIES

Galeria Joan Prats Rambla de Catalunya 54, Dreta de l'Eixample ☎ 932 160 290, @ www.galeriajoanprats .com; Ⓜ Passeig de Gràcia; map p.102. One of the city's best-regarded galleries for the works of contemporary Catalan artists and photographers. Closed Aug.

H2O c/de Verdi 152, Gràcia ☎ 934 151 801, @ h2o.es; Ⓜ Fontana/Lesseps; map p.127. Independent gallery working in the fields of architecture, design, photography and contemporary art.

Sala Parés c/de Petritxol 5–8, Barri Gòtic ☎ 933 187 020, @ salapares.com; Ⓜ Liceu; map p.44. Possibly the most famous gallery in the city, established in the mid-nineteenth century, Sala Parés hosted Picasso's first show. It still deals exclusively in nineteenth- and twentieth-century Catalan art, putting on around twenty exhibitions a year, including its annual "Famous Paintings" exhibition of works by some of the best-known Spanish and Catalan names.

ARENA

LGBT Barcelona

There's a vibrant gay and lesbian scene in Barcelona (or "Gaycelona", as some would have it), backed up by an established organizational infrastructure and a generally supportive city council. Information about the scene – known in Spanish as el ambiente, "the atmosphere" – is pretty easy to come by, while locals and tourists alike are well aware of the lure of Sitges, mainland Spain's biggest gay resort, just forty minutes south by train. Bars, clubs, restaurants and hotels aimed specifically at a gay and lesbian clientele are scattered across Barcelona, though there's a particular concentration in the so-called Gaixample, the "Gay Eixample", an area of a few square blocks just northwest of the university in the Esquerra de l'Eixample. But you'll also be well received at plenty of other nominally straight dance bars and clubs in a city that's generally welcoming to its gay and lesbian visitors.

18

ESSENTIALS

Accommodation Finding sympathetic accommodation in the city isn't a problem, as there's any number of chic, boutique properties with a gay-friendly vibe. Barcelona also has one out-and-out gay hotel, the very cool "hetero-friendly" *Hotel Axel* (see p.173), which is right in the middle of the Gaixample district. Or contact Outlet4Spain (☎ 938 102 711, ⓦ outlet4spain.com), an accommodation agency that specializes in gay-friendly hotels, villas, apartments and flat-shares in Barcelona and Sitges.

Information For up-to-date information and other advice on the gay scene, you can call any of the organizations listed below, or try the lesbian and gay city telephone hotline on ☎ 900 601 601 (toll free; daily 6–10pm only).

What's on Aside from the weekly bar and club listings in *Guía del Ocio* (ⓦ enbarcelona.com, in Spanish) and *Time Out Barcelona* (ⓦ timeout.cat, in English), there's also a good free magazine called *Revista GB* (ⓦ gaybarcelona.net), which carries an up-to-date review of the scene in Barcelona and Catalunya. The single best English-language website is the excellent 60by80 (ⓦ 60by80.com), which has its finger on the pulse of all things hot, from shopping to partying. Also well worth a look is Patroc (ⓦ patroc.com), a guide for gay travellers to 25 European destinations including Barcelona and Sitges.

USEFUL CONTACTS

Antinous c/de Josep Anselm Clavé 6, Barri Gòtic ☎ 933 019 070, ⓦ antinouslibros.com; ⓜ Drassanes. Gay and lesbian bookshop with useful contacts and information board, and a café at the back. Mon–Fri 10am–2pm & 5–8.30pm, Sat noon–2pm & 5–8.30pm.

Ca la Dona c/de Ripoll, Barri Gòtic ☎ 934 127 161, ⓦ caladona.org; ⓜ Urquinaona. A women's centre with library and bar, used for meetings by various feminist and lesbian organizations; information available to callers.

Casal Lambda c/de Verdaguer i Callís 10, Sant Pere ☎ 933 195 550, ⓦ lambda.cat; ⓜ Urquinaona. A gay and lesbian centre with a wide range of social, cultural and educational events.

Cómplices c/de Cervantes 4, Barri Gòtic ☎ 934 127 283, ⓦ libreriacomplices.com; ⓜ Liceu. Exclusively gay and lesbian bookshop; also magazines and DVDs. Mon–Fri 10.30am–8pm, Sat noon–8pm.

Front d'Alliberament Gai de Catalunya (FAGC) c/de Verdi 88, Gràcia ☎ 932 172 669, ⓦ fagc.org; ⓜ Fontana. Association for gay men, with a library, meetings and events.

CAFÉS AND BARS

Aire c/de Valencia 236, Esquerra de l'Eixample ☎ 934 515 812, ⓦ grupoarena.com; ⓜ Passeig de Gràcia; map p.110. The hottest, most stylish lesbian bar in town is a relaxed place for a drink and a dance to pop, house and retro sounds. Gay men are welcome too. Thurs 11pm–2.30am, Fri & Sat 11pm–3am.

Átame c/del Consell de Cent 257, Esquerra de l'Eixample ☎ 934 549 273; ⓜ Universitat; map p.110. Contemporary music bar with a change of pace, from early evening drinks and gentility to late-night hot sounds. Daily 6pm–3am.

La Casa de la Pradera c/de les Carretes 57, El Raval ☎ 934 416 642, ⓦ facebook.com/lacasadelapradera raval; ⓜ Sant Antoni; map pp.58–59. No gimmicks here (well, except that every drink comes with a tapa). Just a relaxed and friendly bar that's a great starting – or ending – point to a night out. Tues–Thurs noon–2am, Fri & Sat noon–3am, Sun noon–midnight.

Dietrich c/del Consell de Cent 255, Esquerra de l'Eixample ☎ 934 517 707; ⓜ Universitat; map p.110. Cornerstone of the Gaixample scene is this well-known music bar and "teatro-café" – *tranquilo* during the week, but ever more hedonistic as the weekend wears on, with drag shows, acrobats and dancers punctuating the DJ sets. Thurs 10pm–2.30am, Fri & Sat until 3am.

People Lounge c/de Villarroel 71, Esquerra de l'Eixample ☎ 935 327 743, ⓦ peoplebcn.com; ⓜ Urgell; map p.110. Stylish café-bar where you shouldn't feel out

---

PARTY TIME

The biggest event of the year – in the country's biggest gay-friendly resort – is **Carnival** in Sitges (see p.144), while the main city bash is Barcelona's annual LGBT **Pride** festival (ⓦ pridebarcelona.org), which has events running over ten days each June, from street parades and stiletto races to Tibidabo fun-fair parties. Barcelona is also often the venue of choice for other international gatherings – in the past, the city has hosted the **Eurogames** (the European Gay and Lesbian Sports Championships), while the gay and lesbian **Circuit** festival (ⓦ circuitfestival.net) is a Barcelona stalwart. For movie buffs there's the annual **Barcelona International Gay and Lesbian Film Festival** (ⓦ cinemalambda.com), usually in July, while the appearance of the sun also sees the city's **Mar Bella** beach come into its own as Barcelona's own gay summer beach zone.

of place if you're over 40. Mon–Thurs 8pm–3am, Fri & Sat 8pm–3.30am, Sun 7pm–3am.

Punto BCN c/de Muntaner 63–65, Esquerra de l'Eixample ☎ 934 536 123, ⓦ grupoarena.com; Ⓜ Universitat; map p.110. A Gaixample classic that attracts a lively crowd for drinks, chat and music. Wednesday happy hour is a blast, while Friday night is party night. Daily 6pm–2.30am.

CLUBS

Arena Madre: c/de Balmes 32, Esquerra de l'Eixample; Classic: c/de la Diputació 233; VIP: Grand Via de les Corts Catalanes 593; Dandy: Grand Via de les Corts Catalanes 593; ☎ 934 878 342, ⓦ grupoarena.com; Ⓜ Passeig de Gràcia; map p.110. The *Madre* "mother" club sits at the helm of the Arena empire, all within a city block (pay for one, get in to all) – frenetic house at *Arena Madre*, high disco antics at *Arena Classic*, more of the same plus dance, r'n'b, pop and rock at the more mixed *Arena VIP* and vintage chart hits at *Arena Dandy*. Madre: daily 12.30–5.30am; Classic: Fri & Sat 12.30–5.30am; Dandy and VIP: Fri & Sat 12.30–6am.

Metro c/de Sepúlveda 158, Esquerra de l'Eixample ☎ 933 235 227, ⓦ metrodiscobcn.com; Ⓜ Universitat;

TOP 5 LGBT-FRIENDLY BARS
Delty Ford's See p.197
La Casa de la Pradera See opposite
La Concha See p.198
Zelig See p.198
Velódromo See p.202

18

map p.110. A gay institution in Barcelona, with cabaret nights and other events midweek, and extremely crowded club nights at weekends, playing current dance, techno and retro disco. Mon–Thurs & Sun 12.15–5am, Fri & Sat 12.15–6.30am.

Pervert Club Ronda de Sant Pere 19–21, Dreta de l'Eixample ⓦ facebook.com/Matineegayclub; Ⓜ Urquinaona; map p.102. The Matinée group – organizers of the Circuit Festival – are behind the Pervert dance club on Saturday nights at *Sala Bloc*. It isn't as kinky as the name suggests – think muscle boys, not whips and chains – but it's always busy and buzzing. Sat midnight–6am.

FESTA MAJOR DE GRÀCIA

Festivals and events

Almost any month you choose to visit Barcelona you'll coincide with a saint's day, festival or holiday, and it's hard to beat the experience of arriving to discover the streets decked out with flags and streamers, bands playing and the entire population out celebrating. Traditionally, each neighbourhood celebrates with its own festa, though the major ones – like Sants' and Gràcia's Festa Majors and the Mercè – have become city institutions, complete with music, dancing, traditional parades and firework displays. The religious calendar has its annual highlights too, with Carnival, Easter and Christmas popular times for parades, events and festivities across the city. Meanwhile, biggest and best of the annual arts and music events are the summer Festival de Barcelona Grec, the ever-expanding Sónar extravaganza of electronic music and multimedia art, and the rock and indie fest that is Primavera Sound.

There's a **month-by-month calendar** below of the best annual festivals, holidays, trade fairs and events, though it's not an exhaustive list. For more information about what's going on at any given time, call into the cultural information office at the **Palau de la Virreina**, Ramblas 99, or check out the Ajuntament's useful **website** (Ⓦbcn.cat/cultura).

Incidentally, not all **public holidays** coincide with a festival, but many do (see p.33). In addition, saints' day festivals – indeed all Catalan celebrations – can vary in date, often being observed over the weekend closest to the dates given.

JANUARY

Cap d'Any New Year's Eve. Street and club parties, and mass gatherings in Pl. de Catalunya and other main squares. You're supposed to eat twelve grapes in the last twelve seconds of the year for twelve months of good luck. The next day, Jan 1, is a public holiday.

Cavalcada dels Reis Afternoon of Jan 5. This is when the Three Kings (who distribute Christmas gifts to Spanish children) arrive by sea at the port and ride into town, throwing sweets as they go. The parade begins at about 5pm on Jan 5; the next day is a public holiday.

Festa dels Tres Tombs Jan 17. The first big festival of the year is the costumed horseback parade through the Sant Antoni neighbourhood, with local saint's day festivities to follow. *Tomb* is the Catalan word for a circuit, or tour, so the riders make three processional turns of the neighbourhood.

Barnasants Dates vary, Jan–April Ⓦbarnasants.com. A singer-songwriter festival (Catalan/Spanish, plus Brazilian and Latin American artists), with more than a hundred gigs held over three months in city clubs and concert venues.

De Cajón! Jan–March Ⓦtheproject.cat. Big-name flamenco stars perform a series of one-off concerts in major city concert halls.

FEBRUARY

Festes de Santa Eulàlia Feb 12 Ⓦbcn.cat/santa eulalia. The depths of winter are interrupted by festivities in honour of Eulàlia, the young Barcelona girl who suffered a beastly martyrdom by the Romans. She's a revered patron of the city, and her saint's day falls on February 12, around which are held a week's worth of celebrations with a focus on children and families – parades of giants, *sardanes*, dances, concerts, *castellers* (see box below) and fireworks. Lots of historic buildings and museums are also open for free on the day.

Carnaval/Carnestoltes Week before Lent, sometimes in March. Costumed parades – where you're encouraged to don a mask and join in – dances, concerts, open-air barbecues and other traditional carnival events take place in every city neighbourhood. However, it's Sitges, on the coast, which has the most outrageous celebrations, though it's a close-run thing with nearby Vilafranca del Penedès.

MARCH/APRIL

Festes de Sant Medir de Gràcia First week in March Ⓦsantmedir.org. A horse-and-carriage parade around Gràcia, which then heads to the Sant Medir hermitage in the Collserola hills. Later, the procession returns to Gràcia, where thousands of sweets are thrown to children along the route, and there's plenty of traditional dancing and feasting.

Setmana Santa Easter, Holy Week. Religious celebrations and services at churches throughout the city. Special services are on Thursday and Friday in Holy Week at

---

CASTLES IN THE SKY

Guaranteed to draw crowds at every festival are the teams of **castellers** – castle-makers – who pile person upon person, feet on shoulders, to see who can construct the highest, most aesthetically pleasing tower. It's an art that goes back over two hundred years, combining individual strength with mutual cooperation – perhaps this is why it was discouraged as an activity under Franco. Nowadays, it's very popular once again, with societies known as *colles* in most Catalan towns who come together to perform at annual festivals and events. There's a real skill to assembling the *castell*, with operations directed by the *cap de colla* (society head) – the strongest members form the crowd at the base, known as the *pinya*, with the whole edifice topped by an agile child, the *anxaneta*, who lifts their palm above their head to "crown" the castle. Ten human storeys is the record. For more, see Ⓦcastellersdebarcelona.cat.

7–8pm, Saturday at 10pm; there's a procession from the church of Sant Agustí on c/de l'Hospital (El Raval) to La Seu, starting at around 4pm on Good Friday; and Palm Sunday sees the blessing of the palms at La Seu. Public holidays on Good Friday and Easter Monday.

Dia de Sant Jordi St George's Day, April 23. St George's Day, dedicated to Catalunya's dragon-slaying patron saint, is a day of national identity – the Catalan flag appears everywhere and red roses (the colour of the dragon's blood) are the bloom of choice, with the two coming together at the Palau de la Generalitat, the home of the Catalan government. The saint's day has been entwined over the years with two other occasions, so that it's also a kind of local Valentine's Day (traditionally, men give their sweethearts a rose…) and International Book Day (…and receive a book in return). You'll be hard pushed to escape stumping up for either as you run the gauntlet of stalls down the Ramblas.

Feria de Abril de Catalunya Last week in April ⓦ fecac.com. The region's biggest Andalucian festival, with ten days of food, drink and flamenco. All the action goes down at the big marquees erected at the Parc del Fòrum plaza (Diagonal Mar).

Festival de Guitarra April & May ⓦ theproject.cat. A spring-season perennial, the annual guitar festival showcases all sorts of musical styles – jazz and Latin, blues and fusion – with some big names playing every year. Gigs are at concert halls across the city.

Saló Internacional del Còmic Dates vary, April or May ⓦ ficomic.com. The International Comic Fair takes place over three days, with stalls, drawing workshops and children's activities at one of the city's exhibition halls.

MAY

Dia del Treball May 1. May Day/Labour Day is a public holiday, with union parades along main city thoroughfares.

Dia de San Ponç May 11. A traditional saint's day, celebrated by a market running along c/de l'Hospital in the Raval, with fresh herbs, flowers, aromatic oils, honey and sweets.

Barcelona Poesia Second or third week ⓦ bcn.cat /barcelonapoesia. Week-long poetry festival with readings and recitals in venues across the city. It incorporates the Jocs Floral (Floral Games), while Spanish and foreign poets converge for the International Poetry Festival at the Palau de la Música Catalana.

Dia Internacional dels Museus May 18. On International Museum Day, there's free entrance to all city-run museums – local press have details of participating museums, opening hours and special events.

Corpus Christi Late May/early June. See box, p.48.

Primavera Sound Usually last week ⓦ primavera sound.com. The city's hottest music festival heralds a massive three-day bash down at the Parc del Fòrum (Diagonal Mar), attracting superstar names in the rock, indie and electronica world. It's extended into the city and Poble Espanyol too, with club gigs and free street gigs now part of the scene.

Festival de Flamenco de Ciutat Vella Usually last week ⓦ flamencociutatvella.com, ⓦ tallerdemusics .com. Annual old-town flamenco bash, organized by the Taller de Músics (music workshop) and Mercat de les Flors. Five days of guitar recitals, singing and dancing, plus DJ sessions and chill-out zone, and lectures and conferences on all matters flamenco.

JUNE

Sónar Usually second or third week ⓦ sonar.es. The International Festival of Advanced Music and Multimedia Art is Europe's biggest and most cutting-edge electronic music, multimedia and urban art festival, attracting up to 100,000 visitors for three days of brilliant noise and spectacle. Sónar by day centres on events at Fira Montjuïc; by night the action shifts to L'Hospitalet, with all-night buses running from the city to the Sónar bars and clubs. Separate day, night and general tickets available – buy well in advance.

Festa de la Música June 21. Every year on this day scores of free concerts are held in squares, parks, civic centres and museums in every neighbourhood across the city – from buskers to orchestras, folk to techno. There are concerts in the two or three preceding days too, so you're bound to catch something you like.

Revetlla/Dia de Sant Joan June 23–24. The "eve" and "day" of St John herald probably the wildest celebrations in the city, with a "night of fire" of bonfires and fireworks across Barcelona. It marks a hedonistic welcome to summer, with parties in full swing in every neighbourhood and pyrotechnics on Montjuïc and Tibidabo. *Coca de Sant Joan*, a sweet flatbread, and cava are the traditional accompaniments to the merriment. The traditional place to end the night is on the beach, watching the sun come up – thankful that the dawning day (June 24) is a public holiday.

Música als Parcs June–Aug ⓦ barcelonacultura.bcn .cat. More than two-dozen parks become venues for evenings of free classical and jazz concerts and performances by the Municipal Orchestra.

JULY

Festival de Barcelona Grec July 1–31 ⓦ barcelona festival.com. Since the 1970s, the summer's foremost arts and music festival has centred its performances on Montjuïc's open-air Greek theatre (see p.92) – a dramatic location for cutting-edge Shakespearean productions or events by Catalan avant-garde performance artists, while music ranges from the likes of Philip Glass to African rap. There are also concerts, plays and dance productions at the CCCB and city theatres – in total, nearly eighty different events held over a five-week period.

AUGUST

Festa Major de Gràcia Mid-Aug ⓦ festamajordegracia .cat. What was once a local village festival is now an annual city highlight, with banging music, boisterous dancing, wackily decorated floats and streets transformed into magical scenes, plus the usual noisy fireworks, parades of giants and devils and human castle-building in main squares. The festivities last a week – don't miss them if you're in town.

Festa Major de Sants Last week of Aug. Another week's worth of traditional festivities in an untouristed neighbourhood, in the streets behind Barcelona Sants station.

San Miguel Mas i Mas Festival ⓦ masimas.com. The quietest summer month gets a shot in the arm with a music festival by promoters Mas i Mas that crosses genres, hip-hop to classical jazz, at a variety of venues across the city.

19

SEPTEMBER

Diada Nacional Sept 11. Catalan national day, commemorating the eighteenth-century defeat at the hands of the Bourbons. It's a public holiday in Barcelona; the last three years have seen overwhelmingly peaceful gatherings of nearly two million people on the city streets, standing in formation and demanding the right to vote on independence from Spain.

Festes de la Mercè Sept 24 ⓦ bcn.cat/merce. The biggest annual festival, held around Sept 24 (a public holiday), is dedicated to Our Lady of Mercy, co-patroness of the city, whose image is paraded from the church of la Mercè near the port. It's an excuse for a week of merrymaking, including costumed giants, breathtaking firework displays and competing teams of *castellers* – not to mention outdoor concerts, bicycle races, children's events and even free admission to city museums and galleries on the saint's day. During the week, the concurrent alternative music festival, known as BAM (ⓦ bcn.cat/bam), puts on free rock, world and fusion gigs at emblematic old-town locations and at Parc del Fòrum.

Festa Major de Sant Miquel Last week. Traditional festivities on the waterfront as Barceloneta celebrates its saint's day with fireworks, parades, *castellers*, music and dancing.

OCTOBER/NOVEMBER

48H Open House BCN Oct (varies) ⓦ 48hopenhouse barcelona.org. Architectural gems, including those that are usually closed to the public, open their doors for one weekend.

LEM Throughout Oct ⓦ gracia-territori.com. Experimental and electronic music and art festival organized by the Gràcia Territori Sonor collective, with free or cheap concerts, events and happenings held in Gràcia's bars, cafés and galleries.

Festival Internacional de Jazz Last week in Oct and through Nov ⓦ barcelonajazzfestival.com. The biggest annual jazz festival in town has been going for more than four decades and attracts superstar solo artists and bands to the clubs and concert halls, as well as putting on smaller-scale street concerts.

CELEBRATING CATALAN-STYLE

Central to any Catalan festival is the parade of **gegants**, the overblown 5m-high giants with a costumed frame (to allow them to be carried) and papier-mâché or fibreglass heads. Barcelona has its own official city *gegants* of King Jaume and his queen (there's more at ⓦ gegantsbcn .cat), while each neighbourhood cherishes its own traditional figures, from elegant noblewomen to turban-clad sultans – the Barri Gòtic's church of Santa María del Pi has some of the most renowned. Come festival time they congregate in the city's squares, dancing cumbersomely to the sound of flutes and drums, and accompanied by smaller, more nimble figures known as **capgrossos** (bigheads) and by outsized lions and dragons. Also typically Catalan is the **correfoc** (fire-running), where brigades of drummers, fire-breathing dragons and demons with firework-flaring tridents cavort in the streets. It's as devilishly dangerous as it sounds, with intrepid onlookers attempting to stop the dragons passing, as firecrackers explode all around – approach with caution.

SOME THINGS YOU MIGHT HAVE MISSED…

If you look beyond the big-name acts and the major annual celebrations, there's a whole world of off-the-radar festive fun in Barcelona, with some events just putting a toe in the water and others growing more elaborate with each year. February's **Minifestival** (⒲minibarcelona .wordpress.com), for example, provides a neat suburban counterpoint to the bigger city music fests, highlighting international indie acts that you've definitely never heard of. In May/June, **Loop** (⒲loop-barcelona.com), the international fair and festival for video art, attracts hundreds of artists from dozens of countries. September sees the ever-improving **Festival Àsia** (⒲casaasia.es), with dance, theatre, music, DJs, children's activities, performance art and workshops showcasing the cultures of Asia and the Pacific region. By October/November, digi-heads and Second Lifers are ready for **Artfutura** (⒲artfutura.org), the digital culture and creativity festival; while alternative Christmas shopping is best done at **Drap-Art** (⒲drapart .net), the Festival of Creative Recycling, which puts on its annual bash and market at the CCCB. Also usually – but not always – near the end of the year is the **Barcelona International Comedy Festival** (⒲barcelonacomedyfestival.com), which attracts top stand-up stars alongside local laughter-merchants in a multilingual and multi-venue programme.

19

Tots Sants All Saints' Day, Nov 1. The day when the Spanish remember their dead with cemetery visits and special meals. It's traditional to eat roast chestnuts (*castanyes*), sold by street vendors, sweet potatoes and *panellets* (almond-based sweets). It's also a public holiday.

DECEMBER

Fira de Santa Llúcia Dec 1–22. For more than two hundred years the Christmas season has seen a special market and crafts fair outside the cathedral. Browse for gifts or watch the locals snapping up Christmas trees, Nativity figures and traditional decorations.

Nadal/Sant Esteve Dec 25–26 ⒲bcn.cat/nadal.

Christmas Day and St Stephen's Day are both public holidays, which Catalans tend to spend at home – the traditional gift-giving is on Twelfth Night (Jan 6). Each year, there's a Christmas Nativity scene erected in Pl. de Sant Jaume, Barri Gòtic, which stays there for the whole of December and the first week in January.

PISCINES PICORNELL

Sports and outdoor activities

Barcelona is well placed for access to the sea and mountains, which is one of the reasons it was picked for the 1992 Olympics – the event that really put the modern city on the map. A spin-off from the games was an increased provision of top-quality sports and leisure facilities throughout Catalunya, which have attracted an increasing number of major games events – half a million spectators watched the European Athletics Championships when they were held here in 2010, the IAAF World Junior Championships hit the city in 2012, and the World Swimming Championships arrived in 2013. However, while there are scores of sports centres and swimming pools in Barcelona, there aren't actually that many that will appeal to tourists or casual visitors. Most people are content to relax on the city beaches or take off for a hike or jog in the surrounding hills of the Parc del Collserola.

ESSENTIALS

Information Servei d'informació Esportiva (☎010, ⋒bcn.cat/oesports), the city council's sports information service, is the main source of information about municipal sports facilities. It also has a drop-in office (Direcció d'Esports) on Montjuïc at Av. de l'Estadi 30 (ⓜEspanya), at the side of the Picornell swimming pool.

Tickets Tickets for all major sporting events can be bought from the agencies, certain ServiCaixa ATMs, Ticketea (☎902 044 226, ⓦticketea.com) or Ticketmaster (☎902 150 025, ⓦticketmaster.es).

BASKETBALL

Second only to football in popularity in Catalunya, basketball has been played in Barcelona since the 1920s. Games are usually played September to June at weekends, with most interest in the city's two main teams. **Club Joventut de Badalona**, founded in 1930, were European champions in 1994, while **FC Barcelona**, founded 1926, finished runners-up five times before finally becoming European champions in 2003, a title they regained in 2010. It's easiest to go and watch FC Barcelona, as Badalona is out in the sticks. The team plays at the Palau Blaugrana, adjacent to the Camp Nou. **Tickets** to games are fairly inexpensive (€9–72, depending on the seat and game), and you can either buy tickets online (ⓦfcbarcelona.com) or go to the stadium (the day before the game).

CYCLING

Cycling is being heavily promoted by the city authorities as a means of transport. There's a successful **bike-sharing scheme** (known as Bicing) while around 180km of cycle paths traverse the city, with plans to double the network. Not all locals have embraced the bike, and some cycle paths are still ignored by cars or are clogged with pedestrians, indignantly reluctant to give way to two-wheelers. But, on the whole, cycling around Barcelona is not the completely hairy experience it was. The nicest place to get off the road is the **Parc del Collserola**, where there are bike trails for varying abilities through the woods and hills. **Montjuïc** is another popular place for mountain-biking – there's a weekend rental outfit up behind the castle. Bikes are allowed on the metro, on FGC trains and on the Montjuïc and Vallvidrera funiculars.

20

Bike tours and rental The best way to see the city by bike – certainly as a first-time visitor – is to take a bike tour (see p.25), bikes and equipment will be provided; or to rent a bike (see p.24).

Maps You might want to pick up the map detailing current cycle paths. It's available from the tourist office, or on the city council's website ⓦbcn.cat/bicicleta.

Races and festivals The city hosts a variety of annual cycling events, including the main regional race, the Volta a Catalunya (ⓦvoltacatalunya.cat) every March. June/July sees the Ajuntament's annual Festa de la Bici (Bicycle Fiesta), while September is another big month, with races during the Mercè festival and a day during the city's "Mobility Week" dedicated to cycling.

Amics de la Bici c/Demóstenes 19, Sants ☎933 394 060, ⓦamicsdelabici.org; ⓜPlaça de Sants. The "Friends of the Bike" organize a full range of events and activities, from rides to bike-mechanic courses.

FOOTBALL

To be honest, there's only one sport in Barcelona and that's football, as played by local heroes **FC** (Futbol Club) **Barcelona**. The team is worshipped at the Camp Nou stadium in the north of the city and, even if you don't coincide with a game, the stadium's football museum and tour alone is worth the trip (see p.132). The other local team – though not to be compared – is **RCD** (Reial Club Deportiu) **Espanyol**, whose games are played at their 40,000-seater stadium at Cornellà, west of the city centre. The season runs from late August until May, with games usually played on Sundays (though live broadcasts on TV now mean that games are also frequently played on Fridays, Saturdays and Mondays). You'll have little

BYE-BYE BULLS

Bullfights are an integral part of many southern Spanish festivals, and while Catalunya too has had a long, if less renowned bullfighting tradition, the more progressive city of Barcelona has always stood somewhat apart. One bullring, the **Plaza de Toros Monumental**, Gran Via de les Corts Catalanes 749 (ⓜMonumental) – site, incidentally, of the Beatles' only ever concert in Barcelona, in 1965 – lasted, with the dwindling support of local aficionados and tourists, until 2011 when bullfighting was banned by the Catalan parliament. The future of the building is still undecided but it may meet a similar fate to the ring in Plaça Espanya, which retained its Moorish facade but was transformed inside into the stylish Arenas de Barcelona shopping centre (see p.113).

TOP 5 GREATEST EVER BARCELONA PLAYERS

Carles Rexach (1965–81)   Xavi (1998–2015)
Johan Cruyff (1973–78)   Lionel Messi (2004–)
Ronaldinho (2003–08)

problem getting a ticket to see an Espanyol game – you can usually just turn up on the day – and, perhaps surprisingly, it's also fairly straightforward to get tickets for FC Barcelona. The Camp Nou seats 98,000, which means it's only really full for big games against rivals like Real Madrid, or for major European ties.

TEAM CONTACTS

FC Barcelona Camp Nou, Av. Aristides Maillol, Les Corts ☎902 189 900, ⓦfcbarcelona.com; ⓜCollblanc/Palau Reial; map pp.130–131. Tickets go on general sale (online or at the stadium) a week or more before each match, or try ServiCaixa or Ticketmaster. Season-ticket holders who aren't attending the match put their seats up for sale through the club, right up until kick-off time, so it's

not advised to buy tickets from touts at the ground. For a typical league game you're likely to pay from €50 (and be seated *very* high up), though prices run as high as €245.
RCD Espanyol Av. Baix Llobregat 100, Cornellà de Llobregat ☎932 927 700, ⓦrcdespanyol.com; ⓜCornellà Centre, then 20min walk. Most tickets cost €40–90; you can buy online and pick your tickets up on the day.

HORSERIDING

Escola Municipal d'Hípica La Foixarda Av. Montanyans 1, Montjuïc ☎934 261 066, ⓦhipicalafoixarda.es; ⓜEspanya, then bus #150; map p.87. The municipal riding school on Montjuïc offers lessons and courses for adults

(beginners especially welcome), children and disabled people, or you can just have a taster with an hour-long riding session from around €22 at the weekends. Office open Mon–Fri 5.30–8pm, Sat & Sun 9am–1.30pm & 5–9pm.

ICE SKATING

There are a couple of ice rinks in the city, including one at FC Barcelona's Camp Nou stadium, and a seasonal rink at Pl. Catalunya over Christmas and New Year (☎933 425 451, ⓦbargelona.cat). At the Roger de Flor rink there's a café-bar from where you can watch the action. It's a good idea to check hours and restrictions before you go, as weekends and holidays especially can see the rinks inundated with children. Note that gloves are compulsory for all skaters and helmets for under-12s, and both can be rented at the rinks.

ICE RINKS

Pavelló Pista Gel Camp Nou, c/d'Aristides Maillol 12, Les Corts ☎902 189 900, ⓦfcbarcelona.com; ⓜCollblanc/Palau Reial; map pp.130–131. Morning and afternoon skating sessions daily throughout the year, times vary; closed Aug. Admission €13.40, including skate rental.

Also a skating school, for classes of all ages and levels.
Skating Pista de Gel c/de Roger de Flor 168, Dreta de l'Eixample ☎932 452 800, ⓦskatingclub.cat; ⓜTetuan; map pp.116–117. Morning and afternoon skating sessions daily throughout the year, times vary. Admission €14, plus €3 for the mandatory gloves, including skate rental.

ROLLERBLADING, SKATING AND SKATEBOARDING

The Passeig Marítim and Port Olímpic area (ⓜCiutadella-Vila Olímpica) see heavy **skate and blade** traffic, while other popular runs include Arc de Triomf (ⓜArc de Triomf), Parc Joan Miró (ⓜTarragona) and Barceloneta, next to the Palau del Mar (ⓜBarceloneta). The Fòrum site down at Diagonal Mar (ⓜEl Marseme Forum) has acres of wide, open space. You're supposed to keep off all marked cycle paths. Meanwhile, *the* place for **skateboarders** is the piazza outside MACBA, the contemporary art gallery in the Raval.

RUNNING AND JOGGING

The **Passeig Marítim** (ⓜCiutadella-Vila Olímpica) is the best place for a seafront run – there's a 5km promenade from Barceloneta all the way to the River Besòs, with a fitness circuit on the way at Mar Bella beach. To get off the beaten track, you'll need to head for the heights of Montjuïc or the Parc del Collserola.

Races and festivals There's a half-marathon (Mitja Marató de Barcelona) held in the city every February or March, while

the full Barcelona Marathon (Marató Barcelona; application forms and details on ⓦzurichmaratobarcelona.com) takes place in March. There are more road races during the September Mercè festival, while La Cursa (ⓦ cursaelcorte ingles.com; April), the annual eleven-kilometre run organized by El Corte Inglés department store, attracts over 50,000 fun-runners onto the streets. It's one of the longest-established city runs, held since 1979, and the 1994 event, attracting 110,000 runners, still holds the Guinness world record for number of participants.

SPORTS CENTRES

Every city neighbourhood has a sports centre, most with swimming pools but also offering a variety of other sports, games and activities. Schedules and prices vary, so it's best to contact the centres directly for any sport you might be interested in. Most have a general daily admission fee (€15–20) if all you want is a swim and use of the gym. For a full rundown call ☎ 010 or consult the sports section database on ⓦ bcn.cat.

CEM Marítim Pg. Marítim 33, Vila Olímpica ☎ 932 240 440, ⓦ claror.cat; ⓜ Ciutadella-Vila Olímpica; map p.83. Large complex by the Port Olímpic with a pool, gym and sauna, plus a wide range of organized activities, games and treatments, from aerobics, dance and yoga to indoor biking, beach tennis and hydrotherapy. Check the website for the other three centres they have in the city. Mon–Fri 7am–midnight, Sat 8am–9pm, Sun 8am–4pm.

CEM Frontó Colom Ramblas 18, Barri Gòtic ☎ 933 023 295, ⓦ frontocolom.com; ⓜ Drassanes; map p.44. Centrally situated sports centre with pool and gym, where you can see traditional Spanish *frontón* (handball) or Basque *jai alai*, reputedly the fastest sport in the world. Mon–Fri 7.30am–10.30pm, Sat 9am–8pm, Sun 9am–2.30pm.

SWIMMING

The city **beaches** are safe, clean and green-flagged but sometimes very crowded. Better swimming can be found at the region's coastal beaches; Sitges is popular but the very fine sand there will still be in your ears weeks later, while Caldetes (Caldes d'Estrach) is probably the best. Barcelona also has scores of municipal **pools** – we've picked out three of the best. You may be required to show your passport before being allowed in, and you'll need to wear a swimming cap. If you're hardy enough, the annual Christmas Swimming Cup involves diving into the port on December 25 and racing other like-minded fools.

20

SWIMMING POOLS

Club Natació Atlètic Barceloneta Pl. del Mar, Barceloneta ☎ 932 210 010, ⓦ cnab.org; ⓜ Ciutadella-Vila Olímpica; map p.79. One indoor pool, two outdoor, plus bar, restaurant and gym facilities. Daily admission for nonmembers is €12, under-10s €7. Mon–Fri 6.30am–11pm, Sat 7am–11pm, Sun 8am–5pm (until 8pm mid-May to Sept).

Piscina Municipal de Montjuïc Av. Miramar 31, Montjuïc ☎ 934 234 041; Funicular de Montjuïc; map p.87. The city's most beautiful outdoor pool, low on facilities but high on Montjuïc with spectacular views – it was built to look good on TV for the Olympic diving

competitions. Admission €6.50, under-15s €4.50. Aug: daily 11am–6.30pm.

Piscines Picornell Av. de l'Estadi 30–38, Montjuïc ☎ 934 234 041, ⓦ picornell.cat; ⓜ Espanya, then bus #150; map p.87. Remodelled and expanded for the Olympics, the fifty-metre indoor pool is open all year, while the outdoor pool is open to the public from June to Sept. Nudist sessions all year on Sat night, plus Sun pm Oct–May. €12 (under-14s €7.30), includes gym and sauna. Indoor pool and other facilities Mon–Fri 6.45am–midnight, Sat 7am–9pm, Sun 7.30am–4pm (until 7.30pm July–Sept); outdoor pool Mon–Fri 9.30am–8.30pm, Sat until 8pm, Sun 10.30am–7pm.

FOLLOW THAT CAR

Catalunya's motor racing circuit, the **Circuit de Catalunya** (ⓦ circuitcat.com), hosts the annual Formula 1 Spanish Grand Prix in April/May, as well as a whole series of other Spanish and Catalan bike and motor races throughout the year, from truck-racing to endurance rallies. The track, which you can tour (€10, pre-purchase tickets online) is out near Granollers, north of the city (trains from Sants/Pg. de Gràcia), a twenty-minute walk from Montmeló station, but during the Grand Prix there are also shuttle-bus services and direct buses from Barcelona. For Formula 1, you need to sort out tickets well in advance (they go on sale the previous Aug; check the website), while sports travel companies can offer special race packages.

SURFIN' BCN

If you've experienced Barcelona's beaches in the summer, you might find it hard to believe that those glass-smooth waters could ever be surf-worthy. However, from September to April, the Mediterranean picks up enough steam to send waves to Barcelona's sandy doorstep. On rare occasions (maybe twice a year), there's enough power to push the waves toward the 2–3m marks, but for the most part, the soft-breaking waves are knee- to waist-high, making the city's beaches – as one local surf instructor put it – a "paradise for beginners". If you're a newbie looking to get your feet wet or are a more experienced surfer in need of gear, try **Pukas Surf Eskola** (Pg. de Joan de Borbó 93, Barceloneta; ☎931 186 021, ⓦpukassurf.com/schools) or **Box Barcelona** (c/de Pontevedra 51–53, Barceloneta; ☎932 214 702, ⓦboxbarcelona.com) – both offer rentals and lessons. For a directory of other surf shops in the city, plus up-to-the-minute surf reports for the region, the website **Barcelona Surf** (ⓦbsurfers.com) can't be beat but is only in Spanish.

TENNIS

Municipal tennis courts, including Vall d'Hebron, are listed on the city council website ⓦbcn.cat or the English-language ⓦbarcelona-tennis.com, while for private clubs consult the website of the Federació Catalana de Tennis (ⓦfctennis.cat). One of these, the Reial Club de Tennis Barcelona-1899 (ⓦrctb1899.es), hosts the **Barcelona Open** every April.

TENNIS COURTS

Centre Municipal de Tenis Pg. Vall d'Hebron 178–196, Vall d'Hebron ☎934 276 500; ⓜMontbau. The main municipal tennis centre at Vall d'Hebron, in the northeastern suburbs, is the best place to play. Unlike many clubs in the city, you can rent courts by the hour without being a member. There are asphalt and clay courts, costing around €20–25 an hour, plus a pool, gym and café. Rackets are available for rent. Check out the special deals after 3pm on Sundays. Public hours Mon–Fri 8am–11pm, Sat until 9pm, Sun until 7pm (Nov–March) & 9pm (April–Oct).

WATERSPORTS

Base Nàutica Municipal Av. Litoral, Platja Mar Bella ☎932 210 432, ⓦbasenautica.org (Catalan only); ⓜCiutadella-Vila Olímpica, then bus #41; map p.83. You can rent kayaks and windsurfers, and there's a popular bar here as well. Prices vary considerably, but you can expect to pay from around €60 for a couple of hours' windsurfer rental or €200 for a two-day elementary sailing course. Open all year: hours vary, though May–Sept daily 10am–8pm.

Centre Municipal de Vela Moll de Gregal, Port Olímpic ☎932 257 940, ⓦvelabarcelona.com (Catalan only); ⓜCiutadella-Vila Olímpica; map p.83. Port Olímpic's sailing club has courses and instruction in catamaran and Laser sailing, kayaking and windsurfing, from two hours to two days. Prices are much the same as at Base Nàutica Municipal. Daily 9am–9pm.

20

LA COMERCIAL

Shopping

While for sheer size and scope Barcelona cannot compete with Paris or other fashion capitals, it is one of the world's most stylish cities – architecture, fashion and decoration are thoroughly permeated by Catalan *disseny* (design). All of this makes for great shopping, whether you're looking for unique clothing by a hot local designer or something stylish for the home. Traditional arts and crafts have a place here too, from basketwork to ceramics, and many artists and craftworkers have workshops that are open to the public. Antiques and curios abound, while souvenirs range from the gloriously tacky to the outrageously wacky – a walk down the Ramblas and through the Barri Gòtic alone throws up anything from Picasso T-shirts to Peruvian bangles, not to mention Barcelona football scarves, handmade soap, carnival masks, designer chocolates and vintage dresses.

21 The best **general shopping area** for clothes, souvenirs, arts and crafts is the Barri Gòtic, particularly between the upper part of the Ramblas and Avinguda Portal de l'Àngel. Established designer and **high-street fashion** is at home in the Eixample, along Passeig de Gràcia, Rambla de Catalunya and Carrer de Pelai, as well as along Avinguda Diagonal in Les Corts. Hot **new designers and boutiques** – including shoe, street- and skatewear specialists – can be found in La Ribera, around Passeig del Born (c/dels Flassaders, c/del Rec, c/de Calders, c/de l'Espartería, c/de la Vidrería, c/del Bonaire), but also down c/d'Avinyó in the Barri Gòtic, between c/del Carme and MACBA in El Raval, and along c/de Verdi in Gràcia. For **secondhand and vintage clothing**, stores line the whole of c/de la Riera Baixa (El Raval), with others nearby on c/del Carme and c/ de l'Hospital, and on Saturdays there's a street market here. More bargains are in the **remainder stores, wholesalers and discount outlets** found along c/de Girona in the Eixample, between the Gran Via and Ronda Sant Pere.

For **antiques** – books, furniture, paintings and artefacts – you need to trawl c/de la Palla, c/dels Banys Nous and surrounding streets in the Barri Gòtic, best combined with the antique market on Thursdays in front of the cathedral. **Delis and specialist food shops** tend to be concentrated around the Passeig del Born in La Ribera. Independent **music and CD stores** are found on and around c/dels Tallers (El Raval), just off the top of the Ramblas. And don't forget the city's **museums and galleries**, where you'll find reasonably priced items ranging from postcards to wall-hangings.

ESSENTIALS

Opening hours Shop opening hours are typically Mon–Sat 10am–1.30/2pm & 4.30–7.30/8pm, though all the bigger shops stay open over lunchtime, while smaller shops close on Saturday afternoons and/or may vary their hours in other ways. Major department stores and shopping malls open Mon–Sat 10am–10pm, though the cafés, restaurants and leisure outlets in malls are usually open on Sunday too. Barcelona's daily food markets, all in covered halls, are generally open from Mon–Sat 8am–3pm & 5–8pm (local variations apply), though the most famous,

La Boqueria on the Ramblas, opens throughout the day.
Sales The annual sales (*rebaixes*, *rebajas*) follow the main fashion seasons – mid-January until the end of February, and throughout July and August.
Tax refunds Non-EU residents can get an IVA (ie VAT) refund on each purchase over the value of €90.16; if there's a "Tax-Free Shopping" sticker displayed at the store (ⓦpremiertaxfree.com), ask for the voucher and claim the refund at the airport before leaving.

ANTIQUES

★**L'Arca** c/dels Banys Nous 20, Barri Gòtic ☎933 021 598, ⓦlarca.es; ⓜLiceu; map p.44. Catalan brides used to fill up their nuptial trunk (*arca*) with embroidered bed

linen and lace, and this shop is a treasure-trove of vintage and antique textiles. Period (eighteenth to early twentieth century) costumes can be rented or purchased as well

CRAFT WORKSHOPS

Crafts have always been central to Barcelona's industry, with a history dating back to the Middle Ages. Many of the street names in the Born (ⓜJaume I/Barceloneta), particularly, refer to the crafts once practised there; eg c/de la Argentería, silversmith's street, c/dels Mirallers, the street where they used to make mirrors, c/de la Vidrería, glassmakers' street, or c/dels Sombrerers, where hats (*sombreros*) were made. Over the last couple of decades, neighbourhoods like the Born, El Raval and Poble Nou have once again become craft centres as empty buildings and warehouses have been opened up as workshops. Some artists work behind closed doors, while others have a space at the front where they sell their limited series or unique pieces.

A good way to see the Ciutat Vella (old town) workshops is to coincide with the **Tallers Oberts**, or open workshops (ⓦtallersobertsbarcelona.cat), usually held over the last two weekends of May, when there are studio visits, exhibitions, children's workshops, guided tours and lots of other events. Or contact Barcelona tour agency My Favourite Things (ⓦmyft.net), who can organize a workshop tour on request, introducing you directly to selected artists.

21

– one of Kate Winslet's *Titanic* costumes came from here. Mon–Sat 11am–2pm & 4.30–8.30pm; closed Mon as well as Sat afternoons in Aug.

Bulevard dels Antiquaris Pg. de Gràcia 55–57, Dreta de l'Eixample ☎ 932 154 499, ⓦ bulevarddelsantiquaris .com; Ⓜ Passeig de Gràcia; map p.102. An arcade with over seventy shops full of antiques of all kinds, from toys and dolls to Spanish ceramics and African art. Mon–Sat 10am–8.30pm; closed Sat in Aug.

Mercantic c/Rius i Taulet 120, Sant Cugat del Vallès ☎ 936 744 950, ⓦ mercantic.com; FGC Sant Cugat. This permanent antiques and collectables market is out in the suburbs but makes a great trip for casual browsers and serious collectors alike. You'll find everything from furniture to farm machinery, old radios to vintage jewellery, postcards to erotic drawings, plus an outdoor flea market (Sun until 3pm), weekly lot auctions (Sat) and trade markets (1st Sun of each month). Tues–Sat 9.30am–8pm, Sun 9.30am–3pm; closed three weeks in Aug.

ARTS, CRAFTS AND GIFTS

Artesanía Catalunya c/dels Banys Nous 11, Barri Gòtic ☎ 934 674 660, ⓦ artesania-catalunya.com; Ⓜ Liceu; map p.44. It's always worth a look in the "Emprentes de Catalunya" showroom of the local government's arts and crafts promotion board. Exhibitions change, but most of the work is contemporary in style, from basketwork to glassware, though traditional methods are still very much encouraged. Mon–Sat 10am–8pm, Sun 10am–2pm.

Cerería Subirà Bxda. de la Llibreteria 7, Barri Gòtic ☎ 933 152 606, ⓦ www.facebook.com/cereriasubira; Ⓜ Jaume I; map p.44. Barcelona's oldest shop (it's been here since 1760) has a beautiful interior, and sells unique handcrafted candles. Mon–Thurs 9.30am–1.30pm & 4–8pm, Fri 9.30am–8pm, Sat 10am–2pm & 5–8pm.

★ **Espai Drap Art** c/d'en Groc 1, Barri Gòtic ☎ 932 684 889, ⓦ drapart.org; Ⓜ Jaume I; map p.44 The Drap-Art creative recycling organization has a shop and exhibition space for artists to show their wildly inventive wares, from trash-bangles to tin bags. Tues–Fri 11am–2pm & 5–8pm, Sat 6–9pm.

Estanc Duaso c/Balmes 116, Esquerra de l'Eixample ☎ 932 151 330, ⓦ www.duaso.com; Ⓜ Diagonal/FGC Provença; map p.110. Owned and run by Jordi Duaso, president of Barcelona's Tobacconist's Guild, this cigar-smoker's paradise features a huge walk-in humidor, expert advice and regular workshops by international cigar-makers, who roll stogies in-store by hand. Mon–Fri 9am–8pm, Sat 10am–2pm.

★ **Fantastik** c/de Joaquín Costa 62, El Raval ☎ 933 013 068, ⓦ fantastik.es; Ⓜ Universitat; map pp.58–59. Beguiling gifts, crafts and covetable objects from four continents. You'll never know how you lived without them, whether it's Chinese robots, African baskets, Russian domino sets or Vietnamese kitchen scales. Mon–Fri 11am–2pm & 4–8.30pm, Sat noon–9pm.

Papirum Bxda. de la Llibreteria 2, Barri Gòtic ☎ 933 105 242, ⓦ papirumbcn.com; Ⓜ Jaume I; map p.44. For all your writing needs – hand-painted paper, draughts-man's pens, leather-bound notebooks, calligraphy sets and more. Mon–Fri 10am–8.30pm, Sat 10am–2pm & 5–8.30pm.

Taller Textil Teranyina c/del Notariat 10, El Raval ☎ 933 179 436, ⓦ teresarosa.com; Ⓜ Catalunya; map pp.58–59. Teresa Rosa Aguayo opened her Raval textile workshop in 1987, and continues to weave striking contemporary carpets, rugs and wall-hangings, and make textile jewellery and other objects. You can call in any time to see the design work being carried out, or sign up for one of the courses. Mon–Fri 11am–3pm & 5–8pm.

BOOKS

GENERAL

Casa del Llibre Pg. de Gràcia 62, Dreta de l'Eixample ☎ 902 026 407, ⓦ casadellibro.com; Ⓜ Passeig de Gràcia; map p.102. Barcelona's biggest book emporium, strong on literature, humanities and travel, with plenty of English-language titles and Catalan literature in transla-tion. Mon–Sat 9.30am–9.30pm.

★ **La Central del Raval** c/d'Elisabets 6, El Raval ☎ 902 884 990, ⓦ lacentral.com; Ⓜ Catalunya; map pp.58–59. Occupying a unique space in the former Misericordia chapel, La Central is a fantastically stocked arts and humanities treasure-trove, with books piled high in every nook and cranny. There's a big English-language section (and other European languages too), while other La Central outlets are found in MACBA (contemporary art museum) and MUHBA (Barcelona History Museum). Mon–Fri 9.30am–9pm, Sat 10am–9pm.

Come In c/de Balmes 129, Esquerra de l'Eixample ☎ 934 531 204, ⓦ libreriainglesa.com; Ⓜ Diagonal; map p.110. Stocks only English-language books and literature, and is also a good place for language-learning and teaching aids. Mon–Fri 9.30am–8.30pm, Sat 9.30am–2pm & 4.30–8pm.

Laie c/de Pau Claris 85, Dreta de l'Eixample ☎ 933 181 739, ⓦ laie.es; Ⓜ Passeig de Gràcia; map p.102. This has been one of Barcelona's favourite bookshops for years, though probably just as much for its café-restaurant, which is a good place to unwind. Other speciality Laie arts outlets are found in galleries like Caixa Forum, CCCB, La Pedrera, Museu Picasso and the Liceu. Mon–Fri 9am–9pm, Sat 10am–9pm.

21

ART, DESIGN AND PHOTOGRAPHY

Museu Nacional d'Art de Catalunya Palau Nacional, Montjuïc ☎ 936 220 360, ⓦ mnac.cat; Ⓜ Espanya; map p.87. The MNAC bookshop has the city's widest selection of books on Catalan art, architecture, design and style. Tues–Sat 10.15am–5.45pm (May–Sept until 7.45pm), Sun 10.15am–2.45pm.

Mutt c/del Comerç 15, Sant Pere ☎ 931 924 438; Ⓜ Jaume I; map p.68. This bookshop and contemporary art gallery has become a hip meeting point for Barcelona's creative set. No wonder – it's a gorgeous space filled with an eclectic array of titles and artwork. Mon–Sat 11am–2pm.

COMICS AND GRAPHIC BOOKS

Norma Comics Pg. de Sant Joan 9, Sagrada Família/ Glòries ☎ 932 448 423, ⓦ normacomics.com; Ⓜ Arc de Triomf; map pp.116–117. Spain's best comic and graphic-novel shop, for everything from manga to the Caped Crusader, plus DVDs and all kinds of related gear and gizmos. Mon–Sat 10.30am–8.30pm.

SECONDHAND

Babelia Books c/de Villaroel 27, Esquerra de l'Eixample ☎ 934 246 681, ⓦ babeliabcn.com; Ⓜ Urgell; map p.110. If the sightseeing gets overwhelming, a cup of tea or coffee and a browse through the books in Babelia will recharge your batteries. There are secondhand titles in English, Spanish and Catalan on the long shelves and home-made pastries to munch as you read. Mon–Sat 10am–10pm.

★**Hibernian Books** c/de Montseny 17, Gràcia ☎ 932 174 796, ⓦ hibernian-books.com; Ⓜ Fontana; map p.125. Barcelona's best secondhand English bookshop has around 40,000 titles in stock, and there are always plenty of giveaway bargains available. There are new titles available as well and you can part-exchange. Mon 4–8.30pm, Tues–Sat 10.30am–8.30pm; Aug: Tues–Sat 11am–2pm & 5–9pm.

TRAVEL, GUIDES AND MAPS

★**Altaïr** Gran Via de les Corts Catalanes 616, Esquerra de l'Eixample ☎ 933 427 171, ⓦ altair.es; Ⓜ Universitat; map p.110. Europe's biggest travel superstore has a massive selection of travel books, guides, maps and world music, plus a programme of travel-related talks and exhibitions. Mon–Sat 10am–8.30pm.

Llibreria Quera c/de Petritxol 2, Barri Gòtic ☎ 933 180 743, ⓦ llibreriaquera.com; Ⓜ Liceu; map p.44. The most knowledgeable place in town for Catalan and Pyrenean maps and trekking guides, plus anything else to do with the great outdoors. Tues 10am–8pm, Wed–Sat 10am–1.30pm & 4.30–8pm; closed Aug.

CLOTHES, SHOES AND ACCESSORIES

DESIGNER FASHION

Antonio Miró c/del Consell de Cent 349, Dreta de l'Eixample ☎ 934 870 670, ⓦ antoniomiro.es; Ⓜ Passeig de Gràcia; map p.102. The showcase for Barcelona's most innovative designer, Antonio Miró – especially good for classy suits, though now also stocks accessories and household design items. Mon–Sat 10.30am–8.30pm.

Armand Basi Pg. de Gràcia 49, Dreta de l'Eixample ☎ 932 151 421, ⓦ armandbasi.com; Ⓜ Passeig de Gràcia; map p.102. Colourful men's and women's jackets, jeans, dresses and casual wear from the hot Spanish designer. There's also a full range of accessories – watches to fragrances – though the must-have items are the designer table- and kitchenware created with super-chef Ferran Adrià. Also an outlet at La Roca Village. Mon–Sat 10am–9pm.

La Comercial c/del Rec 73, La Ribera ☎ 933 192 435, ⓦ lacomercial.info; Ⓜ Jaume I; map p.68. Five boutiques plus a showroom – all clustered around c/del Rec – comprise the fabulous La Comercial, which carries a carefully curated selection of on-trend men's and women's fashion, fragrances and chic home decor. The c/del Rec 77 location is a "pop-up" which houses a different brand each season. Mon–Thurs 11am–9pm, Fri & Sat 11am–9.30pm.

Custo Barcelona Pl. de les Olles 7, La Ribera ☎ 932 687 893; Ⓜ Barceloneta; map p.68; Pl. del Pi 2, Barri Gòtic ☎ 933 042 753; Ⓜ Liceu; map p.44; ⓦ custo-barcelona .com. Selling hugely colourful designer tops and sweaters for men and women, this is where the stars get their T-shirts. There are lots of Custo stores all over the city, but La Ribera's adds a bright splash to the medieval alleys, while last season's gear gets another whirl at the Pl. del Pi discount outlet in the Barri Gòtic. Mon–Sat 10am–9pm, Sun noon–8pm.

Desigual Pl. Catalunya 9, Dreta de l'Eixample ☎ 933 435 940, ⓦ desigual.com; Ⓜ Catalunya; map p.102. The new flagship store for Barcelona's best-known international label offers three floors of bright patchwork and printed clothes for men, women and kids, plus equally colourful home decor. There are other stores around the city. Mon–Sat 10am–10pm.

Jean-Pierre Bua Av. Diagonal 469, Esquerra de l'Eixample ☎ 934 397 100, ⓦ jeanpierrebua.com; Ⓜ Hospital Clinic; map p.110. The city's high temple for fashion victims: a postmodern shrine for Yamamoto, Gaultier, Miyake, McQueen, McCartney, Westwood and other international stars. Mon–Sat 10am–2pm & 4.30–8.30pm.

CLOCKWISE FROM TOP LEFT L'ARCA (P.226); MERCAT DE LA BOQUERIA (P.39); FORMATGERIA LA SEU (P.232); LA CENTRAL DEL RAVAL(P.227) >

21

★ **Natalie Capell** Atelier de Moda c/dels Banys Vells 4, entrance at c/de la Carassa 2, La Ribera ☎ 933 199 219, ⓦ nataliecapell.com; Ⓜ Jaume I; map p.68. Where "each dress carries a story". The boutique stocks Natalie Capell's own very elegant designs, in 1920s- and 1930s-style, every one sewn and colour-dyed by hand. Tues–Sat noon–8.30pm.

Purificación García c/de Provença 292, Dreta de l'Eixample ☎ 934 961 336, ⓦ purificaciongarcia.es; Ⓜ Passeig de Gràcia; map p.102. A hot designer with an eye for fabrics – García's first job was in a textile factory. She's also designed clothes for films, theatre and TV, and her costumes were seen at the opening ceremony of the Barcelona Olympics. The eponymous shop's a beauty, with the more casual items and accessories not particularly stratospherically priced. Mon–Sat 10am–8.30pm.

HIGH-STREET FASHION

Mango Pg. de Gràcia 36, Dreta de l'Eixample ☎ 932 157 530; ⓦ mango.com; Ⓜ Passeig de Gràcia; map p.102. Now available worldwide, Barcelona is where Mango began and prices here are generally a bit cheaper than in North America or other European countries. This is the flagship store, but there are branches all over the city. Mon–Sat 10am–9pm.

Zara Pg. de Gràcia 16, Dreta de l'Eixample ☎ 933 187 675, ⓦ zara.com; Ⓜ Passeig de Gràcia; map p.102. Trendy but cheap seasonal fashion for men, women and children from the Spanish chain. The Pg. de Gràcia branch is the flagship store, but you'll find outlets right across the city. Mon–Sat 10am–10pm.

JEWELLERY, TEXTILES AND ACCESSORIES

★ **Almacenes del Pilar** c/de la Boqueria 43, Barri Gòtic ☎ 933 177 984, ⓦ almacenesdelpilar.com; Ⓜ Liceu; map p.44. A world of frills, lace, cloth and materials used in the making of Spain's traditional regional costumes. You can pick up a decorated fan for just a few euros, though quality items go for a whole lot more. Mon–Sat 10am–2pm & 4–8pm; closed Aug.

Formista c/del Sagristans 9, Barri Gòtic ☎ 933 186 020, ⓦ formista.com; Ⓜ Jaume I; map p.44. Gallery-shop hybrid selling unique handmade objects by international designers and artists. There are sleek leather handbags

alongside porcelain jewellery, hand-printed textiles and more. Mon–Sat noon–9pm.

Iriarte Iriarte c/dels Cotoners 12, La Ribera ☎ 932 690 074, ⓦ iriarteiriarte.com; Ⓜ Jaume I; map p.68. Atelier-showroom for sumptuous handmade leather bags and belts. The alley (off c/dels Cotoners) has several other interesting craft workshops and galleries to browse. Tues–Sat 4.30–8.30pm.

Obach Sombrería c/del Call 2, Barri Gòtic ☎ 933 184 094; Ⓜ Liceu; map p.44. For traditional hats of all kinds, hats and caps to berets and Stetsons. Mon–Fri 9.30am–1.30pm & 4–8pm, Sat 10am–2pm & 4.30–8pm.

SECONDHAND, VINTAGE AND DISCOUNT OUTLETS

Espácio de Creadores c/Comtal 22, Barri Gòtic ☎ 934 127 958; Ⓜ Urquinaona; map p.44. Looking for glad-rags and super-stylish clothes on a budget? This is a fashionista bargain-hunter's dream, selling top-name haute couture from Spanish designers at thirty- to sixty-percent discounts. Mon–Sat 10am–9pm.

Holala! Plaza Pl. de Castella 2, El Raval ☎ 933 020 593, ⓦ holala-ibiza.com; Ⓜ Universitat; map pp.58–59. Vintage heaven in a warehouse setting (up past CCCB) for denim, flying jackets, Hawaiian shirts, baseball gear and much, much more. Mon–Sat 11am–9pm.

★ **Lailo** c/de la Riera Baixa 20, El Raval ☎ 934 413 749, ⓦ lailovintage.es; Ⓜ Liceu; map pp.58–59. Secondhand and vintage clothes shop with a massively wide-ranging stock, plus fancy dress costumes, tuxes and gowns available for rent. If you're serious about the vintage scene, this is your first stop – and if you don't find what you want, just move on down the street to the neighbouring stores and outlets. Mon–Fri 10.30am–2pm & 5–8pm, Sat 10.30am–2pm & 5–8.30pm.

Mango Outlet c/de Girona 37, Dreta de l'Eixample ☎ 934 122 935, ⓦ mangooutlet.com; Ⓜ Girona; map p.102. Last season's Mango gear at unbeatable prices, with items starting at just a few euros. The shop is in the city's "garment district" and there are other outlet stores in the same neighbourhood. Mon–Sat 10am–9pm.

El Mercadillo c/de la Portaferrissa 17, Barri Gòtic ☎ 933 183 872; Ⓜ Liceu; map p.44. The camel at the entrance marks this hippy-dippy indoor street market of shops and stalls selling T-shirts, skatewear, vintage gear and jewellery. Mon–Sat 11am–8.30pm.

La Roca Village La Roca del Vallès ☎ 938 423 939, ⓦ larocavillage.com. The out-of-town outlet mall is one for serious designer discount-hounds, with a hundred stores selling designer gear at up to sixty percent off normal prices. It's half an hour from the city centre and you can get there directly by bus – there are full transport details on the website. Mon–Sat 1–9pm (June to mid-Sept until 10pm).

TOP 5 ONLY-IN-BARCELONA SOUVENIRS

Almacen Marabi See p.234
La Campana See p.232
Els Encants flea market See p.233
Espai Drap Art See p.227
Papabubble See p.233

SHOES

Avarca Castell c/de l'Argentería 61, La Ribera ☎ 932 691 300, ⓦ avarcacastell.com; ⓜ Jaume I, map p.68. A style hailing from Menorca, the simple slingback sandal known as the *avarca* is all the rage, seen on royal and celebrity feet. Mon–Sat 10.30am–11.30pm.

Camper c/de Pelai 13–37, El Triangle ☎ 933 024 124, ⓦ camper.com; ⓜ Catalunya; map p.38. Spain's favourite shoe store opened its first shop in Barcelona in 1981. Providing hip, well-made, casual city footwear at a good price has been the cornerstone of its success – there's a store seemingly on every corner and in every mall, including this one, right at the top of the Ramblas. Mon–Sat 10am–9pm.

★ **La Manual Alpargatera** c/d'Avinyó 7, Barri Gòtic ☎ 933 010 172, ⓦ lamanualalpargatera.com; ⓜ Liceu, map p.44. In this traditional workshop they make and sell *alpargates* (espadrilles) to order, as well as producing other items using straw, rope- and basketwork. Mon–Sat 9.30am–1.30pm & 4.30–8pm.

★ **U-Casas** c/de l'Espaseria 4, La Ribera ☎ 933 100 046, ⓦ casasclub.com; ⓜ Jaume I; map p.68. Casas has four lines of shoe stores across Spain, with the U-Casas brand at the younger end of the market. Never mind the shoes, the stores themselves (right across town) are pretty spectacular, especially at the branch in the Born where an enormous shoe-shaped bench-cum-sofa takes centre-stage. Mon–Thurs 10.30am–8.30pm, Fri & Sat 10.30am–9pm.

DEPARTMENT STORES AND SHOPPING MALLS

Arenas de Barcelona Gran Via de les Corts Catalanes 373–385, Esquerra de l'Eixample ☎ 932 890 244, ⓦ www.arenasdebarcelona.com; ⓜ Espanya; map p.110. This designer mall is a glam refit of a former bull-ring, and while it's bigger on leisure facilities than shops and boutiques, you won't want to miss the view from the circular rooftop promenade. Mon–Sat 10am–10pm.

El Corte Inglés Pl. de Catalunya 14 ☎ 933 063 800; ⓜ Catalunya; map p.38; Av. del Portal de l'Àngel 19–21, Barri Gòtic ☎ 933 063 800, ⓦ elcorteingles.es; ⓜ Catalunya; map p.44. The city's largest department store – visit the flagship Pl. de Catalunya branch for nine floors of clothes, accessories, cosmetics, household goods, toys and top-floor café. For music, books, computers and sports gear, head for the Portal de l'Àngel branch. Mon–Sat 9.30am–9.30pm.

Diagonal Mar Av. Diagonal 3, Diagonal Mar ☎ 902 530 300, ⓦ diagonalmarcentre.es; ⓜ Maresme Fòrum or T4 tram; map p.85. Home to nearly 200 shops, this mall anchors the Diagonal Mar zone, and features the usual high-street suspects (El Corte Inglés, H&M, Zara, Mango, Sephora and FNAC) plus designer clothes and accessories, cafés, restaurants and cinema. Mon–Sat 10am–10pm.

Glòries Av. Diagonal 208 at Pl. de les Glòries Catalanes, Glòries ☎ 934 860 404, ⓦ www.lesglories.com; ⓜ Glòries; map pp.116–117. Huge mall with all the national high-street fashion names (H&M, Zara, Bershka, Mango) as well as a big Carrefour supermarket, children's wear, toys and games, ice-cream parlours, a dozen bars, cafés and restaurants and a seven-screen cinema complex. Mon–Sat 10am–10pm.

L'Illa Av. Diagonal 557, Les Corts ☎ 934 440 000, ⓦ lilla.com; ⓜ María Cristina; map pp.130–131. The landmark uptown shopping mall is stuffed full of designer fashion (including the local Custo), plus Camper (shoes), FNAC (music, film and books), Rituals (home and body), cosmetics, Decathlon (sports), El Corte Inglés (department store), Caprabo (supermarket), gourmet food hall and much more. Mon–Sat 10am–9.30pm.

El Triangle Pl. de Catalunya 4 ☎ 933 180 108, ⓦ eltriangle.es; ⓜ Catalunya; map p.38. Shopping centre at the top of the Ramblas, dominated by the flagship FNAC store, which specializes in books (good English-language selection), music, film and computer stuff. Also a Camper (for shoes), and Sephora (cosmetics), plus lots of boutiques, and a café on the ground floor next to the extensive newspaper and magazine section. Mon–Sat 10am–10pm.

DESIGN, DECORATIVE ART AND HOUSEHOLD GOODS

Cubiña c/de Mallorca 291, Dreta de l'Eixample ☎ 934 765 721, ⓦ cubinya.es; ⓜ Verdaguer; map p.102. The building itself is stupendous – Domènech i Montaner's *modernista* Casa Thomas – while the inside holds the very latest in household design, from slinky CD racks to €5000 dining tables. Mon–Sat 10am–2pm & 4.30–8.30pm (closed Sat June–July); closed in Aug.

Ganivetería Roca Pl. del Pi 3, Barri Gòtic ☎ 933 021 241, ⓦ ganiveteriaroca.cat; ⓜ Liceu; map p.44. Handsome old shop dating from 1911, selling a big range of knives, cutlery, corkscrews and other household goods, including a fine array of gentlemen's shaving gear. Mon–Fri 9.45am–1.30pm &

4.15–8pm, Sat 10am–2pm & 5–8pm.

Germanes García c/dels Banys Nous 15, Barri Gòtic ☎ 933 186 646; ⓜ Liceu; map p.44. Who knew you could make quite so much stuff out of basket-, raffia- and wicker-work? The enormous warehouse-showroom has everything from cradles to tables, plant-holders to wardrobes. Mon 4.30–8pm, Tues–Sat 9.30am–1.30pm & 4.30–8pm.

★ **Gotham** c/de Cervantes 7, Barri Gòtic ☎ 934 124 647, ⓦ gotham-bcn.com; ⓜ Jaume 1; map p.44. The place to come for retro (1950s to 1980s) furniture, lighting, homeware and accessories, plus original designs. Mon–Fri 11am–2pm & 5–8pm, Sat by appointment only.

21

21

Indio c/del Carme 24, El Raval ☎ 933 175 442; Ⓜ Catalunya; map pp.58–59. When locals of a certain age want linen, pillows, blankets, sheets and tablecloths, this is where they come – and the beautiful *modernista* facade, long cutting counters, wood panels and marble floor survive from its nineteenth-century glory days. Mon–Sat 10am–1.30pm & 4.30–8pm.

Vitra Pl. Comercial 5, La Ribera ☎ 932 687 219, Ⓦ vitra .com; Ⓜ Jaume I; map p.68. Home and workplace furniture specialist with stunning chairs and furniture by the likes of Frank Gehry, Philippe Starck, Charles and Ray Eames and Ron Arad. Mon–Thurs 9am–2pm & 5–7pm, Fri 9am–2pm.

FOOD AND DRINK

There's a full list of city **markets** at Ⓦ bcn.cat/mercatsmunicipals. The main local **supermarket** chain is Caprabo (Ⓦ caprabo.es), which has a useful branch in the Mercat de la Barceloneta, though most other branches are located in residential neighbourhoods, away from the tourist sights. The most convenient downtown supermarket is that in the basement of El Corte Inglés (Pl. de Catalunya), and there's also the fairly basic Carrefour Express at Ramblas 113.

DAILY FOOD MARKETS

Mercat de la Barceloneta Pl. de la Font, Barceloneta; Ⓜ Barceloneta; map p.79. See p.81.

Mercat de la Concepció c/de Valencia, Dreta de l'Eixample; Ⓜ Passeig de Gràcia; map p.102. See p.106.

Mercat de Galvany c/de Santaló 65, Sant Gervasi; Ⓜ María Cristina; map pp.130–131. See p.132.

Mercat de la Llibertat Pl. de la Llibertat, Gràcia; Ⓜ Fontana; map p.125. See p.125.

Mercat del Ninot c/de Mallorca 133, Esquerra de l'Eixample; Ⓜ Hospital Clinic; map p.110. See p.112.

Mercat de Sant Antoni Ronda de Sant Antoni, El Raval; Ⓜ Sant Antoni; map pp.58–59. See p.64.

Mercat Sant Josep/La Boqueria Ramblas; Ⓜ Liceu; map p.38. See p.39.

Mercat Santa Caterina Av. Francesc Cambó, Sant Pere; Ⓜ Jaume I; map p.68. See p.67.

SPECIALIST FOOD STORES

★ **La Botifarreria de Santa María** c/de Santa María 4, La Ribera ☎ 933 199 123, Ⓦ labotifarreria.com; Ⓜ Jaume I; map p.68. If you ever doubted the power of the humble Catalan pork sausage, drop by this designer temple-deli where otherwise beautifully behaved locals jostle at the counter for the day's home-made *botifarra*, plus rigorously sourced hams, cheeses, pâtés and salamis. True disciples can even buy the T-shirt. Mon–Fri 8.30am–2.30pm & 5–8.30pm, Sat 8.30am–3pm.

Bubó c/Caputxes 10, La Ribera ☎ 932 687 224, Ⓦ bubo .es; Ⓜ Jaume I; map p.68. There are chocolates and then there are Bubó chocolates – jewel-like creations and playful desserts by pastry maestro Carles Mampel. This very classy shop (with tastings and drinks de rigueur) is complemented by their minimalist new-wave tapas place, *Bubobar*, a couple of doors down at no. 6. Daily 10am–midnight.

La Campana c/de la Princesa 36, La Ribera ☎ 933 197 296, Ⓦ turroneslacampana.com; Ⓜ Jaume I; map p.68. This gorgeous shop from 1890 stocks handmade pralines

and truffles, but it's best known for its beautifully packaged squares and slabs of *torró*, traditional Catalan nougat. Daily 10am–11pm.

★ **Casa Gispert** c/dels Sombrerers 23, La Ribera ☎ 933 197 535, Ⓦ casagispert.com; Ⓜ Jaume I; map p.68. Roasters of nuts, coffee and spices for over 150 years, Casa Gispert have a truly delectable store of wooden boxes, baskets, stacked shelves and tantalizing smells. There are organic nuts and dried fruit, teas and gourmet deli items available too. Tues–Fri 9.30am–2pm & 4–8.30pm (Oct–Dec also Mon, same times), Sat 10am–2pm & 5–8pm.

★ **A Casa Portuguesa** c/de Verdi 58, Gràcia; ☎ 933 683 528, Ⓦ acasaportuguesa.com; Ⓜ Fontana; map p.125. This sleek café and deli on Gràcia's buzziest street is a showcase for the food, wine and culture of Portugal. Call in for a break while trawling the designer and streetwear stores of c/de Verdi – they make Portuguese specialities daily (including the famous *pasteis de Belém*, little custard tarts), and have a full programme of wine tastings, food festivals and other events. Tues–Fri 5pm–midnight, Sat & Sun 11am–3pm & 5pm–midnight.

★ **Formatgeria La Seu** c/de la Dagueria 16, Barri Gòtic ☎ 934 126 548, Ⓦ formatgerialaseu.com; Ⓜ Jaume I; map p.44. Sells the best farmhouse cheeses from independent producers all over Spain. Chatty Scottish owner Katherine is usually on hand to advise, and you can try before you buy with a €2.50 tasting plate – ask about the *formatgelat*, a cheese-ice cream fusion that's unique to the shop. Tues–Thurs 10am–2pm & 5–8pm, Fri & Sat 10am–3.30pm & 5–8pm; closed Aug.

Forn Baluard c/del Baluard 38–40, Barceloneta ☎ 932 211 208, Ⓦ baluardbarceloneta.com; Ⓜ Barceloneta; map p.79. There are scores of bakeries in Barcelona and every neighbourhood has its favourite, but when push comes to shove, foodies pick the *Baluard*, right next to Barceloneta market, where their passion for artisan bread, cakes and pastries knows no bounds. Mon–Sat 8am–9pm.

Olive Pl. de les Olles 2, La Ribera ☎ 933 105 883; Ⓜ Barceloneta; map p.68. The best place to investigate the properties of the humble olive – if you thought that organic, single-estate, cold-pressed, extra-virgin olive oil was as good as it gets, this Mediterranean deli goes a step further with its olive-oil preserves, soaps and face-creams, not to mention Portuguese sea-salt and Provençal herbs. Mon–Fri 11am–3pm & 4.30–9.30pm, Sat 11am–9pm, Sun 1–9pm.

Papabubble c/Ample 28, Barri Gòtic ☎ 932 688 625, ⓦ papabubble.com; ⓜ Drassanes; map p.44. Groovy young things rolling out home-made candy to a chill-out soundtrack. Come and watch them at work, sample a sweetie, and take home a gorgeously wrapped gift. Mon–Fri 10am–2pm & 4–8.30pm, Sat 10am–8.30pm.

Reserva Ibérica Rambla de Catalunya 61, Dreta de l'Eixample ☎ 902 112 641, ⓦ reservaiberica.com;

ⓜ Passeig de Gràcia; map p.102. A ham wonderland specializing in "jamón ibérico de bellota", the finest of all of the Spanish cured hams, which comes from acorn-fed pigs. Pick up pre-packaged samplers or tuck into a plate of paper-thin slices at one of the marble-topped tables. Mon–Sat 9.30am–9pm.

WINE

Vila Viniteca c/dels Agullers 7, La Ribera ☎ 937 777 017, ⓦ vilaviniteca.es; ⓜ Barceloneta; map p.68. A very knowledgeable specialist in Catalan and Spanish wines. Pick your vintage and then nip over the road for the gourmet deli part of the operation. Mon–Sat 8.30am–8.30pm (July & Aug closes Sat at 2pm).

MARKETS

Antiques Av. de la Catedral, Barri Gòtic; ⓜ Jaume I; harbourside, Port Vell; ⓜ Barceloneta. The weekly antiques market outside the cathedral is quite a spectacle but attracts high prices. Better for bargains is the weekend market on the Port Vell harbourside. Cathedral market every Thurs from 10am, closed Aug; harbourside market Sat & Sun from 10am.

Art Pl. Sant Josep Oriol, Barri Gòtic; ⓜ Liceu. The square is filled with stalls and easels every weekend from 11am, with local artists banging out still-lifes, harbour views, and so on.

Christmas Av. de la Catedral and surrounding streets, Barri Gòtic; ⓜ Jaume I. Traditional decorations, gifts, Christmas trees and more at the annual Fira de Santa Llúcia (ⓦ firadesantallucia.cat). Dec 1–22 daily 10.30am–8.30pm.

Coins, books and postcards Mercat Sant Antoni, Ronda de Sant Antoni, El Raval; ⓜ Sant Antoni. The rare coin and secondhand/antiquarian book stalls around Sant Antoni market are also good for posters, trading cards and comic collectables. Sun 8.30am–2pm.

Coins and stamps Pl. Reial, Barri Gòtic; ⓜ Liceu.

Specialist coin and stamp dealers and collectors do regular weekend battle under the arcades of Barcelona's most emblematic old-town square. Sun 10am–2pm.

Farmers' market Pl. del Pi, Barri Gòtic; ⓜ Liceu. Specializes in honey, cheese, cakes and other produce. Also takes place during the Festa de la Mercè (Sept), and the Festa de Sant Ponç in c/de l'Hospital (May 11). First and third Fri–Sun of the month.

Flea market Els Encants, Av. Meridiana 69, Glòries; ⓜ Glòries/Encants. The most entertaining place to trawl through old clothes, jewellery, antiques, junk and furniture is the city's oldest flea market (see p.122), which is now in its shiny (literally) new home on the southwest side of Pl. de les Glòries Catalanes. Every Mon, Wed, Fri & Sat 9am–8pm, plus Dec 1–Jan 5 Sun 9am–3pm.

Flowers Ramblas, between Pl. de Catalunya and Mercat de la Boqueria; ⓜ Liceu; Mercat de la Concepció, c/de Valencia, Dreta de l'Eixample, ⓜ Passeig de Gràcia. The Ramblas flower stalls always put on a pretty show, but locals are more likely to do serious flower and plant shopping at the Mercat de la Concepció.

MUSEUMS, GALLERIES AND ATTRACTIONS

L'Aquàrium Moll d'Espanya, Port Vell ⓦ aquariumbcn.com; ⓜ Drassanes or Barceloneta; map p.79. A fish-related extravaganza, from the mundane (T-shirts, stationery, posters, games, toiletries) to cult must-haves (Mariscal-designed bathroom transfers). Daily: July & Aug 9.30am–11pm; Sept–June 9.30am–9pm, until 9.30pm at weekends.

CosmoCaixa c/Issac Newton 26, Tibidabo ⓦ obrasocial.lacaixa.es; FGC Av. del Tibidabo; map p.138. The shop in the science museum is the place to buy space jigsaws, planet mobiles, model lunar-rovers, dinosaur kits, star charts and natural history books. Tues–Sun 10am–8.30pm.

Fundació Joan Miró Parc Montjuïc, Montjuïc ⓦ miroshop.com; ⓜ Espanya; map p.87. The artist's mark is on most everything, from bibs and beakers to watches and necklaces. July–Sept Tues–Sat 10am–9.30pm, Sun & hols 10am–2.30pm; Oct–June Tues–Sat 10am–7pm.

Museu d'Art Contemporani de Barcelona Pl. dels Àngels, El Raval ⓦ macba.cat; ⓜ Universitat; map pp.58–59. Designer aprons, espresso cups, T-shirts, posters, gifts and toys, plus art and design books. Mon & Wed–Sat 10am–8pm, Sun & hols 10am–3pm.

21

MADE IN BARCELONA

The world owes Barcelona, big time. For a start, in the fashion world there are the global brands **Mango** (women's clothes), **Camper** (shoes) and **Custo** (designer T-shirts), each of which started out in the city. Suitably togged up, you don't just drink a beer here, it's an **Estrella Damm** (tagline, the "beer of Barcelona"), a brew that sponsors everything from the Primavera Sound rock festival to America's Cup yacht racing. And then there are **Chupa Chups** (from the Spanish *chupar*, to lick), the lolly on a stick invented by one Enric Bernat in 1958 – Salvador Dalí, no less, designed the company logo. Kojak in the 1970s TV series wouldn't be seen without one, and Chupa Chups even made it aboard the *Mir* space station. Meanwhile, radical poet, publisher and inventor Alejandro Finisterre (admittedly, born in Galicia) was convalescing outside Barcelona after a bomb injury suffered during the Civil War, when he first came up with the idea for the game of **table football** (*bar football, foosball*). He took out a patent in Barcelona in 1937 and, though there are competing claims, is often regarded as the man subsequently responsible for endless hours wasted in bars worldwide.

MUSIC

Casa Beethoven Ramblas 97 ☎ 933 014 826; Ⓜ Liceu; map p.38. Wonderful old shop selling sheet music, CDs and music reference books – classical, but also rock, jazz and flamenco. Mon–Fri 9am–2pm & 4–8pm, Sat 9am–2pm & 5–8pm; closed Aug.

Discos Paradiso c/de Ferlandina 39, El Raval ☎ 933 296 440, ⓦ discosparadiso.com; Ⓜ Universitat; map pp.58–59. A vinyl-lover's paradise, especially for those with a penchant for electronic music. Techno, dubstep and house aside, there are plenty of offerings for indie, funk and world music fans as well. Mon–Sat 11am–9pm.

Revólver Records c/dels Tallers 11, El Raval ☎ 934 126 248, ⓦ revolverrecords.es; Ⓜ Catalunya; map pp.58–59. Revólver sells the city's best selection of vinyl at the lowest prices. Defiantly old-school, it's a record shop like they used to make them. Next door to its near-identically named but separately run sister shop, Discos Revólver. Mon–Sat 10am–8.30pm.

★**Wah Wah Discos** c/de la Riera Baixa 14, El Raval ☎ 934 423 703, ⓦ www.wah-wahsupersonic.com; Ⓜ Liceu; map pp.58–59. Vinyl heaven for record collectors – rock, indie, garage, 1970s punk, electronica, blues, folk, prog, jazz, soul and rarities of all kinds. Mon–Sat 11am–2pm & 5–8.30pm.

SPORTS

Botiga del Barça FC Barcelona, Camp Nou, Les Corts ☎ 934 923 111, ⓦ fcbarcelona.es; Ⓜ Collblanc/Palau Reial; map pp.130–131. For official merchandise the stadium megastore has it all – including that all-important lettering service for the back of the shirt that elevates you to the squad. Mon–Sat 10am–7pm, Sun 10.30am–3pm, match days until kick-off.

Decathlon c/de la Canuda 20, at Pl. Vila de Madrid, Barri Gòtic ☎ 933 426 161, ⓦ decathlon.es; Ⓜ Catalunya; map p.44. They've got clothes and equipment for 63 sports in the old-town megastore, so you're bound to find what you want. Also bike rental and repair. Mon–Sat 9.30am–9.30pm.

TOYS, MAGIC, COSTUME AND PARTY WEAR

★**Almacen Marabi** c/dels Flassaders 30, La Ribera, no phone ⓦ almacenmarabi.blogspot.com; Ⓜ Jaume I; map p.68. Mariela Marabi, originally from Argentina, makes handmade felt finger-dolls, mobiles, puppets and animals of extraordinary invention. She's often at work at the back, while her eye-popping workshop also has limited-edition pieces by other selected artists and designers. Tues–Sat noon–2.30pm & 5–8.30pm.

Drap c/del Pi 14, Barri Gòtic ☎ 933 181 487, ⓦ drap miniatures.blogspot.com.es; Ⓜ Liceu; map p.44. *Everything* is in miniature in this extraordinary dolls'-house outfitters – asking for a set of bedroom furniture hardly stretches the talents of a place that can fit out a minuscule dentist's surgery or a complete art gallery. Mon–Sat 10am–2pm & 4.30–8pm.

★**El Ingenio** c/d'en Rauric 6–8, Barri Gòtic ☎ 933 177 138, ⓦ el-ingenio.com; Ⓜ Liceu; map p.44. Juggling, magic and street-performer shop with a *modernista* storefront. It's also the place to come for carnival costumes and masks, made in the workshop on the premises. Mon–Fri 10am–1.30pm & 4.15–8pm, Sat 10am–2pm & 5–8.30pm.

El Rey de la Màgia c/de la Princesa 11, Sant Pere ☎ 933 193 920, ⓦ elreydelamagia.com; Ⓜ Jaume I; map p.68. Spain's oldest magic shop contains all the tricks of the trade, from rubber chickens to Dracula capes. They also have an associated magic school and theatre, with events and performances posted on the website. Mon–Fri 11am–2pm & 5–8pm, Sat 11am–2pm.

Children's Barcelona

Taking your children to Barcelona doesn't pose insurmountable travel problems. On the whole, once you're happily ensconced, and have cracked the transport system, you'll find that your children will be given a warm welcome almost everywhere you go. There's plenty to do, whether it's a day at the beach or a daredevil cable-car ride, while if you coincide with one of Barcelona's festivals, you'll be able to join in with the local celebrations, from sweet-tossing and puppet shows to fireworks and human castles. "Children's attractions" rounds up the best of the options for keeping everybody happy; sporting events and outdoor activities might also appeal (see p.221). For plenty more ideas, check out the English-language resource and support site ⓦkidsinbarcelona.com, which is packed with information on everything from safe play areas to babysitting services.

22

PUBLIC TRANSPORT

The metro and FGC With very young children, the main problem is using public transport, especially the metro, which seems almost expressly designed to thwart access for push-chairs and buggies. Most stations are accessed by stairs or escalators, and there are steps and stairs within the system itself – you often face a stiff climb out of stations with the pushchair. However, the stations on lines 1 and 2 – including Universitat, Catalunya, Pg. de Gràcia and Sagrada Família

– are accessible by lift from street level, and many FGC stations have lifts to the platforms, too, including Espanya (for Montserrat trains) and Av. del Tibidabo (for Tibidabo).
Buses All city buses have been adapted for wheelchair access and so have room to handle a buggy.
Tickets Children under 4 travel free on public transport, while there are reduced prices for tickets on the sightseeing Bus Turístic and the cable cars.

PRODUCTS, CLOTHES AND SERVICES

Products Disposable nappies (diapers), baby food, formula milk and other standard items are widely available in pharmacies and supermarkets, though not necessarily with the same range or brands that you will be used to at home. Organic baby food is getting easier to come by, though it's best to look in health-food stores rather than supermarkets – and most Spanish nonorganic baby foods contain small amounts of sugar or salt.
Clothing For relatively cheap, well-made babies' and children's clothing, Prénatal (ⓦ prenatal.es) has an excellent range, and there are branches all over the city. Chicco (branches at Diagonal Mar and La Maquinista shopping centres; ⓦ www.chicco.es) is the place for baby and toddler clothes and gear. Or go to Galeries Malda (c/de

la Portaferrissa 22, Barri Gòtic) or El Corte Inglés (see p.231) for more children's and babies' clothes.
Services Most establishments are baby-friendly in the sense that you'll be made very welcome if you turn up with a child in tow. Many museum cloakrooms, for example, will be happy to look after your pushchair as you carry your child around the building, while restaurants will make a fuss of your little one. However, specific facilities are not as widespread as they are in the UK or US. Baby-changing areas are relatively rare, except in department stores and shopping centres, and even where they do exist they are not always up to scratch. By far the best is at El Corte Inglés, though most major shopping centres now have pull-down changing tables in their public toilets.

RESTAURANTS, ACCOMMODATION AND BABYSITTING

Restaurants Local restaurants tend not to offer children's menus (though they will try to accommodate specific requests), highchairs are rarely provided and restaurants open relatively late for lunch and dinner. Despite best intentions, you might find yourself eating in one of the international franchise restaurants, which tend to be open throughout the day.
Accommodation Suitable accommodation is easy to find, and most hotels and *pensions* will be welcoming. However, bear in mind that much of the city's budget accommodation is located in buildings without lifts; if you're travelling out of

season, it's worth noting that some older-style *pensions* don't have heating systems – and it can get cold. If you want a cot provided, or baby-listening and -sitting services, the larger hotels may be better – though always check in advance about facilities. Renting an apartment is often a good idea as you'll get a kitchen and a bit more space for the kids to play in.
Babysitting You'll pay from around €10–15/hr for babysitting if arranged through your hotel; or contact Tender Loving Canguros (from €9/hr, plus fee; enquiries Mon–Sat 9am–9pm; ☎ 647 605 989, ⓦ tlcanguros.com), whose nannies and babysitters all speak English.

CHILDREN'S ATTRACTIONS

If you've spent too much time already in the showpiece museums, galleries and churches, any of the suggestions below should head off a children's revolt. **Admission charges** are almost always reduced for children, though the cut-off age varies from attraction to attraction.

CINEMA, SHOWS AND THEATRE
Cinema Children's film sessions are held at the FilmoTeca (see p.208), Sat 5pm & Sun 4.30pm, admission €3. Phenomena Experience (see p.208) also regularly shows classic kids' movies in English.
Font Màgica The sound-and-light show in front of the Palau Nacional on Montjuïc (see p.89) is always a hit, though it starts quite late.
Magic shows The magic shop, El Rey de la Màgia (see p.234), has weekend magic shows (Sat 6pm, Sun noon &

6pm; €12–15), with an hour of magic plus a visit to the shop's magic museum.
Theatre There are often children's puppet shows, music, mime and clowns at the Fundació Joan Miró (see p.95), usually at weekends and holidays. Jove Teatre Regina (c/de Sèneca 22, Gràcia; ☎ 932 181 512, ⓦ jtregina.com; ⓜ Diagonal) also puts on music and comedy productions for children (Sat & Sun 6pm; adult admission €10.90, includes children). Children's activities are also held at the Pati Llimona on c/Regomir near the Town Hall (Ajuntament) in Pl. Sant Jaume (ⓦ patillimona.net).

MUSEUMS, GALLERIES AND ATTRACTIONS

L'Aquàrium Adults might find the Aquarium disappointing, but there's no denying its popularity with children. Under-3s get in free, and there are discounts for 4- to 10-year-olds (see p.80).

Museums Most of the major museums and galleries run children's activity programmes, especially in school holidays. The "Niños" section in the weekly *Guía del Ocio* magazine lists the possibilities, from art and craft workshops at the Fundació Joan Miró and MACBA to chocolate-making at the Museu de la Xocolata. Museums with a special interest for children include Museu Blau (see p.84), CosmoCaixa science museum (see p.137), Museu del Futbol, FC Barcelona (see p.132), Museu d'Història de Barcelona (see p.50), Museu de Cera, wax museum (see p.42), Museu Marítim (see p.77) and Museu del Mamut, mammoth museum (see p.72).

Parc Zoològic All the usual suspects, plus children's zoo and dolphin shows; free for under-3s, discounts for under-12s (see p.75).

Poble Espanyol Open-air "museum" of Spanish buildings, craft demonstrations, gift shops and restaurants. Family ticket available (see p.89).

PARKS AND GARDENS

Gardens Top choice is the Parc del Laberint in Horta (see p.128), where the hillside gardens, maze and playground provide a great day out. For a city-centre surprise, seek out the Jardins de la Torre de les Aigües, c/Roger de Llúria 56, Dreta de l'Eixample (see p.106), which from the end of June to the end of August transform from an urban garden into a beach, complete with sand and paddling pool.

Parks Parc de la Ciutadella has the best range of attractions, with a boating lake and a zoo. Older children will love the bizarre gardens and buildings of Gaudí's Park Güell, while the Parc del Collserola is a good target for a walk in the hills and a picnic. At Parc del Castell de l'Oreneta (daily 10am–dusk), behind Pedralbes monastery, there are miniature train rides and pony rides on Sundays and public holidays (not Aug); it's at the end of c/de Montevideo (take bus #66 from Pl. Catalunya or #64 from Pl. Universitat to the end of the line and walk up Av. d'Espasa).

Playgrounds Most city kids use the squares as playgrounds, under parental supervision. In Gràcia, Pl. de la Virreina and Pl. de Rius i Taulet are handsome traffic-free spaces with good bars with attached *terrasses*. Wherever your children play, however, you need to keep an eagle eye out for dog dirt. In the old town, the nicest dog- and traffic-free playground is in Pl. de Vicenç Martorell, in El Raval, where there are some fenced-off swings in front of a great café, *Kasparo* (see p.180). Parc del Fòrum, at Diagonal Mar, also has a good children's playground and lots of other child-oriented attractions.

RIDES AND VIEWS

Cable-cars The two best rides in the city are the cross-harbour cable-car from Barceloneta to Montjuïc (see p.78), and the Telefèric de Montjuïc (see p.88), which then takes you up to the castle at the top of Montjuïc. Neither is for the faint-hearted child or sickly infant.

Las Golondrinas Sightseeing boat rides around the port and local coast (see p.25).

Mirador de Colom See the city from the top of the Columbus statue at the bottom of the Ramblas (see p.77).

Torre de Collserola Stunning views from the telecommunications tower near Tibidabo. Under-3s go free (see p.139).

THEME PARKS

Catalunya en Miniatura Torrelles de Llobregat, 17km southwest of Barcelona (A2 highway, exit 5) ☎ 936 890 960, ⌨ catalunyaenminiatura.com. A theme park with 170 Catalan monuments in miniature, plus mini-train rides, children's shows and playground. March–June & Sept daily 10am–6pm; July & Aug daily 10am–7pm; Oct–Jan Tues– Sun 10am–6pm. Admission €13.50, under-12s €9.50, under-3s free.

Illa Fantasia Vilassar de Dalt, 25km north of Barcelona, just short of Mataró (exit 92 on the main highway) ☎ 937 514 553, ⌨ illafantasia.com. Supposedly the largest water park in Europe, with slides, splash pools, swimming pools, water games and picnic areas. Buy a combined ticket (*billete combinado*) at Barcelona Sants station and you can travel free on the train to Premià de Mar, and then take the free connecting bus to the park. Admission €26, children under 1.2m high €16.50, children under 90cm high free. June to mid-Sept daily 10am–6pm.

Port Aventura 1hr south of Barcelona, near Salou and La Pineda (exit 35 on A7) ☎ 902 202 220, ⌨ portaventura.es. Universal Studios' massive theme park is based on five different cultures – Mexico, the Wild West, Polynesia, China and the Mediterranean – and also features the Costa Caribe water adventure park. There are five on-site hotels, a beach club, shops, restaurants and shows, as well as fairground rides (including the highest rollercoaster in Europe). Two-day (€56, under-10s €48) and three-day/two-park (€79, under-10s €63) combination tickets offer the best value. Renfe trains from Pg. de Gràcia/Barcelona Sants run directly to Port Aventura's own station (1hr 25min; ⌨ renfe.com), or the park is just 15min from Reus airport. Daily April–Oct 10am–7/8pm (July & Aug until midnight); Nov–Dec Sat & Sun only 10am–7/8pm.

Tibidabo Dubbed "La Muntanya Mágica", the rides and shows in the mountain-top amusement park (see p.137) are unbeatable as far as location goes, though tame compared with those at Port Aventura.

22

DETAIL FROM THE MIRADOR DE COLOM

Contexts

History

Catalan cultural identity can be traced back as far as the ninth century, when a powerful dynastic entity, dominated by Barcelona and commonly known as the Crown of Aragón, emerged from the quilt of independent polities of the eastern Pyrenees. It developed over the next six hundred years, before its merger with Castile-León in the late 1400s led to eventual inclusion in the new Spanish empire of the sixteenth century – which marked the decline of Catalan independence and its eventual subjugation to Madrid. Catalunya has rarely been a willing subject, and local yearning for social and cultural divorce from the rest of Spain remains deeply ingrained.

Early civilizations

During the **Upper Paleolithic** period (35,000–10,000 BC), cave-dwelling hunter-gatherers lived in parts of the Pyrenees, and **dolmens**, or stone burial chambers, from around 5000 BC still survive. Although no habitations from this period have been discovered, huts of some sort were erected, and farming had certainly begun. By the start of the **Bronze Age** (around 2000 BC), the Pyrenean people had started to move into fortified villages in the coastal lowlands.

The first of many successive **invasions** of the region came some time after 1000 BC, when the Celtic "urnfield people" crossed the Pyrenees and settled in the river valleys. These people lived side by side with indigenous Iberians, and the two groups are commonly, if erroneously, referred to as **Celtiberians**.

The foundation of Barcelona

The **Greeks** had established Mediterranean trading posts at Roses and Empúries by around 550 BC. Two centuries later, though, the coast and the rest of the peninsula were conquered by the North African **Carthaginians**, who founded **Barcino** (later Barcelona) in around 230 BC, probably on the heights of Montjuïc. The Carthaginians' famous commander, Hannibal, went on to cross the Pyrenees in 214 BC and attempted to invade Italy. However, the Second Punic War (218–201 BC) – much of which was fought in Catalunya – resulted in the expulsion of the Carthaginians from the Iberian peninsula in favour of the **Romans**, who made their new base at the former Carthaginian stronghold of Tarraco (Tarragona).

Roman Catalunya

The Roman colonization of the Iberian peninsula was far more intense than anything previously experienced and met with great resistance from the Celtic and Iberian tribes.

c.230 BC	218–201 BC	304 AD
Carthaginians found the settlement of "Barcino", probably on the heights of Montjuïc	Romans expel Carthaginians from Iberian peninsula in Second Punic War. Roman Barcino is established around today's Barri Gòtic	Santa Eulàlia – the city's patron saint – is martyred by Romans for refusing to renounce Christianity

> ## BARCINO – TARRAGONA'S LITTLE SISTER
>
> Barcelona does its best to champion its Roman remains, and the sketchy ruins of **Barcino** – or Colonia Julia Augusta Faventia Pia, as it was dubbed in 15 BC by the emperor Augustus – can be traced today in a walk around the Barri Gòtic, centred on the cathedral area (see box, p.50). However, Roman Barcino was always second best to the provincial capital of **Tarraco**, whose extremely fine monuments can still be seen in and around today's Tarragona. Imperial Tarraco (see p.153) was home for two years to Augustus himself, and boasted two forums, a theatre and a circus, plus temples and necropolises, not to mention an infrastructure of roads, bridges and aqueducts – much of which was used well into modern times.

It took almost two centuries for the conquest to be complete, by which time Spain had become the most important centre of the Roman Empire after Italy. During the first two centuries AD, the Spanish mines and the granaries of Andalucía brought unprecedented wealth, and **Roman Spain** enjoyed a period of stable prosperity in which Catalunya played an influential part. In Tarraco, Barcino and the other Roman towns, the inhabitants were granted full Roman citizenship; the former Greek settlements on the Costa Brava had meanwhile accepted Roman rule without difficulty, and experienced little interference in their day-to-day life.

By the third century AD, the Roman political framework was showing signs of decadence and corruption, and it became increasingly vulnerable to **barbarian invasions** from northern Europe. The Franks and the Suevi swept across the Pyrenees, sacking Tarraco in 262 and destroying Barcelona. Within two centuries Roman rule had ended, forced on the defensive by new waves of Suevi, Alans and Vandals, and finally superseded by the **Visigoths** from Gaul, former allies of Rome.

Visigothic Spain

The **Visigoths** established their first Spanish capital at Barcelona in 415. They went on to base themselves further south at Toledo, and build a kingdom that encompassed most of what is now Spain and southwestern France. Their triumph, however, was relatively short-lived. Ruling initially as a caste apart from the local people, with a distinct status and laws, the Visigoths lived largely as a warrior elite, and were further separated by their adherence to Arian Christianity, which was considered heretical by the Catholic Church. Under their domination, the economy and the quality of life in the former Roman towns declined, while plots and rivalries within their ranks pitted members of the ruling elite against each other.

Moorish conquest

Divisions within the Visigothic kingdom coincided with Islamic expansion in North Africa, which reached the shores of the Atlantic in the late seventh century. In 711, Tariq ibn Ziyad, governor of Tangier, led a force of several thousand troops across the Straits of Gibraltar and routed the Visigothic nobility. With no one to resist, the stage for the **Moorish conquest of Spain** was set. Within ten years, the Muslim Moors had advanced far to the north, destroying Tarragona and forcing Barcelona to surrender – although the

c.350	415	711
Roman city walls built as threat of invasion grows	Visigoths sweep across Spain and establish temporary capital in Barcino	Moorish conquest of Spain. Barcelona eventually forced to surrender (719)

more inaccessible parts of the Pyrenees retained their independence. In most places, the local population were granted limited autonomy in exchange for payment of tribute. There was no forced conversion to Islam, and Jews and Christians lived securely as second-class citizens. In areas of the peninsula that remained under direct Muslim power during the ninth century, a new ethnic group emerged: the **Mozarabs**, Christians who lived under Muslim rule, and adopted Arabic language, dress and social customs.

The Spanish Marches

Moorish raiding parties reached beyond the Pyrenees as far as Poitiers, where Charles Martel, the de facto ruler of Merovingian France, dealt them a minor defeat in 732 that convinced them to withdraw. Both Martel's son Pepin, and his famous grandson **Charlemagne** (768–814), pushed the invaders further back, with Charlemagne's empire including the southern slopes of the Pyrenees and much of Catalunya. After being ambushed and defeated by the Basques at Roncesvalles in 778, Charlemagne switched his attention to the Mediterranean side of the Pyrenees, attempting to defend his empire against the Muslims. He took Girona in 785 and his son Louis directed the successful siege of Barcelona in 801. With the capture of Barcelona, the Frankish counties of Catalunya became a sort of buffer zone, known as the **Spanish Marches**. Separate territories were established, each ruled by a count and theoretically owing allegiance to the Frankish king or emperor.

The birth of Catalunya

As the Frankish empire of Charlemagne disintegrated in the wake of his death, the counties of the Marches enjoyed greater independence, which was formalized in 878 by Guifré el Pelós – **Wilfred the Hairy**. Wilfred was count of Urgell and the Cerdagne and, after adding Barcelona to his holdings, named himself its first count, founding a dynastic line that was to rule until the 1400s. In the wake of the Muslim withdrawal from the area, **Christian outposts** had been established throughout Catalunya. Wilfred continued the process, founding Benedictine monasteries at Ripoll (about 880) and Sant Joan de les Abadesses (888), where his daughter was the first abbess.

Wilfred was followed by a succession of rulers who attempted to consolidate his gains. Early counts, like **Ramon Berenguer I** (1035–76), concentrated on establishing their superiority over the other local counts, which was bitterly resisted. **Ramon Berenguer III** (1144–66) added considerable territory to his realms with his marriage in 1113 to a Provençal heiress, and made alliances and commercial treaties with Muslim and Christian powers around the western Mediterranean.

The most important stage in Catalunya's development, however, came in 1137 with the marriage of **Ramon Berenguer IV** to Petronella, the 2-year-old daughter of King Ramiro II of Aragón. This led to the **dynastic union of Catalunya and Aragón**. Although this remained a loose and tenuous federation – the regions retained their own parliaments and customs – it provided the platform for rapid expansion over the next three centuries. Ramon also managed to force most of the other counts to recognize his superior status, and subsequently issued the **Usatges de Barcelona**, a code of laws and customs defining feudal duties, rights and authorities – and sneakily put Ramon I's name on them to make

801	878	985
Barcelona retaken by Louis the Pious, son of Charlemagne. Frankish counties of Catalunya become a buffer zone, known as the Spanish Marches	Guifré el Pelós (Wilfred the Hairy) declared first Count of Barcelona, founding a dynastic line that rules until 1410	Moorish sacking of city. Sant Pau del Camp – city's oldest surviving church – built after this date

them appear older than they were. He also captured Muslim Tortosa and Lleida in 1148–49, which mark the limits of the modern region of Catalunya. Now, however, the region began to look east for its future, across the Mediterranean.

The Kingdom of Catalunya and Aragón

Ramon Berenguer IV was no more than a count, but his son **Alfons I**, who succeeded to the throne in 1162, also inherited the title of King of Aragón (where he was Alfonso II), and became the first count-king of what historians later came to call the **Crown of Aragón**. To his territories he added Roussillon and much of southern France, becoming known as "Emperor of the Pyrenees".

Alfons's son in turn, Pere (Peter) the Catholic, gained glory as one of the military leaders in the decisive defeat of Muslim forces at the **Battle of Las Navas de Tolosa** in 1212. Through his ties of lordship to the French counts of Toulouse, however, Pere found himself on the wrong side in the Albigensian wars (the Catholic Church's crusade against the Cathar heresy), and he was killed a year later. These were uncertain times in Catalunya, but a golden age was about to dawn.

Jaume I

Pere was succeeded by his 5-year-old son, **Jaume I** (1213–76), whose extraordinary reign started unpromisingly when he was initially entrusted to the care of the Knights Templar while his crown was disputed by rival counts. Shrugging off the tutelage of his Templar masters at the age of 13, Jaume personally took to the field to tame his rebellious nobles, before embarking on a series of campaigns of conquest, which brought him Muslim Mallorca in 1229, Menorca in 1231 and Ibiza in 1235. Next he turned south and conquered the city of Valencia in 1238, establishing a new kingdom of which he was also ruler. Recognizing Catalunya's future lay in **Mediterranean expansion**, Jaume signed the **Treaty of Corbeil** in 1258, renouncing his rights in France (except for Montpellier, the Cerdagne and Roussillon), in return for the French king Louis' renunciation of claims in Catalunya.

Catalan expansion

On Jaume's death, his kingdom was divided between his sons, one of whom, **Pere II** ("the Great"), took Catalunya, Aragón and Valencia. Connected through marriage to the Sicilian Crown, Pere used the 1282 "Sicilian Vespers" rising against Charles of Anjou to press his claim to the island. In August that year, Pere was crowned in Palermo, and Sicily became the base for Catalan exploits throughout the Mediterranean. Catalan mercenaries, the **almogávares**, took Athens and Neopatras between 1302 and 1311, and famous sea-leaders-cum-pirates such as Roger de Flor and Roger de Llúria fought in the name of the Catalan-Aragónese Crown. Malta (1283), Corsica (1323), Sardinia (1324) and Naples (1423) all fell under the influence of successive count-kings.

Barcelona's medieval mercantile class were quick to see the possibilities of Mediterranean commerce. Maritime customs were codified in the so-called *Llibre del Consolat de Mar*, trade relations were established with North Africa and the Middle East, and Catalan became used as a trading language throughout the Mediterranean.

1137	1213–76	1282–1387	1348
Dynastic union of Catalunya and Aragón established	Reign of Jaume I, "the Conqueror", expansion of empire and beginning of Catalan golden age	Barcelona at centre of a Mediterranean empire. Successive rulers construct most of Barcelona's best-known Gothic buildings	Black Death strikes, killing half of Barcelona's population

CATALAN ROOTS

During the ninth century, conflicting loyalties in the territories of the Spanish Marches sparked the construction of many local fortifications to protect and control the population. That led to the term *catlá* ("lord of the castle") being used to refer to the people of the area – the root of today's "**Catalan**" (Castilian has an analogous root). At around the same time, spoken Latin had taken on geographical particularities, as happened across much of the former Roman Empire, and the "Romance" languages, including Catalan, had begun to develop. A document from 839 recording the consecration of the cathedral at La Seu d'Urgell in the Pyrenees is seen as the first Catalan-language historical document.

Catalunya in the golden age

Catalunya's first parliament, the **Corts** – one of the earliest such bodies in Europe – was established during Jaume I's reign, while in 1249, the first governors of Barcelona were elected, nominating councillors to help them who became known as the Consell de Cent. 1289 saw the first recorded meeting of a body that became known as the **Generalitat**, a sort of committee of the Corts. Within it were represented each of the three traditional estates – commons, nobility and clergy – and the Generalitat gradually became responsible for administering public order, justice and defence of the realm.

By the mid-fourteenth century Catalunya was at its economic peak. Barcelona had impressive new buildings to match its status as a regional superpower – the cathedral, the church of Santa María del Mar, the Generalitat building, the Ajuntament (with its Consell de Cent meeting room) and the Drassanes shipyards all testify to Barcelona's wealth in this period. Catalan became established as a **literary language**, and Catalan works are recognized as precursors of much of the great medieval literature of Europe: Ramon Llull's romance *Blanquerna* was written a century before Chaucer's *Canterbury Tales*. **Architecture** progressed from Romanesque to Gothic styles, with churches displaying features that have become known as Catalan-Gothic, including spacious naves, hexagonal belfries and a lack of flying buttresses.

The rise of Castile

The last of Wilfred the Hairy's dynasty of Catalan count-kings, Martin the Humane (Martí el Humà), died in 1410 without an heir. After nearly five hundred years of continuity, there were six claimants to the succession, and in 1412 nine specially appointed counsellors elevated Ferdinand (Ferran) de Antequera, son of a Catalan princess, to the vacant throne.

Ferdinand ruled for only four years, but his reign and that of his son, Alfons, and grandson, John (Joan) II, spelled the end of Catalunya's influence in the Mediterranean. The Castilian rulers were soon in dispute with the Consell de Cent, and non-Catalans started to be appointed to key positions in the Church, state offices and the armed forces. In 1469 John's son, Prince Ferdinand (Ferran), who was born in Aragón, married Isabel of Castile, a union that would eventually finish off Catalan independence. Both came into their inheritances quickly, Isabel taking Castile in 1474 and the Catalan-Aragónese Crown coming to Ferdinand in 1479.

1391	1410	1469	1479
Pogrom against the city's Jewish population	Death of Martí el Humà (Martin the Humane), last of Catalan count-kings. Beginning of the end of Catalan influence in the Mediterranean	Marriage of Ferdinand of Aragón and Isabel of Castile	Ferdinand succeeds to Catalan-Aragónese Crown. Inquisition introduced to Barcelona, leading to forced flight of the Jews

---

THE INQUISITION IN CATALUNYA

The Catholic monarchs, Ferdinand and Isabel, shared in the religious bigotry of their contemporaries, although Isabel, under the influence of her personal confessor, Tomás de Torquemada, was the more reactionary of the two. In Catalunya, the **Inquisition** was established in 1487, and aimed to purify the Catholic faith by rooting out heresy. It was directed mainly at the secret **Jews**, most of whom had been converted by force after the pogrom of 1391 to Christianity. Their descendants, known as **New Christians**, were suspected of practising their former faith in secret, and in 1492, an edict forced some seventy thousand Jews to flee the country. The Jewish population in Barcelona was completely eradicated in this way, while communities elsewhere – principally in Girona, Tarragona and Lleida – were massively reduced, and those who remained were forced to convert to Christianity.

Ferdinand and Isabel

Under **Ferdinand and Isabel**, the two largest kingdoms in Spain were united under a ruling pair known as **"Los Reyes Católicos"** ("Els Reis Catòlics" in Catalan) – the Catholic monarchs. Devoting their energies to the reconquest and unification of Spain, they finally took back Granada from the Moors in 1492, and initiated a wave of Christian fervour with the **Inquisition** at its heart.

In 1493, the final shift in Catalunya's outlook occurred with the triumphal return of **Christopher Columbus** from the New World, to be received in Barcelona by Ferdinand and Isabel. Castile, like Portugal, looked away from the Mediterranean to the Americas for trade and conquest, and the exploration and exploitation of the New World was spearheaded by the Andalucían city of Seville. Meanwhile, Ferdinand gave the Supreme Council of Aragón control over Catalan affairs in 1494. The Aragonese nobility, who had always resented the success of the Catalan maritime adventures, now saw the chance to complete their control of Catalunya by taking over its ecclesiastical institutions; Catalan monks were thrown out of the great monasteries of Poblet and Montserrat.

Habsburg rule

Charles I, a **Habsburg**, came to the throne in 1516 as a beneficiary of the marriage alliances made by the Catholic monarchs. Five years later he was elected emperor of the **Holy Roman Empire** (as Charles V), inheriting not only Castile, Aragón and Catalunya, but also Flanders, the Netherlands, Artois, the Franche-Comté and all the American colonies. With such responsibilities, attention was inevitably diverted from Spain, whose chief function became to sustain the Holy Roman Empire with gold and silver from the Americas. It was during this era that Madrid was established as capital city of the Spanish empire, and the long rivalry began between Madrid and Barcelona.

Throughout the **sixteenth century**, Catalunya continued to suffer under the Inquisition. Deprived of trading opportunities in the Americas, it became impoverished. Habsburg wars wasted the lives of Catalan soldiers, banditry increased, and the poverty of the mass of the population was a source of perpetual tension.

1493	1516	1640–52
Christopher Columbus received in Barcelona after triumphant return from New World	Spanish Crown passes to Habsburgs and Madrid is established as capital of Spanish empire	Uprising known as "War of the Reapers" declares Catalunya an independent republic. Barcelona besieged and surrenders to Spanish army

With Spain and France at war in 1635, the Catalans took advantage of the situation and revolted, declaring themselves an independent republic under the protection of the French King Louis XIII. This, the **War of the Reapers** – after the marching song *Els Segadors* ("The Reapers"), later the Catalan national anthem – ended in 1652 with the surrender of Barcelona to the Spanish army. The **Treaty of the Pyrenees** in 1659 finally split the historical lands of Catalunya, as the Spanish lost control of Roussillon and part of the Cerdagne to France.

Bourbon repression

In 1700, when the Habsburg king Charles II died heirless, France's Louis XIV saw an opportunity to fulfil his longtime ambition of putting a **Bourbon** (*Borbón* in Castilian, *Borbó* in Catalan) on the Spanish throne. He secured the succession of his grandson, Philippe d'Anjou, on the condition that Philippe renounced his rights to the throne of France. This deal put a Bourbon on the throne of Spain, but led to war with the other claimant, Archduke Charles of Austria: the resulting **War of the Spanish Succession** lasted thirteen years from 1701, with Catalunya lining up on the Austrian side (along with England) in an attempt to regain its ancient rights.

However, the **Treaty of Utrecht** in 1714 gave the throne to the Bourbon Philippe, now **Philip V** of Spain, and initiated a fresh period of repression from which the Catalans took a century to recover. Barcelona lay under siege for over a year, and with its eventual capitulation a fortress was built at Ciutadella to subdue the city's inhabitants – the final defeat, on September 11, is still commemorated every year as a Catalan holiday, **La Diada**. The university at Barcelona was closed, the Catalan language was banned, the Consell de Cent and Generalitat were abolished. In short, Catalunya was finished as even a partially autonomous region.

Napoleonic and Peninsular wars

When neighbouring France became aggressively expansionist following the Revolution of 1789, Spain was a natural target, first for the Revolutionary armies and later for the machinations of Napoleon. In 1805, during the **Napoleonic Wars**, the French fleet (along with the Spanish who had been forced into an alliance) was defeated at Trafalgar. Charles IV was forced to abdicate shortly afterwards, and Napoleon installed his brother Joseph on the throne three years later.

Attempting to broaden his appeal among Spain's subjects, the French emperor proclaimed a separate government of Catalunya – independent of Joseph's rule – with Catalan as its official language. The region's response was an indication of how far Catalunya had become integrated into Spain during the Bourbon period – despite their history the Catalans supported the Bourbon cause solidly during the ensuing **Peninsular War** (1808–14), ignoring Napoleon's blandishments. Girona was defended heroically from the French in a seven-month siege, while Napoleon did his cause no good at all by attacking and sacking the holy shrine and monastery at Montserrat. Fierce local resistance was eventually backed by the muscle of a British army, and the French were at last driven out.

1714	1755	1778
After War of Spanish Succession, Spanish throne passes to Bourbons. Barcelona finally subdued on September 11 (now Catalan National Day); Ciutadella fortress built	Barceloneta district laid out – gridded layout is early example of urban planning	Steady increase in trade with America; Barcelona's economy improves

The slow Catalan revival

Despite the political emasculation of Catalunya, the eighteenth century had seen signs of **economic revival**, not least as (from 1778) Catalunya was allowed to trade with the Americas for the first time. In this way, the shipping industry received a boost and Catalunya was able to export its textiles to a broader market.

After the Napoleonic Wars, Catalunya experienced **industrialization** on a scale like nowhere else in Spain. In the mid-nineteenth century, the country's first **railway** was built from Barcelona to Mataró, later to be extended south to Tarragona and north to Girona and the French border. **Manufacturing** industries encouraged a population shift from the land to the towns; Catalan olive oil production helped supply the whole country; and previously local industries flourished on a wider scale – for example, cava production was introduced in the late nineteenth century, supported closely by the age-old cork industry of the Catalan forests. From 1890, hydroelectric power was harnessed from the Pyrenees, and by the end of the century Barcelona was the fastest-growing city in Spain – one of only six with more than 100,000 inhabitants.

Cultural renaissance

The first stirrings of what became known as the **Renaixença** (Renaissance) came in the mid-nineteenth century. Despite being banned in official use and public life, the Catalan **language** had never died out. Books started to appear again in Catalan, and the language was revived among the bourgeoisie and intellectuals as a means of making subtle nationalist and political points. Catalan **poetry** became popular, and the late medieval **Jocs Florals** (Floral Games), a sort of literary competition, were revived in 1859 in Barcelona: one winner was the great Catalan poet, Jacint Verdaguer (1845–1902). Catalan **drama** developed (although even in the late nineteenth century there were still restrictions on performing wholly Catalan plays), led mainly by the dramatist Pitarra.

Prosperity led to the rapid **expansion of Barcelona**, particularly the mid-nineteenth-century addition to the city of the planned Eixample district. Encouraged by wealthy patrons and merchants, architects such as Josep Puig i Cadafalch, Lluís Domènech i Montaner and Antoni Gaudí i Cornet were in the vanguard of the **modernista** movement that changed the face of the city. Culture and business came together with the **Universal Exhibition** of 1888, based around the *modernista* buildings of the Parc de la Ciutadella, and later the **International Exhibition** on Montjuïc in 1929.

The seeds of civil war

In 1814, the repressive Ferdinand VII had been restored to the Spanish throne. Despite the Catalan contribution to the defeat of the French, he stamped out the least hint of liberalism in the region, abolishing virtually all Catalunya's remaining privileges. On his death, the crown was claimed both by his daughter Isabel II, with liberal support, and by his brother Charles, backed by the Church and the conservatives. The ensuing **First Carlist War** (1833–39) ended in victory for Isabel, who came of age in 1843. Her reign was a long record of scandal, political crisis and constitutional compromise, until liberal army generals under the leadership of General Prim eventually effected a coup in 1868,

1814	1848	1850	1859
After Peninsular War, French finally driven out, with Barcelona the last city to fall	Rapid expansion and industrialization	Plaça Reial – emblematic old-town square – is laid out	Old city walls demolished and Eixample district built to accommodate growing population

forcing Isabel to abdicate. However, the experimental **First Republic** (1873–75) failed, and following the **Second Carlist War** the throne passed to Isabel's son, Alfonso XII.

Against this unstable background, Catalan dissatisfaction increased and the years preceding World War I saw a growth in working-class **political movements**. Barcelona's textile workers organized a branch affiliated to the Communist First International, founded by Karl Marx, and the region's wine growers also banded together to seek greater security. Tension was further heightened by the **loss of Cuba** in 1898, which added to local economic problems, with returning soldiers seeking employment in cities where there was none.

Conflict in Barcelona

A call-up for army reserves to fight in Morocco in 1909 provoked a general strike and, at the end of July, a solid week of rioting in Barcelona, and then throughout Catalunya, in which over one hundred people died. Working-class Catalans objected violently to the suggestion that they should fight abroad for a state that did little for them at home, and Barcelona's streets saw the widespread burning of churches and other religious institutions – symbols of the power of the state that dominated their lives. Battle lines were drawn in the very name given to the disturbances – what to the rioters was a glorious "July revolution" came to be known by the nervous bourgeoisie as the **Tragic Week** (Setmana Tràgica). Mass arrests, executions and repression followed, as the rioters were put down, but seeds were sown as Catalan workers realized the need to be better organized. One direct result was the establishment of the Confederación Nacional del Trabajo – the **CNT** – in 1911, which included many previously unconnected Catalan working-class organizations.

World War I and the start of dictatorship

During **World War I** Spain was neutral, though inwardly turbulent since soaring inflation and the cessation of exports following the German blockade of the North Atlantic hit the country hard. As rumblings grew among the workers and political organizations, the army moved decisively, crushing a general strike in 1917. However, the situation did not improve. Violent strikes and assassinations plagued Barcelona, while the CNT and the union of the socialists, the CGT, both saw huge increases in membership.

In 1923, **General Primo de Rivera**, the captain-general of Catalunya, overthrew the national government in a military coup that had the full backing of the Catalan middle class, and established a dictatorship that at first enjoyed economic success. The general resigned in 1930, dying a few months later, but the hopes of some for the restoration of the monarchy's political powers were short-lived. The success of anti-monarchist parties in the municipal elections of 1931 led to the abdication of the king and the foundation of the **Second Republic**.

The Second Republic

In 1931, Catalunya, under Francesc Macià, leader of the Republican Left, declared itself to be an **independent republic**, and the Republican flag was raised over the Ajuntament in Barcelona. Madrid refused to accept the declaration, though a statute of limited autonomy was granted in 1932. Despite initial optimism, the government

1882	1888	1893	1900
Work begins on Sagrada Família; Antoni Gaudí takes charge two years later	Universal Exhibition held at Parc de la Ciutadella. *Modernista* architects start to make their mark	First stirrings of anarchist unrest. Liceu opera house bombed	Pablo Picasso's first public exhibition held at *Els Quatre Gats* tavern

failed to satisfy raised local expectations. **Anarchism** in particular gained adherents among the frustrated middle classes as well as among workers and peasantry. The **Communist Party** and the left-wing **socialists**, driven into alliance by their mutual distrust of the "moderate" socialists in government, were also forming a growing bloc. On the Right, the **Falangists** (founded in 1923 by José Antonio Primo de Rivera, son of the dictator) made uneasy bedfellows with conservative traditionalists and dissident elements in the army upset by modernizing reforms.

In this atmosphere of growing confusion, the left-wing **Popular Front** alliance, including the Catalan Republican Left, won the general election of January 1936 by a narrow margin, and an all-Republican government was formed. In Catalunya, **Lluís Companys** became president of the Generalitat. But with the economy crippled by strikes, the government singularly failed to exert its authority over anyone.

Finally, on July 17, 1936, the military garrison in Morocco rebelled under the leadership of **General Francisco Franco**, to be followed by uprisings at military garrisons throughout the country. Much of the south and west quickly fell into the hands of the Nationalists, but Madrid and the industrialized northeast remained loyal to the Republican government. In Barcelona, although the military garrison supported Franco, it was soon subdued by local Civil Guards and workers, while local leaders set up militias in preparation for the coming fight.

In October 1936, Franco was declared military commander and head of state; fascist Germany and Italy recognized his regime as the legitimate government of Spain in November. The Civil War was on.

Civil War

The **Spanish Civil War** (1936–39) was one of the most bitter and bloody the world has seen. Both sides visited violent reprisals on their enemies – the Republicans shooting priests and local landowners wholesale, and burning churches and cathedrals; the Nationalists carrying out mass slaughter of the population of almost every town they took. This was also the first modern war – Franco's German allies demonstrated their ability to inflict terror on civilian populations with bombing raids on Gernika and Durango, while radio became an important propaganda weapon, with Nationalists offering starving Republicans the "white bread of Franco".

Despite sporadic help from Russia and the 35,000 volunteers of the **International Brigades**, the Republic could never compete with the professional armies and the massive assistance from fascist Italy and Nazi Germany that the Nationalists enjoyed. Eventually, the nonintervention of other European governments effectively handed victory to the Nationalists. The Republican government fled Madrid first for Valencia, and then moved on to base itself at Barcelona in 1937. The **Battle of the Ebro** around Tortosa saw massive casualties on both sides; Nationalist troops advanced on Valencia in 1938, and from the west were also approaching Catalunya from their bases in Navarre. When Bilbao was taken by the Nationalists, the Republicans' fight on the **Aragón front** was lost. The final Republican hope, that war in Europe over Czechoslovakia would draw the Allies into a war against fascism, evaporated in September 1938 with the British Prime Minister Chamberlain's capitulation to Hitler at Munich. Instead, Franco was able to call on new arms and other supplies from Germany for a final offensive against Catalunya.

1909	**1922**	**1926**	**1929**
Setmana Trágica (Tragic Week) of rioting. Many churches destroyed	Park Güell opens to the public	Antoni Gaudí run over by a tram; Barcelona stops en masse for his funeral	International Exhibition held at Montjuïc

The **fall of Barcelona** came on January 25, 1939 – the Republican parliament held its last meeting at Figueres a few days later. Republican soldiers, cut off in the valleys of the Pyrenees, made their way across the high passes into France, joined by women and children fearful of a fascist victory. Among the refugees and escapees was **Lluís Companys**, president of the Generalitat, who was later captured in France by the Germans, and handed back to Spain. Under orders from Franco, he was shot at the castle prison on Montjuïc in 1940.

Catalunya in Franco's Spain

Although the Civil War left more than half a million dead, destroyed a quarter of a million homes and sent a third of a million people (including 100,000 Catalans) into exile, Franco was in no mood for reconciliation. With his government recognized by Allied powers, including Britain and France, he set up **war tribunals** that ordered executions and created concentration camps in which upwards of two million people were held until "order" had been established by authoritarian means.

The **Catalan language** was banned again, in schools, churches, the press and in public life; only one party was permitted; and censorship was rigorously enforced. The economy was in ruins, and Franco did everything possible to further the cause of Madrid against Catalunya, starving the region of investment and new industry. After **World War II**, during which the country was too weak to be anything but neutral, Spain was economically and politically isolated.

What saved Franco was the acceptance of **American aid**, offered on the condition that he provide land for US air bases. Prosperity increased after this, fuelled in the 1960s and 1970s by a growing tourist industry, but Catalunya (along with the Basque Country, another thorn in Franco's side) remained economically backward. Absentee landlords took much of the local revenue, a situation exacerbated by Franco's policy of encouraging emigration to Catalunya from other parts of Spain, and granting the immigrants land, in an attempt to dilute regional differences.

Despite the **cultural and political repression**, the distinct Catalan identity was never obliterated. The Catalan Church retained a feisty independence, while Barcelona emerged as the most important publishing centre in Spain. Clandestine language and history classes were conducted, and artists and writers continued to produce work in defiance of the authorities. Nationalism in Catalunya, however, did not take the same course as the Basque separatist movement. There was little violence against the state in Catalunya, and no serious counterpart emerged to the Basque terrorist organization ETA. The Catalan approach was subtler: an audience at the Palau de la Música sang the unofficial Catalan anthem when Franco visited in 1960; a massive petition against language restrictions was raised in 1963; and a sit-in by Catalan intellectuals at Montserrat was organized in protest against repression in the Basque Country.

Franco's death and the new democracy

When Franco died in 1975, **King Juan Carlos** was officially designated to succeed as head of state – approved by the powerful army and groomed for the succession by Franco himself. The king's initial moves were cautious in the extreme, though to his

1936–39	1939–75	1975
Spanish Civil War. Barcelona at heart of Republican cause, with George Orwell and other volunteers arriving to fight. City eventually falls to Nationalists in January 1939	Spain under Franco. Generalitat president Lluís Companys executed, Catalan language banned and Catalan identity threatened by Madrid	Death of General Franco, who is succeeded as head of state by King Juan Carlos

credit, Juan Carlos recognized that some real break with the past was inevitable, and, accepting the resignation of his prime minister, set in motion the process of **democratization**. His newly appointed prime minister, Adolfo Suárez, steered through a Political Reform Act, which allowed for a two-chamber parliament and a referendum in favour of democracy, and also legitimized the Socialist Party (the PSOE) and the Communists.

In the elections of 1977, the first since 1936, the **Pacte Democratico per Catalunya** – an alliance of pro-Catalan parties – gained ten seats in the lower house of the Spanish parliament, which was otherwise dominated by Suárez' own centre-right UCD party but also had a strong Socialist presence. In a spirit of consensus, it was announced that Catalunya was to be granted a degree of autonomy, and a million people turned out on the streets of Barcelona to witness the re-establishment of the Generalitat and welcome home its president-in-exile, **Josep Tarradellas**.

A new Spanish constitution of 1978 allowed for a sort of devolution within a unitary state, and the **Statute of Autonomy** for Catalunya was approved in 1979, with the first regional elections taking place in March 1980. The conservative **Jordi Pujol i Soley** and his coalition party **Convergència i Unió** (CiU) gained regional power – and proceeded to dominate the Catalan parliament for the next quarter of a century. In a way, the pro-conservative vote made it easy for the central government to deal with Catalunya, since Catalan demands for autonomy did not have the extreme political dimension seen in the Basque Country.

The 1980s and 1990s

Felipe González' PSOE was elected in 1982 with a massive swing to the left in a country that had for 43 years remained firmly in the hands of the political right; they were given a renewed mandate in 1986, the same year Spain joined the **European Community**. The country also decided by referendum to stay in NATO and boasted one of the fastest-growing economies in western Europe. Barcelona's successful hosting of the **1992 Olympic Games** brought the city to a global audience, galvanizing tourism and sparking development projects including the radical restoration of the old town and port areas. Narrow victories in two more elections kept the Socialists in power, but they failed to win an overall majority in 1993 and were forced to rely on the support of the Catalan nationalist coalition, CiU, to retain power. That state of affairs enabled Jordi Pujol to pursue long-cherished nationalist aims, in particular the right to retain a proportion of Catalunya's own income-tax revenue.

In the wake of allegations of sleaze and the disclosure of the existence of a secret "dirty war" against the Basque terrorists, it was no surprise that the PSOE lost the general election of 1996 to the conservative Partido Popular (PP), under **José María Aznar**. However, the PP came in well short of an outright majority, and Aznar was left with the same problem as his predecessor, relying on the Catalan nationalists and other smaller regionalist parties to maintain his party in power. A resounding victory in the national elections of 2000 finally enabled the PP to govern unconstrained by other parties, but Aznar swiftly lost his way, with ninety percent of Spaniards opposing his support for US and British **military action in Iraq** in 2003.

1977	1978–80	1992
First democratic Spanish elections for forty years	Generalitat re-established and Statute of Autonomy approved. Socialist mayor and municipal government elected (1979); Conservative nationalist government elected (1980)	Olympics held in Barcelona. Massive rebuilding projects transform Montjuïc and the waterfront

---

NO NUDES PLEASE, WE'RE CATALAN

Barcelona is one of Europe's most popular city-break destinations, but tourism has brought its own problems, as Barcelona has acquired a not-always-welcome reputation as a beach resort and party town. The roaming stag parties and antisocial late-night behaviour by visitors causes much hand-wringing at City Hall (and much street-hosing early each morning), while certain old-town areas are now virtual tourist-only zones for much of the year. The city council has banned resort-style behaviour on Barcelona's streets – you can take your shirt off, or walk around in swimwear on the beach or the beach promenade, but strolling up and down the Ramblas as if you're on the Costa del Sol is not tolerated by police. Even so, photographs such as those showing tourists on the Ramblas having sex with prostitutes (in 2009) or running naked through supermarkets (in 2014), continue to be splashed across the world's media.

The tables turned once again in 2004, when the PSOE were unexpectedly victorious in a general election shaped by the deaths of two hundred people in the Madrid **train bombings** of March 11. The Socialists took power in a minority administration led by PSOE prime minister **José Luis Rodríguez Zapatero**, forced to rely on parliamentary support from Catalan separatists and other regional parties. Spectacular economic growth ensued, and Zapatero and the PSOE were re-elected in 2008, though not quite enjoying an absolute majority.

The irresistible rise of Catalan nationalism

The current high profile of the campaign for **Catalan independence** owes much to the impact of the worldwide **economic recession** on Spain as a whole, from 2008 onwards. With his government's **austerity measures** growing increasingly unpopular, Zapatero called time on his leadership in April 2011, and the PP won a resounding victory in the snap election that followed. In its wake, PP prime minister Mariano Rajoy largely abandoned any pretence of seeking political accommodation with Catalunya, and growing numbers of Catalans have lost faith in a future within Spain.

Nationalist fervour has swept across the political spectrum, with those who support independence as a matter of political principle or historical identity finding common cause with those who believe the national austerity programme to have damaged social and economic justice in Catalunya, and others who feel the rest of Spain to be a financial drain on what might otherwise be a prosperous Catalunya.

One and a half million protesters took to Barcelona's streets on La Diada in 2012 to demand independence; a year later, hundreds of thousands of pro-separatists joined hands to create a **250-mile-long human chain** that stretched from the French border to Valencia. And in the wake of the regional parliament's approval of a "**declaration of sovereignty**" in January 2013, Catalan president Artur Mas urged Madrid to allow Catalunya to hold a referendum on independence.

After Rajoy rejected that request, Catalunya staged a non-binding referendum on November 9, 2014. More than eighty percent of the 2.3 million who voted – a turnout of something over 37 percent of the electorate – supported the proposition that Catalunya should be a separate, independent nation. The Spanish government reacted by condemning the poll as unconstitutional, and charging Mas with perverting the

1995	2004	2006
MACBA (contemporary art museum) opens, signalling regeneration of El Raval district	Diagonal Mar hosts Universal Forum of Cultures, heralding transformation of Poble Nou district	New statute of autonomy agreed with Spain

course of justice, misuse of public funds and abuse of power. Barcelona thus appeared to be on a collision course with the central government in Madrid, evoking local memories of quite how often in its history Spain has played the role of an occupying power.

A new era

Following municipal elections in May 2015, **Ada Colau**, who campaigned on a left-wing platform supported by the national anti-austerity movement **Podemos**, became Barcelona's first female mayor. Colau made her name fighting on behalf of tenants evicted for falling into arrears on their mortgages; under Spanish law, banks can continue to demand mortgage payments from customers even after their homes have been repossessed.

Besides targeting corruption, and reducing the salaries of city employees, Colau has promised to shift the emphasis in Barcelona away from promoting tourism at any cost. Barcelona receives more than 7.5 million tourists each year, and many locals feel that the social cost has come to outweigh the economic benefits. The "black economy" of illegal tourist lets, for example, has priced locals out of affordable city-centre rental accommodation. Colau has announced that the city's tourist tax, which has traditionally been used to pay for promoting Barcelona abroad, will instead be spent on providing civic services in the hardest-hit neighbourhoods.

As this book went to press, it was too soon to assess what impact Colau may have; regional elections in September 2015 saw pro-independence parties win a majority of seats, but 47.8% of the vote, making the outlook far from certain. On the one hand such success for the nationalists in Catalunya could make independence look like a very real possibility for the near future. On the other, the election of an anti-austerity "people power" Spanish government in Madrid might turn things around once again, creating a greater sense of solidarity with the rest of Spain – as indeed might a more general European-wide economic recovery. Watch this space.

2010	2014	2015
Catalan parliament bans bullfighting; Catalunya becomes first region in mainland Spain to do so	In an unofficial referendum supported by all major Catalan parties, over eighty percent of voters endorse independence for Catalunya	Anti-eviction campaigner Ada Colau becomes Barcelona's first female mayor

Books

The selection of books reviewed below provides useful background on Barcelona's history, people and institutions. Despite its long pedigree, Catalan literature is hard to find in translation, though novels set in the city by (mostly foreign) authors provide a feel of Barcelona past and present. Most of the major local bookshops (see p.227) carry English-language guides and titles about the city; or look in the museum bookshops (particularly in MNAC, MACBA, Caixa Forum, Museu Picasso and Fundació Joan Miró) for books on art, design and architecture. There's plenty in the archive of online literary magazine ⓦbarcelonareview.com on Spanish and Catalan writers, art, culture and life, and the very useful Lletra (ⓦlletra.net) makes an excellent online resource (in English) for Catalan literature.

HISTORY

BARCELONA

★**Jimmy Burns** *Barça: A People's Passion*. On one level, it's simply an informative history of the city's famous football team, alma mater of Cruyff, Lineker, Maradona, Ronaldinho et al. However, like the club itself, the book is so much more than that, as Burns examines Catalan pride and nationalism through the prism of sport.

Liz Castro (ed) *What's Up With Catalonia?* Excellent anthology of 36 short and very readable essays discussing various political, economic, cultural and historical aspects of the campaign for Catalan independence.

Felipe Fernàndez-Armesto *Barcelona: A Thousand Years of the City's Past*. An expertly written appraisal of what the author sees as the formative years of the city's history, from the tenth to the early twentieth century.

★**Robert Hughes** *Barcelona*. The renowned art critic casts his accomplished eye over two thousand years of Barcelona's history and culture, with special emphasis on the nineteenth and early twentieth centuries – explaining, in his own words, "the zeitgeist of the place and the connective tissue between the cultural icons".

★**Matthew Stewart** *Monturiol's Dream*. A witty and engaging account of the life of Narcís Monturiol, the nineteenth-century Catalan utopian visionary, revolutionary and inventor of the world's first true submarine. Stewart places Monturiol firmly at the centre of Barcelona's contemporary social and political turmoil – printing seditious magazines, manning the barricades in the 1850s, fleeing into exile and returning to pursue his pioneering invention.

Colm Tóibín *Homage to Barcelona*. Echoing Orwell, the Irish writer pays his own homage to the city, tracing Barcelona's history through its artists, architects, personalities, organizations and rulers.

SPAIN

Hugh Thomas *Rivers of Gold: The Rise of the Spanish Empire*. Thomas's scholarly but eminently accessible history provides a fascinating snapshot of Spain's most glorious period – the meteoric imperial rise in the late fifteenth and early sixteenth centuries, when characters such as Ferdinand and Isabel, and Columbus and Magellan, shaped the country's outlook for the next three hundred years.

★**Giles Tremlett** *Ghosts of Spain*. In this warts-and-all look at contemporary Spain, the Madrid-based contributor to *The Guardian* and *The Economist* finds the dark days of the Civil War never very far from the surface, even now. It's a terrific read – if you buy just one book for general background on how modern Spain works and what its people think, this should be it.

THE CIVIL WAR

Gerald Brenan *The Spanish Labyrinth*. First published in 1943, Brenan's record of the background to the Civil War is tinged by personal experience, yet still impressively rounded.

★**George Orwell** *Homage to Catalonia*. Stirring account of the Civil War fight on the Aragón front and Orwell's participation in the early exhilaration of revolution in Barcelona. A forthright, honest and entertaining tale, covering Orwell's injury and subsequent flight from factional infighting in Republican Spain.

Paul Preston *A Concise History of the Spanish Civil War; Franco; The Spanish Holocaust*. From the leading historian of twentieth-century Spain, *Civil War* is an easily accessible introduction to the subject, while *Franco* offers a penetrating, monumental biography of Franco and his regime. *The Spanish Holocaust* is a controversial account of the murders and massacres that took place in Spain during

CATALAN LITERATURE AND WRITERS

Catalan was established as a literary language as early as the thirteenth century, and the **golden age** of medieval Catalan literature lasted until the mid-sixteenth century, with another cultural and literary flowering in the nineteenth century known as the **Renaixença** (Renaissance). However, this long pedigree has suffered two major interruptions: first, the rise of Castile and later Bourbon rule, which saw the Catalan language eclipsed and then suppressed; and a similar suppression under Franco, when there was a ban on Catalan books and publications. In the post-Civil War period, there was some relaxation of the ban, but only since the return of democracy to Spain has Catalan literature once again flourished.

Catalan and Spanish speakers and readers are best served by the literature, since there's little still in translation. The vernacular works of mystic and philosopher **Ramon Llull** (1233–1316) mark the onset of a true Catalan literature – his *Blanquerna* was one of the first books to be written in any Romance language, while the later chivalric epic *Tirant lo Blanc* (*The White Tyrant*) by **Joanot Martorell** (1413–68) represents a high point of the golden age. None of the works of the leading lights of the nineteenth-century Renaixença is readily available in translation, and it's to *Solitud* (*Solitude*) by **Víctor Català** (1869–1966) that you have to look for the most important pre-Civil War Catalan novel. This tragic tale of a woman's life and sexual passions in a Catalan mountain village was published pseudonymously in 1905 by Caterina Albert i Paradís, who lived most of her life in rural northern Catalunya.

During and after the Civil War, many authors found themselves under forcible or self-imposed exile, including perhaps Spain's most important modern novelist, **Juan Goytisolo** (born 1931), a bitter enemy of the Franco regime (which banned his books). Goytisolo has spent most of his life abroad, in Paris and Marrakesh, and his great trilogy – *Marks of Identity*, *Count Julian* and *Juan the Landless* – confronted the whole ambivalent idea of Spain and Spanishness. Other notable exiles included **Pere Calders i Rossinyol** (1912–94), best known for his short stories, and **Mercè Rodoreda i Gurgui** (1909–83), whose *Plaça del Diamant* (*The Time of Doves*), *El Carrer de les Camèlies* (*Camellia Street*) and *La Meva Cristina i Altres Contes* (*My Cristina and Other Tales*) are relatively easily found in translation. For something lighter, there are the works of **Maria Antònia Oliver i Cabrer** (born 1946), novelist, children's author and short-story writer born in Mallorca, whose early novels were influenced by her birthplace, but whose *Estudi en Lila* (*Study in Lilac*) and *Antipodes* introduce fictional Barcelona private eye Lonia Guiu. More detectives – this time, oddball twins Eduard and Pep – comb the city in the work of contemporary Catalan novelist **Teresa Solana** (born 1962).

Some Catalan writers write in Spanish rather than Catalan, including perhaps the best-known of all – **Manuel Vázquez Montalbán** (1939–2003), crime writer *par excellence*, and novelist, poet, journalist, political commentator and committed Communist to boot. His Pepe Carvalho books did much to expose the shortcomings of the new Spanish democracy in fast-changing Barcelona. Montalbán's contemporary **Juan Marse** (born 1933) uses the post-Civil War dictatorship as the background for many of his Barcelona-set novels, and the same period spawned the Barcelona blockbuster *The Shadow of the Wind* by **Carlos Ruiz Zafón** (born 1964), and its prequel *The Angel's Game*. For other new Catalan writers, such as **Albert Sánchez Piñol** (born 1965), nationality seems incidental at best – his well-regarded first novel, *Cold Skin*, is a creepy psychological sci-fi tale of solitude on an Antarctic island, while literary adventure story *Pandora in the Congo* starts in the dark heart of the African jungle.

and after the Civil War – violence that still engenders dark passions on both sides of the argument in contemporary Spain.

ART AND ARCHITECTURE

★ **Gijs van Hensbergen** *Gaudí: The Biography*. A worthy biography of "arguably the world's most famous architect". Van Hensbergen places his work firmly in context, as Spain lost its empire and Catalunya slowly flexed its nationalist muscles.

Hugh Thomas *The Spanish Civil War*. This exhaustive political study is still the best single telling of the convoluted story of the Civil War.

John Richardson *A Life of Picasso*. The definitive multi-volume biography – Volume 1, covering the period 1881–1906, is an extremely readable account of the artist's early years, covering his entire time in Barcelona.

Philippe Thiébaut *Gaudí: Builder of Visions*. Read van

Hensbergen for the life, but pick up this pocket-sized volume for its excellent photographic coverage – not just Gaudí buildings and interiors, but sketches, historical photographs and architectural insights that add up to a useful gateway to his work in the city and surroundings.

FOOD AND WINE

★**Colman Andrews** *Catalan Cuisine*. The best available English-language book dealing with Spain's most adventurous regional cuisine. Full of historical and anecdotal detail, it's a pleasure to read, let alone cook from (no pictures, though).

Penelope Casas *The Foods and Wines of Spain*. Casas roams across every region of Spain in this classic Spanish cookery book, including the best dishes that Catalunya has to offer. Her *Paella* and *Tapas: The Little Dishes of Spain* covers the rest of the bases.

Jan Read *Wines of Spain*. All you need to know to sort out your Penedès from your Priorat – an explanation of regions and producers, plus tasting notes and tips for wine tourists.

NOVELS SET IN BARCELONA

John Bryson *To the Death, Amic*. Barcelona, under siege during the Civil War, is the backdrop for a coming-of-age novel recounting the adventures of 10-year-old twins Enric and Josep.

Miguel Cervantes *Don Quixote*. Barcelona is the only city to which Cervantes gives its real name in his picaresque classic – in the Barcelona chapters, Don Quixote and Sancho Panza see the ocean for the first time, and Quixote fights a duel on Barceloneta beach against the Knight of the White Moon.

Ildefonso Falcones *Cathedral of the Sea*. Barcelona lawyer Falcones set his award-winning first novel in the expansionist years of the fourteenth century, where work is under way on the building of the city's most magnificent church, Santa María del Mar. His highly realistic, excitingly plotted tale lifts the skirts of medieval Barcelona to show an authentic picture of a city on the make.

Juan Marse *Lizard Tails* and *Shanghai Nights*. Marse spent his formative years in a Barcelona scarred by the Civil War, and ruptured childhood and family hardship are themes that emerge in much of his work. *Lizard Tails* is an evocation of post-Civil War childhood, while *Shanghai Nights* – again, Barcelona and war to the fore – is billed as "a tale of the human spirit".

★**Eduardo Mendoza** *City of Marvels*, *The Truth About the Savolta Case* and *The Year of the Flood*. Mendoza's first and best novel, *City of Marvels*, is set in the expanding Barcelona of 1880–1920, full of rich underworld characters and riddled with anarchic and comic turns. The milieu is reused with flair in *The Truth About the Savolta Case*, while *The Year of the Flood* adds a light touch to an unusual amorous entanglement in 1950s Barcelona.

Raul Nuñez *The Lonely Hearts Club*. A parade of grotesque and hard-bitten characters haunt the city in this oddball but likeable romantic comedy.

Colm Tóibín *The South*. Barcelona provided the background for Tóibín's first novel, about an Irish woman looking for a new life.

★**Carlos Ruiz Zafón** *The Shadow of the Wind*. Top holiday read is the international bestseller by the Barcelona-born, one-time LA screenwriter Zafón. A Gothic literary thriller set in the aftermath of the Civil War, full of atmospheric Barcelona locations, it generated rave reviews, and sold over fifteen million copies worldwide. Zafón followed up with a similarly intricate, similarly successful plot-within-plot prequel called *The Angel's Game*.

THRILLERS AND CRIME NOVELS

Bernado Atxaga *The Lone Man*. The noted Basque writer set his well-received psychological thriller during the 1982 World Cup, when two ETA gunmen hole up in a Barcelona hotel.

★**Manuel Vázquez Montalbán** *Murder in the Central Committee*, *Southern Seas*, *The Angst-Ridden Executive*, *An Olympic Death*, *Offside*, *The Man of My Life* and *Tatoo*. Montalbán's greatest creation, the fast-living gourmand-detective Pepe Carvalho, ex-Communist and CIA agent, first appeared in print in 1972, and went on to investigate foul deeds in the city in a series of wry and racy Chandler-esque thrillers. *Murder in the Central Committee* is a good place to start, as Carvalho confronts his Communist past. *Southern Seas* won the Planeta, Spain's biggest literary prize, while the city's businesses, institutions and events come under typical scrutiny in *The Angst-Ridden Executive*, *An Olympic Death* and *Offside*. Twenty-first-century Catalan politics and business come under the spotlight in the last Carvalho novel, *The Man of My Life*, while the early *Tatoo* plunges readers right back into "sex, death and food in 1970s Barcelona".

Teresa Solana *A Not So Perfect Crime; A Shortcut to Paradise*. In her first two Barcelona noir novels, Solana introduces bumbling detective twins Eduard and Pep – they don't look alike and they don't solve cases, but they do skewer contemporary high society, whether in politics (*A Not So Perfect Crime*) or literary circles (*A Shortcut to Paradise*).

Barbara Ellen Wilson *Gaudí Afternoon*. Pacy feminist thriller making good use of Gaudí's architecture as a backdrop for deception and skulduggery.

Language

In Barcelona, Catalan (Català) has more or less taken over from Castilian Spanish (Castellano) as the language on street signs, maps, official buildings and notices, and so on. On paper, it looks like a cross between French and Spanish, and is generally easy to read if you know those two. Spoken Catalan is harder to come to grips with, as the language itself is not phonetic, and accents vary from region to region.

Few visitors realize how important Catalan is to those who speak it: never commit the error of calling it a dialect. However, despite the ubiquity of the Catalan language, you'll get by perfectly well in Spanish, as long as you can learn to understand Catalan in timetables, on menus, and the like. You'll find some basic pronunciation rules below, for both Spanish and Catalan, and a selection of words and phrases in both languages. Spanish is certainly easier to pronounce, but don't be afraid to try Catalan, especially in the more out-of-the-way places – you'll generally get a good reception if you at least try communicating in the local language.

Numerous **Spanish phrasebooks** are available, not least the *Spanish Rough Guide Phrasebook*, laid out dictionary-style, and featuring 24 typical travel scenarios that can also be downloaded as audio files. In Barcelona, *Parla Català* (Pia) is the only readily available English–Catalan phrasebook, though more extensive Catalan–English dictionaries and teach-yourself Catalan guides are available online.

PRONUNCIATION

CASTILIAN (SPANISH)

Unless there's an accent, words ending in "D", "L", "R" or "Z" are **stressed** on the last syllable, all others on the second last. All **vowels** are pure and short; combinations have predictable results.

A somewhere between the "A" sound of "back" and that of "father".

E as in "get".

I as in "police".

O as in "hot".

U as in "rule".

C is lisped before "E" and "I", hard otherwise: "cerca" is pronounced "thairka".

G works the same way, a guttural "H" sound (like the "ch" in "loch" before "E" or "I", a hard "G" elsewhere – "gigante" becomes "higante".

H is always silent.

J the same sound as a guttural "G": "jamón" is pronounced "hamon".

LL sounds like an English "Y": "tortilla" is pronounced "torteeya".

N is as in English unless it has a tilde (accent) over it, when it becomes "NY": "mañana" sounds like "man-yaana".

QU is pronounced like an English "K".

R is rolled, "RR" doubly so.

V sounds more like "B", "vino" becoming "beano".

X has an "S" sound before consonants, normal "X" before vowels.

Z is the same as a soft "C", so "cerveza" becomes "thairbaitha".

CATALAN

With Catalan, don't be tempted to use the few rules of Spanish pronunciation you may know – in particular the soft Spanish "Z" and "C" don't apply, so unlike in the rest of Spain the city is not "Barthelona" but "Barcelona", as in English.

A as in "hat" if stressed, as in "alone" when unstressed.

E varies, but usually as in "get".

I as in "police".

IG sounds like the "tch" in the English scratch; "lleig" (ugly) is pronounced "yeah-tch".

O a round full sound, when stressed, otherwise like a soft "U" sound.

U somewhere between the "U" of "put" and "rule".

Ç sounds like an English "S"; "plaça" is pronounced "plassa".

C followed by an "E" or "I" is soft; otherwise hard.

G followed by "E" or "I" is like the "zh" in "Zhivago"; otherwise hard.

H is always silent.

J as in the French "Jean".

TALKING THE TALK

Catalan (Català) is a Romance language, stemming directly from Latin, and closely resembling the language of Occitan, spoken in southern France. Catalan is spoken by over ten million people in total, in Barcelona and Catalunya, part of Aragón, much of Valencia, the Balearic islands, Andorra and parts of the French Pyrenees – and its use is thus much more widespread than, say, Danish, Finnish and Norwegian. Other Spaniards tend to belittle it by saying that to get a Catalan word you just cut a Castilian one in half but, in fact, the grammar is more complicated and it has eight vowel sounds compared with Castilian's five. Catalan was banned from the radio, TV, daily press and schools during the Franco era, so many older people cannot read or write it, even if they speak it all the time. Virtually every Catalan is bilingual, but most regard Catalan as their mother tongue and it's estimated to be the dominant language in over half of Catalunya's households – a figure that's likely to grow given its amazing recent revival.

L.L is best pronounced (for foreigners) as a single "L" sound; but for Catalan speakers it has two distinct "L" sounds.

LL sounds like an English "Y" or "LY", like the "yuh" sound in "million".

N as in English, though before "F" or "V" it sometimes sounds like an "M".

NY corresponds to the Castilian "Ñ".

QU before "E" or "I" sounds like "K", unless the "U" has an umlaut (Ü), in which case, and before "A" or "O", as in "quit".

R is rolled, but only at the start of a word; at the end, it's often silent.

T is pronounced as in English, though sometimes it sounds like a "D", as in "viatge" or "dotze".

V at the start of a word sounds like "B"; in all other positions it's a soft "F" sound.

W is pronounced like a "B/V".

X is like "SH" or "CH" in most words, though in some, like "exit", it sounds like an "X".

Z is like the English "Z" in "zoo".

USEFUL WORDS AND PHRASES

Words and phrases below are given in the following order: **English** – Spanish – *Catalan*.

BASICS

English	Spanish	*Catalan*
Yes, No, OK	Sí, No, Vale	*Sí, No, Val*
Please, Thank you	Por favor, Gracias	*Si us plau, Gràcies*
Where? When?	Dónde? Cuando?	*On? Quan?*
What? How much?	Qué? Cuánto?	*Què? Quant?*
Here, There	Aquí, Allí/Allá	*Aquí, Allí/Allá*
This, That	Esto, Eso	*Això, Allò*
Now, Later	Ahora, Más tarde	*Ara, Mès tard*
Open, Closed	Abierto/a, Cerrado/a	*Obert, Tancat*
With, Without	Con, Sin	*Amb, Sense*
Good, Bad	Bueno/a, Malo/a	*Bo(na), Dolent(a)*
Big, Small	Gran(de), Pequeño/a	*Gran, Petit(a)*
Cheap, Expensive	Barato, Caro	*Barat(a), Car(a)*
Hot, Cold	Caliente, Frío	*Calent(a), Fred(a)*
More, Less	Más, Menos	*Mes, Menys*
I want	Quiero	*Vull (pronounced "vwee")*
I'd like	Quisiera	*Voldria*
Do you know?	¿Sabe?	*Vostès saben?*
I don't know	No sé	*No sé*
There is (is there?)	(¿)Hay(?)	*Hi ha(?)*
What's that?	¿Qué es eso?	*Què és això?*
Give me (one like that)	Deme (uno así) (a bit brusque)	*Doneu-me*
Do you have?	¿Tiene?	*Té …?*
The time	La hora	*L'hora*
Today, Tomorrow	Hoy, Mañana	*Avui, Demà*

Yesterday	Ayer	*Ahir*
Day before yesterday	Ante ayer	*Abans-d'ahir*
Next week	La semana que viene	*La setmana que ve*
Next month	El mes que viene	*El mes que ve*

GREETINGS AND RESPONSES

Hello, Goodbye	Hola, Adiós	*Hola, Adéu*
Good morning	Buenos días	*Bon dia*
Good afternoon/night	Buenas tardes/noches	*Bona tarde/nit*
See you later	Hasta luego	*Fins després*
Sorry	Lo siento/Disculpéme	*Ho sento*
Excuse me	Con permiso/Perdón	*Perdoni*
How are you?	¿Cómo está (usted)?	*Com va?*
I (don't) understand	(No) Entiendo	*(No) Ho entenc*
Not at all/You're welcome	De nada	*De res*
Do you speak English?	¿Habla (usted) inglés?	*Parleu anglès?*
I (don't) speak Spanish/Catalan	(No) Hablo español	*(No) Parlo Català*
My name is ...	Me llamo ...	*Em dic ...*
What's your name?	¿Como se llama usted?	*Com es diu?*
I am English/	Soy inglés(a)	*Sóc anglès(a)*
... Scottish/	... escocés(a)	*... escocès(a)*
... Australian/	... australiano(a)	*... australian(a)*
... Canadian/	... canadiense(a)	*... canadenc(a)*
... American/	... americano(a)	*... americà (a)*
... Irish	... irlandes(a)	*... irlandès (a)*

FINDING ACCOMMODATION

Do you have a room?	¿Tiene una habitación?	*Té alguna habitació? ... amb*
... with two beds/double bed	... con dos camas/cama	*dos llits/llit per dues persones*
... with shower/bath	matrimonial ... con ducha/baño	*... amb dutxa/bany*
It's for one person (two people)	Es para una persona (dos personas)	*Per a una persona (dues persones)*
For one night (one week)	Para una noche (una semana)	*Per una nit (una setmana)*
It's fine, how much is it?	¿Está bien, cuánto es?	*Esta bé, quant és?*
It's too expensive	Es demasiado caro	*És massa car*
Don't you have anything cheaper?	¿No tiene algo más barato?	*En té de mé sbon preu?*

DIRECTIONS AND TRANSPORT

How do I get to ...?	¿Por donde se va a ...?	*Per anar a ...?*
Left, right, straight on	Izquierda, derecha, todo recto	*A la dreta, a l'esquerra, tot recte*
Where is ...?	¿Dónde está ...?	*On és ......?*
... the bus station	... la estación de autobuses	*... l'estació de autobuses*
... the train station	... la estación de ferrocarril	*... l'estació*
... the nearest bank	... el banco más cercano	*... el banc més a prop*
... the post office	... el correos/la oficina de correos	*... l'oficina de correus*
... the toilet	... el baño/aseo/servicio	*... la toaleta*
It's not very far	No es muy lejos	*No és gaire lluny*
Where does the bus to ... leave from?	¿De dónde sale el autobús para ...?	*De on surt el autobús a ...?*
Is this the train for Barcelona?	¿Es este el tren para Barcelona?	*Aquest tren va a Barcelona?*
I'd like a (return) ticket to ...	Quisiera un billete (de ida y vuelta) para ...	*Voldria un bitlet (d'anar i tornar) a ...*
What time does it leave (arrive in)?	¿A qué hora sale (llega a)?	*A quina hora surt (arriba a)?*

NUMBERS

1	un/uno/una	*un(a)*
2	dos	*dos (dues)*
3	tres	*tres*
4	cuatro	*quatre*
5	cinco	*cinc*
6	seis	*sis*
7	siete	*set*
8	ocho	*vuit*
9	nueve	*nou*
10	diez	*deu*
11	once	*onze*
12	doce	*dotze*
13	trece	*tretze*
14	catorce	*catorze*
15	quince	*quinze*
16	dieciseis	*setze*
17	diecisiete	*disset*
18	dieciocho	*divuit*
19	diecinueve	*dinou*
20	veinte	*vint*
21	veintiuno	*vint-i-un*
30	treinta	*trenta*
40	cuarenta	*quaranta*
50	cincuenta	*cinquanta*
60	sesenta	*seixanta*
70	setenta	*setanta*
80	ochenta	*vuitanta*
90	noventa	*novanta*
100	cien(to)	*cent*
101	ciento uno	*cent un*
102	ciento dos	*cent dos (dues)*
200	doscientos	*dos-cents (dues-centes)*
500	quinientos	*cinc-cents*
1000	mil	*mil*
2000	dos mil	*dos mil*

DAYS AND MONTHS

Monday	lunes	*dilluns*
Tuesday	martes	*dimarts*
Wednesday	miércoles	*dimecres*
Thursday	jueves	*dijous*
Friday	viernes	*divendres*
Saturday	sábado	*dissabte*
Sunday	domingo	*diumenge*
January	enero	*gener*
February	febrero	*febrer*
March	marzo	*març*
April	abril	*abril*
May	mayo	*maig*
June	junio	*juny*
July	julio	*juliol*
August	agosto	*agost*
September	septiembre	*setembre*

October	octubre	*octobre*
November	noviembre	*noviembre*
December	diciembre	*desembre*

FOOD AND DRINK

Words and phrases below are given in the following order: **English** – Spanish – *Catalan*.

SOME BASIC WORDS

To have breakfast	Desayunar	*Esmorzar*
To have lunch	Comer	*Dinar*
To have dinner	Cenar	*Sopar*
The bill	La cuenta	*El compte*
I'm a vegetarian	Soy vegetariano/a	*Sóc vegetarià/vegetariana*
Knife	Cuchillo	*Ganivet*
Fork	Tenedor	*Forquilla*
Spoon	Cuchara	*Cullera*
Table	Mesa	*Taula*
Bottle	Botella	*Ampolla*
Glass	Vaso	*Got*
Menu	Carta	*Carta*
Soup	Sopa	*Sopa*
Salad	Ensalada	*Amanida*
Hors d'oeuvres	Entremeses	*Entremesos*
Omelette	Tortilla	*Truita*
Sandwich	Bocadillo	*Entrepà*
Toast	Tostadas	*Torrades*
Tapas	Tapes	*Tapes*
Butter	Mantequilla	*Mantega*
Eggs	Huevos	*Ous*
Bread	Pan	*Pa*
Olives	Aceitunas	*Olives*
Oil	Aceite	*Oli*
Vinegar	Vinagre	*Vinagre*
Salt	Sal	*Sal*
Pepper	Pimienta	*Pebre*
Sugar	Azucar	*Sucre*

GENERAL MENU TERMS

Assorted	Surtido/variado	*Assortit*
Baked	Al horno	*Al forn*
Char-grilled	A la brasa	*A la brasa*
Fresh	Fresco	*Fresc*
Fried	Frito	*Fregit*
Fried in batter	A la romana	*A la romana*
Garlic mayonnaise	Alioli	*All i oli*
Grilled	A la plancha	*A la plantxa*
Pickled	En escabeche	*En escabetx*
Roast	Asado	*Rostit*
Sauce	Salsa	*Salsa*
Sautéed	Salteado	*Saltat*
Scrambled	Revuelto	*Remenat*
Seasonal	Del tiempo	*Del temps*
Smoked	Ahumado	*Fumat*
Spit-roasted	Al ast	*A l'ast*

Steamed	Al vapor	*Al vapor*
Stewed	Guisado	*Guisat*
Stuffed	Relleno	*Farcit*

FISH AND SEAFOOD/PESCADO Y MARISCOS/PEIX I MARISC

Anchovies	Anchoas/Boquerones	*Anxoves/Seitons*
Baby squid	Chipirones	*Calamarsets*
Bream	Dorada	*Orada*
Clams	Almejas	*Cloïses*
Crab	Cangrejo	*Cranc*
Cuttlefish	Sepia	*Sipia*
Eels	Anguilas	*Anguiles*
Hake	Merluza	*Lluç*
Langoustines	Langostinos	*Llagostins*
Lobster	Langosta	*Llagosta*
Monkfish	Rape	*Rap*
Mussels	Mejillones	*Musclos*
Octopus	Pulpo	*Pop*
Oysters	Ostras	*Ostres*
Perch	Mero	*Mero*
Prawns	Gambas	*Gambes*
Razor clams	Navajas	*Navalles*
Red mullet	Salmonete	*Moll*
Salmon	Salmón	*Salmó*
Salt cod	Bacalao	*Bacallà*
Sardines	Sardinas	*Sardines*
Scallops	Vieiras	*Vieires*
Sea bass	Lubina	*Llobarro*
Sole	Lenguado	*Llenguado*
Squid	Calamares	*Calamars*
Swordfish	Pez espada	*Peix espasa*
Trout	Trucha	*Truita (de riu)*
Tuna	Atún	*Tonyina*
Whitebait	Chanquete	*Xanguet*

MEAT AND POULTRY/CARNE Y AVES/CARN I AVIRAM

Beef	Buey	*Bou*
Boar	Jabalí	*Senglar*
Charcuterie	Embutidos	*Embotits*
Chicken	Pollo	*Pollastre*
Chorizo sausage	Chorizo	*Xoriço*
Cured ham	Jamón serrano	*Pernil serrà*
Cured pork sausage	Longaniza	*Llonganissa*
Cutlets/Chops	Chuletas	*Costelles*
Duck	Pato	*Ànec*
Ham	Jamón York	*Pernil dolç*
Hare	Liebre	*Llebre*
Kid/goat	Cabrito	*Cabrit*
Kidneys	Riñones	*Ronyons*
Lamb	Cordero	*Xai/Be*
Liver	Hígado	*Fetge*
Loin of pork	Lomo	*Llom*
Meatballs	Albóndigas	*Mandonguilles*
Partridge	Perdiz	*Perdiu*

Pigs' trotters	Pies de cerdo	*Peus de porc*
Pork	Cerdo	*Porc*
Rabbit	Conejo	*Conill*
Sausages	Salchichas	*Salsitxes*
Snails	Caracoles	*Cargols*
Steak	Bistec	*Bistec*
Tongue	Lengua	*Llengua*
Veal	Ternera	*Vedella*

VEGETABLES AND PULSES/VERDURAS Y LEGUMBRES/VERDURES I LLEGUMS

Artichokes	Alcachofas	*Carxofes*
Asparagus	Esparragos	*Esparrecs*
Aubergine	Berenjena	*Albergínia*
Avocado	Aguacate	*Alvocat*
Broad/lima beans	Habes	*Faves*
Cabbage	Col	*Col*
Carrots	Zanahorias	*Pastanagues*
Cauliflower	Coliflor	*Col-i-flor*
Chickpeas	Garbanzos	*Cigrons*
Courgette	Calabacín	*Carbassó*
Cucumber	Pepino	*Concombre*
Garlic	Ajo	*All*
Haricot beans	Judías blancas	*Mongetes*
Herbs	Hierbas	*Herbes*
Leeks	Puerros	*Porros*
Lentils	Lentejas	*Llenties*
Mushrooms	Champiñones	*Xampinyons*
Onion	Cebolla	*Ceba*
Peas	Guisantes	*Pèsols*
Peppers	Pimientos	*Pebrots*
Potatoes	Patatas	*Patates*
Spinach	Espinacas	*Espinacs*
Tomatoes	Tomates	*Tomàquets*
Turnips	Nabos	*Naps*
Wild mushrooms	Setas	*Bolets*

FRUIT/FRUTA/FRUITA

Apple	Manzana	*Poma*
Apricot	Albaricoque	*Albercoc*
Banana	Plátano	*Plàtan*
Cherries	Cerezas	*Cireres*
Figs	Higos	*Figues*
Grapes	Uvas	*Raïm*
Melon	Melón	*Meló*
Orange	Naranja	*Taronja*
Peach	Melocotón	*Pressec*
Pear	Pera	*Pera*
Pineapple	Piña	*Pinya*
Strawberries	Fresas	*Maduixes*

DESSERTS/POSTRES/POSTRES

Cake	Pastel	*Pastís*
Cheese	Queso	*Formatge*
Crème caramel	Flan	*Flam*

Fruit salad	Macedonia	*Macedonia*
İce cream	Helado	*Gelat*
Rice pudding	Arroz con leche	*Arròs amb llet*
Tart	Tarta	*Tarta*
Yoghurt	Yogur	*Yogur*

CATALAN SPECIALITIES

Amanida Catalana Salad served with sliced meats (sometimes cheese)

Ànec amb peres Duck with pears

Arròs a banda Rice with seafood, the rice served separately

Arròs a la Cubana Rice with fried egg and home-made tomato sauce

Arròs a la marinera Paella: rice with seafood and saffron

Arròs negre "Black rice", cooked – risotto-style – in squid ink

Bacallà a la llauna Salt cod baked with garlic, tomato and paprika

Bacallà amb mongetes Salt cod with stewed haricot beans

Botifarra (amb mongetes) Grilled Catalan pork sausage (with stewed haricot beans)

Bunyols Fritters, which can be sweet (like little doughnuts, with sugar) or savoury (salt cod or wild mushroom)

Calçots Large char-grilled spring onions, eaten with romesco sauce (available Feb–March)

Canelons Cannelloni

Conill all i oli Rabbit with garlic mayonnaise

Conill amb cargols Rabbit with snails

Crema Catalana Crème caramel, with caramelized sugar topping

Entremesos Hors d'oeuvres of mixed meat and cheese

Escalivada Grilled aubergine, pepper and onion

Escudella i carn d'olla A winter dish of stewed mixed meat and vegetables, served broth first, meat and veg second

Espinacs a la Catalana Spinach cooked with raisins and pine nuts

Esqueixada Salad of salt cod with peppers, tomatoes, onions and olives – a summer dish

Estofat de vedella Veal stew

Faves a la Catalana Stewed broad beans, with bacon and botifarra – a regional classic

Fideuà Short, thin noodles (the width of vermicelli) served with seafood, accompanied by all i olli

Fideus a la cassola Short, thin noodles baked with meat

Fricandó (amb bolets) Braised veal (with wild mushrooms)

Fuet Catalan salami

Llagosta amb pollastre Lobster with chicken in a rich sauce

Llenties guisades Stewed lentils

Mel i mató Curd cheese and honey – a typical dessert

Oca amb naps Goose with turnips

Pa amb tomàquet Bread (often grilled), rubbed with tomato, garlic and olive oil

Panellets Marzipan cakes – served for All Saints' Day

Perdiu a la vinagreta Partridge in vinegar gravy

Perdiu amb col Partridge with cabbage dumplings

Pollastre al cava Chicken with cava (champagne) sauce

Pollastre amb gambes Chicken with prawns

Postres de músic Cake of dried fruit and nuts

Rap amb all cremat Monkfish with creamed garlic sauce

Salsa romesco Spicy sauce (with chillis, ground almonds, hazelnuts, garlic, tomato and wine), often served with grilled fish

Samfaina Ratatouille-like stew (onions, peppers, aubergine, tomato), served with salt cod or chicken

Sarsuela Fish and shellfish stew

Sípia amb mandonguilles Cuttlefish with meatballs

Sopa d'all Garlic soup, often with egg and bread

Suquet de peix Fish and potato casserole

Xató Mixed salad of olives, salt cod, preserved tuna, anchovies and onions

DRINKS

Beer	Cerveza	*Cervesa*
Wine	Vino	*Vi*
Champagne	Champan	*Xampan/Cava*
Sherry	Jerez	*Xerès*
Coffee	Café	*Cafè*
Espresso	Café solo	*Cafè sol*
Large black coffee	Café Americano	*Cafè Americà*
Large white coffee	Café con leche	*Cafè amb llet*
Small white coffee	Café cortado	*Cafè tallat*
Decaff	Descafeinado	*Descafeinat*

Tea	Té	*Te*
Drinking chocolate	Chocolate	*Xocolata*
Juice	Zumo	*Suc*
Crushed ice drink	Granizado	*Granissat*
Milk	Leche	*Llet*
Tiger nut drink	Horchata	*Orxata*
Water	Agua	*Aigua*
Mineral water	Agua mineral	*Aigua mineral*
... (sparkling)	... (con gas)	*... (amb gas)*
... (still)	... (sin gas)	*... (sense gas)*

A GLOSSARY OF CATALAN WORDS

Ajuntament Town hall (city council)

Avinguda Avenue

Barcino Roman name for Barcelona

Barri Suburb or quarter

Bodega Cellar, wine bar or warehouse

Caixa Savings bank

Call Jewish quarter

Camí Path

Capella Chapel

Carrer Street

Casa House

Castell Castle

Cava Catalan "champagne"

Comarca County

Correus Post office

Església Church

Estació Station

Estany Lake

Festa Festival

Font Waterfall

Forn Bakery

Generalitat Catalan government

Gòtic Gothic (eg Barri Gòtic, Gothic Quarter)

Granja Milk bar/café

Guiri Foreigner

Llotja Stock exchange building

Mercat Market

Modernisme Catalan Art Nouveau

Monestir Monastery or convent

Museu Museum

Palau Aristocratic mansion/palace

Passatge Passage

Passeig Promenade/boulevard; also the evening stroll thereon

Pastisseria Cake/pastry shop

Pati Inner courtyard

Plaça Square

Platja Beach

Pont Bridge

Porta Gateway

Rambla Boulevard

Renaixença Renaissance

Ríu River

Sant/a Saint

Sardana Catalunya's national folk dance

Serra Mountain range

Seu Cathedral

Terrassa Outdoor terrace

Small print and index

A ROUGH GUIDE TO ROUGH GUIDES

Published in 1982, the first Rough Guide – to Greece – was a student scheme that became a publishing phenomenon. Mark Ellingham, a recent graduate in English from Bristol University, had been travelling in Greece the previous summer and couldn't find the right guidebook. With a small group of friends he wrote his own guide, combining a highly contemporary, journalistic style with a thoroughly practical approach to travellers' needs.

The immediate success of the book spawned a series that rapidly covered dozens of destinations. And, in addition to impecunious backpackers, Rough Guides soon acquired a much broader readership that relished the guides' wit and inquisitiveness as much as their enthusiastic, critical approach and value-for-money ethos.

These days, Rough Guides include recommendations from budget to luxury and cover more than 120 destinations around the globe, as well as producing an ever-growing range of ebooks.

Visit **roughguides.com** to find all our latest books, read articles, get inspired and share travel tips with the Rough Guides community.

Rough Guide credits

Editor: Alice Park
Layout: Nikhil Agarwal
Cartography: Ashutosh Bharti
Picture editor: Michelle Bhatia
Proofreader: Diane Margolis
Managing editor: Monica Woods
Senior editor: Natasha Foges
Assistant editor: Sharon Sonam

Production: Jimmy Lao
Cover design: Nicole Newman, Michelle Bhatia, Nikhil Agarwal
Editorial assistant: Freya Godfrey
Senior pre-press designer: Dan May
Programme manager: Gareth Lowe
Publisher: Keith Drew
Publishing director: Georgina Dee

Publishing information

This eleventh edition published March 2016 by
Rough Guides Ltd,
80 Strand, London WC2R 0RL
11, Community Centre, Panchsheel Park,
New Delhi 110017, India
Distributed by Penguin Random House
Penguin Books Ltd, 80 Strand, London WC2R 0RL
Penguin Group (USA), 345 Hudson Street, NY 10014, USA
Penguin Group (Australia), 250 Camberwell Road,
Camberwell, Victoria 3124, Australia
Penguin Group (NZ), 67 Apollo Drive, Mairangi Bay,
Auckland 1310, New Zealand
Penguin Group (South Africa), Block D, Rosebank Office
Park, 181 Jan Smuts Avenue, Parktown North, Gauteng,
South Africa 2193
Rough Guides is represented in Canada by DK Canada, 320
Front Street West, Suite 1400, Toronto, Ontario M5V 3B6
Printed in Singapore
© Rough Guides 2016
Maps © Rough Guides

288pp includes index
A catalogue record for this book is available from the
British Library
ISBN: 978-0-24120-435-1
The publishers and authors have done their best to ensure
the accuracy and currency of all the information in **The
Rough Guide to Barcelona**, however, they can accept
no responsibility for any loss, injury, or inconvenience
sustained by any traveller as a result of information or
advice contained in the guide.
1 3 5 7 9 8 6 4 2

Help us update

We've gone to a lot of effort to ensure that the eleventh
edition of **The Rough Guide to Barcelona** is accurate
and up-to-date. However, things change – places get
"discovered", opening hours are notoriously fickle,
restaurants and rooms raise prices or lower standards. If
you feel we've got it wrong or left something out, we'd like
to know, and if you can remember the address, the price,
the hours, the phone number, so much the better.

Please send your comments with the subject line "**Rough
Guide Barcelona Update**" to mail@uk.roughguides.com.
We'll credit all contributions and send a copy of the next
edition (or any other Rough Guide if you prefer) for the very
best emails.

Find more travel information, connect with fellow
travellers and plan your trip on Ⓦ roughguides.com.

ADOUT TIIC AUTIIOR5

Steve Tallantyre is a British journalist and copywriter. He moved to
Barcelona from Italy in the late 1990s, already clutching a Rough Guide with
circles scrawled around the restaurants he planned to visit. Now married to a
Catalan native and with two "Catalangles" children, he writes about the
region's culture and gastronomy for international publications, news agencies
and his own blog: ⓦfoodbarcelona.com.

Greg Ward has written sixteen travel, history and music books for Rough
Guides as sole author, and shared authorship on several more. His specialist
areas include Spain, France, Southwest USA, Hawaii and the Greek islands.

Acknowledgements

Steve Tallantyre: Thanks to Brian McLean for his
assistance, Laura Ramírez for her support, and the cooks,
sommeliers, waiters, hotel staff and PR professionals of
Barcelona who fed, watered, hosted and helped me while
researching the book.

Greg Ward: Thanks to Jules Brown, the original author of
this book; Natasha Foges for giving me the opportunity
to work on it; my wife Samantha Cook for sharing the fun;
Alice Park for a fine editing job; Steven Tallantyre; and
Anna Castan.

Readers' updates

Thanks to all the readers who have taken the time to write in with comments and suggestions (and apologies if we've
inadvertently omitted or misspelt anyone's name):

Paola Castagnino, Claire Hyde, Margaret MacGregor, Sarah Martindale, Amy Ruffle, Paul Webb

Photo credits

All photos © Rough Guides except the following:
(Key: t-top; c-centre; b-bottom; l-left; r-right)

p.1 Alamy Images/Markus Schieder
p.2 Dreamstime.com/Pedritobcn
p.4 Alamy Images/Zoonar GmbH
p.6 Dreamstime.com/Luciano Mortula
p.7 Alamy Images/REDA
p.9 Alamy Images/Mike Hughes (t); Alamy Images/
Barcelona Demonstrations (b)
p.10 Dreamstime.com/Pavel Kirichenko
p.11 Dreamstime.com/Krasnevsky (t); Corbis/Gregorio/
Alterphotos/EXPA/NewSport (b)
p.12 Alamy Images/age fotostock (t); Dreamstime.com/
Jackf (b)
p.13 Getty Images/John Harper (bl)
p.14 Alamy Images/John Kellerman (tl); Corbis/Tom Grill (bl)
p.15 Getty Images/Sylvain Sonnet (t)
p.16 Getty Images/Panoramic Images
p.17 Alamy Images/David Noton Photography
p.18 Alamy Images/wronaphoto.com
p.36 Dreamstime.com/Travel Pix Collection
p.49 Alamy Images/Steve Vidler (tl); SuperStock/Rafael
Campillo (tr); Dreamstime.com/Juan Moyano (b)
p.56 Alamy Images/Kevin Foy
p.63 Alamy Images/Deborah Harmes (t)
p.65 Dreamstime.com/Javarman
p.76 Corbis/Sylvain Sonnet
p.109 Courtesy of *Museu del Modernisme Català*
p.114 SuperStock/Guido Krawczyk

p.119 Getty Images/Sylvain Sonnet
p.140 Getty Images/Xavier Arnau Serrat
p.149 Getty Images/John Miller/Robert Harding (t); Alamy
Images/David Bagnall (c)
p.164 Alamy Images/Kumar Sriskandan
p.175 Courtesy of *Ca L'estevet*
p.185 Courtesy of *Lolita Taperia* (br)
p.199 Travel Pictures (tl); Alamy Images/Christian Bertrand
(tr); Courtesy of *Sala Becool* (bl)
p.204 SuperStock/photononstop
p.214 Alamy Images/Stefano Ginella
p.217 Alamy Images/dpa picture alliance (t); Corbis/
Alberto Estevez/epa (bl); Travel Pictures Ltd/Rafael
Campillo (br)
p.225 Courtesy of *La Comercial*
p.229 Courtesy of *L'Arca* (tl); Courtesy of *La Central del
Raval* (bl)
p.238 SuperStock/Fotosearch

Front cover & spine Detail of the Sagrada Família © AWL
Images/Hemis
Back cover Mercat de la Boqueria © Robert Harding
Picture Library/Rafael Campillo (t); Cable-car on Montjuïc ©
Robert Harding Picture Library/Juergen Stumpe/LOOK (bl);
Park Güell © Robert Harding Picture Library/Tim Langlotz/
Seasons.agency (br)

Index

Maps are marked in grey

Map index

Listings key

■ Accommodation

● Café/tapas bar/restaurant

■ Bar/club/live music venue

● Shop

City plan

The **city plan** on the pages that follow is divided as shown:

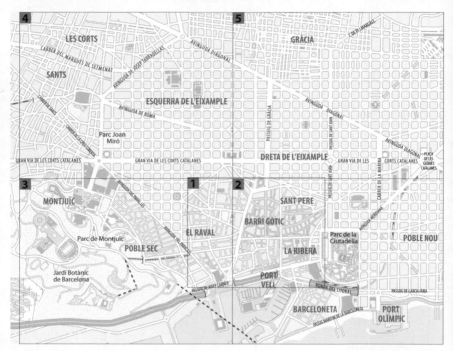

Map symbols

International boundary	Viewpoint	Post office	Building
Railway	Statue	Hospital	Church/cathedral/chapel
Road	Information office	Synagogue	Market
Motorway	Parking	Airport	Park/garden
Pedestrian road	Swimming pool	Metro station	Forest
Cable car	Tram line & stop	FGC station	Beach
Wall	Gardens		Cemetery

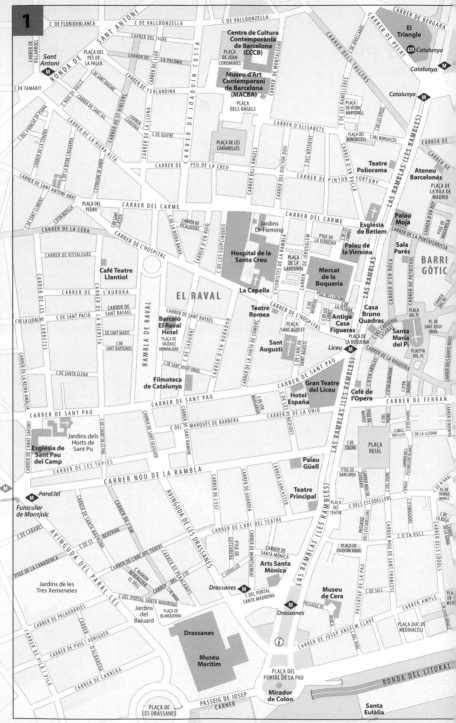

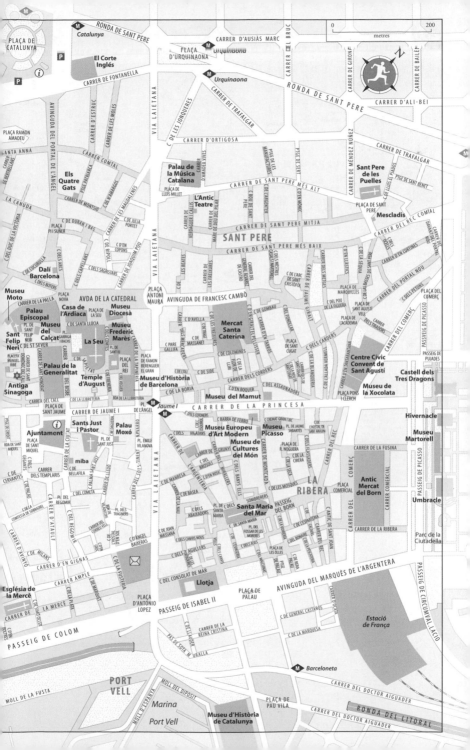

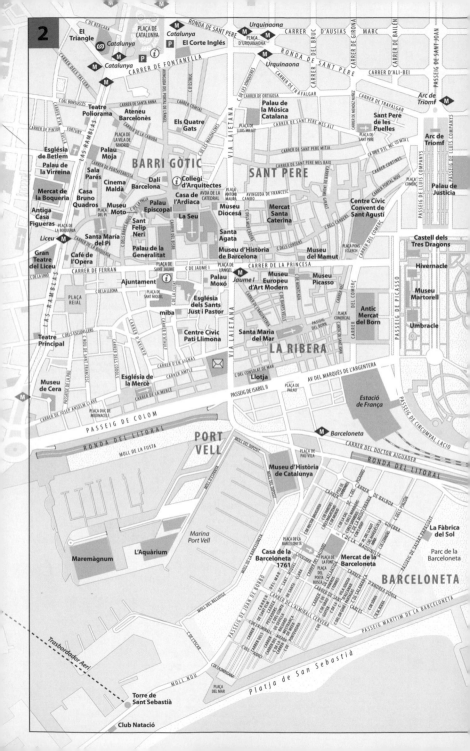

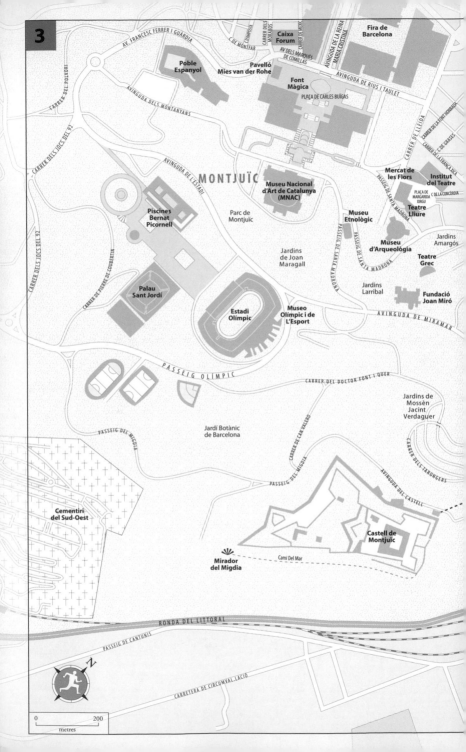

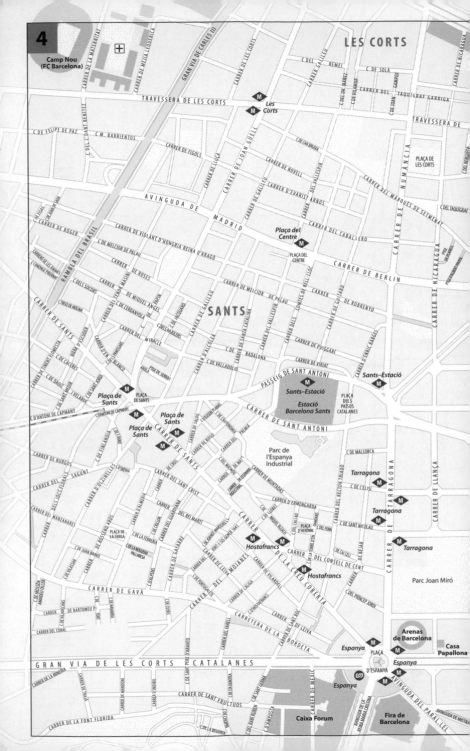

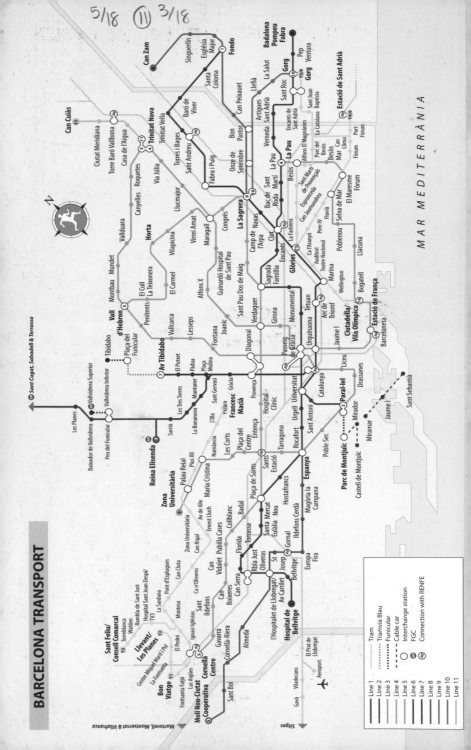